Foundations of International

Foundations of International Economics is a state-of-the-art collection of articles by leading Post Keynesian scholars on international finance and trade. All major areas in international economics are covered, with the Post Keynesian approach giving a welcome fresh perspective.

The chapters feature studies of payment schemes, exchange rate determination, open economy macroeconomics, developing country issues, capital flows, balance of payments constraints, liquidity preference, Fordism and the role of technology in trade. Beyond the specifics of each contribution, this collection as a whole suggests the usefulness of the Post Keynesian paradigm in addressing complex issues of global interdependence.

Representing cutting-edge research, this is the only collection of its kind. Whilst *Foundations of International Economics* is intended for both advanced and undergraduate use, it will also be a useful reference tool for scholars.

The Contributors: Philip Arestis, Robert Blecker, Paul Davidson, Sheila C. Dow, Bruce Elmslie, Ilene Grabel, John S.L. McCombie, Eleni Paliginis, A.P. Thirlwall, Flavio Vieira, L. Randall Wray.

The Editors: Johan Deprez is Visiting Assistant Professor at Whittier College, California. **John T. Harvey** is Associate Professor of Economics at Texas Christian University.

Foundations of International Economics

Post Keynesian perspectives

Edited by Johan Deprez and John T. Harvey

London and New York

First Published 1999 by Routledge
11 New Fetter Lane, London EC4P 4EE

Simultaneously published in the USA and Canada
by Routledge
29 West 35th Street, New York, NY 10001

Routledge is an imprint of the Taylor & Francis Group

© 1999 Selection and editorial matter Johan Deprez and John T. Harvey;
individual chapters © their authors

Typeset in Times by Solidus (Bristol) Ltd, Bristol
Printed and bound in Great Britain by
Creative, Print and Design (Wales), Ebbw Vale

British Library Cataloguing in Publication Data
A catalogue record for this book is available from the British Library

Library of Congress Cataloging in Publication Data
Foundations of international economics : post-Keynesian perspectives /
        [edited by] Johan Deprez and John T. Harvey.
        p. cm.
        Includes bibliographical references and index.
        1. International economic relations. I. Deprez, Johan, 1958– .
        II. Harvey, John T., 1961– .
        HF1359.F677 1998
        337—dc21   98-38603
                                                                        CIP

ISBN 0–415–14650–X (hbk)
ISBN 0–415–14651–8 (pbk)

Contents

Figures

Tables

Contributors

Philip Arestis, University of East London, England.
Robert Blecker, The American University, USA.
Paul Davidson, University of Tennessee, USA.
Johan Deprez, Whittier College, USA.
Sheila C. Dow, University of Stirling, Scotland.
Bruce Elmslie, University of New Hampshire, USA.
Ilene Grabel, University of Denver, USA.
John T. Harvey, Texas Christian University, USA.
John S.L. McCombie, Cambridge University, England.
Eleni Paliginis, Middlesex University, England.
A. P. Thirlwall, The University of Kent at Canterbury, England.
Flavio Vieira, University of New Hampshire, USA.
L. Randall Wray, Jerome Levy Institute and University of Denver, USA.

Acknowledgements

The editors would like to thank, first of all, the contributors. They truly 'wrote' this book, and were kind enough to allow us to put our names on the cover. Any success we have we owe to them. Second, we are indebted to our editor at Routledge, Alison Kirk. She has been ever helpful and patient, while at the same time prodding when necessary. Next, we wish to acknowledge all those teachers, friends, family members, and other mentors who introduced us to scholarship and academics as a life's work. We have them to thank for the fact that we actually get paid for doing what we enjoy doing most. Very special in this realm is Paul Davidson, whose continued support, encouragement, and vision is unparalleled. We are also especially grateful to the late Alfred Eichner, the Post Keynesian economist who served as a special inspiration to us both. He was a kind man, a caring teacher, and an outstanding scholar. He is missed. Last, but most significantly, we thank (and apologize to!) our families (Veronica, Melanie, Meg, and Alex). They were doubly cursed in that they not only had to share our sacrifices, they had to put up with us, too.

1 Introduction

Johan Deprez and John T. Harvey

It is difficult today to read any economic literature, popular or scholarly, without soon encountering references to 'globalization,' 'transnationals,' 'multinationals,' and the like. As we are reminded every day, the world is getting smaller and smaller and, in the process, more interdependent. A financial crisis in East Asia can be a cause of genuine concern to farmers in Iowa. Chinese labor laws significantly affect the economic and social status of workers (employed and unemployed) in Birmingham. The prospect of a European central bank has ramifications well beyond the borders of the European Union. All of this is increasingly evident to both participants and bystanders in this process.

What is not evident, however, is how to fully explain the effects, present and future, of these developments. In fact, one of the chief concerns of the authors in this volume is that a number of dangerously misleading 'truths' have arisen in the subject of international economic relations. Especially frightening is the fact that these myths are not confined to the financial pages or the after-hours conversations of business professionals; instead, they inform and guide public policy. Policy cannot be designed in the absence of theories that adequately explain the underlying relationships. Little wonder so few years pass between crises in the international monetary system.

The chapters in this book offer 'Post Keynesian' perspectives on international economic issues. It is our contention that these essays, because they are based on a more realistic view of the nature of economic activity, are better able to explain the character of the contemporary world economy. Though this Post Keynesian literature has been growing rapidly in recent years, the present volume is the first attempt to assemble the views from the leading Post Keynesian scholars in one work. The chapters address a variety of theoretical, applied, and empirical issues ranging from exchange rates and capital flows to trade and development. Our hope is that this book can serve as a comprehensive reference to others interested in the current state of Post Keynesian research and that it may stimulate other explorations and policy discussions in this direction. The book is also aimed at upper-level undergraduate and graduate students in order that their interest can be stimulated, as well.

We believe that the reader will find that the foundations of Post Keynesian theory are not opaque or mysterious (in fact, to us they seem like common sense), and that the policies Post Keynesians recommend are very reasonable. Indeed, while the programs advocated often require substantial overhauls of existing institutions, they call neither for the collapse of capitalism nor the privatization of all economic functions. Such extremes are not necessary to correct the flaws of our system. The particular topics addressed by the authors are such that the reader should finish this book with an understanding of the theoretical bases of Post Keynesian international economics, an appreciation of the policies those theories would suggest, and a grasp of how the structure of the current system is bound to lead to instability and deflation.

What is Post Keynesian economics? Though there are several strands of thought, a number of commonalities can be identified. First, economic agents are understood to operate in an environment of uncertainty. This creates the conditions that make money important in the macroeconomy, thereby invalidating Say's Law. No other characteristic of Post Keynesian modeling has more far-reaching effects. When money plays a causal role, full employment is no longer guaranteed by free markets. As a consequence, the government plays an important, even vital, role in the economy and microeconomic issues become clouded as the concept of opportunity cost becomes irrelevant. 'Free Traders' can no longer argue that workers whose jobs are destroyed by foreign competition will, after a short period of adjustment, find themselves automatically employed in industries that better reflect their economy's comparative advantage (in the process raising world welfare). Without Say's Law, nations accumulating balance of payments surpluses become antisocial drains on the level of world production and employment, rather than international role models for aspiring capitalists. The whole array of policy choices and consequences is changed when money matters.

Second, Post Keynesians believe that the economy is best modeled as existing in historical rather than logical or mechanical time. This means that they believe that the past has a real, qualitative impact on the future, that economic agents' decisions are affected by past events. As economic outcomes are realized, so market participants take these into account and their behavior is thus changed. When time is important in this way, the general equilibrium framework is not appropriate. At the very least, it must be used with great care, for general equilibrium models typically assume that everything happens simultaneously. That is, prices are set, contracts are struck, wages are earned, inputs are purchased, capital is built, incomes are spent, and output is produced all at the same instant. The economy reaches a state of equilibrium and stays there until one or more parameters change (until a function shifts, for example). The realized equilibrium does not somehow affect future ones by changing parameters (and therefore the underlying behavior). The parameters, the outcome, the equilibrium, and, therefore, the economy are assumed stable in the general equilibrium approach. Not so in the Post Keynesian.

In terms of market structure, Post Keynesians realize that oligopolies play a terribly important political and economic role in the real world. Oligopolists (or 'megacorps') have market power. They set price by marking up over cost, and they use the funds so generated to finance investment. Oligopolists compete with one another not through price, but via purchases of new plant and equipment, product differentiation, erection of barriers to entry, and public relations efforts (Eichner 1976). Because of the nature of the industries that tend toward oligopoly (manufacturing and mining in particular), 'the production subsystem of the economy is essentially dominated by the megacorp' (Arestis 1992: 89).

The fourth distinguishing characteristic of Post Keynesian economics is the recognition of the importance of income distribution in explaining the macrodynamics of modern economies, as well as the socially determined nature of the distribution of income. The split between wages and profits and the rates of each are seen to be determined by investment, growth, historical circumstances, power relationships, institutional conditions, expectations of firms and households, and social policy. The distribution of income and wage and profit rates are not seen as physically determined and to be functions of the marginal products of labor and capital, even if one assumes these are identifiable concepts. While the specific justification for arguing that income distribution is socially determined may vary within Post Keynesian economics, all agree on its general nature and that it is a very appropriate realm for socioeconomic policy.

This book is divided into four parts: Balance of Payments Issues; Open Economy Macroeconomics; International Money and Exchange Rates; and Real and Portfolio Capital Flows and the Role of Technology. The individual chapters run the gamut from theory to empiricism to policy. Whenever possible, technical detail has been kept to a minimum in the hope that this text will be accessible to both scholars and students.

The opening chapter is, appropriately, from the editor of the *Journal of Post Keynesian Economics*: Paul Davidson. Professor Davidson's theme is one that is repeated throughout this volume: capital market activity aimed at earning speculative profits is only coincidentally beneficial to output and employment growth. Indeed, the opposite is far more likely. His specific focus is international portfolio capital movements, and it is his contention that the progressive post-war liberalization of markets, including especially the collapse of the Bretton Woods exchange rate agreement, has created an international economic system with a deflationary bias (that is, a tendency toward economic stagnation and unemployment). What is required is both a reform of the payments system such that surplus countries are punished for the drain they create on world economic activity and a conscious recognition on a national level that governments must work to maintain full employment. Until that is achieved, trade is far more likely to play a predatory role than a constructive one.

The next chapter, by John S.L. McCombie and A.P. Thirlwall, is an excellent review of the literature related to balance of payments growth constraints, or Thirlwall's Law. Their basic premise is that, just as Post Keynesians argue that the gap between desired investment and full-employment saving is an obstacle to economic growth, so is that between export earnings and full-employment imports. They begin with an outstanding historical overview of the theory, then work through a theoretical exposition, and close with implications and empirical evidence. The lesson learned from this chapter is that closed economies exist only on paper and that, in our increasingly interdependent world, the maintenance of full employment requires careful analysis of balance of payments issues in addition to domestic macroeconomic considerations.

The next part of the book is entitled Open Economy Macroeconomics. Johan Deprez's chapter takes Keynes' aggregate supply and demand as it has been articulated and developed by Sidney Weintraub and Paul Davidson for closed economies and extends it to deal with open economies. This model reaffirms the basic Keynesian conclusion that production and employment is constrained by the effective demand that exists in an economy and the role of exports in this. The model is articulated in such a way as to highlight the rarely understood role of firms' expectations in determining employment, output, and patterns of trade. In a manner that is consistent with Post Keynesian explanations of the determination of exchange rates, it is also argued that there is no tendency within modern economies towards a balance of trade. Finally, by having an explicit supply side in the model, it is capable of addressing a wide range of other issues. Specifically, the question of cost reductions as a means of expanding exports is addressed and is found to be much more problematic than usually assumed.

Robert Blecker follows with a Kaleckian open-economy model. While both reviewing Kalecki's contributions to international economics and extending that work, Blecker makes three main points: (a) trade in the presence of oligopolistic industries can be conflictive; (b) in contrast to the implications of closed-economy Kaleckian models, it is possible when a foreign sector is introduced for a redistribution of income from wages to profits to be contractionary rather than expansionary; and (c) the relative effects of a currency devaluation on the trade balance and national income are not clear without taking into account the impact on income distribution. Though he finishes by cautioning the reader that the model needs to be extended, the preliminary results are nonetheless thought provoking. They serve to remind us that however well designed a domestic macro model might be, adding international trade and investment often involves more than simply a new variable or two.

Sheila Dow's chapter opens the next part of the book, International Money and Exchange Rates. She develops a Post Keynesian international finance theory in which liquidity preference and endogenous credit creation play a central role. Dow argues that, though all economic units have balance of payments problems the 'solutions' to which are likely to be deflationary, that bias is made worse in the international context by currency speculation. The solution is to provide financial stability and low interest rates, which may be possible on the necessary scale only given a truly international money.

L. Randall Wray's chapter addresses similar concerns from a different direction. He starts by outlining the orthodox view of money, capital flows, and exchange rates, wherein free markets ensure independent domestic macro policies and rapid adjustments to optimal equilibria. He then presents the Post Keynesian view, which leads him to Keynes' famous bancor proposal for the international monetary system. Wray argues that while the latter is appropriate in a world where money matters, Keynes' original justification for it was flawed. Wray remedies this and thus provides additional support.

In his chapter, John Harvey explains the exchange rate volatility and misalignment characteristic of the post Bretton Woods era. He sees these as a function of the spectacular growth of short-term capital flows and the fact that portfolio investment now, for all intents and purposes, determines exchange rates. He concludes that the effect of this transformation has been payments imbalances, resource misallocation, reduced government policy autonomy, and wasted entrepreneurial skills.

The last part is Real and Portfolio Capital Flows and the Role of Technology. There, Philip Arestis and Eleni Paliginis examine recent economic developments on the periphery of the European Union and the North American Free Trade Area. Their thesis is that these economic unions have not created the institutions necessary to promote convergence, and that as a consequence the peripheral economies remain at a significant disadvantage. Though orthodox theorists and policymakers have argued that multinational capital will be attracted to these regions and therefore spur their development, the reality is that it is too volatile and generally unreliable to be of much help. Arestis and Paliginis suggest that though multinational enterprises could play a positive role if properly controlled, the best solution would be encouragement of indigenous capital accumulation.

Ilene Grabel shows that the pitfalls of dependence on international capital for development are not limited to those described in the previous chapter. Third World reliance on portfolio investment, she shows, tends to adversely constrain macro policy choices and increase risk. Grabel both makes this argument on a theoretical level and uses the 1994–6 Mexican financial crisis to illustrate her points.

The last contribution is from Bruce Elmslie and Flavio Vieira. Unique in the volume, their chapter is the only one to take a closer look at the determinants, rather than the effects, of foreign trade. In particular, they focus on the role technology plays in generating trade patterns, an approach consistent with the Post Keynesian emphasis on the megacorp as the most important representative firm. They start by reviewing the history of technology gap theory, beginning with the mercantilists. They then review modern attempts to reconcile technology gap theory within the framework of both comparative and absolute advantage, discuss testing issues, and review the empirical literature. Their theme is that though technology gap theory is difficult to operationalize, the fact that it is a much more powerful explanation of the real world than the orthodox alternatives more than justifies the efforts to do so.

We hope that the eleven chapters in this volume give the reader a fresh perspective on the international economy. As the world shrinks and nations become more and more interdependent, so the need for penetrating analyses of those conditions becomes more pressing. We believe that the Post Keynesian approach – relying on the non-neutrality of money, the oligopolistic nature of industry, and the existence of the economy in historical time – is best poised to offer these analyses.

References

Arestis, P. (1992) *The Post Keynesian Approach to Economics*, Aldershot, Hants. Edward Elgar.

Eichner, A. (1976) *The Megacorp and Oligopoly: Micro Foundations of Macro Dynamics*, Armonk, N.Y: M.E. Sharpe.

Part I

Balance of payments issues

2 Global employment and open economy macroeconomics

Paul Davidson

Keynes' (1936) *General Theory of Employment Interest and Money*[1] is developed primarily in a closed economy context. Keynes did, however, introduce an open economy analysis when he noted that:

1   trade could modify the magnitude of the domestic employment multiplier (120);
2   reductions in money wages would worsen the terms of trade and therefore reduce real income, while it could improve the balance of trade (263); and
3   stimulating either domestic investment or foreign investment can increase domestic employment growth (335).

In a world where governments are afraid that to deliberately stimulate any domestic spending will unleash inflationary forces, export-led growth is seen as a desirable alternative path for expanding domestic employment. A 'favorable balance [of trade], provided it is not too large, will prove extremely stimulating' to domestic employment (338), even if it does so at the expense of employment opportunities abroad.

In a passage that is particularly *a propos* for today's global economic setting, Keynes noted that 'in a society where there is no question of direct investment under the aegis of public authority [due to fear of government deficits *per se*], the economic objects, with which it is reasonable for the government to be preoccupied, are the domestic interest rate and the balance of foreign trade' (335). If, however, nations were permitted free movement of funds across national boundaries, then 'the authorities had no direct control over the domestic rate of interest or the other inducements to home investment, [and] measures to increase the favorable balance of trade [are] . . . the only *direct* means at their disposal for increasing foreign investment' (336) and domestic employment.

Keynes was well aware that the domestic employment advantage gained by export-led growth 'is liable to involve an equal disadvantage to some other country' (338). When countries pursue an 'immoderate policy' (338) of export led growth (for example, Japan, Germany and the newly industrializing countries (NICs) of Asia in the 1980s), the unemployment problem is aggravated for the surplus nations' trading partners.[2] These trading partners are then forced to engage in a 'senseless international competition for a favourable balance which injures all alike' (338–9). The traditional approach for improving the trade balance is to make one's domestic industries *more competitive* by either forcing down nominal wages (including fringe benefits) to reduce labor production costs and/or by a devaluation of the exchange rate.[3] Competitive gains obtained by manipulating these nominal variables can only foster further global stagnation and recession as one's trading partners attempt to regain a competitive edge by similar policies.

Unlike the classical theorists of his day (and our day as well[4]) Keynes recognized that 'the mercantilists were aware of the fallacy of cheapness and the danger that excessive competition may turn the terms of trade against a country' (345) thereby reducing domestic living standards, so that, as President Clinton noted in his 1992 campaign, 'people are working more and earning less.'

Keynes realized that if *every* nation did not actively undertake a program for public *domestic* investment to generate *domestic* full employment, then the resulting *laissez-faire* system of prudent fiscal finance in tandem with a system of free international monetary flows would create a global environment where *each* nation independently sees significant national advantages in a policy of export-led growth even though pursuit of these policies simultaneously by many nations 'injures all alike' (338–9). This warning of Keynes, however, went virtually unrecognized in the 1980s while mainstream economists waxed enthusiastic about the export-led economic miracles of Japan, Germany and the Pacific rim NICs without noting that these miraculous performances were at the expense of the rest of the world.

In a *laissez-faire* world, when governments do not have the political will to stimulate directly any domestic component of aggregate spending to reduce unemployment, 'domestic prosperity [is] directly dependent on a competitive pursuit of [export] markets' (349). This is a competition in which not all nations can be winners. When, in the late 1980s, the United States began to take steps to reduce its huge trade deficit with the 'miracle economies' of the early 1980s by both depressing its domestic demand and trying to make its industries more competitive in order to gain a larger share of existing world markets, the whole world was plunged into a stagnating slow-growth recessionary era. By 1992, stimulated by a lowering of interest rates and a decline in the exchange rate, the US economy revived, and an undervalued exchange rate permitted it to grow faster than the rest of the OECD nations – at least till early 1997 when a significant increase in the exchange rate and higher interest rates threatened US expansion.

For a nation to break out of a global slow-growth stagnating economic environment, the 'truth,' Keynes insisted, lay in pursuing a

> policy of an autonomous rate of interest, unimpeded by international preoccupations, and a national investment programme directed to an

optimum level of employment which *is twice blessed* in the sense that *it helps ourselves and our neighbours at the same time.* And *it is the simultaneous pursuit of these policies by all countries together which is capable of restoring economic health and strength* internationally, whether we measure it by the level of domestic employment or by the volume of international trade

(349, italics added)

From 1982 to 1986, the Reagan Administration unwittingly pursued this Keynesian truth by increasing military (public investment) spending and cutting taxes to stimulate consumption. By mid-1982, the Federal Reserve helped by reducing interest rates to avoid a massive international debt default. As a result of the US acting as the 'engine of growth' between 1982 and 1986, most of the OECD nations rapidly recovered from the greatest global recession since the Great Depression. Unfortunately, as recovery occurred, most of the major trading partners of the US did not engage in a 'simultaneous pursuit of these policies' of increasing public spending and reducing interest rates. These nations neither remembered nor understood Keynes' recommendation that only by the concurrent public investment policies of all nations could global economic health and strength be restored.[5] Instead, some of America's trading partners took advantage of Reagan's 'Keynesian' policy, which stimulated US demand for imports, to pursue an export-led growth policy.

Until we understand Keynes' *General Theory* lessons in an open economy context, we are doomed to repeat the past errors encouraged by 'the inadequacy of the *theoretical* foundations of the *laissez-faire* doctrine' (339) and by 'orthodox economists whose common sense has been insufficient to check their faulty logic' (349) which presumes global full employment so that free trade must increase the global wealth of nations by reducing each nation's aggregate supply constraints through the law of comparative advantage.[6]

In a passage that is amazingly prescient of the economic environment since Bretton Woods, Keynes warns that the law of comparative advantage is only applicable *after* all nations have domestic demand management policies assuring full employment. Whenever nations operate under a *laissez-faire* mentality that produces significant global unemployment, then

> if a rich, old country were to neglect the struggle for markets its prosperity would droop and fail. But if [all] nations can learn to provide themselves with full employment by their domestic policy ... there need be no important economic forces calculated to set the interest of one country against that of its neighbours. There would still be room for the international division of labour and for international lending in appro- priate conditions. But there would no longer be a pressing motive why one country need force its wares on another or repulse the offerings of its neighbour, not because this was necessary to enable it to pay for what it

wished to purchase, but with the express object of upsetting equilibrium in the balance of payment so as to develop a balance of trade in its own favour [that is, export-led growth policy]. *International trade would cease to be what it is, namely, a desperate expedient to maintain employment at home by forcing sales on foreign markets and restricting purchases, which, if successful, will merely shift the problem of unemployment to the neighbour which is worsted in the struggle*, but a willing and unimpeded exchange of goods and services in conditions of mutual advantage.

(382–3, italics added)

Unfortunately, as is evident from the political slogans that surrounded the successful conclusion of the North American Free Trade Agreement (NAFTA) and the Uruguay round of the GATT talks in 1993, most governments have been led by mainstream economists to believe that free trade *per se* is job creating globally. Keynes' *General Theory* suggests otherwise.

The post-Bretton Woods international payments system has created perverse incentives that set trading partner against trading partner to perpetuate a world of slow growth (if not stagnation). Generalizing Keynes' *General Theory* to an open economy provides a rationale for designing an international payment system that creates incentives for each nation to pursue domestic demand policies which ensure full employment without the fear of a balance of payments constraint. Only then will the gains from the law of comparative advantage become relevant.

A consistent theme throughout Keynes' *General Theory* is that classical logic has assumed away questions that are fundamental to a market-oriented, money-using economy. These problems are particularly relevant to understanding the current international payments relations that involve liquidity, persistent and growing debt obligations, and the importance of stable rather than flexible exchange rates.

An example of the sanguine classical response to Post Keynesians who raise these issues is that of Professor Milton Friedman to me in our 'debate' in the literature. Friedman (1974: 151) stated: 'A price may be flexible . . . yet be relatively stable, because demand and supply are relatively stable *over time* . . . [Of course] violent instability of prices in terms of a specific money would greatly reduce the usefulness of that money.' It is nice to know that as long as prices or exchange rates remain relatively stable, or 'sticky' over time, there is no harm in permitting them to be flexible. The problem arises when exchange rates display volatility. Should there be a deliberate policy that intervenes in the market to maintain relative stability or should we allow a free market to determine the exchange rate? Keynes helped design the Bretton Woods Agreement to foster action and intervention to stabilize exchange rates and control international payment flows. Friedman sold the public on the beneficence of government inaction and the free market determination of exchange rates.

Nowhere is the difference between the Keynes view and the view of those who favor *laissez-faire* arrangements more evident than in regards to these questions of international capital movements and payments mechanisms and the desirability of a flexible exchange rate system. Keynes' *General Theory* analysis suggests that government monitoring and, when necessary, control of capital flows is in society's interest. Such controls are not an infringement on the freedom of economic agents any more than the control of people's right to shout 'fire' in a crowded theater is an infringement of the individual's right of free speech.

Capital movements

New Keynesians have little to say about exogenous capital movements and their potentially detrimental effects on the balance of payments and global employment.[7] Keynes, on the other hand, recognized that large unfettered capital flows can create serious international payments problems for nations whose current accounts would otherwise be roughly in balance. Unfortunately, in a *laissez-faire* system of capital markets there is no way of distinguishing between the movement of floating and speculative funds that take refuge in one nation after another in the continuous search for speculative gains, or for precautionary purposes, or for hiding from the tax collector, or to launder illegal earnings *vis-à-vis* funds being used to promote genuine new investment for developing the world's resources.

The international movement of speculative, precautionary, or illegal funds (hot money), if it becomes significantly large, can be so disruptive to the global economy as to impoverish most, if not all, nations who organize production and exchange processes on an entrepreneurial basis. Keynes (1980: 25) warned: 'Loose funds may sweep round the world disorganizing all steady business. Nothing is more certain than that the movement of capital funds must be regulated.'

One of the more obvious dicta that follows from Keynes' (1980: 81) revolutionary vision of the importance of liquidity in open economies is that:

> There is no country which can, in future, safely allow the flight of funds for political reasons or to evade domestic taxation or in anticipation of the owner turning refugee. Equally, there is no country that can safely receive fugitive funds which cannot safely be used for fixed investments and might turn it into a deficiency country against its will and contrary to the real facts.

Tobin is one of the few economists with high visibility in the profession who has, since the early 1970s, been arguing that flexible exchange rates and free international financial flows can have devastating impacts on industries and even whole economies.

Currency speculation

In the classical model, where agents know the future with perfect certainty or, at least, can form statistically reliable predictions without persistent errors (that is, rational expectations), speculative market activities can be justified as stabilizing. When, on the other hand, the economic future is uncertain (nonergodic), today's agents 'know' they cannot reliably predict future outcomes. Hicks (1979: vii) has argued that if economists are to build models which reflect real world behavior, then the agents in these models must 'know that they just don't know' what is going to happen in the future.

In the uncertain world we live in, therefore, people cannot rely on historical or current market data to reliably forecast future prices (that is, in the absence of reliable institutions that assure orderly spot markets, there can be no reliable existing anchor to future market prices). In such a world, speculative activities cannot only be highly destabilizing in terms of future market prices, but the volatility of these future spot prices can have costly real consequences for the aggregate real income of the community. Nowhere has this been made more obvious than in the machinations of the foreign exchange markets since the end of the Bretton Woods era of fixed exchange rates.

Eichengreen, Tobin, and Wyplosz (hereafter ETW) (1995) have recognized the potential high real costs of speculative destabilizing economic activities that can occur if governments permit unfettered flexible exchange markets. They suggest that foreign exchange markets have become the scene of a number of speculative attacks against major currencies.

At approximately the same time the ETW article appeared in print, the winter 1994–5 Mexican peso crisis exploded and spilled over into a US dollar problem. In international financial markets, where image is often more important than reality, the dollar was dragged down by the peso during the late winter and early spring of 1995 while the German mark and Japanese yen appeared to be the only safe harbors for portfolio fund managers.

Portfolio fund managers in search of yields and 'safe harbors' can move funds from one country to another in nanoseconds with a few clicks on their computer keyboard. In today's global economy any whiff of currency weakness becomes a conflagration spreading along the information highway. Federal Reserve Chairman Alan Greenspan was quoted in the *New York Times* as testifying that 'Mexico became the first casualty ... of the new international financial system' which permits hot portfolio money to slosh around the world 'much more quickly.' Can the real economies of the twenty-first century afford to suffer many more casualties in this new international financial system?

If initially the major central banks do not dispatch sufficient resources to intervene effectively in order to extinguish any speculative currency fire, then the resultant publicity is equivalent to hollering 'fire' in a theater. The consequent panic worsens the situation and central banks whose currencies are seen as safe havens may lose any interest in a coordinated response to the increasing inferno.

What Tobin and his associates are worried about is that with electronically linked international financial markets and an interconnected global economy there is a strong possibility, which even advocates of free international capital markets have begun to admit, that 'hot money' portfolio flows can have massive disruptive real economic effects.

In this real world in which we live, pragmatists such as Tobin and his associates are implicitly arguing that, because of the possibility of speculative portfolio changes, the social costs of freely flexible exchange rates far exceed the social benefits. Accordingly, there is a role for some form of government intervention in the foreign exchange market. In contrast, orthodox economic theory traditionally argues for unfettered exchange rate markets on the presumption that the social benefits of such markets exceed the social costs of government interference. Mainstream theorists typically reach this conclusion because they conflate the concept of speculation with the concept of arbitrage. Since the latter is always a stabilizing force, orthodoxy insists that the former is also always a stabilizing factor.

If the social costs of free exchange markets exceed the social benefits, then what is required in this global economy with computer-linked financial markets is not a system of *ad hoc* central bank interventions while what Greenspan calls the 'new international financial system' burns the real economy. What is necessary is to build into the international system permanent fireproofing rules and structures that prevent imagery-induced currency fires. *Crisis prevention rather than crisis rescues must be the primary long-term objective.* If the developed nations do not hang together on a currency-fire prevention system, then they will all hang separately in a replay of the international financial market crisis of the Great Depression.

Reasonable people do not think it is a violation of civil liberties to prohibit people from boarding an airplane with a gun. Moreover, no one would think we were impinging on individual rights if society prohibited anyone from entering a movie theater with a Molotov cocktail in one hand and a book of matches in the other – even if the person indicated no desire to burn down the theater. Yet, in the name of free markets, fund managers can imagine an exploding Molotov cocktail and then yell 'fire' in the crowded international financial markets any time the 'image' of a possibly profitable fire moves them.

Fifty years ago, Keynes recognized what the best and the brightest economists are only beginning to recognize today, namely that 'there is not a country which can . . . safely allow the flight of funds [hot money] . . . Equally there is no country that can safely receive . . . [these portfolio] funds which cannot safely be used for fixed investment' (Keynes 1980: 25).

Tobin has taken up this Keynesian theme and argued for fire prevention in the form of 'sand in the wheels of foreign exchange markets,' that is, to levy a tax on moving funds from one currency to another. (This is equivalent to taxing, rather than banning, the Molotov cocktail member of the theater audience.) ETW have also explored the possibility of imposing compulsory interest-free deposits or other capital requirements (therefore creating an 'opportunity cost' tax) to 'discourage short-term round tripping, but not long term investment' (Greenway 1995: 160).

A published discussion between ETW (1995), Garber and Taylor (1995) and Kenen (1995) did not focus on the economic rationale in terms of a Tobin tax (or any other form of government intervention). Rather, Garber and Taylor raised the issue of the institutional feasibility of a foreign exchange transaction tax, while Kenen concentrated specifically on capital controls and why he perceived the impossibility of such controls at this time. Little discussion of the theoretical rationale for any controls was provided.

Keynes, on the other hand, who distinguished the speculative motive for liquidity preference from the marginal efficiency demand for real investment, analyzed this problem in some detail in the 1940s and concluded, as the citation above suggests, that a system of outright prohibition of international hot money flows would be required. With the help of the formula developed below, it is easy to see why Keynes reached this conclusion.

Capital uncertainty and speculative flows

In order for any asset to be considered as a liquid store of value over time that asset must be readily resalable in a well-organized, orderly spot market. The institution of 'market-maker' is a necessary condition for the existence of well-organized, orderly spot markets (Davidson 1972: 64–71). Since the spot market price of any liquid asset in such a market can change over time, savers who are storing claims on resources must contemplate the possibility of an appreciation or a depreciation in the asset's spot market price at a future date when the holders wish to liquidate their holdings. This potential capital gain or loss is obtained by subtracting today's spot price (p_s^{t0}) from the expected spot price at a future date (p_s^{t1}) when the asset will be resold. If ($p_s^{t1} - p_s^{t0}$) > 0, a capital gain is expected from holding the asset till $t1$; if ($p_s^{t1} - p_s^{t0}$) < 0, a capital loss will be expected.

Offsetting the possible capital loss on choosing any liquid asset is the future earnings (q) that can be obtained from owning the asset during a period of time net of carrying costs (c) incurred by holding this asset. Both q and c tend to increase with the time period the asset is held. There are also transactions costs (T_s) incurred in both buying and reselling a liquid asset. These transactions costs are usually independent of the time interval that the liquid asset is held. These transactions costs, however, normally increase at a decreasing rate as the value of the asset increases.

If an unforeseen liability becomes due in the immediate future, then the transactions cost of taking a position and then liquidating it can easily swamp any net income flow ($q - c$) received from holding the asset for such a short time while the capital gain (or loss) is likely to be negligible. It is, therefore, normal to prefer to hold some saving in the form of the money in which near-term contractual obligations will come due to cover planned and some possible unforeseen obligations (Hicks 1967).

The more uncertain the future appears, the more unforeseeable liabilities may come due. The more desirable, therefore, it will be to minimize transactions costs by storing saving in the form of money or other safe short-term assets denominated in terms of the currency of contractual settlement. This soothes our fears of becoming illiquid if anything unpredictable occurs during the period.[8]

Savers find a capital loss repugnant but the lure of capital gains seductive. Let q be the future expected income to be received from holding a financial security over a period of time, and c be the carrying costs where both q and c are denominated in terms of the specific currency of the issuer of the financial asset. Let us allow foreign currencies and stocks and bonds denominated in foreign currencies be included in the choice of assets to be held in any portfolio.

If, for a specific liquid asset, the portfolio manager expects:

$$(q - c) + (p_s^{t1} - p_s^{t0}) - T_s > 0, \tag{2.1}$$

then the manager is a 'bull.' If it is expected that:

$$(q - c) + (p_s^{t1} - p_s^{t0}) - T_s < 0, \tag{2.2}$$

then the fund manager is a 'bear.' In the simplest case, for example, if $(q - c)$ minus T_s equals zero, then if:

$$p_s^{t1}/p_s^{t0} > 1 \tag{2.3}$$

then the person is a bull, while if:

$$p_s^{t1}/p_s^{t0} < 1 \tag{2.4}$$

the person is a bear.

If one holds one's own domestic money there is no future net income $(q - c = 0)$, no capital gain or loss $(p_s^{t1} - p_s^{t0} = 0)$, and no transactions costs $(T_s = 0)$.

In a flexible exchange rate system, fund managers estimate the expected future income plus capital gain or loss on all domestic and foreign liquid securities. For ease of exposition in analyzing portfolio decisions in a multination open economy context, let us include the fund manager's expected capital gains and losses for each security (in terms of the currency the security is denominated in) in the magnitude of $(q - c)$. Accordingly, the term $(p_s^{t1} - p_s^{t0})$ can be reserved for the *ceteris paribus* effect of an expected change in the spot exchange rate. Thus, besides expected capital gains (or losses) and all the transactions costs (T_s) associated with the purchase and sale of a liquid asset, including the usual cost of converting currencies, expected changes in the exchange rate must also be factored into the decision as to which international liquid assets to hold.

Obviously, the portfolio manager will choose to move money into those assets that are expected to yield the highest positive values as in inequality (2.1) and sell those assets that have negative perspective yields as in inequality (2.2).

In orthodox economic theory, when interest rates are equalized, if similar financial assets denominated in different currencies are perfect substitutes, then the $(q - c)$ term for these securities is assumed to be equal, given the state of expectation about future exchange rates *vis-à-vis* today's rate. Under these stylized circumstances, international speculative hot money flows will occur whenever there is, *ceteris paribus*, a sudden change in sentiment involving the expected value of the future spot exchange rate relative to the current rate, that is, the portfolio manager's evaluation of the $p_s^{t1} - p_s^{t0}$ term changes.

If one or more portfolio managers who control significant portfolio sums suddenly change their expectations regarding future exchange rates, then there can be a massive movement of funds from one country to another. Once a significant international flow of funds occurs, this can encourage other fund managers to change their expectations of $p_s^{t1} - p_s^{t0}$ until either:

1   the foreign reserves of the central bank of the nation suffering the outflow of hot money are nearly exhausted.[9] Then the nation cannot maintain an orderly exchange rate market. Consequently fund managers who are late-comers cannot readily convert their holdings into foreign assets; or
2   the country being drained of reserves increases its interest rate (that is, the $q - c$ term) sufficiently to offset the expected potential capital gain $(p_s^{t1} - p_s^{t0})$; or
3   central banks deliberately intervene in the exchange market in an attempt to change private sector expectations regarding $(p_s^{t1} - p_s^{t0})$; or
4   some form of taxation is added to increase the value of the T_s term to offset the expected increase in capital gains from an exchange rate change; or
5   some form of outright prohibition of hot money portfolio flows is successfully introduced.

The Tobin tax falls under item (4) where governments use taxation in an attempt to stop speculative flows of hot money. The belief behind the Tobin tax is that adding a marginal tax will increase social costs until they coincide with social benefits, so that private decisions will become socially optimum. By using the above equational relationships, however, it can be shown that the usual suggested magnitude of a 'Tobin tax' or other similar 'opportunity cost' capital tax will only marginally increase the cost of speculating. Consequently a Tobin tax will stop speculation on relatively *small* movements in the exchange rate (independent of the time horizon of the fund manager) while it will have a significantly larger impact on stemming real international trade. In other words, the Tobin tax is not able to solve the problem whenever speculative portfolio flows become significantly large conflagrations, but simultaneously they induce large and permanent private costs (in excess of social costs) on real international trade flows.

The 'half percent tax' used by ETW (1995: 164) as an illustration is equal to 1 percent of a round-trip transaction. Thus the relationship for determining one's bullishness (or bearishness) requires evaluating the following terms:

$$(q - c) + (p_s^{t1} - p_s^{t0}) - x\,(p_s^{t1} + p_s^{t0}) - T_s$$

where x equals the magnitude of the Tobin tax rate. If:

$$(q - c) + (p_s^{t1} - p_s^{t0}) - x\,(p_s^{t1} + p_s^{t0}) - T_s > 0 \qquad (2.5)$$

the person is a bull, while if:

$$(q - c) + (p_s^{t1} - p_s^{t0}) - x\,(p_s^{t1} + p_s^{t0}) - T_s < 0 \qquad (2.6)$$

the portfolio manager is bearish. When:

$$(q - c) + (p_s^{t1} - p_s^{t0}) - x\,(p_s^{t1} + p_s^{t0}) - T_s = 0 \qquad (2.7)$$

the agent is neither bullish nor bearish and will not engage in any speculative activities.

Equations (2.5)–(2.7) show that given the values of $q - c$ and T_s, the Tobin tax merely increases slightly the differential between the expected future spot price and the current spot price before speculative bull or bear responses are induced.

If we assume the simplest case that $q - c = T_s$, then if:

$$p_s^{t1}/p_s^{t0} > (1 + x/\,(1 - x)) \qquad (2.8)$$

then the person is a bull, while no bullish speculative flows will be induced even if expected p_s^{t1} was greater than p_s^{t0} up to the point where:

$$p_s^{t1}/p_s^{t0} = (1 + x/(1 - x)) \qquad (2.9)$$

Thus, for example, if the magnitude of the Tobin tax is 0.5 percent, then the expected future spot price must be at least 1.1 percent higher than the current spot exchange rate[10] to make the agent willing to speculate on any foreign currency.

As long as the spot price is expected to change, *ceteris paribus*, by much more than 1.1 percent during any period where there is a 0.5 percent Tobin tax, speculative flows still have a significant positive payoff. Consequently any Tobin tax less than 100 percent *of the expected capital gain* (on a round trip) is unlikely to stop hot money sloshing around.

Whenever there is a speculative run on a currency, one expects dramatic changes in the currency. For example, the Mexican peso fell by approximately

60 percent in the winter of 1994–5. A Tobin tax of over 23 percent would have been required to stop the speculative surge that created the peso crisis. At best, the Tobin tax might slow down the speculative fever when small exchange rate changes are expected.

The grains of sand of a Tobin tax might be the straw that breaks the speculative back of very small portfolio managers, since normal transactions costs (T_s) of foreign transactions are essentially regressive. An additional proportional (Tobin) tax on top of a large regressive transactions cost might keep more very small speculators out of the market. For movements of larger sums, however, the normal transactions costs quickly shrink to a negligible proportion of the total transaction. In today's free-wheeling financial markets, individuals with even small portfolio sums may join mutual funds that can speculate on foreign currencies; therefore a Tobin tax is unlikely to constrain even small investors – who can always join a large mutual fund to reduce the impact of total transactions costs sufficiently to reduce the remaining Tobin tax to relative insignificance whenever speculative fever runs high.

Finally, there is a rule of thumb which suggests that under the current flexible exchange rate system, there are five normal hedging trade transactions in every real final goods trade compared to two for every speculative flow in international finance. If this ratio is anywhere near correct, then a 0.5 percent Tobin tax could imply levying up to a 2.5 percent tax on normal real trade flow transactions compared to a 1 percent round-trip speculative tax. It would appear then that a Tobin transaction tax might throw larger grains of sand into the wheels of international real commerce than it does into speculative hot money flows. A 0.5 percent Tobin tax could be equivalent to instituting a 2.5 percent universal tariff on all goods and services traded in the global economy.[11]

Independently of questions of the political and economic feasibility of instituting a ubiquitous Tobin tax, therefore, proposals to increase marginal transactions costs in foreign exchange by either a Tobin tax or a small feasible opportunity cost tax on capital is unlikely to prevent speculative feeding frenzies that lead to attacks on major currencies and their economic neighbors while it may inflict greater damage on international trading in goods and services.

Such considerations led Keynes to suggest an outright prohibition of all significant international portfolio flows through the creation of a supra-national central bank and his 'bancor' plan. At this stage of economic development and global economic integration, however, a supranational central bank is not politically feasible. Accordingly, what should be aimed for is a more modest goal of obtaining an international agreement among the G7 nations. To be economically effective and politically feasible, this agreement, while incorporating the economic principles that Keynes laid down in his 'bancor' plan, should not require any nation to surrender control of local banking systems and fiscal policies.

Keynes introduced an ingenious method of directly prohibiting of hot money flows by a 'bancor' system with fixed (but adjustable) exchange rates and a trigger mechanism to put more of the onus of resolving current account deficits on surplus nations. It is possible to update Keynes' prohibition proposal to meet twenty-first century circumstances. In the next section such a system will be proposed. Moreover, this system will be in the best interests of all nations for it will make it easier to achieve global full employment without the danger of importing inflationary pressures from one's trading partners.

There is not enough space in this chapter to debate all possible alternative proposals for fire prevention in currency speculation. Instead I hope to raise the public consciousness for the potential tremendous real benefits that can accrue from establishing currency-speculation fire prevention institutions rather than merely relying on either fire-fighting intervention such as the suggested emergency fund financed by contributions of the G7 nations and managed by the IMF, or a *laissez-faire* policy on international capital markets that can produce currency fires to burn the free world's real economies. We must recognize the very real possibility that there can be no safe harbor when a major currency is attacked.

The golden age of economic development

The Bretton Woods years were an era of unsurpassed economic global prosperity. Economist Irma Adelman of the University of California has characterized the period as a 'Golden Age of Economic Development . . . an era of unprecedented sustained economic growth in both developed and developing countries.' Table 2.1 provides the statistical evidence that Adelman used in reaching her conclusion about our economic golden age.

Although we do not possess reliable statistics on GDP per capita before 1700, it is probably true that from biblical times until the Renaissance the average standard of living in the world showed little improvement from year to year or even from generation to generation. Improvement in global economic living standards began with the development of merchant capitalism during the Renaissance period in Europe. Between 1700 and 1820 (see Table 2.1) the per capita slice of the economic pie was increasing at an average annual rate of 0.2 percent. Thus if people lived on average approximately 45 years, their standard of living increased less than 10 percent from birth to death.

Living standards started to increase substantially early in the nineteenth century. The Industrial Revolution period was truly revolutionary. During the years 1820–1913, annual living standards improved ten times faster than in the previous century as the annual growth rate of 1.2 percent compounded year after year. The average increase in labor productivity was almost seven times greater than during the previous 100 years. The per capita income of the advanced nations of the world more than trebled in less than 100 years. No wonder this period is often portrayed in western literature as the era of growth of the common man.

Table 2.1 Real GDP (annualized growth rate, %)

Years	Real GDP per capita OECD nations		
1700–1820	0.2		
1820–1913	1.2		
1919–1940	1.9		
1950–1973	4.9		
1973–1981	1.3		
	Major industrial nations	New industrializing nations	Developing nations
1973–1990	2.5	3.5	−0.1
	Total real GDP		
	OECD nations	Developing nations	
1950–1973	5.9	5.5	
	Real GDP per capita		
	OECD nations	Developing nations	
1950–1973	4.9	3.3	

During this 1820–1913 period the volume of world exports grew thirty-fold as a global economy and financial system were created with a fixed exchange rate under a gold-sterling standard. The growth rate during the Golden Age of Bretton Woods, however, was almost double the previous peak annual growth rate of the industrializing nations during the Industrial Revolution (from 1820 to 1913). Annual labor productivity growth between 1950 and 1973 was more than triple that of the Industrial Revolution. Moreover, between 1950 and 1973, real GDP per capita in the developed (or OECD) nations grew 2.6 times faster than between the wars.

The resulting prosperity of the industrialized world was transmitted to the less developed nations through world trade, aid, and direct foreign investment. From 1950–73, annual growth in per capita GDP for *all* developing nations was 3.3 percent, almost triple the growth experienced by the industrializing nations during the Industrial Revolution. The total GDP pie of the less developed countries (LDCs) increased at almost the same rate as that of the developed nations, 5.5 percent and 5.9 percent respectively, but the higher population growth of the LDCs caused the lower per capita income growth.

By comparison, the economic record of the flexible rate systems between the world wars and since 1973 is dismal. The growth rate of the major developed nations since 1973 is approximately half of what it was during Bretton Woods, not much better than the experience of the nineteenth and early twentieth centuries. Moreover, the OECD nations have suffered through persistently higher rates of unemployment and, especially during the 1970s, recurrent bouts of inflation. The contrast for the LDCs since 1973 is even more startling, with annual real income per capita declining. The best performances since 1973 have been turned in by the newly developing nations along the

Pacific rim, but even with their 'economic miracle' the per capita improvements are significantly lower than those experienced by the industrial nations between 1950 and 1973.

Finally, it should be noted that during the Bretton Woods period there was a better overall record of price level stability than during the post-1973 period, or between the wars, or even under the international gold standard.

The lesson that should have been learned

What can we conclude from these facts? First, fixed exchange rate systems are associated with better global economic performance than are flexible systems. Second, during the post-war period until 1973, global economic performance was nothing short of spectacular. It exceeded the remarkable performance of the Industrial Revolution and the gold standard fixed exchange rate system. This unparalleled 'Golden Age' experience required combining a fixed exchange rate system with another civilizing principle, namely that creditor nations must accept a major share of the responsibility for solving any persistent international payments imbalances that might develop. Third, the Bretton Woods period was a remarkably crisis-free economic era.

Since the breakdown of Bretton Woods, on the other hand, the global economy has stumbled from one global economic crisis to another. Economic growth around the world has slowed significantly while the increasing global population menaces standards of living. The number of mouths to be fed is threatening to increase at a faster rate than global GDP. Economics has once more become the dismal science with its Malthusian overtones.

Instead of bringing the utopian benefits promised by conservative economics, the post-Bretton Woods system has generated a growing international monetary crisis. As early as 1986 *New York Times* columnist Flora Lewis noted that government and business leaders recognize that 'the issues of trade, debt, and currency exchange rates are intertwined.' Lewis warned that the world is on a course leading to an economic calamity, yet 'nobody wants to speak out and be accused of setting off a panic . . . the most sober judgment is that the best thing that can be done now is to buy more time for adjustments to head off a crash . . . decision makers aren't going to take sensible measures until they are forced to by crisis.'

The current international payments system does not serve the emerging global economy well. *The Financial Times* of London and *The Economist*, both previously strong advocates of today's floating rate system, have acknowledged that this system is a failure and was sold to the public and the politicians under false advertising claims.[12] Yet no leader is calling for a complete overhaul of a system that is far worse than the one we abandoned in 1973. No one has the courage to speak out in public forums and suggest that the conservative philosophy which has governed our economic affairs in recent decades is a formula for economic disaster.

The responsibility for resolving international trade imbalances in a civil global community: the Marshall Plan example

During World War II, Europe's productive capacity was ravaged. Immediately after the war, Europeans required huge quantities of imports to feed themselves and to rebuild their factories and cities. During 1946 and 1947 European nations used up almost all of their pre-war savings (their foreign reserves) to pay for imports from the United States, the only nation that had available productive capacity.

Under any conventional conservative international monetary system, once their reserves were exhausted the Europeans would have either to accept the burden of adjustment by 'tightening their belts,' that is by reducing demand for imports to the negligible amount they could earn from exports, or to borrow dollars to pay for imports. The Catch 22 of these alternatives was:

1   Europeans could not produce enough to feed their population. To tell starving people to tighten their belts is not only an uncivilized suggestion but it imposes an impossible condition. Had the necessary 'belt tightening' been undertaken, the result would have been to depress further the war-torn standard of living of western Europeans. This would have induced political revolutions in Europe, not to mention recession in America's export industries.

2   During the Great Depression, European export earnings were so low that they defaulted on most of their international debts. Given this experience and the fact that their post-war industries were in shambles and could not produce enough in exports to service their debt, American banks would not make the massive loans needed by Europeans. It was also obvious that any direct US government loans could not be repaid.

As a civilized strategy to avoid the political and economic chaos that would probably have occurred in Europe, the United States offered to pay for the European potential trade deficits (of imports over exports) necessary to rebuild Europe through the Marshall Plan and other aid programs. In essence, the Marshall Plan permitted foreigners to buy United States exports without either drawing down their last pennies of foreign reserve savings or going into debt that could not be repaid in the foreseeable future. Through the Marshall Plan and other aid programs, the United States was demonstrating a civilized attitude to the entire global community.[13]

If the United States had left the deficit nations to adjust to the vast looming trade imbalance by reducing imports, then (a) the standard of living of Europeans and Asian residents would have been substantially lower; *and* (b) the United States would have slipped into a great recession as there would have been too little international demand for the products of its surplus industrial capacity.

The Marshall Plan and large-scale foreign military and economic aid programs *gave* foreigners large sums of American dollars, *as a gift*, so that they could buy American products. The result was that:

1 huge benefits accrued to both foreigners and US citizens. Foreigners used these gifts to buy the American goods necessary to rebuild their economies and to feed their people. Americans obtained additional jobs and earned more income by selling exports to these foreigners;
2 by its generosity the United States invigorated, enriched and strengthened the international community to the immense economic gain of all nations outside the Iron Curtain.

The Marshall Plan gave away a total of $13 billion in four years. (In 1994 dollars this is equivalent to $139 billion.) This 'giveaway' represented 2 percent *per annum* of United States GDP. Nevertheless, American consumers experienced no real pain. During the first year of the Marshall Plan, US real GDP per capita was 25 percent greater than in 1940 (the last peacetime year). Employment and per capita GDP grew continuously between 1947 and 1957 as these foreign aid funds financed additional demand for US exports. These exports were produced by employing what otherwise would have been idle American workers, and factories created jobs and incomes for millions of Americans. For the first time in its history, the United States did not suffer from a severe recession immediately after the cessation of a major war.

The entire free world experienced an economic 'free lunch' as both the debtors and the creditor nation gained from this United States 'giveaway.' The Bretton Woods system in tandem with the Marshall Plan, whereby the United States took deliberate steps to prevent others from depleting their foreign reserves and become overindebted internationally, resulted in a global golden age of economic development.

By 1958, however, the US international position of being able to export more than it imported was coming to an end. Foreign aid grants exceeded the United States' trade surplus of demand for US exports over US imports. Unfortunately, the Bretton Woods system had no mechanism for automatically encouraging emerging trade surplus (creditor) nations to step into the civilizing adjustment role the US had been playing since 1947. Instead, these creditor nations converted a portion of their annual dollar export earnings into calls on the gold reserves of the United States. In 1958 alone, the US lost over $2 billion of its gold reserves. In the 1960s, increased US military and financial aid responses to the Berlin Wall and Vietnam accelerated this trend.

The seeds of destruction of the Bretton Woods system were sown and the golden age of global economic development ended as the trade surplus nations continually drained gold reserves from the United States. When the US closed the gold window in 1971 in order to avoid a continuing reduction in its foreign reserves and then in 1973 unilaterally withdrew from Bretton Woods, the last vestige of a potentially enlightened international monetary approach was lost

– apparently without regret or regard as to how well it had served the global economy.

Comparing the Marshall Plan and the Treaty of Versailles

This civilized historical episode enhancing a post-war international civil community can be compared to the barbaric policy and the resultant fragmented international system that followed World War I. Under the 1919 Treaty of Versailles, the victorious Allies imposed a harsh settlement on the defeated nations. Massive reparations were imposed on Germany as the European Allies attempted to obtain compensation for the costs of the war that they had incurred.

In his book *Economic Consequences of the Peace*, John Maynard Keynes spoke out against the uncivilized policy of imposing reparations on these war-torn nations. Perhaps the victorious European nations whose citizens had suffered through years of war cannot be blamed for mistrusting Keynes' civilized economic arguments or the political ideals of President Woodrow Wilson. The evils of waging war may have eroded the civilized values of the European Allies to the point where they felt compelled to demand barbaric financial retribution.

The result of this Allied barbarism may have been initially satisfying to the warlike passion for revenge by humiliating a former enemy; but barbaric treatment can breed more barbarism, as the evils imposed by the oppressor shape the values of the oppressed. Although the primary responsibility for Nazi Germany does not lie with the British and French economic policies after the war, to the extent that they helped shape German society's values of the 1920s and '30s, the harsh Allied terms for peace did have a significant role in the outcome that occurred in the 1930s and '40s in Europe.

The United States was the only victorious nation to pursue a civilized policy of not claiming reparations. The United States developed a loan plan (the Dawes Plan) for aiding the Germans to meet the Allied claims. Unlike the other victorious Allies, the United States enjoyed an economic boom in the 1920s as the Allies bought American goods with these Dawes Plan dollars. The European victors, even with the boost of war reparations, experienced much tougher economic times.

Reforming the world's money

Fifty years ago, Keynes (1980: 168) provided a clear outline of what is needed when he wrote:

> We need an instrument of international currency having general acceptability between nations ... We need an orderly and agreed upon method of determining the relative exchange values of national currency units ... We need a quantum of international currency ... [which] is

governed by the actual current [liquidity] requirements of world commerce, and is capable of deliberate expansion . . . We need a method by which the surplus credit balances arising from international trade, which the recipient does not wish to employ can be set to work . . . without detriment to the liquidity of these balances.

What is required is a *closed*, double-entry bookkeeping, clearing institution to keep the payments 'score' among the various trading regions plus some mutually agreed upon rules to create and reflux liquidity while maintaining the international purchasing power of the international currency. The eight provisions of the clearing system suggested in this section meet the criteria laid down by Keynes. The rules of this Post Keynesian proposed system are designed: (a) to prevent a lack of global effective demand[14] due to any nation(s) either holding excessive idle reserves or draining reserves from the system; (b) to provide an automatic mechanism for placing a major burden of payments adjustments on the surplus nations; (c) to provide each nation with the ability to monitor and, if desired, to put boulders into the movement of international portfolio funds in order to control movements of flight capital;[15] and finally (d) to expand the quantity of the liquid asset of ultimate international redemption as global capacity warrants.

Elements of such a clearing system would include:

1 The unit of account and ultimate reserve asset for international liquidity is the International Money Clearing Unit (IMCU). All IMCUs are held *only* by central banks, not by the public.

2 The central bank of each nation or unionized monetary system (UMS) central bank is committed to guarantee one-way convertibility from IMCU deposits at the clearing union to its domestic money. Each central bank will set its own rules regarding making available foreign monies (through IMCU clearing transactions) to its own bankers and private sector residents.[16] Since central banks agree to sell their own liabilities (one-way convertibility) against the IMCU only to other central bankers and the International Clearing Agency while they simultaneously hold only IMCUs as liquid reserve assets for international financial transactions, there can be no draining of reserves from the system. Ultimately, all major private international transactions clear between central banks' accounts in the books of the international clearing institution.

3 The exchange rate between the domestic currency and the IMCU is set *initially* by each nation – just as it would be if an international gold standard were instituted. Since enterprises that are already engaged in trade have international contractual commitments which would span the change-over interval, then, as a practical matter, one would expect that the existing exchange rate structure (with perhaps minor modifications) would provide the basis for initial rate setting. Provisions 7 and 8 below indicate when and how this nominal exchange rate between the national

currency and the IMCU would be changed in the future.

4   Contracts between private individuals will continue to be denominated in whatever domestic currency is permitted by local laws and agreed upon by the contracting parties. Contracts to be settled in terms of a foreign currency will therefore require some announced commitment from the central bank (through private sector bankers) of the availability of foreign funds to meet such private contractual obligations.

5   An overdraft system to make available short-term unused creditor balances at the clearing house to finance the productive international transactions of others who need short-term credit. The terms will be determined by the *pro bono* clearing managers.

6   A trigger mechanism to encourage a creditor nation to spend what is deemed (in advance) by agreement of the international community to be *'excessive' credit balances accumulated by running current account surpluses*. These excessive credits can be spent in three ways: (a) on the products of any other member of the clearing union; (b) on new direct foreign investment projects; and/or (c) to provide unilateral transfers (foreign aid) to deficit members. Spending on imports forces the surplus nation to make the adjustment directly through the balance on goods and services. Spending by way of unilateral transfers permits adjustment directly by the current account balance; while direct foreign investment provides adjustment by the capital accounts (without setting up a contractual debt that will *require* reverse current account flows in the future).

Provision 6 provides the surplus country with considerable discretion in deciding how to accept the 'onus' of adjustment in the way it believes is in its residents' best interests. It does not permit the surplus nation to shift the burden to the deficit nation(s) through contractual requirements for debt service charges independently of what the deficit nation can afford.[17] The important thing is to make sure that continual oversaving[18] by surplus nations cannot unleash depressionary forces and/or a building up of international debts so encumbering as to impoverish the global economy of the twenty-first century.

In the unlikely event that the surplus nation does not spend or give away these credits within a specified time, then the clearing agency would confiscate (and redistribute to debtor members) the portion of credits deemed excessive.[19] This last-resort confiscatory action by the managers of the clearing agency would make a payments adjustment through unilateral transfer payments in the current accounts.

Under either a fixed or a flexible rate system, nations may experience persistent trade deficits merely because trading partners are not living up to their means – that is because other nations are continually hoarding a portion of their foreign export earnings (plus net unilateral transfers). By so doing, these oversavers are creating a lack of global effective demand. Under provision 6, deficit countries would no longer have to deflate their real economy merely to adjust payment imbalances because others are oversaving. Instead, the system would seek to remedy the payment deficit by increasing opportunities for deficit nations to sell abroad and thereby earn their way out of the deficit.

7   A system to stabilize the long-term purchasing power of the IMCU (in terms of each member nation's domestically produced market basket of goods) can be developed. This requires a system of fixed exchange rates between the local currency and the IMCU that changes only to reflect permanent increases in efficiency wages.[20] This assures each central bank that its holdings of IMCUs as the nation's foreign reserves will never lose purchasing power in terms of foreign-produced goods, even if a foreign government permits wage-price inflation to occur within its borders. The rate between the local currency and the IMCU would change with inflation in the local money price of the domestic commodity basket.

If increases in productivity lead to declining nominal production costs, then the nation with this decline in efficiency wages (say of 5 percent) would have the option of choosing either (a) to permit the IMCU to buy (up to 5 percent) fewer units of domestic currency, thereby capturing all (or most of) the gains from productivity for its residents while maintaining the purchasing power of the IMCU; or (b) to keep the nominal exchange rate constant. In the latter case, the gain in productivity is shared with all trading partners. In exchange, the export industries in this productive nation will receive an increased relative share of the world market.

By altering the exchange rate between local monies and the IMCU to offset the rate of domestic inflation, the IMCU's purchasing power is stabilized. By restricting use of IMCUs to central banks, private speculation regarding IMCUs as a hedge against inflation is avoided. Each nation's rate of inflation of the goods and services it produces is determined solely by the local government's policy towards the level of domestic money wages and profit margins *vis-à-vis* productivity gains, that is, the nation's efficiency wage. Each nation is therefore free to experiment with policies for stabilizing its efficiency wage to prevent inflation. Whether the nation is successful or not, the IMCU will never lose its international purchasing power. Moreover, the IMCU has the promise of gaining in purchasing power over time if productivity grows more rapidly than money wages and each nation is willing to share any reduction in real production costs with its trading partners.

Provision 7 produces a system designed to maintain the relative efficiency wage parities amongst nations. In such a system, the adjustability of nominal exchange rates will be primarily (but not always, see provision 8) to offset changes in efficiency wages among trading partners. A beneficial effect that follows from this proviso is that it eliminates the possibility of a specific industry in any nation put at a competitive disadvantage (or secure a competitive advantage) against foreign producers solely because the nominal exchange rate was changed independently of changes in efficiency wages and the real costs of production in each nation.

Nominal exchange rate variability will no longer create the problem of a loss of competitiveness due solely to the overvaluing of a currency as, for example, was experienced by the industries in the American 'rust belt' during the period 1982–5. Even if temporary, currency appreciation can have significant permanent real costs, for example, industries may abandon markets and the resulting idle existing plant and equipment may be cast aside as too costly to maintain.

Provision 7 also prevents any nation from engaging in a beggar-thy-neighbor, export-thy-unemployment policy by pursuing a real exchange rate devaluation that does not reflect changes in efficiency wages. Once the initial exchange rates are chosen and relative efficiency wages are locked in, reductions in real production costs that are associated with a relative decline in efficiency wages are the main factors (with the exception of provision 8) justifying an adjustment in the real exchange rate.

Although provision 6 prevents any country from piling up persistent excessive surpluses this does not mean that it is impossible for one or more nations to run persistent deficits. Proposal 8 below provides a program for addressing the problem of persistent export–import deficits in any one nation.

8   If a country is at *full employment* and still has a tendency towards persistent international deficits on its current account, then this is *prima facie* evidence that it does not possess the productive capacity to maintain its current standard of living. If the deficit nation is a poor one, then surely there is a case for the richer nations which are in surplus to transfer some of their excess credit balances to support the poor nation.[21] If it is a relatively rich country, then the deficit nation must alter its standard of living by reducing the relative terms of trade with major trading partners. Rules, agreed upon in advance, would require the trade-deficit rich nation to devalue its exchange rate by stipulated increments in each period until evidence becomes available to indicate that the export–import imbalance is eliminated without unleashing significant recessionary forces.[22]

If, on the other hand, the payment deficit persists despite a continuous positive balance of trade in goods and services, then there is evidence that the deficit nation might be carrying too heavy an international debt service obligation. The *pro bono* officials of the clearing union should bring the debtor and creditors into negotiations to reduce annual debt service payments by (a) lengthening the payments period, (b) reducing the interest charges, and/or (c) debt forgiveness.[23]

If any government objects to the idea that the IMCU provisions provide governments with the ability to limit the free movement of 'capital' funds, then that nation is free to join other nations of similar attitude in forming a regional currency union (UMS), thereby assuring a free flow of funds among the residents of the currency union.

Conclusion

In normal times with free capital markets, 'speculators may do no harm as bubbles on a steady stream of enterprise. But the position is serious when enterprise becomes the bubbles on a whirlpool of speculation' (Keynes 1936: 159). The grains of sand of a Tobin tax may prick the small bubbles of speculation, but the sand is likely to restrict significantly the flow of real trade. On the other hand, the sands of the Tobin tax will be merely swept away in whirlpools of speculation. Boulders are needed to stop the destructive currency speculation from destroying global enterprise patterns, for 'it is enterprise which builds and improves the world's possessions' (Keynes 1930: 148).

Notes

1 All page references to passages from this book will be cited in the text of this chapter accompanying the relevant quote or discussion. References to any other writings of Keynes or any other will appear as endnotes.
2 Nations with banking institutions which make it difficult for foreign authorities to obtain information regarding bank accounts held by their residents are likely to encourage the influx of funds trying to escape national tax collectors, criminal investigators, and the central banks of nations that try to limit capital outflows. Thus, it is not surprising, that often exchange rates reflect speculative and flight capital flows rather than purchasing power parities.
3 For example, in 1977 the Carter Administration attempted to 'talk down the dollar.' In the spring of 1993, Secretary of Treasury Bentsen tried to talk up the yen. In January 1994, the *New York Times* quoted Secretary Bentsen as saying that 'allowing the yen to decline would not be an acceptable way for Japan to try to escape from its recession.'
4 Most mainstream economists were appalled by President Reagan's boasts regarding the higher dollar that was achieved in the early years of his Administration.
5 Even in the 1990s, as this is being written, nations are still ignoring this Keynesian 'truth' to the detriment of over 38 million unemployed people in the OECD nations and many more in Eastern Europe and the former Soviet Union.
6 In this matter, Keynes (1936: 339) pointed out, 'the [orthodox] faculty of economists prove to have been guilty of presumptuous error.'
7 As I point out in my book (Davidson 1994), both Old and New Keynesian analysis is based on the restrictive classical axioms that Keynes threw out in developing his *General Theory*. It is no wonder, therefore, that these 'Keynesians' subscribe to the classical view of international trade – if they think about it at all.
8 Transactions costs (of holding alternative liquid assets) in the broadest sense – that is including the *fear* of rapid *unpredictable* changes in spot prices, or operating in a thin spot market where no financial institution will act as a residual

buyer and seller – are basic to determining the magnitude of transactions, precautionary and speculative demands for money in the current income period. If all assets were instantaneously resalable without any costs, there would never be a need to hold 'barren money' rather than a productive asset, except for the necessary nanosecond before it was necessary to meet a contractual commitment that came due. In the real world, the magnitude of actual costs of moving between liquid assets and the medium of contractual settlement is related to the degree of spot market organization and the existence of financial institutions that 'make' spot markets and that thereby assure reasonable moment-to-moment stickiness in spot prices.

9   In flexible exchange rate markets, the central bank typically provides foreign exchange support for private (commercial) banks who make the market in foreign exchange.

10   Or 1.1 percent higher than the agent's expectation of the future spot exchange rate in the absence of the tax, if the agent requires a risk premium.

11   Even if the 5 to 1 ratio overestimates the number of real trade transactions compared to speculative flows, as long as there is some multiple, the Tobin tax is likely to impact trade flows more than speculative flows.

12   *The Economist* magazine (January 6, 1990) indicated that the decade of the 1980s will be noted as one in which 'the experiment with floating currencies failed.' Almost two years earlier (February 17, 1987), *The Financial Times* admitted that 'floating exchange rates, it is now clear, were sold on a false prospectus . . . they held out a quite illusory promise of greater national autonomy . . . [but] when macropolicies are inconsistent and when capital is globally mobile, floating rates cannot be relied upon to keep the current accounts roughly in balance.'

13   The Marshall Plan was even offered to the Soviet Union, which refused it.

14   Williamson (1987: 200) recognizes that when balance of payments 'disequilibrium is due purely to excess or deficient demand,' flexible exchange rates *per se* cannot facilitate international payments adjustments.

15   This provides an added bonus by making tax avoidance and profits from illegal trade more difficult to conceal.

16   Correspondent banking will have to operate through the International Clearing Agency, with each central bank regulating the international relations and operations of its domestic banking firms. Small-scale smuggling of currency across borders, and so on, can never be completely eliminated. But such movements are merely a flea on a dog's back – a minor, but not debilitating, irritation. If, however, most of the residents of a nation hold and use (in violation of legal tender laws) a foreign currency for domestic transactions and as a store of value (for example, it is estimated that Argentineans hold close to $5 billion US dollars), this is evidence of a lack of confidence in the government and its monetary authority. Unless confidence is restored, all attempts to restore economic prosperity will fail.

17   Some may fear that if a surplus nation is close to the trigger point it could short-circuit the system by making loans to reduce its credit balance *prior* to setting off the trigger. Since preventing unreasonable debt service obligations is an important objective of this proposal, a mechanism which monitors and can restrict such pre-trigger lending activities may be required.

One possible way of eliminating this trigger-avoidance lending loophole is as follows: An initial agreement is established as to what constitutes sensible and flexible criteria for judging when debt servicing burdens become unreasonable is established. Given these criteria, the clearing union managers would have the responsibility for preventing additional loans which push debt burdens beyond reasonable servicing levels. In other words, loans that push debt burdens too far could not be cleared through the clearing union, that is, the managers would refuse to release the IMCUs for loan purposes from the surplus country's account. (I am indebted to Robert Blecker for suggesting this point.)

The managers would also be required to make periodic public reports on the level of credits being accumulated by surplus nations and to indicate how close these surpluses are to the trigger point. Such reports would provide an informational edge for debtor nations, permitting them to bargain more successfully regarding the terms of refinancing existing loans and/or new loans. All loans would still have to meet the clearing union's guidelines for reasonableness.

I do not discount the difficulties involved in setting up and getting agreement on criteria for establishing unreasonable debt service burdens. (For some suggestions, however, see the second paragraph of provision 8.) In the absence of cooperation and a spirit of goodwill that is necessary for the clearing union to provide a mechanism assuring the economic prosperity of all members, however, no progress can ever be made.

Moreover, as the current international debt problems of African and Latin American nations clearly demonstrates, creditors ultimately have to forgive some debt when they have previously encouraged excessive debt burdens. Under the current system, however, debt forgiveness is a last-resort solution acceptable only when both debtor and creditor nations suffer from faltering economic growth. Surely a more intelligent option is to develop an institutional arrangement which prevents excessive debt servicing burdens from ever occurring.

18 Oversaving is defined as a nation persistently spending less on imports plus direct equity foreign investment than the nation's export earnings plus net unilateral transfers.

19 Whatever 'excessive' credit balances are redistributed shall be apportioned among the debtor nations (perhaps based on a formula which is inversely related to each debtor's per capita income and directly related to the size of its international debt) to be used to reduce debit balances at the clearing union.

20 The efficiency wage is related to the money wage divided by the average product of labor; it is the unit labor cost modified by the profit mark-up in domestic money terms of domestically produced GNP. At this preliminary stage of this proposal, it would serve no useful purpose to decide whether the domestic market basket should include both tradable and non-tradable goods and services. (With the growth of tourism more and more non-tradable goods become potentially tradable.) I personally prefer the wider concept of the domestic market basket, but it is not obvious that any essential principle is lost if a tradable only concept is used, or if some nations use the wider concept while others the narrower one.

21 This is equivalent to a negative income tax for poor, fully employed families within a nation.

22 Although relative prices of imports and exports would be altered by the change in the terms of trade, the adjustment is due to the resulting income effect, not a substitution effect. The deficit nation's real income will fall until its import surplus disappears.

23 The actual program adopted for debt service reduction will depend on many parameters including: the relative income and wealth of the debtor *vis-à-vis* the creditor, the ability of the debtor to increase its per capita real income, etc.

References

Adelman, I. (1991) *Long-term Economic Development*, Working Paper no. 589, Berkeley, Cal.: California Agricultural Experiment Station.

Davidson, P. (1972) *Money and the Real World*, London: Macmillan.

—— (1994) *Post Keynesian Macroeconomic Theory*, Cheltenham: Edward Elgar.

Eichengreen, B., Tobin, J. and Wyplosz, C. (1995) 'The Case for Sand in the Wheels of International Finance,' *Economic Journal* 105, 428: 162–72.

Friedman, M. (1974) 'A Response to His Critics,' in R.J. Gordon (ed.) *Milton Friedman's Monetary Framework: A Debate With his Critics*, Chicago: University of Chicago Press.

Garber, P. and Taylor, M.P. (1995) 'Sand in the Wheels of Foreign Exchange Markets: a Skeptical Note,' *Economic Journal* 105, 428: 173–80.

Greenway, D. (1995) 'Policy Form: Sand in the Wheels of International Finance. Editorial Note,' *Economic Journal* 105, 428: 160–2.

Hicks, J.R. (1967) 'A Suggestion for Simplifying the Theory of Money,' in *Critical Essays in Monetary Theory*, Oxford: Clarendon Press.

—— (1979) *Causality in Economics*, New York: Basic Books.

Kenen, P. (1995) 'Capital Controls, the EMS and the EMU,' *Economic Journal* 105, 428: 181–92.

Keynes, J.M. (1930) *A Treatise on Money*, vol. II, London: Macmillan.

—— (1936) *The General Theory of Employment, Interest and Money*, London: Macmillan.

—— (1980) *The Collected Writings of John Maynard Keynes*, vol. 25, D. Moggridge (ed.), London: Macmillan.

Lewis, Flora (1986) *New York Times*, November.

Williamson, J. (1987) 'Exchange Rate Management: the Role of Target Zones,' *American Economic Review Papers and Proceedings* 77, 2: 200–4.

3 Growth in an international context

A Post Keynesian view

John S. L. McCombie and A. P. Thirlwall

Introduction

The purpose of this chapter is to discuss and analyse how the balance of payments impinges on the growth performance of countries. This is important because mainstream growth theory still largely ignores the balance of payments. In classical growth theory, the balance of payments was assumed to look after itself through internal or external price adjustment, thereby severing any possible link between the state of the balance of payments and the use or accumulation of resources for economic growth. Harrod's growth model (Harrod 1939) was a closed economy model, and so was the neoclassical growth model (see, for example, Solow 1956) with the added objection that the demand side of the economy was completely ignored. Savings determine investment and aggregate demand equals aggregate supply. 'New' growth theory, or endogenous growth theory (see Romer 1986; Lucas 1988) is also supply orientated and there are no demand constraints either internal or external. Many of the 'new' growth models are closed economy models, and in those which are not, the focus is on growth and trade, not on growth and the balance of payments. In the history of economic thought, the only school to have emphasised the importance of foreign exchange and a strong balance of payments for economic growth was the Mercantilists.

In more recent times, a handful of eminent economists has highlighted foreign exchange as a scarce resource which may not be easily substitutable by domestic saving, but their voices have not constituted a coherent school of thought. John Maynard Keynes in *The General Theory* (1936) defended mercantilism on the grounds that the interest rate required for external balance might be inappropriate to secure a domestic balance between saving and investment, leading to unemployment, but the idea was not seriously developed into a theory of balance-of-payments constrained growth. Roy Harrod (1933) before him had developed the concept of the (static) foreign trade multiplier, but the idea put forward, that the pace and rhythm of industrial growth in an open economy are determined by export performance relative to the propensity to import, was eclipsed by Keynes's investment multiplier for the closed economy. Raul Prebisch (1950), in thinking about the problems of developing countries, challenged the doctrine of the mutual profitability of free trade by arguing that the gains from specialisation in primary production may be offset by the balance-of-payments consequences of such specialisation, but his argument for viewing trade from a monetary standpoint, rather than from the viewpoint of real resource augmentation, was too unorthodox for the profession to grasp. Hollis Chenery and his collaborators (Chenery and Bruno 1962; Chenery and Adelman 1966; Chenery and Macewan 1966), developed the concept of dual-gap analysis, also in a development context, which showed that if the foreign exchange gap to achieve a target rate of growth was greater than a domestic savings–investment gap, foreign inflows would need to fill the larger of the two gaps, otherwise growth would be constrained by the most limiting resource (that is, foreign exchange) and domestic saving would go unutilised. This idea was also attacked by the neoclassical orthodoxy on the grounds that it ignores the substitution possibilities between imports of consumption and investment goods, and between domestic saving and foreign exchange. Excess domestic saving can be used to produce more exports. In the long run, a separate foreign exchange gap is impossible. Finally, Nicholas Kaldor (1975) attempted to revive the doctrine of the Harrod trade multiplier, particularly in the context of the United Kingdom, as an explanation of the UK's poor growth performance relative to the rest of Europe in the post-war period, but with little impact. The UK's weak balance of payments was viewed by the economics establishment as a supply problem, ostensibly reinforcing the neoclassical model that growth is supply determined rather than demand constrained.

Growth and the balance of payments: an historical overview

The traditional and conventional (classical and neoclassical) approach to the analysis of the growth performance of countries is to focus on resource availability and the supply of factor inputs, and to explain growth rate differences between countries in these terms. Heavy emphasis is placed on investment and technical progress. It should be obvious, however, that resource availability is not a sufficient condition for growth because resources may be unemployed or underutilised. It should be equally apparent that most resources for growth are not fixed in supply or exogenously given to an economic system, which conventional growth and trade theory tends to assume. Most resources for growth, such as the quantity and quality of labour inputs, capital accumulation and improved productivity through technical progress, are elastic in supply and endogenous to an economic system, dependent on the growth of output itself. This insight provides the starting point for the debate between those who believe that growth is supply driven (and analyse growth in this way) and those who believe that growth is demand driven, and that it is constraints on demand – be they economic or institutional – that explain growth rate differences between countries. If a balance-of-payments deficit, or foreign exchange shortage, is not automatically eliminated through a change in the relative prices of domestic and foreign goods, it immediately becomes a constraint on demand if the deficit cannot be indefinitely financed at a constant rate of interest, and therefore will affect the growth process.

In both traditional and 'new' growth theory, no particular emphasis is placed on demand constraints within either a closed or an open economy. Pre-Keynesian modes of thinking die hard. Classical growth theory, as epitomised by Ricardo, was a supply-orientated model. Profits determined investment, and investment determined growth. The pervasive classical belief in Say's Law that 'supply creates its own demand' implied that all output produced would be sold, and all resources would be employed, assuming, also, flexibility in the labour market. The fact that industry would have to sell ('exports') to agriculture to obtain wage (or consumption) goods ('imports') for workers was assumed to present no problems because any imbalance between the supply of and demand for 'exports' and 'imports' would be rectified by adjustment of the internal terms of trade.

Keynes, in his *General Theory*, undermined Say's Law in the static closed economy and showed that output is not determined by supply but by effective demand, which may, within limits, generate its own supply. In the growing closed economy, Harrod (1939) then showed that there was no automatic mechanism which ensured that a country would necessarily grow at its assumed capacity rate, which he called the natural rate of growth. Plans to save may exceed the rate of *induced* investment at the natural rate, leading to secular stagnation. Not only the level of output, but also the growth of output, is determined by demand, not by available supplies. It is true that the natural rate of growth in the Harrod model sets the *upper* limit to growth, but there is nothing to say that the natural rate of growth is immutable and independent of demand. For example, it is well documented (see Cornwall 1977; Kindleberger 1967) that labour force growth differs between countries partly as a result of net immigration/emigration which responds to differences in the demand for labour between countries. Neither Keynes in the *General Theory* nor Harrod in his dynamic extension of Keynes's theory explicitly addressed themselves to the open economy and the possibility that an imbalance between plans to export and import may present as much of a problem for demand as divergencies between plans to save and plans to invest.[1]

Not only did classical growth theory ignore demand,[2] but classical trade theory also ignored the balance of payments. In classical economics, much emphasis is given to the importance of trade for growth, but it is all *real* trade theory, and again supply orientated. The monetary consequences of trade for growth are ignored. We owe to Ricardo the doctrine of comparative advantage which shows that countries specialising in what they are best at producing in an opportunity cost sense can increase total production and, by trading, improve the welfare of all. His was a very powerful and influential theorem, but it is based on several special and restrictive assumptions. One assumption is full employment; another is continuous balance-of-payments equilibrium. The full employment assumption is crucial to the predictions of the theorem, because if unemployment were to arise in the process of specialisation and resource reallocation, the resource gains from specialisation might be offset by resource losses from unemployment. Full employment is taken for granted in the model because all activities are assumed to be subject to constant costs of production per unit of output so that there is no limit to the employment of labour in each activity as resource reallocation takes place. But suppose that some activities are subject to diminishing returns so that the marginal product of labour falls and the marginal cost of labour rises. There will then be a limit to the level of employment in these activities given by the minimum (subsistence) wage. Countries forced to specialise in these activities through the pursuit of static comparative advantage may find themselves with unemployment owing to their inability to absorb all the labour from the activities in which they have a comparative disadvantage. The mutual profitability of the free trade argument breaks down.

More important for the argument here, however, is the neglect of the effect of the structure and pattern of trade on the balance of payments of a country, because in classical theory the balance of payments is assumed to be self-equilibrating. If the balance of payments is not self-adjusting, however, this is another reason why unemployment may develop, and why trade and growth cannot be looked at simply from the point of view of the augmentation of the supply of resources. Early classical thinking was based on the price-specie flow mechanism outlined by David Hume (1752). Gold movements were the instrument by which payments balance was supposed to be achieved. Countries with a payments deficit would lose gold, causing an internal price deflation which would induce a rise in exports and a fall in imports, and the opposite for surplus countries. This is also sometimes referred to as the Ricardo–Mill adjustment mechanism, retaining the classical presumption of continuous full employment. More refined versions of the gold standard story were developed in the late nineteenth century when the operation of the system was at its zenith, recognising the fact that in practice no gold standard country operated a rigid 100 per cent reserve monetary system backed by gold. Fiduciary issues of currency were permitted. But a fixed relation between the monetary base and the total quantity of money was assumed so that the theory of balance-of-payments adjustment stayed essentially the same. The model was also extended to capital flows where gold moved in the same direction as the capital transfer, and the trade surplus generated in the country 'exporting' capital was the real counterpart of the capital transfer. Again, there was no adjustment of income or output. Monetary historians (for example, Triffin 1964; McClosky and Zecher 1976; Cooper 1982) have noted, however, that instead of the price levels of deficit and surplus countries moving in *opposite* directions, there was a tendency in the nineteenth century for countries' price levels to move together. In practice, it was not relative price changes that operated to achieve payments balance, but expenditure and output changes associated with interest rate differentials. Capital importing countries (in current account deficit) with high interest rates had expenditure damped relative to capital exporting countries (in current account surplus) with lower interest rates. Income adjustment is therefore implied. Even as late as the 1930s, however, very few economists were teaching this story; one notable exception was P. Barrett Whale at the London School of Economics (see Barrett Whale 1932, 1937). The story of how flexible exchange rates are supposed to rectify balance-of-payments disequilibrium is as equally open to doubt as is the old gold standard mechanism, and we return to this issue later.

In the context of developing countries, the Argentinian economist Raul Prebisch (1950) made an early challenge to the practical relevance of the predictions of real trade theory, on the grounds that the Ricardian gains from trade may be offset by terms of trade deterioration and by an underutilisation of resources because the pattern of trade leads developing countries into perpetual balance-of-payments difficulties. If there is unemployment, the opportunity cost of the use of resources is zero, and this leads to the possibility of welfare gains from protection, which Prebisch advocated for Latin America. In this field, too, classical and neoclassical thinking dies hard. Harry Johnson (1964) in his classic paper on tariffs and development calls protection for balance of payments reasons a 'non-argument.' Yet, if balance of payments problems impose demand constraints and lead to unemployment, this implies a distortion in the labour market which provides an *economic* argument for protection, as Johnson himself recognises, because the social cost of labour is zero.

Another tack used by neoclassical economists is to invoke the 'small country' assumption that countries can sell any amount of goods they choose in world markets so that, by definition, there are no demand constraints on output growth, only supply constraints. There are two responses that can be made to this argument. The first is that, at least in the markets for manufactured goods, producers are rarely, if ever, price takers. Even within 'small' countries, most producers produce heterogeneous goods within fairly narrow product ranges and are not small suppliers relative to total supply. Each producer is a 'monopolist' of his own differentiated product: the well-known concept of monopolistic competition. Second, even in the case of small suppliers of homogeneous goods, it does not follow that there is an unlimited demand for *all* goods. Producers, in total, will be affected in the amount they can sell by shifts in the world demand for output. It can be seen during periods of fluctuation in the world economy that the demand and sales of all homogeneous primary commodities varies cyclically with world economic activity.

Notwithstanding the Keynesian revolution, and the manifest balance of payments difficulties experienced by many countries, the prevailing orthodoxy is still to analyse growth from the supply side. This is epitomised in the neoclassical approach to the analysis of growth and in the more recent 'new' or endogenous growth theory. The neoclassical approach uses the aggregate production function and attempts to explain the growth of output in terms of the growth of factor inputs and their productivity. Differences in the growth of output between countries are thus accounted for in terms of differences in the rates of growth of labour inputs, capital accumulation and technical progress as the determinant of productivity growth. Major empirical studies that have used this approach are Denison (1967) and Matthews *et al.* (1982) (see also Crafts 1988). There is no doubt that the approach is very versatile, in the sense that any variable can be included in the production function that is thought to influence the growth process and can yield interesting results, but it does not answer the fundamental question of why factor supplies and productivity grow at different rates between countries. The approach treats factors of production and technical progress as essentially exogenous to an economic system, whereas in practice what is happening to the growth of the labour force, capital accumulation and technical progress is to a large extent endogenous to an economic system since their growth depends, at least in part, on the strength of demand. The response of labour supply (partly through migration and increases in the participation rate) to demand has already been mentioned. One of the best examples is the immigration into Germany and Switzerland during the 1950s and 1960s. Capital accumulation has a large induced element through the accelerator mechanism. (The growth of capital is also endogenous in steady-state growth in the neoclassical approach, but these models lack an independent investment function. The rate of investment is determined by savings.) We know also from studies of productivity growth that through the mechanism of static and dynamic returns to scale, productivity growth is induced by output growth itself – the so-called Verdoorn Law (see Thirlwall 1983a; Bairam 1987). So we are back to the question of what determines output growth. In neoclassical growth analysis, demand constraints – either internal or external through the balance of payments – never enter the picture in an explicit manner. Long-run growth is determined by the rate of growth of the labour force in efficiency units, exogenously determined.

'New' growth theory, or endogenous growth theory, retains all the essential features of the neoclassical approach to growth except that the assumption of diminishing returns to capital is relaxed. If the marginal product of capital does not decline as more investment takes place, the investment ratio will also be a determinant of long-run growth. In this sense, growth is said to be endogenous. The question then is: what are the forces that prevent the marginal product of capital from falling as countries get richer? Some models stress the role of research and development (Romer 1986); others stress the role of human capital formation (Lucas 1988). But it is clear from the definition of the capital–output ratio (which is equal to the capital–labour ratio divided by the productivity of labour) that anything which raises the productivity of labour in the same proportion as the capital–labour ratio will keep the capital–output ratio, or the productivity of capital, unchanged. Embodied technical progress of all types (including learning by doing) is sufficient, as Kaldor (1957) pointed out in his early growth model which included the innovation of the technical progress function to replace the neoclassical production function. None of the 'new' growth theory models address the issue of demand. Savings determines investment, and aggregate demand equals aggregate supply. Most of the models of endogenous growth are also closed economy models. Where trade is included (see Grossman and Helpman 1990) it is to capture the technological spillovers from trade which may also keep the marginal product of capital from falling as capital accumulation takes place. In the empirical studies which attempt to test 'new' growth theory, trade is measured as the ratio of trade to GDP as a measure of the openness of an economy. Sometimes the variable is statistically significant (see Knight *et al.* 1993), but often it is fragile (Levine and Renelt 1992). One statistical problem seems to be that investment performance is closely correlated with the measure of openness. From an economic viewpoint, however, the ratio of trade to GDP is a very static measure of the potential role of trade in the growth process. To capture the dynamic effects of trade from both the demand side and the supply side, the growth of exports would be a much more appropriate variable to take, and, indeed, it turns out to be highly significant (Thirlwall and Sanna 1996). Exports are important from the demand side both directly and indirectly because they allow other components of demand to grow faster than otherwise would be the case in accordance with the Hicks supermultiplier (McCombie 1985). Exports are the only component of demand that can pay for the import requirements associated with growth. Export growth is important from the supply side because it allows a faster growth of imports, and imports may be more productive than domestic resources, particularly if they allow the fuller use of domestic resources in accordance with dual-gap theory mentioned earlier.

In the demand-orientated approach to growth that we shall develop here, long-run output growth in the open economy will be shown to be fundamentally determined by export growth in accordance with the workings of the dynamic Harrod trade multiplier. This model captures the twin ideas that, in the open economy, exports are the only true component of autonomous demand, and that in the long run balance-of-payments equilibrium on current account (or basic balance equilibrium including sustainable long-run capital flows) is a requirement. It will be argued, in turn, that the growth of exports, at least for developed countries, is mainly determined by the non-price characteristics of goods which are captured in the measurement of the income elasticity of demand for exports, that is, all those factors that cause the demand curve for exports to shift *outwards* over time, as distinct from movements *along* the demand curve through relative price and exchange rate changes. This view of growth performance could potentially unite 'supply-siders' and 'demand-siders.' Demand, determined by export performance and the balance-of-payments position, governs output growth; but supply factors such as investment in new technology, research and development effort, education and training in skills determine the income elasticity of demand for exports, and therefore how fast a country's exports grow as world demand grows. The view which cannot be accepted is that a mere augmentation of the supply of resources will necessarily improve the growth performance of a country if it does not at the same time improve the long-run balance-of-payments position. If exports remain static and imports rise, the deficit on the balance of payments may be unsustainable, demand would have to be contracted and resources would remain underutilised. It is in this sense that the balance of payments becomes the ultimate constraint on growth.

We turn now to the ways in which this argument has been recognised in the history of economic thought, but which has invariably come under attack and gone against the mainstream. The exposition here also goes against the mainstream, but it does have historical antecedents. We consider first the Mercantilists.

Mercantilism

Mercantilism was a doctrine that dominated both economic and political thinking for over a century from the publication of Machiavelli's *The Prince* in 1532 to Thomas Mun's *England's Treasure by Foreign Trade* published posthumously in 1664. Politically, the doctrine was associated with the concept of a strong State, with a positive balance of trade and the accumulation of foreign exchange (gold and other precious metals) seen as the means of acquiring political strength and national prosperity. Edward Misselden, who appears to have been the first writer to use the term 'balance of trade' in his book *The Centre of the Circle of Commerce* (1623), explicitly argued that the policies of the State should be to secure a favourable balance of trade by promoting exports and discouraging imports, the country thereby receiving treasure and growing rich. The precise means by which the accumulation of treasure would make a country rich, however, was not always clear in mercantilist writing, and it was one of Adam Smith's critiques of mercantilism that not only was it anti-free trade, but also that it confused money and wealth or money and capital. Neither of Smith's main criticisms of mercantilism, however, appears to be entirely fair. If Thomas Mun is taken as typifying mercantilist thinking in the seventeenth century, Mun did not confuse money and wealth, and he was against protection because of the fear of retaliation. In Mun, the emphasis is not on treasure for its own sake (as it tended to be in earlier writings), but on the beneficial effect that treasure can have in stimulating economic activity in a country by keeping the rate of interest low and encouraging investment. Suviranka (1923) in his book, *The Theory of the Balance of Trade in England*, concludes:

> much in the appreciation of money by mercantile writers does not, therefore, appear unreasonable . . . As long as paper currency had not been introduced, there existed permanently, even at the time of the largest supply of money, a *potential* scarcity of money. A stoppage or even a substantial slackening in the supply of the precious metals would have, by the steadily growing demand for money, changed, sooner or later, the imminent danger of a scarcity into a painful reality. It is against this

background that the mercantile psychology must be seen and that the anxiety for a steady supply of money only becomes fully intelligible for us, who are living in greatly changed conditions . . . Instead of reproving them for a theory, fallacious, and insufficient, we may, on the contrary, grant that we find in their writings much common sense and also, often, fine theoretical judgement.

These views come the closest to anticipating Keynes's interpretation and defence of mercantilism which is considered below.

On the question of protection, it was only later that mercantilism tended to take on a protectionist character for the promotion of infant industries and for the creation of domestic employment. It is also interesting in the light of debates about deindustrialisation that some mercantilists stressed the importance of industry relative to other activities. For example, the Italian mercantilist Serra (1613) identified three advantages of industry: first, it was more reliable because it was not dependent on the weather; second, it had a more secure market because industrial goods were not perishable; and third (and most significantly), Serra recognised the phenomenon of increasing returns. Industry can always be multiplied, as he put it, with *proportionately less expense* (*'con minor proporzione di spesa'*). It was not, in other words, Nicholas Kaldor (1966) who first brought to the fore the role of manufacturing industry in the growth process, nor for that matter Adam Smith (1776), but an Italian mercantilist writing in the seventeenth century.

The mercantilist belief that countries can become rich by generating balance of trade surpluses and accumulating foreign exchange (gold) is supposed to have been first and decisively exposed as fallacious by David Hume's essays (1752) 'Of Money' and 'Of the Balance of Trade,' which outlined the crude quantity theory of money that an increase in precious metals will simply increase the price level proportionately with no effects on the real economy. The neutrality of money argument, however, ignores two important considerations. First, if the rate of interest is partly a monetary phenomenon, money will have real effects working through variations in the capital stock. Second, if there are unemployed resources, the impact of increases in the money supply will be on output, not on prices. It was, indeed, Keynes's view expressed in the *General Theory* that throughout history the propensity to save has been greater than the propensity to invest, and that uncertainty and the desire for liquidity have in general made the rate of interest too high.

Given the prevailing economic conditions of the 1930s, it was no accident that Keynes should have devoted part of Chapter 23 in the *General Theory* to a partial defence of mercantilism as containing important germs of truth. In response to a comment from Harrod on drafts of the *General Theory*, Keynes replied: 'what I want is to do justice to schools of thought which the classicals have treated as imbeciles for the last hundred years and, above all, to show that I am not really being so great an innovator, except as against the classical school, but have important predecessors and am returning to an age-long tradition of common sense' (Moggridge 1973). The Mercantilists recognised that the rate of interest is a monetary phenomenon, and that it could be too high to secure full employment, and in relation to the needs of growth. As Keynes (1936: 341) put it in the *General Theory*, mercantilist thought never supposed, as later economists did, 'that there was a self-adjusting tendency by which the rate of interest would be established at the appropriate level.'

Investment is of two types: domestic and foreign. Domestic investment depends on the rate of interest; foreign investment depends on the balance of trade (including the accumulation of precious metals). To the extent that interest rates depend on the quantity of precious metals, a positive balance of trade serves both purposes, permitting both foreign investment and low domestic interest rates. The optimal trade balance and interest rate is a delicate matter. Too low a rate of interest may be too expansionary and worsen the trade balance and also cause a capital outflow which would offset the favourable balance of trade. Too high a rate of interest to finance a balance of trade deficit and/or to protect an exchange rate would be very damaging to domestic investment. This latter situation was exactly the dilemma Britain faced after the return to the gold standard in 1925 at the pre-1914 rate of exchange. Keynes spelt out this dilemma with great force in oral evidence to the Macmillan Committee on Finance and Industry 1929, of which he was also a member. He demonstrated how the economic system generated a high equilibrium level of unemployment as a result of high interest rates enforced by the Bank of England, made necessary by the need to limit *net* overseas investment to the amount that the level of net exports permitted. Ideally, two interest rates are required: one for external lenders and another, lower, rate for internal borrowers. The difficulty of doing this, however, led him reluctantly to advocate protection, and he converted the majority of the Macmillan Committee. It is worth quoting his argument at length:

> Protection is another way of increasing the amount of our foreign investment and that is how it profoundly works in with my argument. The other way is by increasing our exports. We can increase our favourable foreign balance on income account by diminishing our imports, and the real contribution that protection makes is that, by diminishing our imports, it increases the amount of our foreign investment and brings exactly the same sort of relief as the first four remedies I was discussing [namely, gold revaluation, money wage reductions, export bounties and increased efficiency] . . . If it is essential for equilibrium that we should invest abroad on a larger scale than at present, the protectionist way of doing it may be the method of least resistance, because it does not require reductions of money wages and it has less effect . . . in turning the terms of trade against us . . . It may be that the free trade method of increasing our foreign investment has broken down; if so there may be something to be said for the protectionist method of attaining the same result . . .; free trade . . . assumes that if you throw men out of work in one direction you

re-employ them in another. As soon as that link in the chain is broken the whole of the free trade argument breaks down.

(Moggridge 1981: 522)

Later in the *General Theory*, Keynes continued to criticise the inadequacy of the theoretical foundations of the *laissez-faire* doctrine for not recognising that there may not be sufficient inducement to invest in an economic system, which a more favourable balance of trade could remedy. Keynes thus concludes:

the methods of the early pioneers of economic thinking in the 16th and 17th centuries may have attained the fragments of practical wisdom which the unrealistic abstractions of Ricardo first forgot and then obliterated. There was wisdom in their intense preoccupation with keeping down the rate of interest by means of usury laws . . ., by maintaining the domestic stock of money and by discouraging rises in the wage unit; and in their readiness in the last resort to restore the stock of money by devaluation, if it had become plainly deficient through an unavoidable foreign drain, a rise in the wage unit, or any other cause.

(Keynes 1936: 340)

The Keynesian approach to economic growth

In Keynesian theory, it is demand that 'drives' the economic system and supply, within limits, adapts to it. Taking this approach, growth rates differ because the growth of demand differs between countries. The question then becomes: why does demand grow at different rates between countries? One explanation may be the inability of economic agents, particularly governments, to expand demand. This explanation by itself, however, is not very satisfactory. The more probable explanation lies in constraints on demand. In an open economy, the dominant constraint is likely to be the balance of payments.

The importance of a healthy balance of payments for growth can be stated quite succinctly. If a country gets into balance-of-payments difficulties as it expands demand before the short-term capacity growth rate is reached, then demand must be curtailed; supply is never fully utilised; investment is discouraged; technological progress is slowed down; and a country's goods compared with foreign goods become less desirable so worsening the balance of payments still further; and so on. A vicious circle is started. By contrast, if a country is able to expand demand up to the level of existing productive capacity without balance-of-payments difficulties arising, the pressure of demand upon capacity may well raise the capacity growth rate. There are a number of possible mechanisms through which this may happen: the encouragement to investment which would augment the capital stock and bring with it technological progress; the supply of labour increased by the entry into the workforce of people previously outside it or from abroad; the movement of factors of production from low-productivity to high-productivity sectors; and the ability to import more, increasing capacity by making domestic resources more productive. It is this argument that lies behind the advocacy of export-led growth, because it is only through the expansion of exports that the growth rate can be raised without the balance of payments deteriorating at the same time. Believers in export-led growth are really postulating a balance-of-payments constraint theory of why growth rates differ. However, the same rate of export growth in different countries will not necessarily permit the same rate of growth of output because the import requirements associated with growth will differ between countries, and thus some countries will have to constrain demand sooner than others for balance-of-payments equilibrium. The relation between a country's growth rate and its rate of growth of imports is the income of elasticity of demand for imports. Consequently, as we shall see, a country's long-run growth rate will be determined by the ratio of its rate of growth of exports to its income elasticity of demand for imports, which reflects the workings of the (dynamic) Harrod foreign trade multiplier.

Sir Roy Harrod (1933) first brought to the fore the idea that it may be income or output, and not relative prices, that adjusts to preserve balance-of-payments equilibrium, in a little-read, but prescient, book, *International Economics*. In this book, Harrod put forward the view that the level of output of industrial countries is to be explained by the principle of the foreign trade multiplier which at the same time provides the mechanism for keeping the balance of payments in equilibrium. The Harrod foreign trade multiplier predates the Keynesian investment multiplier (although not, of course, the Kahn 1931 employment multiplier), but was eclipsed by it. In practice, however, it may be the more important mechanism in the real world for understanding not only income determination and the growth experience of countries, but also the structural transformation of economies in the throes of development, and the ups and downs of the world economy at large (see Thirlwall 1982). In general, in an open economy, the potential imbalance between export earnings and full employment imports may be a much more difficult and stubborn gap to span than the difference between investment and the full employment saving, especially as the power of governments to bridge a foreign exchange gap, at least in a world of free trade, is much more limited than the power to fill a gap between investment and saving. For many developed and developing countries in the post-war period, there is reason to believe that the inability of exports to pay for full employment imports has been a much more pervasive force determining the level of employment and growth experience. If exports fall short of full employment imports, either income and employment will fall automatically at a given terms-of-trade if other sectors of the economy are in overall balance; or, if other sectors of the economy are in overall deficit (with spending in excess of income), income may be forced to contract by government deflationary measures if a balance-of-payments deficit cannot be financed. The international evidence suggests that the Harrod foreign trade multiplier works in many countries and that differences in export growth performance are an important source of international growth rate differences (see McCombie and Thirlwall 1994, 1997). Kaldor (1975), who did much to revive the idea and significance of the Harrod trade multiplier, once argued: 'In some ways I think it may have been very unfortunate that the very success of Keynes's ideas in explaining unemployment in a depression – essentially a short period analysis – diverted attention from the foreign trade multiplier which over long periods is a far more important principle for explaining the growth and rhythm of industrial development.'[3] In the next section, we derive the balance-of-payments growth rate and will show how it reflects the workings of the (dynamic) Harrod foreign trade multiplier.

The determination of the balance-of-payments equilibrium growth rate

To commence, we consider the case where there is an initial current account disequilibrium in the balance of payments. This may be expressed as:

$$P_d X + F = P_f M E \tag{3.1}$$

where X is the volume of exports, P_d is the domestic price of exports, M is the volume of imports, P_f is the foreign price of imports, E is the exchange rate (measured as the domestic price of foreign currency), and F is the value of nominal capital flows measured in domestic currency. $F > 0$ measures capital inflows and $F < 0$ measures capital outflows. Taking rates of change of the variables in equation (3.1) gives:

$$\theta(p_d + x) + (1 - \theta)f = p_f + m + e \tag{3.2}$$

where the lower-case letters represent rates of growth of the variables, and θ and $(1 - \theta)$ represent the shares of exports and capital flows as a proportion of total receipts (or the proportions of the import bill 'financed' by export earnings and capital flows).

$\theta = P_d X/R$ and $(1 - \theta) = F/R$, where R is total overseas receipts and equals $P_d X + F$.

The normal multiplicative import and export demand functions with constant elasticities are assumed:

$$M = a \left[\frac{P_f E}{P_d} \right]^{\psi} Y^{\pi} \tag{3.3}$$

and

$$X = b \left[\frac{P_d}{P_f E} \right]^{\eta} Z^{\varepsilon} \tag{3.4}$$

where a and b are constants; ψ is the price elasticity of demand for imports ($\psi < 0$); η is the price elasticity of demand for exports ($\eta < 0$); Y is domestic income; Z is the level of 'world' income; π is the income elasticity of demand for imports, and ε is the income elasticity of demand for exports. Expressing equations (3.3) and (3.4) in terms of growth rates, substituting into equation (3.2) and rearranging, we obtain:

$$y = [\theta \, \varepsilon \, z + (1 - \theta) \, (f - p_d) + (1 + \theta\eta + \psi) \, (p_d - e - p_f)] / \pi \tag{3.5}$$

The first term in the square brackets gives the effect on income growth of exogenous changes in income growth abroad, the second term gives the effect of the rate of growth of real capital flows, and the last term gives the effect of changes in the terms of trade.

We shall show below that it is unlikely that a country will be able to run a current account deficit of any size for any length of time, with one or two possible exceptions.[4] Under these circumstances $\theta = 1$ and $(f - p_d) = 0$. Equation (3.5) then reduces to:

$$y = [\varepsilon \, z + (1 + \eta + \psi) \, (p_d - e - p_f)] / \pi \tag{3.6}$$

Remembering the signs of the parameters ($\eta < 0$; $\psi < 0$; $\varepsilon > 0$; and $\pi > 0$), equation (3.6) expresses several familiar economic propositions.

First, inflation in the home country relative to abroad will lower the balance-of-payments equilibrium growth rate if the sum of the price elasticities of demand for exports and imports is greater than unity in absolute value (that is, if $|\eta + \psi| > 1$).

Second, a continuous devaluation or currency depreciation, that is, a sustained rise in the home price of foreign currency ($e > 0$), will improve the balance-of-payments equilibrium growth rate provided the sum of the price elasticities of demand for imports and exports exceeds unity in absolute value, which is the Marshall–Lerner condition (that is, if $|\eta + \psi| > 1$). Notice, however, the important point that a once-for-all depreciation of the currency will not raise the balance-of-payments equilibrium growth rate permanently. After the initial depreciation, e will equal zero and the growth rate would revert to its former level. To raise the balance-of-payments equilibrium growth rate permanently would require continuous depreciation, that is, $e > 0$ in successive periods.

Third, a faster growth of world income will raise the balance-of-payments equilibrium growth rate, but by how much depends crucially on the size of ε, the income elasticity of demand for exports.

Finally, the higher the income elasticity of demand for imports (π), the lower the balance-of-payments equilibrium growth rate.

However, we shall show below that relative prices, expressed in a common currency, do not change greatly in the long run, because of pricing to market or real wage resistance or both. Furthermore, with most trade occurring in highly differentiated goods and services, the price elasticities are likely to be small. Consequently, the contribution to economic growth of the price term, $(1 + \eta + \psi)$ $(p_d - e - p_f)/\pi$, is also likely to be small. If we assume that it has no effect, then the growth of income is given by

$$y_B = x/\pi = \varepsilon z/\pi \tag{3.7}$$

In other words, what may be termed a country's 'balance-of-payments equilibrium growth rate' equals the rate of growth of its export volume divided by the income elasticity of demand for imports. We mean by the term 'balance-of-payments constraint' that a country's performance in overseas markets, and the response of the world financial markets to this performance, constrains the growth of the economy to a rate which is below that which internal conditions (such as the rate of both recorded and disguised unemployment and the degree of capacity utilisation) would warrant.

If $x \cong \varepsilon z$, the balance-of-payments equilibrium growth rate is a function of the ratio of the world income elasticity of demand for a country's exports to that country's income elasticity of demand for its imports.

Estimates of ε and to a lesser extent of π, show considerable variation between countries and these disparities largely reflect differences in non-price competitiveness.

The estimates of the income elasticities are derived from regression analyses of conventional export and import demand functions which contain relative prices as a regressor (see, for example, Houthakker and Magee 1969; Goldstein and Khan 1978). Consequently, differences between countries in their income elasticities of demand reflect all those factors other than relative prices that affect the demand for a country's exports and imports: quality, reliability, delivery dates, the effectiveness of marketing, the extent of the overseas sales and distribution networks, and so on. (Estimates of ε for the early post-war period for the advanced countries vary from 3.55 for Japan to 0.86 for the UK (Houthakker and Magee 1969).)

Clearly, for a country to be potentially balance-of-payments constrained, the change in relative prices cannot have a significant effect on the growth of exports or imports. For example, consider the extreme case of the assumption of the neoclassical 'law of one price' which underlies the monetarist approach to the balance of payments. This postulates that countries' exports are homogeneous and consequently the price elasticities of demand for exports are infinite. Under these circumstances, a country could never be balance-of-payments constrained since the growth of exports is essentially endogenously determined. Any increase in the growth of imports, for example, would automatically result in an increase in the growth of exports through the effect of changes in relative prices. (If the price elasticities are infinite, these changes would be infinitesimally small.) Economies are always at, or near, the full employment level. A corollary of this is that we should expect the income elasticities of demand for imports and exports to be statistically insignificant in the estimated import and export demand functions.

A second requirement necessary for a country to face the possibility of being balance-of-payments constrained is that the growth of capital inflows should not be able to finance ever-growing balance-of-payments deficits.

If the two above conditions are met and the growth of productive potential exceeds the balance-of-payments equilibrium growth rate, which in turn is equal to the actual growth rate (that is, $y_P > y_B = y_A$, with obvious notation), then the country is balance-of-payments constrained.

One test of the balance-of-payments constrained model is to determine statistically how closely the simple rules given by equation (3.7) match the observed growth rates of the various countries. If there is a close relationship, then the contribution of the rate of change in relative prices and capital flows to economic growth must be assumed to be either negligible or offsetting. (We shall show below that the latter case is most implausible.) There is not space here to review all the empirical evidence and the statistical tests that have been undertaken and which suggest that, for most countries, there is no statistical difference between y_B and y (see McCombie and Thirlwall 1997, for a brief review). Instead, we shall restrict ourselves to reporting the actual and balance-of-payments equilibrium growth rates for the major advanced countries for the periods, 1951–73 and 1970–85 (Table 3.1).

Apart from the case of West Germany for 1951–73, where there are reservations about the reliability of the estimate of y_{B2},[5] the only case where the rule does not give a good approximation to the actual growth rate is Japan for both periods, where the balance-of-payments equilibrium growth overstates the observed growth of income. However, during these periods Japan was accumulating substantial surpluses on the current account. While Japan could not be considered to have been balance-of-payments constrained, this does not mean that the neoclassical growth theory comes into its own. Rather, the growth of demand was still crucial in determining the growth of income, except that there was a limit to the speed of transfer of labour from the low-productivity agricultural sector to the high-productivity manufacturing sector, and also a limit to the rate of capital accumulation. This is to say that even in this case growth was not determined exogenously by supply factors, independently of the growth of demand.

In addition to the statistical tests involving the simple rules $y_B = x/\pi = \varepsilon z/\pi$, there is also a great deal of other evidence suggesting the limited importance of relative prices and the growth of capital flows in international trade, to which we now turn.

Table 3.1 The actual and balance-of-payments equilibrium growth rate: selected advanced countries

Country	Growth of GNP (% per annum)	$y_{B1} = \hat{x}/\hat{\pi}$ (% per annum)	$y_{B2} = \hat{\varepsilon}z/\hat{\pi}$ % per annum)
1951–73			
Canada	4.6	5.7	5.2
France	5.0	5.0	4.0
Italy	5.1	5.2	5.4
Japan	9.5	12.5	12.7
West Germany	5.7	5.7	2.2[a]
United Kingdom	2.7	2.7	3.0
United States	3.7	3.4	2.6
1970–85			
Canada	3.4	2.8	3.0
France	3.5	2.6	2.3
Italy	2.6	1.8	1.5
Japan[b]	5.7	11.3	10.1
West Germany	2.4	2.6	1.0[c]
United Kingdom	1.9	2.2	1.6
United States	2.5	2.5	2.1

Sources: Bairam and Dempster (1991); McCombie and Thirlwall (1994: Tables 3.2, 3.3, and 5.5)

Notes:
[a] The estimates of ε and π have been obtained when there has been a correction for autocorrelation. If this adjustment is not made, $y_B = 5.1$. These etimates are from Houthakker and Magee (1969). Using the estimate of ε from Goldstein and Khan (1978) gives a value for y_{B2} of 4.4 per cent.
[b] 1961–85.
[c] Using the estimate of ε from Goldstein and Khan (1978) gives a value of $y_{B2} = 2.5$ per cent.

Price versus non-price competition in international trade

Since the onset of floating exchange rates in 1972, it is clear from the historical evidence that the massive nominal exchange rate movements that have taken place have not rectified balance-of-payments disequilibria. Indeed, in some cases the balance-of-payments response has been perverse; and in the case of the American dollar in recent years, the movement in the exchange rate itself has also been perverse. For the early years of floating from 1972 to 1977, both Triffin (1978) and Kaldor (1978) showed how the surpluses and deficits remained largely impervious to both nominal and real exchange rate movements. According to Triffin:

> the most striking feature of the last six to eight years of floating rates is that they scarcely changed the broad pattern of previous disequilibrium among the major trading countries. The countries that experienced the

largest surpluses before the increase of oil prices have about doubled them, in spite of the strong appreciation of their currencies, and the countries then in deficit saw their deficits more than triple in the following years, in spite of the sharp depreciation of their currencies.

Kaldor makes the same point:

> The general picture that emerges from a study of the trade record of the last five or six years is that the main industrialised countries remained remarkably impervious to very large changes in effective exchange rates. The surplus countries tended to remain in surplus, and the deficit countries to remain in deficit in much the same way as in the 1960s . . . The important thing is that Britain and America, who seemed to be losing out to new industrial giants, Germany and Japan, continued to do so after the real exchange rates between them underwent drastic alterations.

We show the same phenomenon for later years (McCombie and Thirlwall 1994).

It is important to stress from the outset that we do not argue that changes in relative prices, when measured in a common currency, have *no* effect on the balance of payments. Indeed, there are cases where a devaluation has undoubtedly improved the current account, *for a given trend rate of growth*, as, for example, in the cases of the franc in 1957 and 1958 and of sterling in 1967 and 1992. However, to raise the rate of growth of income consistent with the balance of payments being in equilibrium requires an increase in the *growth* of exports or a reduction in the *growth* of imports or both. Given the conventional export and import demand functions, this requires a *continuous* improvement in the country's relative price competitiveness. What is denied is that, for a number of reasons discussed below, this is a feasible option.

The first problem is that it may be difficult for a nominal depreciation to be converted into a real depreciation if there is inflationary feedback from higher import prices to higher domestic prices. This may occur because of real wage resistance as workers increase their money wage claims to prevent a cut in the real wage caused by the higher import prices. If they are successful, domestic prices will eventually increase to the same extent as import prices and there will be no gain in price competitiveness (Wilson 1976; Knoester 1995). For example, in the NIESR and LBS forecasting models of the UK economy it is assumed that the advantage of a once-and-for-all nominal depreciation would progressively diminish, until after five years or so it would be entirely lost.

Knoester (1995) has conducted a number of simulations, using a small macroeconomic model, which traces the effect of a once-and-for-all 10 per cent evaluation. He found, not surprisingly, that under the assumption that employees are fully compensated for an increase in consumer prices, the devaluation only affects the price level and has no impact on real variables. This is true whether the economy is very open (which he defines as where import costs make up 33 percent of total variable costs) or relatively closed (10 per cent of total variable costs). Consequently, the ineffectiveness of nominal exchange rate adjustment is equally applicable to the relatively closed economies such as the US as to the more open economies such as Belgium and the Netherlands. The simulation results confirm that, with complete compensation, the size of the price elasticities (the Marshall–Lerner condition) becomes irrelevant.

Much of the empirical evidence suggests that 'up till now a full compensation of prices in wages – at least in the medium and longer run – seems to be supported by empirical evidence for the majority of the OECD countries including the United States' (Knoester 1995). Studies that support this view and cited by Knoester include Coe (1985), Coe and Gagliardi (1985), Klau and Mittlestaüdt (1986), Chan-Lee *et al.* (1987), Knoester and Van der Windt (1987), Blanchard (1987) and Kawasaki *et al.* (1990).

While real wage resistance may have been important in the past, especially when high rates of inflation occurred with floating exchange rates, nevertheless, it is now sometimes argued that, for the UK at least, this is a thing of the past. It is held that changes in the labour market, especially the weakening of trade union power, have effectively undermined real wage resistance. Moreover, even if it were important, the appropriate policy response would be an effective (and permanent) incomes policy. If this were introduced, so the argument goes, then the balance-of-payments constraint could be lifted. The fundamental cause of the UK's, and indeed the US's, poor economic performance is not the balance-of-payments constraint but rather the unrealistic wage demands of workers. The problem with this argument, as we shall show, is that the basic problem of the UK and the US lies more in their poor non-price competitiveness, than in their lack of price competitiveness.

It is true that the 1980s did see swings in real exchange rates that have made the devaluations of the 1960s and the 1970s seem small by comparison, and this would seem to confirm that real wage resistance may now be unimportant for many countries. But as Krugman (1989a) concedes: 'One of the most puzzling, and therefore one of the most important, aspects of floating exchange rates has been the huge swings in exchange rates that have had only muted effects on anything real.' Consequently, even in the absence of any inflationary feedback, trade flows still appear unresponsive to changes in real exchange rates.

One early hypothesis as to why exchange rate depreciations may be ineffective was put forward by Balogh and Streeten (1951), who argued that the elasticities which form the basis for the famous Marshall–Lerner condition were not, as commonly assumed, independent of each other. They asserted that the elasticity of supply of exports depended upon the elasticity of supply of domestically produced goods that were import-competing. The elasticity of supply of these goods in turn depended on the elasticity of the foreign supply of these goods. Consequently, with a fall in the real exchange rate, the greater the reduction in the supply of imports, the more domestic resources would be diverted into the production of import-competing products and the less would be available for increasing the volume of exports. For this to be a significant factor at less than full employment requires a short-run capacity constraint in manufacturing.

But more importantly, Balogh and Streeten were among the first to stress the importance of oligopolistic competition in manufacturing and to suggest that this might lead to a resistance on the part of exporters to see their market shares decline. It is surprising just how long it has taken for international trade theory, with the development of the 'new' trade theory based on the Chamberlin–Robinson imperfect competition model, to recognise that product markets are not perfect. Exporters to the UK, for example, will try for as long as possible to maintain market share in the face of a decline in sterling, absorbing changes in the exchange rate in their price-cost margins. This policy is sometimes known as 'pricing to market' and a possible theoretical basis for it has been put forward by, *inter alios*, Dornbusch (1987).

There is increasing empirical evidence of the importance of this oligopolistic response to exchange rate changes. Cowling and Sugden (1989) develop a general model in which the reaction of prices to changes in costs is analysed within asymmetric oligopolistic markets. They argue that 'contrary to the usual assumption, the implication of this [market] structure is that exchange rate changes may leave prices unaltered.' They find that the pricing policy in the European car market is compatible with this model. The substantial appreciation of sterling in 1979–80 led neither to a fall in the domestic price of imported cars in the UK nor to an increase in the foreign prices of UK car exports. They conclude that 'adjustments are more likely to appear via non-price mechanisms such as advertising and product policies and also via the sourcing policies of the transnational corporations.' Strong support for the pricing to market hypothesis is also found by Marston (1990) with respect to Japanese manufacturing.

Firms are unlikely to increase their efforts in exporting if they believe that a depreciation of a currency, even though it may be substantial, is likely to be short-lived. The huge swings of the real exchange rate in the 1980s were more likely to have been interpreted by firms as the consequences of temporary capital flows and speculative bubbles than as earlier exchange rate changes.

If there is not full wage compensation, a nominal devaluation, *ceteris paribus*, will lead to an improvement in competitiveness. If foreign firms are to preserve their export sales, then the mark-up must decline at a rate necessary to offset this decline in their price competitiveness (see Blecker 1994 for an analysis in terms of changes in the mark-up). While this may be an important short-run adjustment mechanism, it is implausible that this could be effective in the long run, as it implies that profits of the importer are increasingly squeezed. Indeed, evidence for the United States suggests that there is a complete pass-through after about a year (Krugman and Baldwin 1987). Nevertheless, to the extent that it prevents the current account from adjusting in the short run, this may lead to income adjustment in the form of a slowdown in the growth rate. If this improves the current account and reverses the initial depreciation, it will reinforce the balance-of-payments constraint.

Even if relative prices do alter, price elasticities are likely to be low if there is a high degree of product differentiation, so that even a large change in relative prices has little effect on the volume of imports and exports demanded. The early elasticity pessimism, where a change in the exchange rate was thought to have had no effect on the current account during the 1950s, is now considered to have been unfounded. (If trade is balanced and the sum of the absolute values of the price elasticities equals unity, equation (3.6) demonstrates that changes in the terms of trade will have no effect on economic growth.) But there are two points to note concerning this. First, even if the traditional Marshall–Lerner conditions are satisfied, what is important is the *size* of the elasticities, as these determine the quantitative response of exports and imports to a change in the exchange rate. Second, with the development of greater product differentiation over the post-war period in both manufactured goods and services, the size of the price elasticities is likely to have declined over time. Low price elasticities are especially true of the capital goods industries where technical specifications are often of greater importance than the price. To take just one example, a study by Kravis and Lipsey (1971) found that, of the various factors accounting for factory equipment imports into the US from Germany and for US exports in 1964, in both cases only 7 per cent of purchases could be attributable to price, and about three-quarters of purchases were for reasons of product specification.

Consequently, even when relative prices do change, they have quantitatively little effect on trade flows, and, indeed, superficially seem to have a perverse impact. This is sometimes known as the 'Kaldor Paradox.' As noted above, Kaldor (1978) was one of the first to observe that changes in relative prices could explain very little by way of the observed changes in trade shares over the early post-war period. The paradox is that those countries with the greatest relative *improvement* in price competitiveness also experienced the greatest *loss* in their world market shares and vice versa. While undoubtedly any improvement in price competitiveness would have led to an improvement in market shares, *ceteris paribus*, the effect of declining non-price competitiveness more than offset any such gains. Further statistical evidence is provided by Fetherston *et al.* (1977).

In a survey of competition in international trade, Posner and Steer (1979) summarized their findings as follows: 'Historically there is no doubt that non-price changes have dominated – the proportion of total change they "explain" is an order of magnitude greater than the explanatory power of price competitiveness.' This is echoed by Stout (1979), who also concluded that 'the differences between the British and German or French income elasticities of demand for manufactured imports support the quite widespread evidence that non-price competitive disadvantages underlie Britain's industrial decline.' Why countries differ in their non-price competitiveness is a complex question but is undoubtedly related to the poorly understood reasons why firms differ in *x*-inefficiency (Leibenstein 1966).

Finally, an interesting study by Brecht and Stout (1981) suggests that a depreciation of the exchange rate may actually worsen non-price competitiveness as it may lead to 'trading down,' or the substitution of low for high unit value goods. This is because an improvement in relative prices will have a greater effect on relatively homogeneous goods which tend to have low value added. A depreciation may also reduce the incentive for producers to engage in the risky but essential process of developing superior high-quality products. Brecht and Stout find some support for this argument in their analysis of the UK's export performance during the substantial depreciation of sterling in the mid-1970s.

These issues are all discussed at much greater length in McCombie and Thirlwall (1994). The fact that attempts to relax the balance-of-payments constraint through large exchange rate adjustments may be thwarted by real wage resistance and the resulting depreciation–inflation vicious circle, by competitive devaluations, by pricing to market or by low price elasticities – all demonstrating that there is little scope for an individual country to improve its rate of growth through exchange rate adjustments.

Capital flows and the balance-of-payments equilibrium growth rate

A question then arises of the extent to which capital flows (or, strictly speaking, their growth) can relax, or indeed eliminate, the balance-of-payments constraint on economic growth. A somewhat sceptical view is given by an OECD paper:

> Some countries can be in current account deficit for many years, while others may be in persistent surplus. But for most a *change* in the current account position equivalent to 1 per cent of GNP over one or two years would, depending upon the starting point, be considered significant and could well set in motion a train of adjustment.
>
> (Larsen, Llewellyn and Potter 1983: 51)

Larsen *et al.* consider that the train of adjustment most likely to be set in motion is the deflation of domestic demand (that is, income adjustment) rather than a depreciation of the exchange rate which they consider to be largely ineffective.

Nevertheless, the late 1970s and the 1980s saw the progressive de-regulation and liberalisation of the international financial markets, and an assumption often made is that a country can now borrow as much as it requires on the international capital markets at the going world rate of interest. This is sometimes qualified by the assumption that as the degree of indebtedness of a country increases, so the actual interest rate may rise because of the increase in risk premiums. Nevertheless, it is still argued that the international adjustment process works. The ready accessibility to international capital, it is held, has greatly reduced, if not completely eliminated, the balance-of-payments constraint. Deficit countries can now borrow to give themselves the necessary breathing space before a depreciation of the exchange rate putatively works. There are problems with this argument. First, it overlooks the serious difficulties posed by the accumulation of excessive foreign debt. Second, the portfolio approach to the balance of payments shows that foreigners' portfolios will eventually adjust fully to, for example, an increase in a country's interest rate that takes it above the world interest rate. Investors will be unwilling to increase indefinitely the share of their portfolios devoted to overseas assets, notwithstanding this positive interest rate differential. Consequently, with stock equilibrium, there will not be persistent capital flows, even with sustained differences in interest rates.

We shall show that, under plausible assumptions, the growth of capital flows is likely to have only a quantitatively small effect in raising the balance-of-payments equilibrium growth rate. A more detailed breakdown of the balance-of-payments identity in nominal values than that given by equation (3.1) is:

$$P_d X + F = P_f E M + r^* k D + r(1 - k) D + e k D \qquad (3.8)$$

where $F > 0$ is the net capital inflow; r^* is the nominal interest rate paid on the foreign currency component of the net stock of overseas debt, D, with the latter denominated in the domestic currency; r is the interest rate paid on the domestic currency component of the debt; k is the proportion of the stock of debt denominated in foreign currency; and e is the rate of change of the exchange rate. Rearranging equation (3.8), and assuming that uncovered interest rate parity holds, so that $r^* = r - e$, we obtain:

$$dB = F = - TB + r D = F_1 + F_2 \qquad (3.9)$$

where dD is the increase in the debt; F, as noted above, is net capital inflows which comprise borrowings from abroad to cover the deficit on the trade balance (TB) ($P_f E M - P_d X = -TB = F_1$) and the interest repayments (F_2). It is useful to term F_1 'active' debt accumulation since it involves a real resource transfer into the country. F_2 may be regarded as 'passive' debt accumulation as it merely represents the increase in debt due to past trade deficits. (We assume for convenience that there is no amortization of the debt.) Over time, as a country runs a persistent balance-of-payments deficit, the passive contribution is likely to become progressively more important and increasingly to dominate the active debt accumulation. For example, one indicator of the capacity of a country to service and repay its debt commonly used by the financial markets is the debt to GDP ratio, namely, $\gamma \equiv D/GDP$. It will need only a few years of current account deficits of, say, 4 per cent for a country, which is initially neither an overseas debtor nor creditor, to accumulate a debt to GDP ratio of 20 per cent. If the interest rate is 10 per cent, the interest payments (increase in passive debt) will be 2 per cent of GDP, or about half of a current account deficit of 4 per cent of GDP, which would normally be considered substantial.

The growth of the debt to GDP ratio (denoted by $\dot{\gamma}$ is given by:

$$\dot{\gamma} = d - gdp = F / D - gdp = -TB / D + r - gdp \tag{3.10}$$

where d and gdp are the rates of growth of D and GDP, both measured in nominal terms.

For sustainability, the debt ratio has eventually to stabilise, so that $d = 0$. Consequently, this implies that:

$$- TB / DF = gdp - r \tag{3.11}$$

From equation (3.11), it may be seen that if the nominal rate of interest equals the growth of nominal GDP, a deficit on the trade balance is not sustainable – the trade balance must be in equilibrium. If the nominal interest rate exceeds the growth of GDP, the trade balance must be in surplus for the debt–GDP ratio not to increase indefinitely. It is only when the growth of GDP exceeds the nominal interest rate that a permanent deficit trade balance is sustainable (Howard 1985). These results follow through for real values, as $y \equiv gdp - p$ and $r' \equiv i - p$, where p and r' are the rate of inflation and the real rate of interest, respectively. Thus, the condition for sustainability is $- TB/D = y - r'$.

If it is assumed that the maximum sustainable level of debt to GDP is γ^*, then in real terms we have from the relation that $d(D/P_d)/Y = \gamma^* y$, (where Y is the level of real income) the condition that:

$$\frac{(- TB + rD)/P_d}{Y} = \frac{- C A B/P_d}{Y} = \gamma^* y \tag{3.12}$$

From equation (3.12), it can be seen that, if the real interest rate equals the growth of real income, the trade balance must be in equilibrium confirming the analysis couched in nominal terms. Thus, while a country may run a temporary trade deficit while the debt to GDP ratio increases, this is not sustainable if the debt to GDP ratio is eventually to stabilise. A country can, however, run a current account deficit equivalent to the 'passive' debt accumulation multiplied by the maximum debt–GDP ratio, γ^*. While there is no hard and fast rule as to the maximum value of γ, the financial markets usually become increasingly nervous if it exceeds about 0.40 for any length of time (Coutts *et al.* 1990). Thus, if the rate of growth of income is 2 per cent per annum, the maximum sustainable current account deficit as a proportion of GDP is about 0.8 per cent. If γ^* is lower, say 0.25, then the maximum current account deficit is also smaller, in this case 0.5 per cent of GDP. Thus, only a relatively small current account deficit is likely to be sustainable in the long run.

We may consider the implications of these arguments in terms of the balance-of-payments equilibrium growth rate. Consider first the case where the accumulation of debt has occurred to such an extent that the financial markets dictate that there can be no further increase in the debt to GDP ratio. This implies that $d' = y$ (where the superscript $'$ denotes measurement in real terms). Since $dD' = F'$, it follows that $\gamma^* = F'/D' = y$. If we assume that the growth of income is constant, then it follows that the growth of capital flows, measured in real terms, must also equal the growth of income. Hence, the balance-of-payments equilibrium growth rate becomes:

$$y = \frac{\theta x}{\pi - (1 - \theta)} \tag{3.13}$$

which will give a reasonably close approximation to the simple rule, $y_B = x/\pi$. This may be shown as follows. Consider a relatively open economy where the proportion of output exported is 30 per cent of GDP. Suppose this country persistently runs a relatively large current account deficit of 4 per cent of GDP, that is, $F/Y = 0.04$, and that π takes a value of 1.5. Consequently, since $\theta = X/(X + F) = (X/Y)/[(X/Y) + (F/Y)]$, it follows that $[\theta/(\pi - (1 - \theta))]x$ equals $0.64x$ compared with the value for x/π of $0.67x$. If, for example, 50 per cent and 15 per cent of GDP are exported, then the equilibrium growth rates are $0.65x$ and $0.61x$, respectively, and these are again close to the values given by the simple dynamic Harrod foreign trade multiplier.

It is important to make a distinction between long-term capital flows and short-run speculative capital flows. The former will be beneficial if they are used for productive investment that will eventually generate increased export earnings and the foreign exchange necessary to cover the interest and amortisation payments. Australia, for example, has experienced a substantial balance-of-payments deficit over much of the post-war period as foreign investment has moved in to develop its extensive resource base. Indeed, an alternative definition of the balance-of-payments equilibrium growth rate would be where the 'basic balance' (current account plus long-term capital flows) is in equilibrium.

However, the conclusion of a study by Feldstein and Horioka (1980) is that, notwithstanding the much greater integration in the international financial markets, there are considerable institutional barriers that greatly restrict the international mobility of long-term investment in response to differences in rates of return. If there were perfect world capital mobility, there should be no correlation between a country's investment–output ratio and its savings ratio. Saving in each country should respond to the international possibilities of investment, while investment in a country should be able to draw on the global pool of available capital. When Feldstein and Horioka regress investment ratios on savings ratios using a sample of advanced countries, they find that, far from there being no statistical relationship, the slope coefficient is highly significant and does not differ significantly from unity. This leads them to conclude that 'while a small part of the total world capital stock is held in liquid form and is available to eliminate short-term interest rate differentials, most capital is apparently not available for arbitrage-type activity among long-term investments.'

Their paper has generated a great deal of controversy, and a number of objections have been raised, although none has invalidated the broad thrust of their conclusions. (See, for example, Dooley *et al.* 1987 and the references therein.) As Dooley *et al.* point out, Feldstein and Horioka's statistical results prove to be robust, and conclude that 'we do not know why the apparent isolation of national markets has persisted in the face of substantial expansion of trade in goods and services and in financial capital.' However, Feldstein and Horioka advance some plausible explanations. Investors do not have equal knowledge of the likely returns of investing abroad and at home. For most investors, the perceived risks of investing in a foreign country will be much greater than investing domestically. Feldstein and Horioka further point to the existence of official restrictions on the export of capital that still exist in some countries and the fear of adverse changes in the taxation of foreign capital. In the US, moreover, the savings institutions are required by law to invest only in domestic mortgages on local real estate.

The only finding that runs counter to Feldstein and Horioka's results concerns a number of less developed countries which are heavily dependent on aid. This confirms Thirlwall and Hussain's (1982) findings, using the balance-of-payments equilibrium growth rate model, that the growth of capital flows is important for some less developed countries.

The problem with short-term capital flows is that they are highly volatile. They respond rapidly to small changes in international interest rate differentials and the exchange rate, especially as the latter may lead to substantial capital gains or losses. The danger of a capital flight is that it may lead to a rapid depreciation of a currency and initiate a vicious depreciation–inflation circle. With a current account deficit and the possibility of an exchange rate depreciation that will bring a capital loss to foreign investors, the interest rate is likely to have to be increased in an attempt to prevent a capital flight. This, in turn, is likely to have an adverse effect on domestic investment and, hence, reduce the growth rate. Moreover, there are limits to the extent to which interest rates can be raised to defend the currency.

To summarise, the implication is that capital flows cannot permit an individual country to increase its growth rate above y_B by very much or for very long.

The Harrod foreign trade multiplier and the Hicks super-multiplier

We remarked earlier that the simple growth rule, specified in equation (3.7), namely, that growth will approximate to $y = x/\pi$ in the long run, can be shown to be the dynamic analogue of the static foreign trade multiplier. Harrod originally derived the static foreign trade multiplier on the assumptions of no saving and investment, and no government spending and taxing. Output or income is generated by the production of consumption goods (C) and exports (X), and all income is spent either on home consumption goods (C) or imports (M). On these assumptions, trade is always balanced and income adjusts to preserve equilibrium. We have:

$$Y = C + X \tag{3.14}$$

and

$$Y = C + M \tag{3.15}$$

$$X = M \tag{3.16}$$

Now let the import function be:

$$M = M_0 + \mu Y \tag{3.17}$$

where M_0 is the level of autonomous imports and μ is the marginal propensity to import. (We use μ rather than the conventional notation, m, since the latter is used by us to denote the rate of growth of imports.) Setting M equal to X, expressing equation (3.17) with Y on the left-hand side and differentiating, we obtain:

$$dY/dX = dY/dM_0 = 1/\mu \tag{3.18}$$

This is the static Harrod foreign trade multiplier. The multiplier, $1/\mu$, will always bring the balance of payments back into equilibrium through changes in income following a change in exports or autonomous imports.

Equation (3.18), when it is made 'dynamic', becomes the growth rule $y_B = x/\pi$. If the real terms of trade remain unchanged, we can use the equilibrium condition under which the Harrod foreign trade multiplier works and multiply the left-hand side of equation (3.18) by X/Y and the right-hand side by M/Y (since $X = M$) to give:

$$\frac{dY}{dX} \frac{X}{Y} = \frac{dY}{dM} \frac{M}{Y} \tag{3.19}$$

or

$$\frac{dY}{Y} = \frac{dX}{X} \left[\frac{dY}{dM} \frac{M}{Y} \right] = \frac{dX}{X} \frac{1}{\pi} \tag{3.20}$$

Equation (3.20) is none other than the rule, $y_B = x / \pi$.

The assumptions underlying this approach can be relaxed and the same result obtained if, first, all saving is done for investment or all investment is assumed to generate its own saving and governments run balanced budgets, or, second, if any surplus/deficit in the private sector is exactly offset by a corresponding deficit/surplus in the public sector. If leakages exceed injections, exports will exceed imports and there is no balance-of-payments constraint, but if injections exceed leakages there will be a payments deficit and the question is then how long the deficit can persist without corrective action having to be taken. If relative price changes (including exchange rate changes) are ineffective, output would have to be depressed through government contraction of demand. We would be back in a Harrod trade multiplier world, with the level and growth of income fundamentally determined by the level and growth of export demand in relation to the propensity to import.

The model can be illustrated in diagrammatic form, as in Figure 3.1. GDP growth is measured on the horizontal axis, and export and import growth on the vertical axis. Export growth (denote by the line x_1x_1) is autonomous, while import growth (m_1m_1) is a function of GDP growth as measured by the income elasticity of demand for imports (π). The steeper the m_1m_1 curve, the higher the income elasticity of imports. The GDP growth rate consistent with balance-of-payments equilibrium is defined where the x_1x_1 and m_1m_1 curves cross. The higher the x_1x_1 curve and the flatter the m_1m_1 curve, the higher the equilibrium growth rate will be, and vice versa.

The equation $y = x/\pi$ turns out to be the basis of some of the well-known 'centre–periphery' models of growth and development associated with the names of Prebisch (1950), Seers (1962) and Kaldor (1970) (see Thirlwall 1983b). In other words, one country will grow faster than another if its

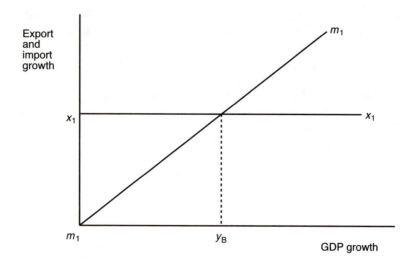

Figure 3.1 Export and import growth

productive structure is such that it exports goods with a high income elasticity of demand in world markets relative to the goods it imports. Industrial countries, with sophisticated technology, tend to export goods with a higher income elasticity of demand than primary producing countries, and herein lies a very basic explanation of the emergence and persistence of the development gap in the world economy.

Some of the assumptions underlying the foreign trade multiplier are clearly unrealistic. Nevertheless, if we generalise the analysis and use an extended Keynesian model, we can demonstrate that the rule reflects the workings of the Hicks super-multiplier, of which the Harrod foreign trade multiplier is a component.

The traditional multiplier of a Keynesian model that includes a consumption function, a linear import demand function, an investment function, government expenditure and taxation is:

$$k = 1/(1 - c + c\, t_d + t_i - i + \mu) \tag{3.21}$$

where c, t_d, t_i, i and μ are the marginal propensity to consume, the marginal propensity to tax (direct and indirect), the marginal propensity to invest and the marginal propensity to import. Assuming that the prices of imports and exports, expressed in the domestic currency, are constant, the growth of income is described by the equation:

$$y = (1/k)\,(\omega_X x + \omega_A\, a) \tag{3.22}$$

where ω_X and ω_A are the shares of exports and autonomous expenditure in income; x and a are the growth rates of exports and autonomous expenditure. The latter includes the autonomous components of consumption, government expenditure, investment and imports.

If the only exogenous increase in expenditure comes from exports, the rate of growth of income is given by $y = (1/k)\omega_X x$. This represents the direct impact of export growth on income growth, via the operation of the Harrod foreign trade multiplier. It may be questioned from a consideration of equation (3.22) why an increase in export growth should assume greater importance than an equivalent increase in the growth of other autonomous expenditures. The answer is, of course, that the growth of exports is the only element that simultaneously relaxes the balance-of-payments constraint while increasing the growth of income. The argument advanced by, for example, Kaldor (1971) is that export-led growth enables the rate of investment to be increased, thereby raising the growth of productive potential. Consumption-led growth, on the other hand, by eventually precipitating a balance-of-payments crisis which requires correction through deflation (and thereby reducing the rate of growth of income) does not raise the propensity to invest. This leads to a lower investment–output ratio than would be obtained through export-led growth.

The direct influence of an increase in exports (or an increase in their rate of growth) through the foreign trade multiplier is only one mechanism by which income (or its growth rate) will be increased. A secondary route is one through which an increase in exports, by initially relaxing the balance-of-payments constraint, will allow other autonomous expenditures to be increased until income has risen by enough to induce an increase in imports equivalent to the initial increase in exports.

We have seen that, in the short run, the increase of income generated by the increase in exports through the foreign trade multiplier is given as $dY = (1/k)dX$. The increase in imports induced by the expansion of income is given by the marginal propensity to import as $dM = \mu dY$. From these two expressions we obtain the relationship $dM = (\mu/k)dX$. As $k > \mu$, the increase in imports will be less than the increase in exports and there will be an improvement in the balance of trade, namely,

$$dBT = dX - dM = (k - \mu) \, dX/k > 0 \tag{3.23}$$

In the long run, however, the super-multiplier operates and increases the level of economic activity until the induced increase in imports equals the increase in exports. In other words, income will increase until the balance of payments is brought back into equilibrium. This secondary increase in demand may occur, for example, through a faster rate of capital accumulation induced by entrepreneurs' expectations of a sustained faster growth rate or an increased growth of government expenditure, or both. Wealth effects arising from the acquisition of overseas assets as a result of the initial excess of exports over imports may also result in an increase in consumption.

We have seen from the import demand function $M = \mu Y$ that $dM = \mu dY$. If there is balance-of-payments equilibrium, it follows that $dM = dX$ and, hence, $dY = (1/\mu)dX$. This may be expressed equivalently as:

$$\frac{d Y}{Y} = \frac{1}{\mu} \frac{X}{Y} \frac{d X}{X} \tag{3.24}$$

or $y = (1/\mu)(\omega_x x)$. Since $\mu = dM/dY$ and $X/Y = M/Y$, it follows that $(1/\mu)(\omega_x) = 1/\pi$, the reciprocal of the income elasticity of demand for imports. Consequently, equation (3.24) is nothing other than the balance-of-payments equilibrium growth rate $y_B = x/\pi$. From equation (3.22), we obtain an alternative expression for the balance-of-payments equilibrium growth rate:

$$y_B = (1/k) (\omega_X x + \omega_A a_B) = x/\pi \tag{3.25}$$

where a_B is the rate of growth of autonomous expenditures necessary, for a given growth of exports, to maintain the growth of income at the balance-of-payments equilibrium rate. ω_A is the share of the level of this autonomous expenditure in total income.

Equation (3.25) represents the working of the Hicks super-multiplier. It may be seen that, apart from the direct growth in output through the foreign trade multiplier, namely $(1/k)\omega_X x$, the initial relaxation of the balance-of-payments constraint permits (rather than necessarily automatically causes) a growth in 'autonomous' expenditure given by:

$$a_B = k\left(\frac{1}{\mu} - \frac{1}{k}\right)\left(\frac{\omega_X}{\omega_A}\right)x \tag{3.26}$$

If autonomous expenditure does not grow as fast as the rate implied by equation (3.25), then the growth of output will be commensurately less and an increasing balance-of-payments surplus will occur. (See McCombie and Thirlwall 1994, ch. 6 appendix, for a simple numerical example illustrating this argument.)

The balance-of-payments equilibrium growth rate of income is thus determined jointly by the growth of exports, via the dynamic foreign trade multiplier (ω_X/k), and the growth of 'induced' autonomous expenditures working through its associated dynamic domestic multiplier (ω_A/k). This is identical to the effect of the growth of exports working through the super-multiplier $(1/\pi)$. It is interesting to note that once we allow for the operation of the super-multiplier, the effect on the growth of income of an increase in the growth of exports has a much greater impact, especially on relatively closed economies, than it does solely through the foreign trade multiplier. For example, in 1980 an increase in the US in the growth of exports of one percentage point would, through the foreign trade multiplier, have raised the growth of GDP by 0.14 percentage points. When the working of the super-multiplier is taken into account, this figure rises to 0.66 percentage points. The values for a relatively open economy, namely Belgium, were 0.39 and 0.73 percentage points, respectively.

Krugman's interpretation of the rule

In McCombie and Thirlwall (1997), we survey the substantial empirical evidence now available in support of the relations given by equation (3.7). The closeness of the results would seem to support the assumptions made in arriving at equation (3.7), namely that long-run balance-of-payments equilibrium is a requirement and that substitution effects in trade are weak. If relative price changes were adjusting the balance of payments quickly and efficiently there would be no reason to expect any systematic relation between a country's growth performance and the performance of exports relative to the income elasticity of demand for imports. We would be in a neoclassical non-demand-constrained world where growth is determined from the supply side alone.

Indeed, this is the message of Krugman (1989b), who attempts to justify the close fit of $y = x/\pi$ – and its corollary equation $y = \varepsilon z/\pi$ which he calls the 45-degree rule – by presenting a model that purports to show a systematic relation between fast growth as the *independent* variable and high export elasticities and low import elasticities as the *dependent* variables. He dismisses the possibility of demand constraints in one sentence by saying: 'I am simply going to dismiss *a priori* the argument that income elasticities determine growth, rather than the other way round.' He continues:

> It just seems fundamentally implausible that over stretches of decades balance-of-payments problems could be preventing long term growth, especially for relatively closed economies like the US in the 1950s and 1960s. Furthermore, *we all know* [our italics] that differences in growth rates among countries are primarily determined in the rate of growth of total factor productivity, not differences in the rate of growth of employment; it is hard to see what channel links balance of payments due to unfavourable income elasticities to total factor productivity growth.

It is worth briefly considering the Krugman argument, and what is wrong with it. He is essentially reversing the direction of causation that has been argued up to now, maintaining that faster growth in one country leads to a greater supply of exports, which causes what he calls the 'apparent' income elasticity of demand for exports to be higher and the 'apparent' income elasticity of demand for imports to be lower. As a country's relative growth rate changes, its 'apparent' income elasticities change as well, preserving the 45-degree rule, namely, $y = ez/\pi$. This is a trade model based on monopolistic competition and increasing returns in which the price of representative goods is equalised between countries and the number of product varieties produced in a country is proportional to its effective labour force as a measure of resource availability. If then the labour force grows at different rates between countries, the faster-growing country will be able to increase its share of world markets by increasing the number of goods faster than other countries, allowing it to sell more without a reduction in its relative prices, therefore giving the faster-growing country an apparently higher income elasticity for demand for its exports. In developing the model, Krugman makes the unusual frank admission that 'no effort will be made at realism,' and herein lies the problem. It is tautologically true that *if* faster-growing countries manage to sell more exports, they will be observed to have a higher income elasticity of demand for exports, but the model does not explain how faster growth arises in the first place (except by the assumption of a faster growth of the labour force, apparently autonomously determined), or why a faster-growing country will necessarily export more independently of the characteristics of the goods it produces. Greater supply availability or variety, or both, are not sufficient if demand is relatively lacking.

Krugman dismisses far too readily the idea that growth may be demand constrained by the balance of payments and that slow growth may itself affect adversely total productivity growth. In practice there are many channels linking slow growth imposed by a balance-of-payments constraint to low productivity growth, and the opposite where the possibility of fast output growth unhindered by demand constraints leads to fast productivity growth. There is a rich literature on export-led growth models, including the Hicks super-multiplier, just discussed, incorporating the notion of circular and cumulative causation (Myrdal 1957), working through induced investment, embodied technical progress, learning by doing, scale economies, and so on, that will produce fast productivity growth in countries where exports and output are growing fast (Dixon and Thirlwall 1975). The evidence from testing Verdoorn's Law shows a strong feedback from output growth to productivity growth (Thirlwall 1983b; Bairam 1987).

In the final analysis it is a question of the extent to which income elasticities can be considered as exogenously determined in the medium term, and are instantaneously endogenously determined by the growth process itself. In this respect, it should not be forgotten that in many instances countries' income elasticities are largely determined by natural resource endowments (or static comparative advantage) and the characteristics of the goods produced, which are the product of geography and history and independent of the growth of output. An obvious example is the contrast between the production of primary and industrial products, where primary products tend to have an income elasticity of demand less than unity (Engel's Law) while most industrial products have an income elasticity greater than unity. Even between industrial countries, with which Krugman's model is basically concerned, feedback mechanisms associated with Verdoorn's Law will tend to perpetuate initial differences in income elasticities associated with 'inferior' industrial structures on the one hand and 'superior' industrial structures on the other. (Indeed, the cumulative causation nature of growth may actually cause these disparities in income elasticities to widen, albeit relatively slowly.) To escape this syndrome requires an exogenous shock which Krugman fails to explain.

Growth is not simply a question of current supply availability. For many countries, both developing and developed, the evidence is consistent with the view that growth is demand-constrained by the need to maintain current account balance-of-payments equilibrium before supply constraints bite. Moreover, many of the resources for growth can be considered endogenous. This is not to say, of course, that supply-side factors do not matter in the growth process. Income elasticities determine the balance-of-payments constrained growth rate, but the supply characteristics of goods determine relative income elasticities. This seems much more plausible than the view that long-run growth rate differences are determined by exogenous differences in the rate of growth of the effective labour supply between countries (in accordance with neoclassical growth theory), and that these growth rate differences lead to a constellation of income elasticities that just keeps the balance of payments in equilibrium without any long-run shifts in real exchange rates (which is what the Krugman model amounts to). The model would imply, for example, that if for some reason Japan's growth rate slowed down, this would so change its income elasticities of exports and imports as to leave the trade balance unchanged with no upward pressure on the exchange rate. This seems implausible. Even more implausible is the presumption that faster growth in the UK would so change the income elasticities of exports and imports as to prevent a deficit arising with no downward pressure on the exchange rate. The historical experience suggests otherwise.

Economic growth in a two-country model

Up to now, our modelling of the relationship between the balance of payments and economic growth has been essentially a partial equilibrium approach, with the growth of GDP specified as a function of export growth which, in turn, is determined primarily by the exogenously given rate of growth of 'world' income. It is now necessary to make explicit allowance for trade interlinkages and to show how the economic performance of one group of countries may deleteriously affect that of another group, working through the balance-of-payments constraint.

When a country expands its domestic demand, it simultaneously increases the demand for its imports. This induces an increase in demand in the countries supplying those imports which, in turn, increases the import supplying countries' demand for the initiating country's exports. This sets up a secondary multiplier effect and so on. The 'linked' multiplier explicitly allows for these feedback effects from the rest of the world. However, the values are not radically different from the conventional multiplier estimates. The value of the linked multiplier for the United Kingdom, for example, is only about 1.16, which compares with the unlinked multiplier of 1.10 (authors' estimates).

The total effect, however, of a number of countries simultaneously expanding or contracting demand can be much larger than these linked multiplier figures suggest. The multiplier for the OECD countries as a whole is of the order of 3, more than double the average value for the individual countries. Thus, the expansionary (deflationary) impact acting through the foreign trade multiplier on a particular country, which results from a number of the larger OECD countries simultaneously increasing (reducing) their growth rates, can be substantial. This is even before we consider the ramifications of the super-multiplier.

While numerous countries correctly consider many of their growth difficulties as originating overseas, for the OECD countries as a whole such problems are largely internally generated. This is because the OECD in aggregate only trades about 7 per cent of its GDP with the rest of the world – a figure which is exceeded by all the individual advanced countries, with the exception of the United States. (The United States has the smallest share of exports in output of the advanced countries, with a figure of 7 per cent, while at the other extreme Belgium exports about 65 per cent of its output.)[6]

Consequently, to understand the causes of, for example, the post-1973 slowdown in output growth, it is necessary to consider the interlinkages between, in particular, the advanced countries. Of particular importance, especially since 1973, is the 'deflationary bias' that the asymmetry in balance-of-payments adjustment has imparted to the international economy. This asymmetry results from the fact that a country is able to run a balance-of-payments surplus almost indefinitely, while there are strong pressures on a country to correct a deficit, normally through deflationary measures to reduce the growth of output and, hence, the growth of imports. The severe deflationary pressures that were introduced in the 1970s, supposedly to reduce the inflation generated by the commodity boom and oil price rises of 1973–74 and 1979, led to a global recession from which it became difficult for any one country to escape through the use of domestic demand management policies (Davidson 1991). It will be shown that, when we consider the interlinkages between the advanced countries, the export-led growth theory and the balance-of-payments constrained growth model have to be extended. Attempts by any one country to relax its balance-of-payments constraint by expenditure switching policies (if, indeed, this is possible) may well lead to *competitive growth*, that is, to an increase in output which is at the expense of another country's production. This is a situation which may eventually lead to reciprocal devaluation and other protectionist measures to control trade that may ultimately render such expenditure switching policies self-defeating. An implication is that the most effective way of increasing growth and reducing unemployment is the generation of *complementary* growth: this involves the politically more difficult problem of coordinated reflation. Only by nations acting in concert in a manner analogous to a closed economy (which obviates the balance-of-payments constraint) can a faster rate of growth be generated.

In the next section, we extend the Harrod dynamic multiplier model to a two-sector case. We consider two groups of countries. The growth of one group is either at its maximum potential ('resource constrained' growth) or at a rate which the relevant governments do not wish to increase for policy reasons, such as to combat inflation ('policy constrained' growth). The model shows how the growth of this group limits the growth of the second group through the balance-of-payments constraint, and the latter group may therefore be described as being 'balance-of-payments constrained.' We next introduce capital flows and relative prices into the model. If the change in relative prices is sufficiently important in determining the growth of exports and imports, the balance of payments ceases to act as a constraint. Likewise, a sufficiently fast growth of long-term capital flows may achieve the same result. Nevertheless, we have argued earlier that both these conditions are very unlikely to be met in practice. But this extension of the analysis does demonstrate how the change in both relative prices and capital flows may be incorporated into the model and how these factors may partially relax the balance-of-payments constraint. We next show how import controls may enable a country to circumvent the balance-of-payments constraint. In the long run, however, the imposition of such controls may reduce a country's competitiveness through encouraging 'featherbedding' and x-inefficiency in the domestic economy.

Resource constrained, policy constrained and balance-of-payments constrained growth

In this section, we discuss how the existence of international trade flows is an important factor in determining the maximum growth rate that a number of advanced countries is able to achieve. Notwithstanding the fact that the industrialised countries, in aggregate, are almost a closed economy, all that is necessary for the balance of payments to act as a factor constraining growth is for one country (or group of countries) to have an exogenously determined growth of output.

Prior to 1973, this condition was fulfilled by such countries as Japan and possibly West Germany, both of which achieved growth rates that were sufficiently fast to induce domestic factor supply shortages.[7] These countries may be termed 'resource constrained.' It is difficult to argue convincingly that any country has been resource constrained since the mid-1970s in the sense that the factor supplies have, in the long run, limited the growth of GDP. (There have been times, of course, when short-term capacity shortages may have restricted a country's rate of expansion.) Nevertheless, various countries have, at different times and to differing degrees, resorted to deflationary policies in the belief that therein lay the solution to the problem of inflation. From the point of view of the remainder of the advanced countries, the result is similar to the effect of resource constrained economies: it restricts the degree of freedom possessed by these countries to pursue policies to raise their individual rates of growth.

For expositional purposes, it is convenient to divide the countries into two categories. Group One consists of those countries which are growing below their maximum potential and are constrained from growing faster by their balance-of-payments problems. Group Two comprises those countries which are either resource or policy constrained and hence are either unable or unwilling to increase their growth rate. Clearly, the composition of the two groups will vary from time to time. For example, the United Kingdom from 1945 to 1979 should be classified as being balance-of-payments constrained (Group One), whereas for the period 1979–86 it was policy constrained (Group Two). Since 1986, the United Kingdom has again encountered severe balance-of-payments problems, putting the country once more into Group One.

We may illustrate the operation of the balance-of-payments constraint using a very simple numerical example involving the two groups of countries. Let us assume that relative prices measured in a common currency do not change. The growth of the imports of Group Two are given by the (long-run) import demand function, $m_2 = \pi_2 y_2$, and $\pi_2 \equiv \varepsilon_1$, where ε_1 is the income elasticity of demand for the exports of Group One. For illustrative purposes, we assume that π_2 takes a value of unity. Let us further assume that Group Two is the resource or policy constrained group and grows at its maximum, or productive potential, growth rate of 5 per cent per annum. Consequently, the rate of growth of Group Two's imports (and Group One's exports) is 5 per cent per annum.

Turning next to Group One, the growth of its imports is given by $m_1 = \pi_1 y_1$. Let us assume that Group One is the more uncompetitive group in terms of its non-price characteristics and that π_1 takes a value of 2. In other words, the income elasticity of demand for Group One's exports is unity while the value for the more (non-price) competitive Group Two is 2. Let us further assume that Group One's growth of productive potential is also 5 per cent per annum. If Group One were to grow at this rate, the growth of its imports would be a rapid 10 per cent per annum. However, a condition for balance-of-payments equilibrium is that $m_1 = m_2$, where $m_1 \equiv x_2$ and $m_2 \equiv x_1$. Clearly, this is incompatible with both groups growing at their productive potential. If Group One were to grow at 5 per cent per annum, it would be running an ever-increasing current account deficit, as the growth of its imports would be 10 per cent while that of exports would be only 5 per cent per annum. If relative prices cannot adjust because of real wage resistance, or are ineffective if they do alter because of low price elasticities, the only way that the balance of payments can be brought into equilibrium is through quantity or income adjustment. It is here that an asymmetry in the adjustment process comes into play. There is much greater pressure on a deficit country to take measures to bring its balance of payments back into equilibrium compared with a surplus country. The result is that Group One has to curtail its rate of growth, in this illustration, to 2.5 per cent, which is well below its growth of productive potential with all the consequences that this implies. Once this reduction in growth is achieved, its imports and exports grow at the same rate, namely, 5 per cent per annum and so the balance of payments will be brought into equilibrium. In these circumstances, Group One is balance-of-payments constrained and its maximum sustainable growth rate is dependent upon the growth of Group Two. The example is summarised in Table 3.2.

If, for some reason such as an increase in the rate of technical progress, Group Two increases its growth rate to, say, 6 per cent per annum, then Group One's balance-of-payments growth rate will increase to 3 per cent per annum. Conversely, if Group Two's growth rate slows because, for example, deflationary policies are introduced putatively to reduce inflation, then Group One will find that its maximum growth rate will also fall, even if it does not share Group Two's concern over inflation.

We may examine this argument in more detail as follows. If we express the reduced-form Keynesian model in terms of growth rates, assume for the moment that the terms of trade do not alter in the long run and make use of the definition that the growth of exports of Group One is equal to the growth of imports of Group Two (that is, $x_i = m_j = \pi_j y_j$ where $i, j = 1, 2; i \neq j$), the growth of income may be expressed as:

$$y_i = \alpha_i a_i + \beta_i \pi_j y_j \qquad i, j = 1, 2; i \neq j \tag{3.27}$$

Table 3.2 Balance-of-payments constrained growth: an illustrative example

	Output y_P (%)	Growth y_B (%)	π	ε	Growth of imports (m)	Growth of exports (x)
Initial growth rates						
Group 2	5	n/a	1	2	5	10
Group 1	5	n/a	2	1	10	5
Balance-of-payments equilibrium growth rates						
Group 2	5	5.0	1	2	5	5
Group 1	5	2.5	2	1	5	5

Notes:
1 y_P is growth of productive potential and y_B is the balance-of-payments constrained growth rate.
2 n/a = not applicable.

α and β are the (dynamic) domestic expenditure and foreign trade multipliers, respectively;[8] a_i is the growth of domestic autonomous expenditure. The interpretation of equation (3.27) is straightforward. The growth of income of, say, Group One is not only a function of the growth of its autonomous expenditure (as in a closed economy), but is also dependent upon the growth of Group Two. As the growth of Group Two increases, so does the growth of its demand for Group One's exports, which, in turn, increases the growth of Group One's income through the dynamic foreign trade multiplier.

The relationships for Groups One and Two given by equation (3.27) may, for convenience, be termed their 'growth equations' and are shown diagrammatically in Figure 3.2(a) as the lines A and B, respectively. The actual growth rates of the two groups are determined by the intersection of the two lines. (This is assumed to occur initially at point a in Figure 3.2(a) where the lines A_0 and B_0 intersect.)

Given any value of y_2, namely the growth of Group Two's income, equation (3.27) (where $i = 1$ and $j = 2$) suggests that Group One could achieve any desired rate of growth by simply determining the appropriate rate of growth of its own autonomous expenditure through government policy and achieving this through domestic demand management policies. This may not be possible, however, because of the existence of a balance-of-payments constraint which it is now necessary to incorporate into the model. The line BP in Figure 3.2(a) is the locus of points where the growth of the two groups is such that there is no change in the balance of payments. In other words, it is the familiar balance-of-payments equilibrium growth rate (see equation (3.7)). Assuming, for the moment, that there is no change in relative prices or in the exchange rate, and that Group One has an initial trade deficit, the equation of the BP locus is given by:

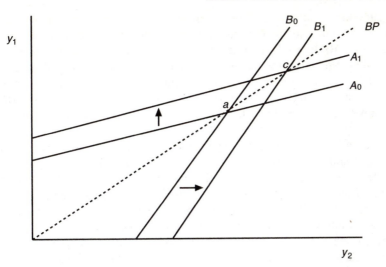

Figure 3.2(a) Balance of payments and growth

$$y_1 = \frac{\varphi \pi_2}{\pi_1} y_2 + \frac{(1 - \varphi)}{\pi_1} (f - p_1) \qquad (3.28)$$

where φ is Group One's share of exports in its total foreign exchange receipts; f is the growth of long-term or autonomous net nominal capital flows from Group Two to Group One. The growth of these capital flows is assumed to be independent of the growth of Group One.

For expositional ease, it is convenient to assume $\varphi = 1$, which means that there are no autonomous capital flows and that trade between the two groups is initially balanced. The equation of the BP locus is now given by:

$$y_1 = \frac{\pi_2}{\pi_1} y_2 \qquad (3.29)$$

which is formally equivalent to the dynamic Harrod trade multiplier (or the Hicks super-multiplier) result.

In terms of Figure 3.2(a), the *BP* locus given by equation (3.29) passes through the origin, whereas if there is a growth of capital inflows to Group One as in equation (3.28) this will cause the *BP* line to be shifted upwards. Thus, a growth of long-term capital inflows enables the balance-of-payments equilibrium growth of Group One to be commensurately higher for any given growth of Group Two.

It may be seen from equations (3.28) and (3.29) that the greater the degree of non-price competitiveness of Group Two compared with Group One (that is, the smaller the ratio π_2/π_1), the lower will be the growth of Group One that is compatible with balance-of-payments equilibrium for a given growth of Group Two.

In Figure 3.2(a), both the groups are growing at their balance-of-payments equilibrium growth rates as the intersection of lines A_0 and B_0 is at point a which is on the BP locus. If the intersection is above the *BP* line, Group One will be running an increasing balance-of-payments deficit which will have to be financed by a growth of short-term capital flows, or accommodating transfers, from Group Two. Conversely, if the intersection is below the *BP* line, Group One will be experiencing an increasing balance-of-payments surplus.

An increase in the growth of Group One's autonomous expenditure causes the line A_0 to shift upwards, through the domestic expenditure multiplier, to become, for example, the line A_1. For the moment, let us assume that Group Two is neither policy nor resource constrained. Consequently, the resulting increased growth of its exports to Group One will, through the dynamic foreign trade multiplier, lead to an increase in the growth of output of Group Two. The growth rates of the two groups are given by point b. Group One has a growing balance-of-payments deficit that has to be financed by a growth in short-term capital flows from Group Two. If, however, Group Two takes the opportunity of increasing its growth of domestic autonomous expenditure so that the output growth rates are given by point c, the balance of payments will be brought back into equilibrium. The overall movement from a to c represents the working of the Hicks super-multiplier. We have previously termed this type of economic growth as complementary and we shall return to its importance.

Figure 3.2(b) depicts the situation where Group Two is resource or policy constrained and has a constant growth rate of y_2^*. An expansion in the growth of Group One's autonomous expenditure now results in a movement from a to d. Once again, the growth of short-term capital flows from Group Two has to finance Group One's growing trade imbalance. In the short run, the growth of Group Two's autonomous domestic expenditure has to decrease to release resources for the increased growth of exports sold to Group One (that is, the line B_0 shifts to B_2).

In the long run, however, the increasing balance-of-payments deficit becomes unsustainable as the ratio of international debt to GDP increases. In the absence of effective expenditure-switching policies to increase the growth of Group One's exports and reduce its import growth, the only remedy is to reduce its growth of output. Thus, in Figure 3.2(b), Group One's balance-of-payments constrained growth is that given by the point a. It would be purely fortuitous and highly unlikely if this rate of growth were such as to be associated with a full utilisation (or a desired level of utilisation) of Group One's factors of production. It is more likely that Group One's rate of growth would be below its full employment rate of growth leading to rising unemployment (either overt or disguised) over time.

Since Group One is constrained by the balance of payments to grow below its maximum potential, if Group Two is policy constrained but decides to raise its rate of growth, it is assumed that Group One will simultaneously increase

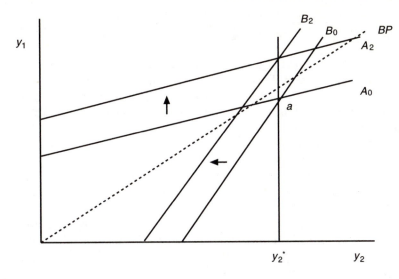

Figure 3.2(b) Balance of payments and growth

its own rate of growth to the greatest extent compatible with balance-of-payments equilibrium. Hence, the growth of Group One is fundamentally determined by the growth of Group Two's autonomous expenditure. If, on the other hand, Group Two is resource constrained, then Group One's own growth rate is ultimately determined by the supply conditions in Group Two.

While it has been argued that in the long run a depreciation of the exchange rate is unlikely to be effective in overcoming the balance-of-payments constraint, nevertheless, it may provide some amelioration in the short run. In the next section, the effect of a depreciation on the growth rates of the two groups is considered.

The impact of a sustained depreciation

In order to analyse the effect of a depreciation or devaluation of Group One's currency, it is convenient to assume that trade is initially balanced. Under these circumstances the growth equations are given by:

$$y_1 = \alpha_1 a_1 + \beta_1 \pi_2 y_2 - \beta_1 (1 + \eta + \psi)(e + p_2 - p_1) \qquad (3.30a)$$

and

$$y_2 = \alpha_2 a_2 + \beta_2 \pi_1 y_1 - \beta_2 (1 + \eta + \psi)(e + p_2 - p_1) \qquad (3.30b)$$

The balance-of-payments equilibrium growth rate becomes:

$$y_1 = \frac{\pi_2}{\pi_1} y_2 - \frac{(1 + \eta + \psi)(e + p_2 - p_1)}{\pi_1} \tag{3.31}$$

It is important to note that in order to alter the growth rate of Group One, given the growth of Group Two, as mentioned above, a *continuous* real depreciation is required rather than a once-and-for-all devaluation because of the multiplicative nature of the demand functions. (For convenience, we shall henceforth take the term 'depreciation' as referring to a continuous depreciation of the currency.)

If the Marshall–Lerner condition just fails to be satisfied in the sense that the price elasticities sum to minus unity, it follows from equations (3.30a), (3.30b) and (3.31) that a depreciation will have no effect upon the equilibrium growth rate of either group of countries. The growth equations and the balance-of-payments equilibrium locus are in this case given by equations (3.27) and (3.29). Empirical studies, however, suggest that the sum of the price elasticities for aggregate exports and imports falls within the range of –1.5 to –2.5, although the estimates are sometimes found to be statistically insignificant. (See, for example, Houthakker and Magee 1969; Stern *et al.* 1976; and Bairam 1988.)

In the circumstances where the Marshall–Lerner condition is satisfied, equation (3.30a) demonstrates that, in terms of Figure 3.3, a depreciation will have the effect of shifting the *BP* locus upwards from BP_0 to B_1. The depreciation also results in the line A_0 moving upwards to A_3. The shift of the *BP* line exceeds that of the line A_0. A corollary is that, from equation (3.30b), the depreciation, *ceteris paribus*, shifts the line B_0 to the left to become line B_3.

The direct impact of a depreciation is to increase the growth of Group One at

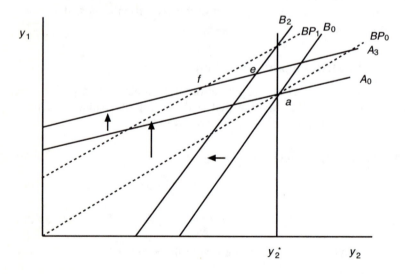

Figure 3.3 Balance of payments and growth

the expense of Group Two: growth is *competitive*. Group Two, seeing its growth rate being adversely affected by the depreciation, may engage in a retaliatory depreciation, thus rendering Group One's initial attempt to raise its rate of growth self-defeating. Moreover, Group One experiences an increasing surplus on the balance of payments whereas the other group suffers from a worsening deficit. With reference to Figure 3.3 again, the effect is that the growth rates move from the values given by point *a* to those designated by point *e*.

The eventual equilibrium position depends upon the reaction of both groups to the depreciation. To take one example: Group Two, in the face of an increasing balance-of-payments deficit, may consider that the most effective remedy is to engage in a competitive depreciation. If this were successful, it would return the economies to point *a*. Alternatively, Group Two might seek to improve its balance of payments by reducing its growth rate even further than that induced by the initial depreciation. In this case, the line B_3 would shift to the left (not shown in Figure 3.3 for clarity) and the equilibrium solution would be given by point *f*.

If, on the other hand, the desired rate of growth of Group Two is its original rate, y_2^*, and Group One simultaneously increases its rate of growth of autonomous expenditure thereby shifting the line A_3 upwards (not shown), the eventual equilibrium will be at point *g*. Thus, with a sufficiently fast rate of currency depreciation, Group One may be able to achieve its own resource or policy constrained rate of growth. Given this, the question arises why flexible exchange rates do not seem to have de-linked the national economies and removed the balance-of-payments constraint.

In fact, the introduction of flexible exchange rates with the breakdown of Bretton Woods has not proved to be the panacea originally envisaged. As we have noted above, the existence of real wage resistance makes it difficult, if not impossible, to translate variations in the nominal exchange rate into long-run changes of the real exchange rate. Associated with this is the possibility of a vicious circle developing which comprises rising inflation, initially generated by the depreciation, and a depreciating exchange rate. Oligopolistic pricing and the effect of uncertainty induced by exchange rate changes also make trade flows unresponsive to changes in relative prices. The experience since the 1970s has shown that all these factors have effectively prevented flexible exchange rates from de-linking the national economies. The failure of flexible exchange rates is perhaps best seen by the emergence of the Exchange Rate Mechanism (ERM) of the European Community, which represents a substantial move back to the type of regime experienced under the Bretton Woods arrangement. (Nevertheless, the failure of sterling to remain in the ERM in 1992 shows just how destabilising speculative capital flows can be.) There is, however, still exchange rate flexibility between countries in the Exchange Rate Mechanism and the US and Japan. Moreover, the evidence cited earlier in this chapter suggests that the magnitude of real exchange rate adjustments would have to be substantial to compensate for the differences in non-price competitiveness between countries.

The imposition of import controls

The second method by which a country may attempt to relax the balance-of-payments constraint is through the imposition of import controls. These may take the form of tariffs or quotas.

The imposition of tariffs by, for example, Group One, would raise the price of imports in terms of domestic currency. (It should be noted that in order to reduce the rate of growth of imports the tariff must be increasing over time: once again the term 'tariff' will be taken to refer to a continuously increasing tariff. A continuously increasing tariff, however, does not seem plausible.) The effect of a tariff is thus analogous to that of a devaluation, with the exception, of course, that there is not the direct stimulus to export growth that a devaluation provides. As the case of a devaluation has been discussed in the last section, the impact of a tariff will not be dealt with separately here. (It is perhaps worth pointing out, though, that the effect of a retaliatory tariff imposed by Group Two may well vitiate any advantage provided to Group One by the original tariff.)

We assume that quotas are introduced to reduce the growth of imports. This may be viewed as a fall in the income elasticity of demand for imports. It is normally postulated that the licences to import would be auctioned off, thus providing a source of revenue.

If Group One introduces a quota, its income elasticity of demand for imports will fall and hence the slope of the BP locus will increase and the BP locus will rotate from BP_0 to BP_2 in Figure 3.4. The slope of the line A_0 will also increase, but it can be shown that the increase is not so great as that of the BP locus. The size of the dynamic foreign trade multiplier increases as there is less leakage of the growth of expenditure into imports. There is also an increase in the contribution that autonomous expenditure growth makes to output growth because the size of the dynamic domestic autonomous expenditure multiplier increases. The post-import quota situation from Group One is given by the line A_4, where we assume that the growth of Group One's autonomous expenditure growth is the same as in the pre-quota case, but its contribution to economic growth is larger for the reason noted above. (Note that, for clarity, the corresponding line B for Group Two is not shown in Figure 3.4.)

Group Two now faces a decline in the rate of growth of demand due to a fall in the growth of its exports. Let us suppose it attempts to maintain its rate of growth at y_2^* by increasing its autonomous expenditure to compensate (Figure 3.4). In this case, the intersection of the line A_4 and the corresponding line for Group Two will occur at point h. In the long run, this is not sustainable, since Group Two is now running a growing balance-of-trade deficit. The reason for this is simple. The imposition of quotas by Group One has reduced the growth of its imports, which are, of course, the exports of Group Two, while the imports of Group Two remain at their pre-quota rate of growth. Unless Group Two is willing to finance an increasing inflow of capital, it will have to take measures to correct this disequilibrium.

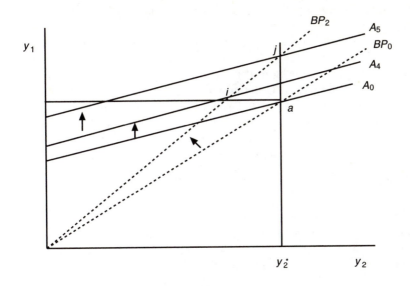

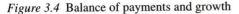

Figure 3.4 Balance of payments and growth

There are fundamentally two choices open to Group Two. First (and more likely, as the experience of the 1930s suggests), Group Two can retaliate by imposing its own import quotas in an attempt to return the ratio of the import elasticities to its original value. Even if this were successful, it should be noted that the growth of world trade would have fallen since the absolute values of π_1 and π_2 would have decreased. This would reduce both the benefits of international specialisation of production and the welfare gains of the increased diversity of choice brought by trade. A likely outcome is a trade war with a progressive move towards autarky. Growth would again have become competitive.

Second, Group Two can pursue deflationary policies until the intersection of the two growth lines occurs on the BP_2 locus. This occurs at point i in Figure 3.4, where Group One's growth rate is the same as that which it experienced before it introduced quotas. The outcome is thus that Group One obtains no benefit from the imposition of quotas, while Group Two finds that its growth rate is reduced. The question then arises why Group One should ever introduce quotas. The answer is that, if at the same time as introducing quotas, Group One increases its growth of autonomous expenditure then its balance-of-payments equilibrium growth rate will be higher than in the pre-quota situation, even though this is not true for Group Two.

Moreover, the growth rate of Group Two need not fall if Group One, at the same time as imposing quotas, takes other measures to increase its growth of autonomous demand *and thereby ensures that its growth of imports remains at the previous rate*. (This was the policy prescription argued by the Cambridge Economic Policy Group. See, for example, Cripps and Godley 1978.) This action ensures that Group Two will no longer be faced with a trade deficit. In terms of Figure 3.4, Group One's growth line shifts up to A_5 and the post-import control growth rates are given by the point j. The outcome is that both countries are growing at their maximum or desired growth rates. The gains for Group One include a greater utilisation of labour, a faster rate of capital accumulation and an increase in the growth of income.

The Cambridge Economic Policy Group argued that the major advantage of import controls, compared with a devaluation, is that they are likely to be less inflationary. If Group One were to introduce reflationary measures to accompany a devaluation so that, assuming no retaliation, the end result would be a growth rate equivalent to that obtained with import controls, the former would be likely to set up larger inflationary pressures. The depreciation would, as we have mentioned above, lead to an increase in the growth of the prices of imported goods (in terms of the domestic currency), resulting in an inflationary wage–price spiral. On the other hand, under import controls, all the tariff and quota revenues could be returned to the economy through tax reductions and so the effect would be likely to be less inflationary than with a devaluation.

The effectiveness, however, of import controls is controversial, not least because of the problem of retaliation. Even the advocates of import controls regard them as necessary only because of the lack of a better alternative. A devaluation would be preferable if it had a sufficiently large quantitative impact on trade flows, but, for the reasons already discussed, this is not seen as a feasible remedy. Import controls are, though, superior to the only other policy which consists of restricting the growth of Group One to the rate determined by the value of its income elasticities of demand for imports and exports, together with the growth of Group Two. In the long term, it is possible that increased inefficiency induced by protectionism may eventually cause π_2 to fall and π_1 to rise, thus offsetting any short-run gains in the growth rate due to the imposition of the quotas.

The post-1973 slowdown in economic growth

The model outlined above may be used to illustrate the post-1973 recession and the slowdown from that date in the economic growth of the advanced countries. The oil crisis of 1973–4 exacerbated the 'deflationary bias' inherent in the asymmetry of the adjustment pressures on deficit and surplus countries. Given the high savings propensities of the OPEC countries, the initial quadrupling of oil prices meant that, to sustain growth, the OECD countries collectively would have to maintain a substantial current account deficit; indeed, this was appreciated by the policy makers at the time. Nevertheless, countries such as Japan and West Germany, accustomed to low inflation rates and annual surpluses on the balance of payments, introduced restrictive monetary and fiscal policies to curtail the rate of price increases (through a belief in some sort of short-run Phillips curve trade-off). The US initially pursued expansionary policies, but this led to a marked deterioration of its current account between 1975 and 1978. The counter-inflationary policies that were introduced in October 1978 were not sufficient to prevent a speculative run on the dollar, which necessitated the corrective action of marked tightening of monetary policy. As Larsen *et al.* (1983: 56) commented: 'This episode suggests that even the largest OECD country, with a relatively small share of trade in GNP, is not immune from the pressures of international linkages.' The inevitable result of the Japanese, West German, and, later, United States policies was that deflationary pressures were transmitted to the advanced countries as a whole.

This is shown in Figure 3.5, where the policy constrained rate of growth of Group Two falls from y_2^* to y_2^{**} in an attempt, for example, to restrain inflation. Given the ineffectiveness of expenditure-switching policies for the reasons outlined earlier, the growth of Group One has also to fall (regardless of whether or not this is a desired objective) to bring the balance of payments back into equilibrium. Thus, for the advanced countries as a whole, the balance-of-payments deficit fell as the growth of output declined.

This may have given the misleading impression that there was no longer a 'balance-of-payments problem.' Although, *ex post*, the balance-of-payments deficits were extinguished, this occurred at the cost of increasing under-utilisation of resources and the social cost of rising and prolonged unemployment. Nevertheless, there were some explicit balance-of-payments crises of countries that tried to expand faster than their balance-of-payments equilibrium growth rate permitted. These included the UK's sterling crisis of 1976 which led to IMF intervention and consequent deflationary policies, Italy in 1980–1, and France in 1982. During the 1980s, there were still the large structural imbalances of the US deficit and the Japanese and West German surpluses. In the 1980s, the US went from being the world's largest

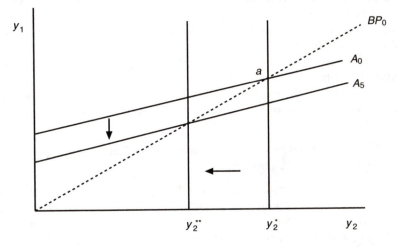

Figure 3.5 Balance of payments and growth

net creditor to the largest net debtor as a result of a growth rate that was faster relative to Japan and Europe than it had been in the past. However, there was increasing pressure from the world financial markets for the US to undertake restrictive measures to reduce the external deficit. Once again, even the US was not immune from the balance-of-payments constraint. (See Stewart 1983 for a discussion of the problems facing the international management of demand subsequent to 1973.)

Conclusions

In this chapter, we have focused on the monetary aspects of trade theory and have argued that the balance of payments can play a major role in the determination of the growth performance of countries through its effect and influence on the growth of demand in an economic system. The model outlined here contrasts with mainstream growth and trade theory in which output growth is supply determined; the role of trade is looked at from the point of view of real resource augmentation, and the balance of payments is assumed to look after itself through relative price adjustment. It is argued here that there are many reasons why the balance of payments is not easily rectified by relative price changes, and that if current account deficits cannot be perpetually financed by capital inflows, it is the growth of output that must adjust to balance imports and exports. We trace this idea back to Harrod's foreign trade multiplier; and the role of the balance of payments itself in determining economic performance we trace back to the doctrine of Mercantilism, with which Keynes in the *General Theory* had some sympathy because a healthy balance of payments permits lower interest rates which are necessary to encourage domestic investment. When we extend the model to more than one country we show how growth in one country can, through the balance-of-payments constraint, affect adversely the overall performance of all countries. We, thus, present a Keynesian open-economy demand-driven model of economic growth in which the supply of factors of production and productivity growth are treated as largely endogenous and in which the major constraint on demand is the growth of exports relative to the income elasticity of demand for imports. The model presents a serious challenge not only to old (neoclassical) growth theory, but also to 'new' growth theory which ignores the balance of payments and has yet to accept the Keynesian revolution.

Appendix A: Real wage resistance and the ineffectiveness of nominal exchange rate changes

In this appendix, we illustrate the role of real wage resistance in thwarting the effect of a nominal devaluation as follows. The growth of consumer prices (p_c) is defined as a weighted function of the growth of the prices of domestically produced consumer goods (p_d) and imported goods, expressed in the domestic currency (p_f').

$$p_c = \sigma \, p_d + (1 - \sigma)p_f' \qquad\qquad (A3.1)$$

where σ is the share of domestically produced consumer goods and services in total consumption expenditure; p_f' is equal to $p_f + e$, where p_f and e are the growth rates of foreign prices and the exchange rate. Domestic prices are determined by a mark-up on total prime costs:

$$P_d = (1 + \tau)[(WL/Y) + (P_n \, N/Y) + (P_f^* M^* R/Y)] \qquad\qquad (A3.2)$$

where the upper case denotes the level of the relevant variable; $(1 + \tau)$ is the mark-up, W is the nominal wage rate, L is the number employed, P_n is the price of domestically produced raw materials (N). P_f^* and M^* are the price in the domestic currency and volume of imported raw materials. The other variables have their conventional meaning.

Expressing equation (A3.2) in terms of proportionate growth rates and assuming that the ratios of domestically and foreign sourced raw materials to output are constant, the following expression is obtained:

$$p_d = \upsilon + (a_w \, w - a_w \, q + a_n \, p_n + a_m^* \, p_f^*) \qquad\qquad (A3.3)$$

where υ is the rate of change of the mark-up, q is the growth of labour productivity, and a_w, a_n, and a_m^* are the shares of the variables in total output.

We further assume for the moment that the mark-up does not change (that is, $\upsilon = 0$) and, for expositional ease, the growth of prices of domestically produced raw materials is assumed to be the same as the growth of prices of domestically produced consumer goods ($p_d = p_n$). It is similarly postulated that the prices of imported raw materials and imported consumer goods grow at the same rate (that is, $p_f' = p_f^*$). Under these circumstances, the growth of domestic prices is given by:

$$p_d = \acute{a}w - \acute{a}q + \hat{a}p_f' \qquad\qquad (A3.4)$$

where $\acute{a} = a_w /(a_w + a_m^*)$ and

$$\hat{a} = a_m^*/(a_w + a_m^*).$$

Substituting equation (A3.4) into (A3.1), we obtain:

$$p_c = \sigma(\acute{a}w - \acute{a}q + \hat{a}p_f') + (1 - \sigma)p_f' \qquad\qquad (A3.5)$$

The growth of wages is given by:

$$w = \tilde{a} \, p_c + q \qquad\qquad (A3.6)$$

The coefficient $\tilde{a}$ is a function of a number of factors affecting the labour market including the level of unemployment, the degree of trade union bargaining power, and so on. If there is real wage resistance, $\tilde{a} = 1$, and it follows that the growth of the real wage equals the growth of labour productivity. Labour thus bargains for, and obtains, an increase in nominal wages equal to an increase in the retail price index. This implies that the share of labour in national income is constant. Under these circumstances:

$$p_c = \sigma(\acute{a}\, p_c + \hat{a}\, p_f') + (1 - \sigma)\, p_f' \tag{A3.7}$$

and

$$P_c = \frac{(1 - \sigma + \hat{\alpha}\, \sigma)}{(1 - \sigma\, a')}\, P_f' \tag{A3.8}$$

However, it may be simply shown that $(1 - \sigma + \hat{a}) = (1 - \sigma\, \acute{a})$, and it therefore follows that $p_c = p_d = p = p_f$ last term satisfies the condition that:

$$(1 + \varphi\, \eta + \psi)\, (p_d - e - p_f) = 0. \tag{A3.9}$$

Thus, a continuous depreciation of the currency cannot relax the balance-of-payments constraint as it will merely lead to a growth in domestic prices which will completely offset any initial gain in price competitiveness.

Appendix B: Dual-gap analysis and the Harrod foreign trade multiplier

There is also a link-up between the dynamic foreign trade multiplier model and models of dual-gap analysis applied to developing countries made famous by Hollis Chenery and his associates in the 1950s and 1960s (see, for example, Chenery and Adelman 1966; Chenery and Bruno 1962; Chenery and Macewan; 1966). The essence of dual-gap analysis is to show that growth may be constrained either by domestic saving or by foreign exchange, and that the role of foreign borrowing is to relieve whichever is the dominant constraint. Chenery's view (like Prebisch's) was that for most developing countries, at least in the intermediate stage of development, the dominant constraint is likely to be a shortage of foreign exchange associated with balance-of-payments deficits, so that growth would be balance-of-payments constrained.

Consider the following model. Growth requires investment goods which may either be provided domestically or purchased from abroad. The domestic provision requires saving; the foreign provision requires foreign exchange. If it is assumed that some investment goods for growth can only be provided from abroad, there is always a minimum amount of foreign exchange required to sustain the growth process. In Harrod's (1939) growth model, the relation between growth and saving is given by the incremental capital–output ratio (c), which is the reciprocal of the productivity of capital (p) that is, $y = s/c$ or

$y = s\,p$, where y is the growth rate and s is the savings ratio. Likewise, the growth rate can be expressed as the product of the incremental output–import ratio $(dY/M = m')$ and the ratio of investment good imports to income $(M/Y = i)$ that is, $y = im'$. If there is a lack of substitutability between domestic and foreign resources, growth will be constrained by whatever factor is more limiting: domestic saving or foreign exchange. Suppose, for example, that the growth rate permitted by foreign exchange is less than the growth rate permitted by domestic saving. In this case, growth would be foreign exchange constrained, and if the constraint were not lifted there would be unemployed domestic resources and a proportion of domestic saving would be unused. For example, suppose that the product of the import ratio (i) and the productivity of imports (m') gives a permissible growth rate of 3 per cent, and the product of the savings ratio (s) and the productivity of capital (p) gives a permissible growth rate of 4 per cent. Growth is constrained to 3 per cent, and for a given productivity of capital a proportion of savings available cannot be absorbed. Ways must be found of using unused domestic resources to earn more foreign exchange or to raise the productivity of imports, or both. As many developing countries will testify, however, this is easier said than done. It is not easy to sell more on world markets if external conditions are unfavourable and price elasticities are low.

The correspondence between the dynamic Harrod trade multiplier result of $y = x/\pi$, and the Chenery model of $y = im'$ is immediately apparent. If balance-of-payments equilibrium is a requirement so that an increase in imports for growth requires an increase in exports, an increase in x will raise i and the foreign exchange constraint is relaxed. The Chenery model was never applied to developed countries, and it is interesting to ask why. But when it was applied to less developed countries it came under attack from neoclassical economists because of its rigid assumptions relating to the lack of substitutability between types of imports and between foreign and domestic resources. Yet we continue to witness in the world economy so many developing countries with huge balance-of-payments difficulties, desperate for foreign exchange, which could grow faster if the foreign exchange constraint were relaxed. The critics do not have the evidence on their side.

Notes

1   As mentioned previously, Harrod (1933) had earlier addressed the question of the open economy and argued that output is determined by the foreign trade multiplier. We take this up later.
2   With the exception of Malthus; but as Keynes (1936: 32) says in the *General Theory*: 'Ricardo conquered England as completely as the Holy Inquisition conquered Spain.'
3   As a matter of historical interest, the Harrod trade multiplier was precisely anticipated by a Danish parliamentarian, Julius Wulff in 1896 (see Hegeland 1954; and Shackle 1967) and by the Australian economist, L.F. Giblin in 1930 (Giblin 1930).
4   Most notably, these are the countries which receive either substantial foreign aid

(normally the LDCs) or long-term private investment from abroad.

5   The estimates of ε for West Germany from Houthakker and Magee (1969) used in calculating y_{B2} for 1953–76 and Bairam and Dempster (1991) for 1970–85 are implausibly low; the estimate of ε from Goldstein and Khans (1978) is better determined.

6   The ratio of the exports of goods and services to GDP at current prices in 1986.

7   Through the cumulative causation nature of growth (the Verdoorn effect), these resource constrained countries were also those whose competitiveness in overseas trade increased over the post-war period. They tended to run persistent balance-of-payments surpluses.

8   The expressions for the multipliers are:

$$\alpha_i = \frac{\omega_{Ai}}{(1 - \omega_{Bi} + \omega_{Mi}\pi_i)}$$

and

$$\beta_i = \frac{\omega_{Xi}}{(1 - \omega_{Bi} + \omega_{Mi}\pi_i)}$$

where ω denotes the share of a variable in total income. A and B denote autonomous and endogenous expenditure, respectively. The derivation of these expressions may be found in McCombie and Thirlwall (1994: ch. 7).

References

Bairam, E. (1987) 'The Verdoorn Law, Returns to Scale and Industrial Growth: a Review,' *Australian Economic Papers* 26, 48: 20–42.

—— (1988) 'Balance-of-Payments, the Harrod Foreign Trade Multiplier and Economic Growth: the European and North American Experience, 1970–85,' *Applied Economics* 20, 12: 1635–42.

—— and Dempster, G. (1991) 'The Harrod Foreign Trade Multiplier and Economic Growth in Asian Countries,' *Applied Economics* 23, 11: 1719–24.

Balogh, T. and Streeten, P.P. (1951) 'The Inappropriateness of Simple "Elasticity" Concepts in the Analysis of International Trade,' *Bulletin of the Oxford University Institute of Statistics* 13: 65–77.

Barrett Whale, P. (1932) *International Trade*, London: Thornton Butterworth.

—— (1937) 'The Workings of the Pre-war Gold Standard,' *Economica* 4: 18–32.

Blanchard, O.J. (1987) 'Aggregate and Individual Price Adjustment,' in W.J. Brainard and G.L. Perry (eds), *Brookings Papers on Economic Activity*, Washington, D.C.: Brookings Institution 1: 57–122.

Blecker, R.A. (1994) 'Relative Wages and the Balance of Payments Constraint,' (mimeo).

Brecht, M.J. and Stout D. (1981) 'The Rate of Exchange and Non-price Competitiveness: a Provisional Study Within UK Manufactured Exports,' *Oxford Economic Papers* (supplement) 33: 268–81.

Chan-Lee, J.H., Coe, D.T. and Prywes, M. (1987) 'Macroeconomic Changes and Macroeconomic Wage Disinflation in the 1980s,' *OECD Economic Studies* 5: 87–126.

Chenery, H. and Adelman, I. (1966) 'Foreign Aid and Economic Development: the Case of Greece,' *Review of Economics and Statistics* 48: 1–19.

Chenery, H. and Bruno, M. (1962) 'Development Alternatives in an Open Economy: the Case of Israel,' *Economic Journal* 72: 79–103.

Chenery, H. and Macewan, A. (1966) 'Optimal Patterns of Growth and Aid: the Case of Pakistan,' *Pakistan Development Review* 6: 209–42.

Coe, D.T. (1985) 'Nominal Wages, the NAIRU and Wage Flexibility,' *OECD Economic Studies* 5: 87–126.

—— and Gagliardi, F. (1985) 'Nominal Wage Determination in ten OECD Countries,' *OECD Economics and Statistics Working Paper* no. 19.

Cooper, R.N. (1982) 'The Gold Standard: Historical Facts and Future Prospects,' *Brookings Papers on Economic Activity* 11: 1–45.

Cornwall, J. (1977) *Modern Capitalism: Its Growth and Transformation*, London: Martin Robertson.

Coutts, K., Godley, W., Rowthorn, R. and Zessa, G (1990) 'Britain's Economic Problems and Policies for the 1990s,' Economic Study no. 6, London: Institute for Public Policy Research.

Cowling, K. and Sugden, R. (1989) 'Exchange Rate Behaviour and Oligopoly Pricing Behaviour,' *Cambridge Journal of Economics* 13, 3: 373–93.

Crafts, N. (1988) 'British Economic Growth Before and After 1979: a Review of the Evidence,' CEPR Discussion Paper no. 292, reprinted in N. Crafts, B. Duckham and N. Woodward (eds), *The British Economy since 1945*, Oxford: Oxford University Press 1990.

Cripps T.F. and Godley, W. (1978) 'Control of Imports as a Means to Full Employment and Expansion in World Trade: the U.K.'s Case. Comment,' *Cambridge Journal of Economics* 2, 3: 327–34.

Davidson, P. (1991) *International Money and the Real World*, 2nd edn, Basingstoke: Macmillan.

Denison, E. (1967) *Why Growth Rates Differ: Postwar Experience in Nine Western Countries*, Washington, D.C.: Brookings Institution.

Dixon, R.J. and Thirlwall, A.P. (1975) 'A Model of Regional Growth Rate Differences on Kaldorian Lines,' *Oxford Economic Papers* 27, 2: 201–14.

Dooley, M., Frankel, J. and Mathieson, D. J. (1987) 'International Capital Mobility: What Do Saving–Investment Correlations Tell Us?,' *IMF Staff Papers* 34, 3: 503–30.

Dornbusch, R. (1987) 'Exchange Rates and Prices,' *American Economic Review* 77, 1: 93–106.

Feldstein, M. and Horioka, C. (1980), 'Domestic Saving and International Capital Flows,' *Economic Journal* 90, 358: 314–29.

Fetherston, M., Moore, B. and Rhodes, J. (1977) 'Manufacturing Export Shares and Cost Competitiveness of Advanced Industrial Countries,' *Economic Policy Review* 30: 62–70.

Giblin, L.F. (1930) *Australia, 1930: An Inaugural lecture*, Melbourne: Melbourne University Press.

Goldstein, M. and Khan, M.S. (1978) 'The Supply and Demand for Exports: a Simultaneous Approach,' *Review of Economics and Statistics* 60, 2: 275–86.

Grossman, G. and Helpman, E. (1990) 'Trade, Innovation and Growth,' *American Economic Review Papers and Proceedings* 80, 2: 86–91.

Harrod, R. (1933) *International Economics*, Cambridge: Cambridge University Press.

—— (1939) 'An Essay in Dynamic Theory,' *Economic Journal* 49: 14–33.

Hegeland, H. (1954) *Multiplier Theory*, Lund: G. W. K. Gleerup.

Houthakker, H. and Magee, S. (1969) 'Income and Price Elasticities in World Trade,' *Review of Economics and Statistics* 51, 2: 111–25.

Howard, D.H. (1985) 'Implications of the US Current Account Deficit,' *Journal of Economic Perspectives* 3: 153–65.

—— (1989) 'Implications of the US Current Account Deficit,' *Journal of Economic Perspectives* 3, 4: 153–65.

Hume, D. (1752) 'Of Money,' and 'Of the Balance of Trade,' in *Political Discourses*, Edinburgh: A. Kincaid & A. Donaldson.

Johnson, H.G. (1964) 'Tariffs and Economic Development: Some Theoretical Issues,' *Journal of Development Studies* 1: 3–30.

Kahn, R.F. (1931) 'The Relation of Home Investment to Unemployment,' *Economic Journal* 41: 173–98.

Kaldor, N. (1957) 'A Model of Economic Growth,' *Economic Journal* 67: 591–624.

—— (1966) *Causes of the Slow Rate of Economic Growth of the United Kingdom: An Inaugural Lecture*, Cambridge: Cambridge University Press.

—— (1970) 'The Case for Regional Policies,' *Scottish Journal of Political Economy* 17, 3: 337–48.

—— (1971) 'Conflicts in National Economic Objectives,' *Economic Journal* 81, 321, 1–16.

—— 1975) 'What is Wrong with Economic Theory?,' *Quarterly Journal of Economics* 89, 3: 347–57.

—— (1978) 'The Effects of Devaluation on Trade in Manufactures,' in N. Kaldor *Further Essays on Applied Economics*, London: Duckworth.

Kawasaki, K., Hoeller, P. and Poret, P. (1990) 'Modelling Wages and Prices for the Smaller OECD Countries,' *OECD Economics and Statistics Department Working Papers*, no. 86.

Keynes, J.M. (1936) *The General Theory of Employment, Interest and Money*, London: Macmillan.

Kindleberger, C.P. (1967) *Europe's Postwar Growth: The Role of Labour Supply*, Cambridge, MA: Harvard University Press.

Klau, F. and Mittelstaüdt, A. (1986) 'Labour Market Flexibility,' *OECD Economic Studies* 6: 7–45.

Knight, M., Loayza, N. and Villanueva, D. (1993) 'Testing the Neoclassical Theory of Economic Growth,' *IMF Staff Papers* 40, 3: 512–41.

Knoester, A. (1995) 'Why a Depreciating Currency Does Not Improve the Current Balance,' Erasmus University, Rotterdam, Research Memorandum 9506.

—— and van der Windt, N. (1987) 'Real Wages and Taxation in Ten OECD Countries,' *Oxford Bulletin of Economics and Statistics*, 49, 1: 151–69.

Kravis, I.B. and Lipsey, R.E. (1971) *Price Competitiveness in World Trade*, New York: National Bureau of Economic Research.

Krugman, P.R. (1989a) *Exchange Rate Instability*, Cambridge, MA: MIT Press.

—— (1989b) 'Differences in Income Elasticities and Trends in Real Exchange Rates,' *European Economic Review* 33, 5: 1031–46.

Krugman, P.R. and Baldwin, R.E. (1987) 'The Persistence of the US Trade Deficit,' in W.C. Brainard and G.L. Perry (eds), *Brookings Papers on Economic Activity*, Washington, D.C.: Brookings Instituition, 1–55.

Landesmann, M. and Snell, A. (1989) 'The Economic Consequences of Mrs Thatcher for UK Manufacturing Exports,' *Economic Journal* 99, 394: 1–27.

Larsen, F., Llewellyn, J. and Potter, S. (1983) 'International Economic Linkages,'

OECD Economic Studies 1: 43–91.

Leibenstein, H. (1966) 'Allocative Efficiency vs "X-efficiency",' *American Economic Review* 56: 392–415.

Levine, R. and Renelt, D. (1992) 'A Sensitivity Analysis of Cross-country Growth Regression,' *American Economic Review* 82, 4: 942–63.

Lucas, R. E. (1988) 'On the Mechanics of Economic Development,' *Journal of Monetary Economics* 22, 1, 3–42.

Machiavelli, N. (1532) *Il Principe*, Rome: A. Blado.

Maddison, A. (1980) 'Western Economic Performance in the 1970s: a Perspective and Assessment,' *Banca Nazionale del Lavoro Quarterly Review* 33, 134: 247–90.

—— (1982) *Phases of Capitalist Development*, Oxford: Oxford University Press.

Marston, R.C. (1990) 'Pricing to Market in Japanese Manufacturing,' *Journal of International Economics* 29, 3-4: 217–36.

Matthews, R., Feinstein, C. and Odling-Smea, J. (1982) *British Economic Growth 1856–1973*, Stanford, CA: Stanford University Press.

McClosky, D. and Zecher, R. (1976) 'How the Gold Standard Worked: 1880–1913,' in J.A. Frenkel and H.G. Johnson (eds), *The Monetary Approach to the Balance of Payments*, London: Allen & Unwin.

McCombie, J.S.L. (1985) 'Economic Growth, the Harrod Foreign Trade Multiplier and the Hicks Super-multiplier,' *Applied Economics* 17, 1: 55–72.

—— and Thirlwall, A.P. (1994) *Economic Growth and the Balance-of-Payments Constraint*, Basingstoke: Macmillan.

—— (1997) 'The Dynamic Harrod Foreign Trade Multiplier and the Demand-orientated Approach to Economic Growth: an Evaluation,' *International Review of Applied Economics* 11, 1: 5–26.

Misselden, E. (1623), *The Centre of the Circle of Commerce*, London: J. Dawson for N. Bourne.

Moggridge, D. (1973) *The Collected Writings of J.M. Keynes*. Vol. XIII: *The General Theory and After: Part I Preparation*, London: Macmillan.

—— (1981) *The Collected Writings of J.M. Keynes*. Vol. XX : *Activities 1929–1931: Rethinking Employment and Unemployment Policies*, London: Macmillan.

Mun, T. (1664) *England's Treasure by Foreign Trade*; reprinted Oxford: Basil Blackwell, 1923.

Myrdal, G. (1957) *Economic Theory and Underdeveloped Regions*, London: Duckworth.

Posner, M.V. and Steer, A. (1979) 'Price Competitiveness and Performance of Manufacturing Industry,' in F. Blackaby (ed.), *De-industrialisation*, London: Heinemann.

Prebisch, R. (1950) *The Economic Development of Latin America and its Principal Problems*, New York: ECLA, UN Department of Economic Affairs.

Romer, R.M. (1986) 'Increasing Returns and Long Run Growth,' *Journal of Political Economy* 94, 5: 1002–37.

Seers, D. (1962) 'A Model of Comparative Rates of Growth of the World Economy,' *Economic Journal* 72, 45–78.

Serra, A. (1613) *Breve Trattato della Cause che Possono far Abbondare li Regni d'Oro e Argento dove non Sono Miniere, con Applicazione al Regno di Napoli* [A Brief Treatise on the Causes which Can Make Gold and Silver Abound in Kingdoms where there are no Mines].

Shackle, G.L.S. (1967) *The Years of High Theory*, Cambridge: Cambridge University Press.

Smith, A. (1776) *An Inquiry into the Nature and Causes of the Wealth of Nations*, London: Strachan & Cadell.

Solow, R. (1956) 'A Contribution to the Theory of Economic Growth,' *Quarterly Journal of Economics* 70, 65–94.

Stern, R.M., Francis, J. and Schumacher, B. (1976) *Price Elasticities in International Trade*, London: Macmillan.

Stewart, M. (1983) *Controlling the Economic Future: Policy Dilemmas in a Shrinking World*, Brighton: Wheatsheaf.

Stout, D.K. (1979) 'De-industrialisation and Industrial Policy,' in F. Blackaby, (ed.), *De-industrialisation*, London: Heinemann.

Suviranka, B. (1923), *The Theory of the Balance of Trade in England*.

Thirlwall, A.P. (1979) 'The Balance of Payments Constraint as an Explanation of International Growth Rate Differences,' *Banca Nazionale del Lavoro Quarterly Review* 128, 791: 45–53.

—— (1980) 'Regional Problems are Balance-of-Payments Problems,' *Regional Studies* 14, 419–25.

—— (1982) 'The Harrod Trade Multiplier and the Importance of Export-led Growth,' *Pakistan Journal of Applied Economics* 1, 1–21.

—— (1983a) 'Symposium on Kaldor's Growth Laws,' *Journal of Post Keynesian Economics* 5, 341–429.

—— (1983b) 'Foreign Trade Elasticities in Centre–Periphery Models of Growth and Development,' *Banca Nazionale del Lavoro Quarterly Review* 36, 146, 249–62.

—— and Hussain, M.N. (1982) 'The Balance-of-Payments Constraint, Capital Flows and Growth Rate Differences Between Developing Countries,' *Oxford Economic Papers* 34, 3, 498–510.

—— and Sanna, G. (1996) 'The Macro Determinants of Growth and "New" Growth Theory: an Evaluation and Further Evidence,' in P. Arestis (ed.), *Employment, Economic Growth and the Tyranny of the Market: Essays in Honour of Paul Davidson*, Aldershot: Edward Elgar.

Triffin, R. (1964) 'The Evaluation of the International Monetary System: Historical Reappraisal and Future Perspectives,' *Princeton Studies in International Finance* 18, June.

—— (1978) 'Gold and Dollar Crisis: Yesterday and Tomorrow,' *Essays in International Finance* no. 132, Princeton University, December.

Wilson, T. (1976) 'Effective Devaluation and Inflation,' *Oxford Economic Papers* 28, 1, 1–24.

Part II

Open economy macroeconomics

4   Aggregate supply and demand in an open economy framework

*Johan Deprez**

In the literature on open-economy macroeconomic models there exist many models of a purported 'Keynesian' nature. The Keynesian characteristics of such models are often limited to including the possibility of a short-run unemployment situation. These models invariably fail to capture the full richness of Keynes' general theory because they do not make use of Keynes' own aggregate supply and demand model. Consequently, standard interpretations of Keynes' general theory do not recognize that his model:

1   has a complete supply side that is fully capable of incorporating alternative technology, cost, and firm structure considerations;
2   can include short-term and long-term expectational elements, including user cost considerations;
3   includes a theory of aggregate price determination and inflation;
4   incorporates a complete theory of income distribution that is social in nature and rejects the neoclassical technology and thrift view of income distribution; and
5   provides the foundation for a comprehensive theory of long-term dynamics and economic growth.

Despite its obvious strengths, Keynes' aggregate supply and demand approach is the model of choice of only a minority of economists. It is primarily people within the Post Keynesian school of economic thought who have persistently pointed to the richness of Keynes' own method (cf. Weintraub 1958, 1966; Davidson 1978, 1994; Davidson and Smolensky 1964; Kregel 1976; Wells 1977; Casarosa 1981; King 1994; Deprez 1989, 1994, 1998). Because only this small group of economists has consistently worked with Keynes' approach, there still exists a significant amount of confusion in the profession at large as to the structure of the model and the appropriate ways in which it can be applied. As a consequence, much time has been spent re-articulating the basic approach and there have been only limited extensions and applications of the model. A key underexplored area is the theoretical

*The author would like to thank John Harvey for his extensive comments on this chapter.

development of an open-economy version of Keynes' system, as well as applications of the approach to international problems. The most comprehensive undertaking to develop the approach and its applications to the international realm is by Davidson (1992). Attempts to internationalize Keynes' aggregate supply and demand system in order to look at a specific component of the model includes Deprez (1997), while work that makes particular applications of the method includes Davidson (1992–3), Deprez (1995), and Deprez and Deprez (1997).

This chapter presents the basic structure, workings, and implications of Keynes' aggregate supply and demand model as extended to an open economy. In doing so, it builds upon the work that has been done on the closed-economy version of this system, as well as the limited extensions to the international domain. The initial parts of the chapter develop the three central components of the model: (a) the aggregate supply function; (b) the aggregate expected demand function; and (c) the aggregate (actual) expenditures function. These constituent elements of this approach are presented with the aid of simple and, possibly, familiar formal examples. The model is used to illustrate how aggregate production and employment decisions are made in an open economy. Subsequently explored are actual market outcomes in terms of sales and prices, the nature of short-period equilibria in an open economy, and the use of the model to address macrodynamic questions. Advanced considerations that could be built into the basic model, as well as underexplored areas of study, are ultimately suggested.

The general structure of the model

Keynes created his aggregate supply and demand model in *The General Theory of Employment, Interest, and Money* (*CWJMK* VII) in order to explain the equilibrium determination of employment, output, and income in a modern monetary production economy. By recognizing that the investment component of aggregate demand is negatively influenced by the liquidity preferences of firms and households, Keynes was able to conclude logically that aggregate supply and demand equilibrium generally occurs at levels of employment well below full employment (*CWJMK* VII: 28, 254). Consequently, social action is required to compensate for this systemic shortcoming of modern capitalism.

The basic model has three central component parts: (a) the aggregate supply function; (b) the aggregate expected demand function; and (c) the aggregate (actual) expenditures function or aggregate actual demand function. The first two generate the aggregate output and employment decisions of firms, while adding in the third generates the actual sales, market prices, and profits.

The aggregate supply function incorporates the technological and cost considerations that go into the production process. These could include expectations of future costs involved with current production. This first element of the model also involves a desired pricing scheme of firms. The most common pricing scheme is one based on marginal cost pricing, but the model can incorporate alternative mechanisms (cf. Davidson and Smolensky 1964: 126–35; Deprez 1989). Keynes' own aggregate supply function was derived directly from competitive Marshallian microfoundations (cf. Weintraub 1958; Casarosa 1981) 'involving few considerations which are not already familiar' (*CWJMK* VII: 89). In the present, open-economy version of the model no special additions are made to this approach and all production by firms is assumed to take place in their 'home' countries.

The aggregate expected demand function is made up of the firms' short-term expectations of what sales will be in the market for the output that they are about to produce. Firms need to create such expectations in order to make their production decisions because the output that they create takes time to produce and is usually only sold sometime after production is finished (cf. Davidson 1978: 33–43). The first and second considerations of the model lead the firms to decide on a particular production plan to follow. A certain amount and mix of output is produced, requiring the hiring of a particular amount of labor and of other inputs, as well as the payment of the associated wage-bill and the cost of working capital inputs.

In an open economy, this second component is extended to reflect the fact that short-term sales expectations are generated with respect to the sales that may occur in different international market areas (Deprez 1997). Within a unionized monetary system (UMS) in which one has the same unit of account or fixed exchange rates between currencies that are expected to remain fixed (Davidson 1992: 80–2), the inclusion of sales expectations in the additional market areas is sufficient. Within a non-unionized monetary system (NUMS) where various nominal units of account are used to settle contracts and have flexible exchange rates between them that are expected to vary, expectations of exchange rate variations need to be part of placing a value on expected sales in the different market areas. In other words, exchange rate uncertainty must be part of this component of an open-economy version of the aggregate supply and demand model (Davidson 1992: 83).

The third component of the model is the aggregate (actual) expenditures function or the aggregate actual demand function (Casarosa 1981). The output produced on the basis of the information contained in the first two functions is brought to market where it comes to face this component of the model. The aggregate actual expenditures function captures the desired expenditures of the different categories of economic agents in the economy for whom the output is being produced. This third component, in conjunction with the results generated by the interaction of the first and second components, creates the actual sales, prices, profits, and related results.

In an open economy, the aggregate (actual) expenditures function generally incorporates only the usual open-economy extensions. Part of the output that can be bought by the resident households, firms, and government entities (that is, the income recipients of the economy) of a particular economy is produced outside of that economy. These purchases are the imports into that country.

Only part of what is actually purchased by these entities is produced by firms resident within the same economy. In addition, in a world of open economies the firms of a particular nation state will sell part of their output to residents of other economies. The sale of such output is the exports from the country under consideration.

These three components are the necessary elements to Keynes' aggregate supply and demand approach. The specific ways in which they are filled in is open. To round out a complete Keynes model one also needs to have (a) investment as independent from the past in some fundamental way and as being dependent upon forward-looking long-term expectations; and (b) money and liquidity preference influencing production and investment decisions in a crucial manner. An open-economy version of Keynes' approach requires the appropriate extensions in each component area.

The aggregate supply function

The aggregate supply function presents the aggregate supply value of output, measured in a monetary unit, as a function of the level of employment. The aggregate supply value of output is equal to the maximum quantities of output that could be supplied at the different employment levels times the unit supply (minimum acceptable) prices associated with the different quantities of output:

$$Z = f(N) = \sum_{i=1}^{n} Z_i = \sum_{i=1}^{n} f_i(N_i) = \sum_{i=1}^{n} P_i^s Q_i^s \tag{4.1}$$

Following Davidson (1962), a most simple example that incorporates a short-run Cobb–Douglas production function is used in this chapter to illustrate the basic relationships of the open-economy Keynes model.[1] The production function itself presents the aggregate quantity of output, Q, as a function of the level of employment, N, and the stock of capital goods in existence, K_0. The output elasticities of labor and capital are, respectively, represented by α and $1 - \alpha$, while A is the Solow (1956) technological shift parameter:

$$Q = A N^\alpha K_0^{1-\alpha} \tag{4.2}$$

Under perfect competition, profit maximization, and no intertemporal considerations, the unit supply price is equal to the marginal factor cost, *mfc* (*CWJMK* VII: 52–61). For a given money-wage rate, W, associated with the above Cobb–Douglas production function, the unit supply price is:

$$P^s = mfc = \frac{W}{\alpha A} \left(\frac{N}{K_0} \right)^{1-\alpha} \tag{4.3}$$

By assuming that there is only one type of output in an economy and using the above information, the aggregate supply function becomes:

$$Z = P^s Q^s$$

$$= \left[\frac{W}{\alpha A} \left(\frac{N}{K_0} \right)^{1-\alpha} \right] [A N^\alpha K_0^{1-\alpha}] \tag{4.4}$$

$$= \frac{1}{\alpha} W N$$

In this specific example, the aggregate supply function is a linear function of the level of employment. Per unit of employment, the value of supply increases at the rate of $(1/\alpha)W$. This is illustrated in Figure 4.1.

For an open economy, the aggregate supply function as formulated above implies that (a) domestic firms produce only domestically, do not have production facilities abroad, and do not consider moving their production facilities abroad; (b) all costs incurred are domestic costs denominated in the domestic currency; and (c) no firm decisions as to financial investments are considered.

The aggregate expected demand function

The aggregate expected demand function captures the value of sales, measured in a monetary unit, expected by the firms in producing in a particular country, presented as a function of the domestic level of employment.

In an open economy, the expected sales of the firms producing in a particular country are a combination of (a) those that are expected to occur domestically, and (b) those that are expected to occur in all the other countries

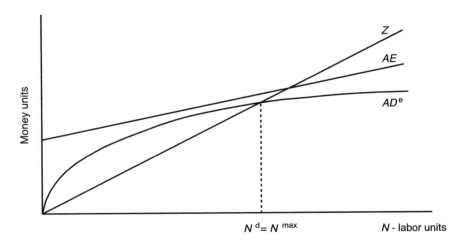

Figure 4.1 Aggregate supply, expected demand, and actual expenditure

of the system. The sales that occur in the other economies are made in terms of currencies that are different from the one in which the firms incur their costs. Consequently, the expected aggregate demand function must include how these revenues are expected to translate back into the currency in which the costs were incurred.

Firms which operate under conditions of pure competition expect that they will be able to sell all that they produce. With no need to form an expectation of the quantity that can be sold, the purely competitive firms only need to form an expectation of what the market price will be for their output. Given the usual assumption of increasing marginal cost, this expectation determines the amount of output that the firms produce and the amount of labor they need to hire to produce this output.

Within a closed economy, the purely competitive firms of a homogeneous-output industry need to create only a unit price expectation with respect to the one particular market in which they are operating. To generalize this to an open economy, NUMS, the short-term expectations of sales by firms producing in a particular economy and selling to the 'world' can be captured by a composite expected unit price. This composite expected unit price is made up of:

1   the unit price that is expected to exist domestically;
2   the unit prices that are expected to exist in all the foreign economies that the firms expect to sell to;
3   the exchange rates between the foreign currencies and the domestic currency that are expected to prevail when the sales occur and the revenues are repatriated;
4   the market share that the firms are expected to have domestically (one minus the share that foreign firms are expected to have in the domestic market); and
5   the market share that the firms expect to have in each of the foreign countries that they expect to sell to.

Formally, this composite expected unit price can be expressed (Deprez 1997: 604) as:

$$P^e = (1 - \phi_d^e) P_d^e + \sum_{i=1}^{n} \phi_{d,i}^e \, e_i^e \, P_i^e \qquad (4.5)$$

The symbols in the above equation are:

P^e – composite expected unit price
P_d^e – expected unit price in the domestic economy (measured in the domestic economy's unit of account)
P_i^e – expected unit price in the ith foreign economy, $i = 1, 2, 3, \ldots, n$ (measured in that economy's unit of account)

e^e_i – expected exchange rate; number of units of the domestic currency expected to be obtained by one unit of the ith economy's currency

ϕ^e_d – expected degree of openness of the domestic economy; $0 \leq \phi^e_d < 1$

$\phi^e_{d,i}$ – expected degree of openness of the ith foreign economy to imports from the 'domestic' economy (the 'domestic' economy's exports); $0 \leq \phi^e_{d,i} < 1$

The composite unit expected price is a weighted average of the unit prices expected in the different market areas. The weights are the expected market shares in each one of the economies. The degree of openness expected in the domestic economy effectively indicates the market share that the domestic firms expect to lose to the foreign competition. The remaining fraction is what the domestic firms expected to sell. The openness of the foreign economy to the imports of the country under study indicates expected market share in those economies. The inclusion of these degrees of openness is founded on Davidson's (1992: 69–84) use of these to explain pricing, costs, inflation, and income categories in an open economy.

Under a UMS, there is either only one monetary unit of account that all economies use or there is a fixed exchange rate (Davidson 1992: 80–2). Either way, there is no expected variation in the exchange rates in the equation above, reducing one source of uncertainty. If one has a world of closed economies, then the different degrees of openness in this equation are all zero. The composite expected unit price then reduces down to the domestic expected unit price.

With this formulation of the composite expected price, it is important to note that there are five different types of expectations involved, compared to the one in a closed economy, each bringing with it a degree of uncertainty and each one being susceptible to disappointment. In a closed economy, the unit price turning out as expected is the only requirement for short-period equilibrium in a flex-price context. In an open economy, the domestic expectations are of the unit sales prices plus the market share that is expected to go to foreign-produced output. Each additional country to which sales could be made that is added to the model adds three expectational variables. For short-period equilibrium in an open-economy, NUMS context the expectations of all five components have to turn out as expected within a flex-price context. The magnitude of uncertainty does more than just double when even a second economy is added to the mix.

The aggregate expected demand function is the aggregate expected sales value of output expressed as a function of employment, N. It is the expected price of output multiplied by the quantities of output supplied. For the Cobb–Douglas case and the composite expected price previously raised, the aggregate expected demand function is, formally:

$$AD^e = P^e \, Q^s$$

$$= \left[(1 - \phi_d^e) \, P_d^e + \sum_{i=1}^{n} \phi_{d,i}^e \, e_i^e \, P_i^e \right] A \, N^\alpha \, K_0^{1-\alpha} \tag{4.6}$$

In contrast to the aggregate supply function that, in this case, is a linear function of employment, the aggregate expected demand function increases at a decreasing rate with respect to changes in employment. This occurs because of the diminishing marginal product of labor and is illustrated in Figure 4.1.

The point of effective demand

On the basis of the firms' short-term sales expectations captured in the aggregate expected demand function and the cost, technology, and desired pricing considerations embodied in the aggregate supply function, they decide on a level of output to produce, employment to offer, and variable costs to incur. For an economy of short-run, expected profit-maximizing, perfectly competitive firms, these decisions are based upon the point of equality of the two functions. This equality is the aggregate equivalent of marginal cost equaling marginal revenue. Diagrammatically, this aggregate production decision by firms in the economy occurs when the aggregate expected demand function intersects the aggregate supply function (see Figure 4.1). Formally, this may be expressed as:

$$Z = AD^e$$

$$P^s \, Q^s = P^e \, Q^s$$

$$\frac{1}{\alpha} \, WN = \left[(1 - \phi_d^e) \, P_d^e + \sum_{i=1}^{n} \phi_{d,i}^e \, e_i^e \, P_i^e \right] A \, N^\alpha \, K_0^{1-\alpha}$$

$$P^s = P^e$$

$$\frac{1}{\alpha A} \left(\frac{N}{K_0} \right)^{1-\alpha} W = (1 - \phi_d^e) \, P_d^e + \sum_{i=1}^{n} \phi_{d,i}^e \, e_i^e \, P_i^e \tag{4.7}$$

This intersection is the *point of effective demand* (*CWJMK* VII: 25).

The above equality solves for the profit-maximizing quantity of labor required in production, which is usually taken to be the labor demand function:

$$N^d = N^{\max} = \left[\alpha A \, \frac{(1 - \phi_d^e) \, P_d^e + \sum_{i=1}^{n} \phi_{d,i}^e \, e_i^e \, P_i^e}{W} \right]^{\frac{1}{1-\alpha}} K_0 \tag{4.8}$$

From the profit maximizing quantity of labor required in production one obtains by the profit-maximizing quantity of output, which is usually taken to be the output supply function:

$$
Q_d^s = Q_d^{max} = A \left[\alpha A \ \frac{(1 - \phi_d^e) P_d^e + \sum_{i=1}^{n} \phi_{d,i}^e e_i^e P_i^e}{W} \right]^{\frac{\alpha}{1-\alpha}} K_0 \qquad (4.9)
$$

The level of employment and the ancillary level of output increase with an increase (upward shift) in aggregate expected demand and/or an increase (rightward shift) in aggregate supply. A higher level of aggregate expected demand occurs when there is a higher

1   domestic expected unit price of output;
2   expected unit price of output in the foreign markets;
3   degree of openness of the foreign economies;
4   value of foreign currencies measured in terms of the domestic one;

and when there is a lower

5   degree of openness of the domestic economy.

A higher level of aggregate supply occurs when:

1   there is a lower money wage;
2   there is a larger stock of capital goods available; and
3   when there is higher level of technological knowledge.

The level of employment and the ancillary level of output decrease with a decrease (downward shift) in aggregate expected demand and/or a decrease (leftward shift) in aggregate supply. A lower level of aggregate expected demand occurs when there is a lower

1   domestic expected unit price of output;
2   expected unit price of output in the foreign markets;
3   degree of openness of the foreign economies;
4   value of foreign currencies measured in terms of the domestic one;

and when there is a higher

5   degree of openness of the domestic economy.

A lower level of aggregate supply occurs when:

1   there is a larger money wage;
2   there is a lower stock of capital goods available; and
3   when there is lower level of technological knowledge.

The approach above makes it clear that the output produced by the firms within a particular country, as well as the employment and the labor income that this generates, is determined by the interaction of the component parts of the aggregate supply and expected demand functions. Key in the latter are the firms' expectations of sales domestically and abroad. Once produced, the question arises of how the firms split up the total output between the different markets.[2]

The aggregate expected demand function has embodied in it a particular rule for dividing up the output between the alternative markets. In constructing the composite expected unit price, the expected unit prices – expressed in terms of the domestic currency – have each a weight associated with them. When the weight associated with each market is divided by the sum of all the different weights one has the fraction of total output that will be shipped to that particular market. For each country within which production occurs these fractions, of course, sum to one. Formally:

$$sh_{d,d} = \frac{(1 - \phi_d^e)}{(1 - \phi_d^e) + \sum_{i=1}^{n} \phi_{d,i}^e}$$

$$sh_{d,i} = \frac{\phi_{d,i}^e}{(1 - \phi_d^e) + \sum_{i=1}^{n} \phi_{d,i}^e} \qquad (4.10)$$

On this basis all the output produced by the domestic firms is fully divided up between the domestic market, $Q_{d,d}^s$, and each of the different foreign markets, $Q_{d,i}^s$:

$$Q_d^s = Q_{d,d}^s + \sum_{i=1}^{n} Q_{d,i}^s = sh_d Q_d^s + \sum_{i=1}^{n} sh_i Q_d^s \qquad (4.11)$$

The output that is available in the domestic market, Q_d^a, is the sum of what the domestic producers allocate to home market, $Q_{d,d}^s$, plus what the producers from each of the foreign economies decide to ship to the country under consideration, $Q_{i,d}^s$. Formally:

$$Q_d^a = Q_{d,d}^s + \sum_{i=1}^{n} Q_{i,d}^s \tag{4.12}$$

The aggregate expenditures function

The aggregate expenditures function or aggregate actual demand function (Casarosa 1981: 190–3) presents the money value of the aggregate expenditures that firms, households, and government entities resident in the particular country under consideration wish to make on final goods and services as a function of the aggregate level of employment. In that we have seen that the variations in the level of employment and production generate different levels of wage income and expected profit income, the aggregate expenditures are implicitly also a function of these actual and expected components of income.

Because of its innovative nature, Keynes devoted a large part (Books III and IV) of *The General Theory* to the details of the aggregate demand function. This function incorporates the idea that demand depends partially upon employment and income, and partially upon considerations that are independent of current and past economic circumstances. While Keynes (*CWJMK* VII: 29) labeled these influences 'consumption' and 'investment,' Davidson (1994: 24–7) points out that all that is necessary for the basic Keynesian argument is that some portion of spending is independent of current (and past) employment and income, no matter what the specific source or function thereof may be. The special components of the aggregate demand function were seen to be the propensity to consume, the inducement to invest, and the monetary influences on the latter. These component parts allowed Keynes (*CWJMK* VII: 25–6) to reject Say's Law and arrive at his revolutionary conclusion concerning the logical persistence of equilibrium involuntary unemployment. A simple discussion and illustration of the component parts of the aggregate expenditures function is given below.

The consumption function

The value of the consumer good expenditures by households is a positive function of:

1   wage income of workers, WN;
2   expected profits, Π_g^e, if these are seen to influence rentier or capitalist consumption;
3   the level of wealth holdings, Ω;
4   an inverse function of households' desire for liquidity, LP_h; and
5   an indeterminate function of the unit demand price of household for consumer goods, P_h^d.

The latter consideration depends upon the own-price elasticity of demand of such goods. All of the component parts of the consumption function could be broken down further in more advanced models. The general consumption function can be expressed as:

$$C = f(WN; \Pi_g^e; \Omega; LP_h; P_h^d) \tag{4.13}$$

A most simple specific consumption function can be made use of in the current presentation. The basic idea that only part of current income is directly related to current expenditures can be captured by the specification of a consumption function in which all current wage income is spent on consumption goods. No other consumption influences are explicitly considered. Formally, this consumption function can be written as:

$$C = WN \tag{4.14}$$

The investment function

The money of value of the gross investment expenditures by firms is a positive function of:

1   the long-term expectations – the expectations of gross profits over a multi-period planning horizon, $\sum_{t=2}^{m} \Pi_{g,t}^e$ – that firms hold; and
2   the rate of technological obsolescence of capital equipment, RO;
3   a negative function of the rate of interest on loans, i;
4   the capital stock already in existence, K_0;
5   the liquidity desires of firms, LP_f; and
6   an indeterminate function of the unit demand price of firms for capital goods, P_f^d.

This may be formally expressed as:

$$I_g = f\left(\sum_{t=2}^{n} \Pi_{g,t}^e ; RO, i; K_0; LP_f; P_f^d \right) \tag{4.15}$$

A simple specification of this investment function captures the gross profit expectations over the planning horizon of all the firms and discounts these on the basis of the interest rate on loans:

$$I_g = \left(\sum_{t=2}^{n} \frac{\Pi_{g,t}^e}{(1 + i)^t} \right) \tag{4.16}$$

In an open economy, the expectation of gross profits relates to sales that are expected to occur domestically and in the foreign countries to which the firms expect to be exporting. In addition, when a NUMS exists, the long-term expectations of profits arising from sales in other countries is also susceptible to exchange rate uncertainty. In other words, this function is a lot more complicated than it would be in a closed economy. As such these expectations are more likely to be disappointed.

The government expenditures function

The value of expenditures by government entities, *G*, is made up of

1   the government's discretionary expenditures, $G_{ds,0}$;

and is a negative function of

2   the level of employment, *N*, due to the operation of automatic stabilizers; and
3   an indeterminate function of the unit demand price of the government for its purchases of goods and services.

Assuming unit own-price elasticity of demand for the government's purchases, this gives the following government expenditures function:

$$G = G_{ds} + G_{as} = G_{ds,0} + \Theta[N_f - N] \qquad (4.17)$$

In the above equation N_f is the full employment level of employment and Θ is a coefficient related to automatic stabilizer expenditures.

Adding the component parts

The aggregate (actual) expenditures of economic entities resident in the economy under consideration is the sum to the three elements presented above:

$$AE = C + I_g + G$$
$$= WN + \left(\sum_{t=2}^{n} \frac{\Pi_{g,t}^e}{(1+i)^t} \right) + G_{ds,0} + \Theta[N_f - N] \qquad (4.18)$$

The shape of the aggregate expenditures function is significantly different than the aggregate expected demand function (see Figure 4.1). The aggregate expenditures function has a positive intercept because of the investment expenditures and part of the government expenditures being independent of the level of employment. The part of government expenditures that captures the automatic stabilizers also contributes to the positive value of the intercept. Increases in the consideration that determine the value of the intercept shift the aggregate expenditures function upward, and the reverse generates a downward shift in this function. As the level of employment becomes larger consumption, expenditures increase. Expenditures as a whole increase with the level of employment because the increases in consumption expenditures dominate the decreases in government expenditures brought about by the automatic stabilizers. In that expenditures depend only upon part of the sum of actual and expected income generated by current production – the value of aggregate supply – the aggregate expenditures function increases at a slower rate than the aggregate supply function. Consequently, there is a level of employment at which these two functions intersect.

The specific level of aggregate expenditures that exists depends upon the levels of output and employment. These magnitudes are generated by the interaction of the aggregate supply function and the aggregate expected demand function. The specific employment level generated by these first two functions of the model is then substituted into the third function to find the level of aggregate actual expenditures. As is illustrated in Figure 4.1, this level of expenditures does not have to match the level of demand that was expected nor coincide with the point of effective demand.

Market outcomes in an open economy

The way the model has been set up, where both domestic and foreign firms provide output to the domestic market, means that we only need to consider the expenditures of domestic firms, households, and government entities in understanding the actual market outcomes. In other words, foreign entities only buy in their own markets. In those markets, they may buy goods and services produced abroad. So the British consumer is seen to buy American goods in the British market. The British consumer is not buying American goods in the American market in competition with the American consumer.[3]

Market outcomes, even if they occur with the market clearing of a pure flex-price market, are not necessarily equilibrium outcomes. Short-period equilibrium is the situation where short-period expectations are exactly met. In that market-clearing does not depend upon these expectations being met, the coincidence of market-clearing and short-period equilibrium is only a theoretically special case. Furthermore, it was Keynes' argument that equilibrium would generally not occur at an employment level that is consistent with full employment.

Aggregate supply and demand equilibrium

Within a closed economy, short-period equilibrium occurs if there is an employment level at which each of the three constituent functions of the model – the aggregate supply function, the aggregate expected demand function, and the aggregate expenditures function – take on the same value (cf. Deprez 1998). Speaking diagrammatically, this occurs if all three functions intersect at the same employment level. As pointed out above, the production decisions and plans of firms are based upon their short-term expectations interacting with their supply decisions: the intersection of the aggregate supply function and the aggregate expected demand function. The actual expenditures based upon the level of employment generated by the carrying out of these plans come in contact with the output that was produced and create actual market results, including actual market prices. If these actual market results match the short-term expectations that created the output, there is a short-period equilibrium. If the actual results do not match the short-term expectations, then there is a disequilibrium situation.

In an open economy, the conditions for a short-period equilibrium become significantly more complicated. Just as in a closed economy, this also requires that all the short-term expectations are exactly met. In an open economy, however, this means that:

1   the expected unit price in the home market;
2   the expected unit prices in all the foreign markets;
3   the expected exchange rates;
4   the expected degree of openness of the home economy; and
5   the expected degree of penetration in the foreign countries

all need to be exactly met by the actual market outcomes. Expectations can be disappointed by the results in many different situations.

When flex-price markets are assumed in all the countries of the model, then all the output that has been produced and brought to market will be sold. When fix-price markets are brought into the model output can remain unsold or queues for output can result. In flex-price markets the actual prices at which the output is sold may be different than the prices that were expected and used to make the production decisions.

The actual sales that occur generate actual profits.[4] The total revenue generated by firms producing in a particular country is the sum of the revenues generated in the different markets, translated into the home currency. Gross profit is these revenues minus the cost of variable inputs. In the basic model this involves only direct labor cost and is completely incurred in terms of the home currency. Formally:

$$\Pi_g^a = Q_{dd}^s \, P_d^a + \sum_{i=1}^{n} Q_{d,i}^s \, e_i^a \, P_i^a - WN \tag{4.19}$$

Firms try to maximize the expected value of these gross profits in determining their output and employment decisions. Consequently, actual market outcomes may be such that these profit expectations are exactly met or are disappointed. When the actual profits exceed the expected profits there are windfall profits and when actual profits are less than expected there are windfall losses (*CWJMK*). Formally:

$$W\Pi_g = \Pi_g^a - \Pi_g^e \tag{4.20}$$

When the actual price is higher than the expected price in a particular market, windfall profits – profits that are higher than what was expected (*CWJMK* VII: 57–8) – are the result. If actual prices are lower than what was expected, there exist windfall losses. In an open economy it is possible for the firms producing in a particular economy to have windfall profits in certain markets coexisting with windfall losses in other markets or the exact meeting of short-term expectations in yet other markets. Thus firms producing with a particular economy can have:

1   the exact meeting of short-term expectations in all their market and, thus, have short-period equilibrium;
2   windfall profits in all their markets;
3   windfall losses in all their markets; or
4   some combination of the three types of results.

The latter situation can be consistent with the aggregate amount of profits for the firms producing in an economy being exactly as expected, higher than expected, or lower than expected.

In an open economy, the production decisions made by firms are partially based upon expected exchange rates. Thus, within a NUMS, it is possible to have windfall profits or losses that come solely from the exchange rates being different than expected. If the domestic currency ends up with a higher value relative to the foreign currency (a lower exchange rate as written in the equations) as compared to the expected value of the exchange rate, then there will be windfall losses. If the domestic currency depreciates to a larger extent than expected or does not appreciate as much as expected, then there will be windfall profits. Just as is the case with respect to unit price expectations, if unit price expectations turn out exactly as expected:

1   exchange rate expectations can be exactly met in all markets, resulting in profits turning out just as expected;
2   unexpected exchange rate changes can result in windfall profits in all markets;
3   unexpected exchange rate changes can result in windfall losses in all markets; or
4   exchange rates can result in some combination of the first three possibilities.

Again, the latter situation can be consistent with the aggregate amount of profits for the firms producing in an economy being exactly as expected, higher than expected, or lower than expected.

Other monetary magnitudes face the same issues as profits. The value of exports is the actual value of sales by the domestic firms in the foreign markets. Formally this may be expressed as:

$$X = \sum_{i=1}^{n} Q_{d,i}^{s} \, e_{i}^{a} \, P_{i}^{a} \qquad (4.21)$$

These exports may turn out to be different than what was expected based upon what happens in terms of the actual prices relative to the expected prices in the foreign market and in terms of the actual exchange rate relative to the expected exchange rate.

The sales of firms producing in the other economies within the domestic market of the country in question is the value of imports into that country. In other words, part of the production of foreign firms was shipped into the economy in question. When the actual market prices are determined, that actual value of imports can then be determined. Formally, imports are:

$$M = \sum_{i=1}^{n} Q_{i,d}^{s} \, P_{d}^{a} \qquad (4.22)$$

The value of imports may be different than what the firms from the different foreign countries expected because the actual domestic price is different than expected or because exchange rates differ from their expected values.

The actual results in terms of prices and exchange rates, and their derivative indicators such as gross profits, exports, and imports, serve as the key feedback mechanism for the formulation of the next period's short-term expectations. Any or all component parts of the composite expected unit price can be modified in response to the actual results. Similarly, any expectation-based components of aggregate supply or aggregate actual expenditures may also be modified by the previous period's actual results and the degree of disappointment of the previously held expectations. The degree to which each expected magnitude is modified by the deviation of the corresponding actual result from the previously held expectation can be captured by the appropriate elasticity of expectations (Davidson 1978: 379–88). In an open economy there are, of course, many more such feedback paths affecting employment and output decisions than exist in a closed economy.

When one has a short-period equilibrium, what are some of its characteristics? Most importantly, such an equilibrium will tend to be one that exhibits involuntary unemployment. A short-period equilibrium at full employment is only one possible equilibrium situation and it is one that generally will not exist (*CWJMK* VII: 289–91).

Dynamic analysis

Keynes' aggregate supply and demand model is fully capable of dealing with movements over time by the application of his theory of shifting equilibrium (*CWJMK* VII: 293). This means that the model can deal with questions of dynamics, including the theory of growth and technical change (Weintraub 1966).

The model of shifting equilibrium is 'Keynes's complete dynamic model' (Kregel 1976: 215). Both long-term and short-term expectations can be disappointed; both long-term and short-term expectations and the decisions based on them may therefore change over time in unpredictable ways. Moreover, the disappointment of either type of expectation may have effects on the formation of either type of expectation. Long-term and short-term expectations are interdependent. For Keynes, 'the theory of shifting equilibrium ... [is] the theory of a system in which changing views about the future are capable of influencing the present situation' (*CWJMK* VII: 293).

For each set of expectations there exists a short-period equilibrium outcome consistent with the expectations that the economy is 'chasing.' The problem is that if the economy does not immediately hit the equilibrium position then the resulting change in expectations that occurs defines a new equilibrium for the next period. The actual results are likely to again disappoint the expectations, leading to a further shift. The shifting equilibrium model is therefore seen as one where:

> failure to hit on the point of effective demand may mean not only that the system has missed the intersection of the aggregate demand and supply curves, but that it will cause the curves themselves to shift, since their underlying determinants (propensity to consume, liquidity preference, marginal efficiency of capital) will be readjusted to disappointment
>
> (Kregel 1976: 215)

And so we move on and on in a shifting equilibrium model without the real world ever having actually reached the equilibrium that is newly defined for each period.

Expectations, actions, and outcomes create ever-changing aggregate supply and demand conditions and a dynamic sequence of shifting equilibria consistent with these conditions. The sequence of short-period situations that the economy generates has no underlying long-run equilibrium or center of gravitation driving it (cf. Deprez 1985–6). The shifting equilibrium sequence that the economy is going through has fluctuating levels of output, employment, income, and prices that are rarely, if ever, consistent with full employment. These fluctuations are not extreme; the economy neither 'explodes' nor contracts into nothingness. The boundedness of the fluctuations exists because of limits to the changes in expectations, usually reflected in the set of elasticities of expectations being less than one (Davidson 1978: 385–6).

The cumulative processes created by the changes in expectations in the shifting equilibrium model are constrained by the institutional constraints on actions and on expectations formation (*CWJMK* VII: 147–64), an overlapping structure of wage, debt, and other contracts (Davidson 1978: 388–401), and an overlapping structure of fixed capitals in both the real and monetary sense (cf. Deprez 1985–6).

Subjective price elements and the terms of trade

A key set of considerations in extending the model forward arise from the expectational and subjective elements that Keynes raised to affect the absolute and relative prices embodied in the model. There are four such considerations that are important (Deprez 1995). First, Keynes' (*CWJMK* VII:) introduction of liquidity premiums into the asset choices of investors means that the relative prices will settle into an equilibrium where the relative prices of liquid assets will be higher and illiquid assets lower than would exist under a classical equilibrium. Second, because exchange rates are determined in a similar fashion where liquidity premiums and speculative considerations dwarf trade influences (cf. Harvey, Chapter 8 in this volume), these elements inject subjective and expectational components into international relative prices. Third, as has already been brought out above, long-term expectations and the marginal efficiency of capital are keys in generating demand and, thus, the actual price patterns that exist internationally. Fourth, in a dynamic economy Keynes' notion of user cost enters the determination of relative prices from both the supply and the demand side.

Keynes (*CWJMK* VII: 67) pointed out that under pure competition the unit supply price is equal to the marginal prime cost associated with producing the output. Marginal prime cost is the sum of marginal factor cost – which was made use of above – and marginal user cost. The user cost of current production is the expected future loss in profitability arising from the use of fixed capital or natural resources as compared to leaving these resources unused. In industrial production such user costs may result from current production (a) depreciating the current capital stock; (b) altering the expected productivity of capital or labor; (c) changing the expected conditions for the firm's output; and (d) changing the expected costs for the future capital and labor inputs of the firm. By introducing these subjective considerations, unit supply prices can vary even when marginal factor cost is a given. In other words, variation in marginal user cost affects both absolute and relative prices.

In an open economy, these considerations become more complicated and increasingly subject to variation because of the multiple markets that firms consider and the exchange rate uncertainty that they have to deal with. As a consequence, even when objective cost considerations are identical in different economies, the subjective elements listed above can create different relative price patterns in different countries, as well as creating different international relative prices. This means that these subjective elements can (a) affect the employment and output levels; (b) change income generated; (c) alter demand levels and patterns; (d) affect comparative advantage conditions and the resulting patterns of trade; (e) change the international terms of trade and the resulting value of exports and imports; and (f) alter the international allocation of resources.

Implications of the model

The results brought out in the chapter include a number of interesting and potentially important ones for the development of this approach. Within (neo)classical models, trade is commonly looked at as the trading of goods for goods. Money is only a neutral intermediary. In this chapter, goods are sold for money. Consequently, even in a one-good example, it is possible to have international trade arising from firms' desire to obtain monetary profits in whatever markets are available. Short-period equilibrium is not a situation of export equaling imports, but of the short-term expectations of firms being met. This can occur regardless of the type of trade balance in existence. While not all components of a full-blown model are specified, there is no necessary mechanism that creates a balance between exports and imports over time. At the very least this requires an examination of the determination of exchange rates. From a Post Keynesian perspective (cf. Davidson 1992: 105–15) there is no reason to expect exchange rates to function so as to balance trade.

Conclusions and ways forward

This chapter has presented the central components of Keynes' aggregate supply and demand model as extended to deal with open-economy considerations. Each of the three constituent functions of the basic model – the aggregate supply function, the aggregate expected demand function, and the aggregate actual expenditures function – was explained in turn. On the assumption of firms producing only within the home country, there are no special extensions to the aggregate supply function. The first special reformulation is of the expected aggregate demand function via the inclusion of a composite expected unit price that incorporates the expected unit prices in all the economies the firms expect to sell in, the expected value of all relevant exchange rates, and the expected market shares in each of the markets the firms expected to sell to. The combination of these two functions generates the levels of employment, output, and wage income in an open economy.

The aggregate (actual) expenditures function includes the demand for both domestically and foreign-produced goods that are available in the domestic market. The level of demand depends partially upon the domestic level of employment, production, and wage income and partially upon considerations fully independent of current and past production. The long-term expectations and monetary considerations that determine investment are central to such consideration. The actual market results depend not only upon this level of demand, but also upon the quantity of goods that has been supplied to the domestic market by foreign firms.

Within the open-economy version of Keynes' model there is no tendency for equilibrium to occur at full employment. On the contrary, the tendency is for investment to be insufficient for such a result. In an open economy, sales to foreign markets may compensate for this systemic shortcoming. Of course, if the general insufficiency of investment demand is a world-wide problem, then only some economies benefit from international trade. Japan and certain other Asian economies are generally cited as the ones which have persistently benefited from such export-led growth. The Asian financial crisis of the late 1990s has painfully reminded us of the fragility of such a path and its susceptibility to the types of monetary uncertainties discussed in this chapter.

In that modern international economic relations are not based on the barter of goods, there is also no tendency for trade to balance within the monetary production economy of Keynes' model. This is consistent with the fact that some countries – like the ones mentioned above – have persistently experienced trade surpluses, while others – like the United States – have been dealing with continuous trade deficits. The logical corollary to this is that activist policies are needed to manage such situations when they are deemed to be problematic. Much of international trade negotiations and the pressure to 'open up' certain markets are better understood from this perspective.

Finally, the model implies that changing patterns of trade are not simply adjustments to take advantage of more efficient processes. Such relatively benign adjustments can only take place in a Say's Law world. In Keynes' model, changing trade patterns create and destroy employment, income, and wealth. No wonder that international macrodynamics are seen by policy makers and the public as such a crucial area for political discourse and action!

Certain extensions of the basic model are pointed out. It is recognized that the supply side of the model can be extended to incorporate alternative firm structures, technology considerations, and pricing behavior. Similarly, the aggregate expected demand function can incorporate alternative specifications on the formulation of short-term expectations, including different market structure specifications. For the aggregate actual expenditures function, one can conceive of more detailed specifications of the three component functions: the consumption function, the investment function, and the government expenditures function. Additional potential extensions of the model can be found by its systematic application to dynamic and growth questions via the method of shifting equilibrium. The other area that was explicitly discussed involves the extended inclusion in the model of expectational and subjective elements, via liquidity premiums and user costs. Additionally, a more detailed and formal discussion of subsidiary components of the model, such as the labor market, financial markets, and monetary and banking institutions, would also be illuminating. Hopefully, this chapter, as well as the other contributions to this volume will help stimulate such work.

Notes

1   The use of this production function in no way endorses it as an appropriate representation of aggregate production relationships, especially in the long run. It is used because of the high degree of familiarity that many readers may have with this function. It should be recognized that Keynes' own approach is not limited by the constraints that this specific function puts on the model.
2   If firms' sales expectations include a quantity component, then the answer may be more straightforward than under the perfect competition assumption used in this chapter.
3   The implicit assumption in many models is just the opposite of what is made here: British consumers buy part of their goods in the American market.
4   This relatively basic observation differs from the assumption of a Say's Law economy where it is the act of production which is assumed to generate profits.

References

Casarosa, C. (1981) 'The Microfoundations of Keynes's Aggregate Supply and Expected Demand Analysis,' *Economic Journal* 91, 361: 188–94.

Davidson, P. (1962) 'Income and Employment Multipliers, and the Price Level,' *American Economics Review* 52: 738–52.

—— (1978) *Money and the Real World*, 2nd edn, London: Macmillan.

—— (1991) 'Is Probability Theory Relevant for Uncertainty? A Post Keynesian Perspective,' *Journal of Economic Perspectives* 5: 29–43.

—— (1992) *International Money and the Real World*, 2nd edn, New York: St. Martin's Press.

—— (1992–3) 'Reforming the World's Money,' *Journal of Post Keynesian Economics* 15, 2: 153–79.

—— (1994) *Post Keynesian Macroeconomic Theory*, Aldershot, Hants.: Edward Elgar.

—— (1997) 'Are Grains of Sand in the Wheels of International Finance Sufficient To Do the Job When Boulders are Often Required?' *Economic Journal* 107, 442: 671–86.

—— and Smolensky, E. (1964) *Aggregate Supply and Demand Analysis*, New York: Harper & Row.

Deprez, J. (1985–6) 'Time in a Multi-industry, Fixed Capital World', *Journal of Post Keynesian Economics* 8, 2: 249–65.

—— (1989) 'Income Distribution in Keynes' Aggregate Supply Function with Vintage Fixed Capital,' *Journal of Economics* 15: 70–9.

—— (1993a) 'Fixed Capital and Inflation: an Analysis Applying Keynes' Notion of User Cost,' *Review of Radical Political Economics* 25, 3: 34–42.

—— (1993b) 'The User Cost of Fixed Capital in Keynes' Theory of Investment,' in P. Davidson (ed.), *Can the Free Market Pick Winners? What Determines Investment*, Armonk, NY: M.E. Sharpe.

—— (1994) 'Aggregate Supply,' in P. Arestis and M. C. Sawyer (eds), *The Elgar Companion to Radical Political Economy*, Aldershot, Hants.: Edward Elgar.

—— (1995) 'Technology and the Terms of Trade: Considering Expectational, Structural, and Institutional Factors,' *Journal of Economic Issues* 29, 2: 435–42.

—— (1996) 'Davidson on the Labour Market in a Monetary Production Economy,' in P. Arestis (ed.), *Keynes, Money and the Open Economy: Essays in Honour of Paul*

Davidson, Cheltenham, Glos.: Edward Elgar.

—— (1997) 'Open-economy Expectations, Decisions, and Equilibria: Applying Keynes' Aggregate Supply and Demand Model,' *Journal of Post Keynesian Economics* 19, 4: 599–615.

—— (1998) 'Aggregate Demand and Supply,' in P. O'Hara (ed.), *Encyclopedic Dictionary of Political Economy*, Oxford: Basil Blackwell.

Deprez, P. and Deprez, J. (1997) 'The Monetary Dynamics of Economic Integration,' in S.D. Gupta and N.K. Choudhry (eds), *Dynamics of Globalization and Development*, Boston, MA: Kluwer Academic Publishers.

Harvey, J.T. (1991) 'A Post Keynesian View of Exchange Rate Determination,' *Journal of Post Keynesian Economics* 14, 1: 61–71.

—— (1993) 'The Institution of Foreign Exchange Trading,' *Journal of Economic Issues* 27, 3: 679–98.

Keynes, J.M. (1971–83) *The Collected Writings of John Maynard Keynes*, ed. D. Moggridge, London: Macmillan, and Cambridge: Cambridge University Press. (Volumes are referred to in the text as *CWJMK* followed by the volume number.)

King, J.E. (1994) 'Aggregate Supply and Demand Analysis since Keynes: a Partial History,' *Journal of Post Keynesian Economics* 17, 1: 3–31.

Kregel, J.A. (1976) 'Economic Methodology in the Face of Uncertainty,' *Economic Journal* 86, 342: 209–25.

Solow, R.M. (1956) 'A Contribution to the Theory of Economic Growth,' *Quarterly Journal of Economics* 70, 1: 65–94.

Weintraub, S. (1958) *An Approach to the Theory of Income Distribution*, Philadelphia: Chilton.

—— (1966) *A Keynesian Theory of Employment, Growth and Income Distribution*, Philadelphia: Chilton.

Wells, P. (1977) 'Keynes' Disequilibrium Theory of Employment,' in S. Weintraub (ed.), *Modern Economic Thought*, Philadelphia: University of Pennsylvania Press.

5   Kaleckian macro models for open economies

*Robert Blecker**

Introduction

Michal Kalecki (1899-1970) has long been recognized as one of the main progenitors of what has come to be known as the 'Post Keynesian' approach in economics (see Weintraub 1978; Eichner and Kregel 1975). Kalecki had a strong personal influence on Joan Robinson, Josef Steindl, and other major contributors to this approach, and is considered to have anticipated important aspects of John Maynard Keynes' *General Theory* (1936).[1] Kalecki's contributions to the post-Keynesian tradition include his theory of mark-up pricing by oligopolistic firms, his concept of financial constraints on business investment, his model of the distribution of income between wages and profits, and his analysis of the determination of the level of profits through a multiplier mechanism. Kalecki also influenced the theories of monopoly capitalism and the profit squeeze in the Marxian and radical tradition (Baran and Sweezy 1966; Glyn and Sutcliffe 1972; Boddy and Crotty 1975). In addition, Kalecki made major contributions to the 'structuralist' tradition in development economics (Taylor 1983, 1991; FitzGerald 1993) and some of Kalecki's ideas have entered mainstream, neoclassical economics – although often without recognition of Kalecki's priority.[2]

In contrast, Kalecki's contributions to international economics are less well known. Like Keynes, he is best known for his work from the 1930s, which was a time of relatively closed economies in which the paramount issue was the causes of the Great Depression. More like Adam Smith than David Ricardo, Kalecki did not develop a separate 'trade theory,' but simply incorporated the implications of international trade relations into his models where it seemed important. Nevertheless, two of his earliest essays were on international topics ('On Activating the Balance of Trade', 1929, and 'Consequences of Dumping', 1931, in Kalecki 1990: 15–20, 26–34).[3] His earliest formulations of the profit multiplier model, written in the 1930s (collected in Kalecki 1990), included the stimulative effects of trade surpluses, which he recognized to be analogous to the effects of deficit spending by governments.[4] His work on

* The author would like to acknowledge helpful comments from Amit Bhaduri and Malcolm Sawyer on an earlier draft.

economic development emphasized the role of foreign capital inflows in financing capital accumulation as well as the problems created for the balance of payments by rising import demand in developing countries.

In recent years, there has been a notable revival of interest in Kalecki's work and a new generation of neo-Kaleckian theoretical models has been developed.[5] There have been empirical tests of some of Kalecki's 'micro' theories, especially in regard to the determinants of profit mark-ups and investment spending (see Karier 1988, and Fazzari and Mott 1986–87, respectively), as well as macroeconometric models that incorporate Kaleckian assumptions about how income distribution affects aggregate demand (for example, Gordon 1995, 1997; Stanford 1996). This growing literature includes several contributions that have advanced our understanding of international economic issues, including: the potential for contractionary effects of currency devaluations (Krugman and Taylor 1978); the possibility of conflicting national interests with free trade (Robinson 1978: 201–12; Bhaduri 1986: 132–50); the effect of international competition in squeezing profit mark-ups (Cowling 1982; Blecker 1989b; Arestis and Milberg 1993–4); and the greater likelihood of having profit-led rather than wage-led economic growth in more open economies (Blecker 1989a; Bhaduri and Marglin 1990; You 1991; Bowles and Boyer 1995). To date, however, there has been no complete synthesis of Kaleckian ideas in international economics, and Kalecki's contributions to this field have often been neglected in surveys of his life and work.[6]

This chapter seeks to fill this void in the literature by providing an account of Kalecki's main contributions to international economics and their extensions in the new, neo-Kaleckian literature. In order to highlight the role of international trade and finance in Kalecki's work, we abstract from certain other complexities of Kalecki's original formulations, including: his emphasis on overhead costs; his incorporation of raw materials costs into the 'prime costs' on which mark-ups are calculated; his emphasis on agriculture–industry interlinkages in developing countries; his frequent use of the Marxian distinction between sectors producing capital goods, wage goods, and luxury goods; and his efforts to model the cyclical and long-run dynamics of capitalist economies. We also limit ourselves to Kalecki's work on capitalism; his ideas about the role of foreign trade in socialist planning are not considered. Although these limitations make the present account somewhat less than comprehensive, it is hoped that what follows will cover the fundamentals of the Kaleckian approach to international economics and will solidify the foundations for further extensions of this approach.

The next section begins by discussing Kalecki's own ideas on international trade and finance in more detail. Then, the subsequent three sections develop a series of neo-Kaleckian open-economy macro models addressed to three main issues: how international competition over market shares can make international trade relations conflictive rather than cooperative; how the 'profit-squeeze' effects of international competition affect the relationship between income distribution and economic growth; and the effects of currency devaluation on both national income and the balance of payments (that is, whether a devaluation is expansionary or contractionary and whether it is effective or ineffective in improving the trade balance). Although most of the results of these models have been developed previously, they are presented here together for the first time. Some new implications of and connections between the models will be discussed, and interesting points of commonality or contrast with mainstream macro models will be brought out. The concluding section summarizes the results developed here and briefly discusses their limitations as well as directions for future research.

Kalecki's contributions to international economics

Kalecki's contributions to international economics arise in three main parts of his work: his analysis of the role of net exports in the determination of the level of profits and national income; his analysis of the financing of investment in developing countries; and his analysis of causes of changes in profit mark-ups. We now examine each of these in turn.

Net exports and profit realization

In his earliest work that foreshadowed Keynesian macro theory, Kalecki explored the role of net exports of goods and services (that is, the trade balance) in regard to national income determination – with special emphasis on the profit income of corporate enterprises, which Kalecki saw as the key to financing capital investment. In his complete model with a government sector and foreign trade, Kalecki saw that the following identity (he called it a 'balance sheet relationship') must hold:[7]

$$R + W + T = C_K + C_W + I + G + (X - M) \qquad (5.1)$$

The left-hand side of (5.1) is national income, disaggregated into after-tax profits R and wages W plus tax revenue T (transfers are ignored for simplicity). This sum must be equal to aggregate demand on the right-hand side, which consists of capitalists' and workers' consumption (C_K and C_W, respectively), private investment I, government spending G, and the trade balance (exports X minus imports M). Subtracting ($W + T$) from both sides, and representing workers' saving by $S_W = W - C_W$, (5.1) becomes Kalecki's famous expression of the accounting identity for profits in a capitalist economy:

$$R = C_K + I - S_W + (G - T) + (X - M). \qquad (5.2)$$

The total profits that owners of capital collectively receive must be equal to the sum of their own consumption and investment spending ($C_K + I$), less workers' saving S_W, plus two crucial balances: the government *deficit* $(G - T)$ and the trade *surplus* $(X - M)$.

To appreciate the significance of this relationship, Kalecki also studied a simplified version of (5.2), which assumes a closed economy with no government and no workers' saving:

$$R = C_K + I. \tag{5.2'}$$

In this simplified model, it is literally true that 'the workers spend what they get and the capitalists get what they spend.'[8] That is, workers don't save and aggregate profit income is determined by the capitalists' willingness to spend on consumption and investment. Now, returning to (5.2), and assuming (as Kalecki usually did) that workers' saving S_W is negligible, we can see the significance of the government deficit and the trade surplus: either of these (if positive) enables capitalists to earn profits in excess of their own expenditures on luxury consumption and private investment. The reason for this is quite clear in the case of the trade surplus: the extra profits come from the excess of national income over domestic expenditure due to a surplus of export earnings over import spending. By analogy, Kalecki was able to give a simple and straightforward explanation of why a government deficit is expansionary: a government deficit is equivalent to a private sector surplus with the government, and the extra profits come from the excess of private sector earnings over private sector spending (financed by private lending to the government, which increases the public sector debt). As Kalecki more colorfully put it, deficit-financed government purchases are like 'domestic exports' (Kalecki [1933] 1990: 168), and 'the budget deficit can be considered as an artificial export surplus' (Kalecki [1954] 1991: 245).

Equation (5.2) is merely an identity, in which Kalecki implied that causality ran from the right to the left, that is, from the expenditures that generate profits (that is, the demand for profit finance) to the amount of profits realized. To demonstrate this point, Kalecki offered a model of profit determination that closely paralleled (and anticipated) Keynes' (1936) model of income determination. To specify this model, Kalecki postulated separate functions for workers' and capitalists' consumption:

$$C_W = W - S_W \tag{5.3a}$$

$$C_K = A + c_r R \tag{5.3b}$$

Kalecki tended to assume that workers' saving S_W in (5.3a) was a constant amount (often assumed to be zero for simplicity), which could simply be subtracted from total wage income W to obtain workers' consumption C_W. The function (5.3b) for capitalists' consumption C_K, in contrast, has the familiar linear form of the textbook 'Keynesian' consumption function:[9] it is equal to a constant term A plus the product of the capitalists' marginal propensity to consume out of profit income c_r times the level of profits R.

By substituting (5.3a) and (5.3b) into (5.1), or, equivalently, using (5.3b) in (5.2), we obtain the solution for the equilibrium level of R as follows:

$$R = \frac{A + I - S_W + (G - T) + (X - M)}{1 - c_r} \qquad (5.4)$$

where all the variables in the numerator are taken as given (or, in the case of investment, predetermined by past decisions). In essence, (5.4) is a 'multiplier' formula, with a *profit* multiplier of $1/(1 - c_r)$, and the solution for R can be graphed in a diagram analogous to the famous 45-degree 'cross' of the macro textbooks, as shown in Figure 5.1, in which the vertical axis shows the demand for profit finance and the horizontal axis represents profit income realized. The equilibrium level of profits is found at the point where the demand for profit finance line intersects the 45-degree line, that is, where $R = A + c_r R + I - S_W + (G - T) + (X - M)$. This equilibrium is stable as long as $c_r < 1$, which implies that the demand for profit finance line is flatter than the 45-degree line.

The solution for profits (5.4) can easily be transformed into a solution for total national income Y, using the identity that $R = \pi Y$ (where π is the profit share of national income),[10] which yields Kalecki's famous result that the level of national income is inversely related to the profit share:

$$Y = \frac{A + I - S_W + (G - T) + (X - M)}{(1 - c_r)\pi} \qquad (5.5)$$

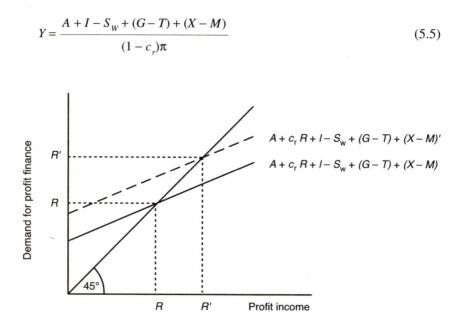

Figure 5.1 Kalecki's profit multiplier model, showing the effect of increasing the trade surplus

Equation (5.5) is very similar to the standard textbook Keynesian model of income determination, except that the equilibrium level of total national income Y is shown to depend on its *distribution* between wages and profits. This is still consistent with Keynes, however, in the sense that income distribution enters the denominator of (5.5) via its effect on the marginal propensity to save out of national income as a whole, which equals $(1 - c_r)\pi$. Kalecki's treatment of workers' saving, the government deficit, and the trade surplus as exogenously given magnitudes is primitive, but this is a deficiency that is easily remedied and we will make these variables endogenous in the extensions of Kalecki later in this chapter. When we do, and when we also make investment I endogenous, we will see that the simple, inverse relationship between Y and π in (5.5) becomes more complex and that national income may become positively related to the profit share in some cases.

Leaving these problems aside for the moment, the important point for present purposes is the political-economic conclusions that Kalecki drew from the preceding analysis. Figure 5.1 shows that a rise in the trade surplus from $(X - M)$ to $(X - M)'$ shifts the 'demand for profit finance' line up, as the higher trade surplus must be matched by increased net capital outflows, which in turn must be financed out of higher profits (assuming a given level of workers' saving S_W and a given budget deficit $G - T$). In equilibrium, the higher aggregate demand implied by the net export surplus generates additional sales of firms that increase their profits, until a new, higher equilibrium level of profits is reached (at profit level $R' > R$ in Figure 5.1). The increase in profits is a multiple of the increase in net exports:

$$\Delta R = \frac{1}{1 - c_r} \Delta(X - M)$$

with $1/(1 - c_r) > 1$, since capitalists' consumption rises endogenously and this creates additional demand for profit finance as well as extra aggregate demand which generates the requisite profits.

Thus, Kalecki's model implies that there is a rational basis to countries' efforts to achieve and maintain trade surpluses, insofar as these tend to boost the profits of domestic firms (holding other factors constant). In Kalecki's words:

> The capitalists of a country which manages to capture foreign markets from other countries are able to increase their profits at the expense of the capitalists of the other countries. Similarly, a colonial metropolis may achieve an export surplus through investment in its dependencies.
>
> (Kalecki [1954] 1991: 245)

In this way, Kalecki thought he had finally solved the puzzle of 'economic imperialism,' which had eluded earlier thinkers such as Hobson, Luxemburg, Bukharin, and Lenin (see Brewer 1980, for a survey). All of these had emphasized the importance of export markets in supporting capital accumulation in the industrialized countries, and Luxemburg had even argued that capitalist accumulation would come to a standstill in the absence of 'external' markets (including domestic non-capitalist sectors as well as foreign underdeveloped countries). Kalecki ([1967] 1991: 451–8) replied that only a *net export surplus* would enable developed capitalist countries to increase the profits of their capitalist classes and thus avert economic stagnation. However, by treating the trade balance as an exogenous magnitude, and not recognizing how it is affected (negatively) by aggregate demand, Kalecki failed to see that not all trade surpluses are stimulative. For example, a trade surplus caused by an exogenous rise in exports or by a real devaluation is stimulative, while a surplus caused by a fall in import demand during a recession is not (although it may lessen the severity of the recession).

Foreign capital and development finance

The analysis in the previous subsection is intended to apply only in an industrialized economy characterized by excess productive capacity. In such an economy, firms can expand their output in response to greater demand for their products, and in the process generate the extra profits that provide the additional savings required to finance the demand stimulus (whether the source of the stimulus is increased investment, net exports, or deficit spending). Kalecki did not believe that such a model applied to the 'underdeveloped' countries of the 1950s and 1960s. As he explained:

> in developed capitalist economies . . . unemployment arises on account of inadequacy of effective demand . . . The situation may, therefore, be tackled by measures designed to stimulate effective demand, such as loan financed government expenditure.
>
> Unemployment and underemployment in underdeveloped countries are of an entirely different nature. They result from the shortage of capital equipment rather than from a deficiency of effective demand.
>
> (Kalecki [1960] 1993: 3)

> The crucial problem facing the underdeveloped countries is thus to increase investment considerably, not for the sake of generating effective demand, as was the case in an underemployed developed economy, but in order to accelerate expansion of productive capacity indispensable for the rapid growth of the national income.
>
> (Kalecki [1966] 1993: 16)

In this context, the balance of trade is seen from an entirely different perspective, which Kalecki developed in his essay on 'The Problem of Financing Economic Development' ([1954] 1993: 23–44). With some rearranging (and a few changes in the definitions of variables to make them more appropriate for developing countries), the national income identity (5.1) can be written as:

$$I = S + (T - G) + (M - X),\qquad(5.6)$$

where I is *total* investment (public and private), $S = (R + W) - (C_K + C_W)$ is total private saving, $(T - G)$ is the budget *surplus* for operating or 'administrative' expenses (that is, G is government consumption only), and $(M - X)$ is the trade *deficit*. Equation (5.6) shows how investment is financed by the sum of private saving, public sector saving, and net capital inflows (or foreign saving, $F = M - X$). Kalecki tended to assume that the 'administrative' budget was balanced (thus $T - G = 0$), but allowed for extra tax revenue T' to finance part of government investment (which was included in I). Thus, Kalecki wrote (5.6) as:

$$I = S + T' + F.\qquad(5.6')$$

However it is written, equation (5.6) or (5.6') led Kalecki to the conclusion that foreign capital inflows allowed a given amount of domestic investment to be financed by a smaller amount of national saving (or taxation). In addition, Kalecki realized that foreign capital inflows F also fulfill another function for a developing country: 'to relieve the shortage of foreign exchange' that results from the fact that 'the process of development tends to strain the balance of payments' by increasing demand for imports of capital goods, raw materials, and basic foods (Kalecki [1954] 1993: 37). In this way, Kalecki anticipated what later became known as the 'two-gap' analysis in the development literature, in which investment I was constrained by the more binding of the two constraints – saving and foreign exchange (see Chenery and Bruno 1962; McKinnon 1964; and Taylor 1979: 123–6).

In either equation (5.6) or (5.6'), the budget and trade balances play fundamentally different roles than they play in equation (5.2) for a developed country. In an underdeveloped country, a budget surplus or a trade deficit is needed to provide extra savings to finance domestic investment since the shortage of capital is the binding constraint on production, whereas in a developed country a budget deficit or trade surplus is needed to provide extra demand to stimulate profits and output since the lack of effective demand is the binding constraint. However, Kalecki ([1966] 1993: 15–16) acknowledged that effective demand problems were not entirely absent in underdeveloped countries. Later writers in the Kaleckian tradition have sometimes assumed that effective demand problems have become the binding constraints on production in developing countries, albeit ones that are more industrialized (or 'semi-industrialized') than they were at the time of Kalecki's writings on development. Thus, for example, Taylor (1983) assumes excess capacity in his benchmark 'structuralist' macro model of a developing economy, and Dutt (1984) does likewise in his 'stagnationist' macro model of India.[11] In any event, Kalecki's framework provides a methodological foundation for a structuralist approach to economic analysis, which presumes that economic models have to be tailored to the particular conditions of a specific country in a specific historical situation, rather than spun out of *a priori* assumptions about what rational agents would do in idealized market conditions (see Taylor 1991).

International competition and profit mark-ups

When we turn to the 'micro' side of Kalecki's work – his theory of mark-up pricing by oligopolistic firms – we encounter a striking paradox. On the one hand, Kalecki himself never explicitly considered international competition as a factor influencing mark-ups. On the other hand, Kalecki's theory of mark-up pricing has inspired numerous analyses of how international competition 'squeezes' profits (see earlier citations).

Much of the explanation for this paradox lies in the historical period in which Kalecki developed this theory. The period from the 1930s to the 1950s, when Kalecki wrote most of his work on the capitalist economies, was a period of relatively closed economies in which national oligopolies were insulated from international competition by a combination of trade protection, technological gaps, transportation costs, and political conflict. In this context, international competitive pressures must have seemed like a remote possibility, not worth emphasizing in models of oligopolistic behavior.[12]

Nevertheless, Kalecki's own discussion of factors influencing mark-ups can easily be extended to incorporate international competition. In his most definitive treatment of the subject, Kalecki ([1954] 1991: 215–16) listed four 'causes of change in the degree of monopoly,' where the 'degree of monopoly' referred essentially to the price–cost margin (ratio of price to variable or 'prime' costs) and is thus positively related to the mark-up rate.[13] These four causes were:

1   the concentration of industry;
2   advertising and other sales efforts;
3   the level of overheads; and
4   the power of trade unions.

The first three factors affect mark-ups (or margins) positively while the last factor affects them negatively. Of these factors 1 and 4 provide points of entry for the analysis of international competition.

In a closed (or heavily protected) economy, an 'industry' can be defined at the national level and hence its degree of concentration can be measured by the distribution of output among domestic firms (using either a crude measure, such as a four-firm ratio, or a more complex measure, such as a Herfindahl index). Opening up an economy to imports and exports requires redefining an 'industry' at the global level, consisting of those producers in various nations that are capable of making competitive products which are at least imperfect substitutes for each other. Thus, for any given degree of domestic concentration, the effective concentration of an industry open to foreign competition must be lower. Hence, one would expect increased international competition – whether due to liberalization of domestic trade barriers, improvements in foreign productivity, or reductions in transportation and communications costs – to reduce domestic firms' 'degree of monopoly' and hence their price–cost margins (or profit mark-ups).

The relationship of trade unions to mark-ups is a subtle one, which was expressed in somewhat greater detail in Kalecki's posthumous essay on 'Class Struggle and the Distribution of National Income' (Kalecki [1971] 1991: 96–103) referred to earlier. There, Kalecki argued that if nominal wages increase proportionally in all firms in all industries in a closed economy, the higher costs will simply be passed on in the form of higher prices and (*ceteris paribus*) mark-ups will remain constant. However, if wages rise more in a particular industry, due to relatively stronger bargaining power of the unions in that industry, then the firms in that industry are also likely to raise prices but in a smaller proportion than the wage increase in order to avoid loss of market share. In Kalecki's words, such an industry will not want its products to become 'more and more expensive and thus less competitive with products of other industries,' and therefore 'the power of trade unions restrains the mark-ups' – especially in industries that have higher mark-ups to begin with, where unions are likely to be more bold in their bargaining since they think firms can afford to pay higher wages (Kalecki [1971] 1991: 100–1).

In this discussion, Kalecki seems to have in mind the market shares of different industries producing different products in the same national economy (for example, steel versus other metals and materials that could be substituted for steel). However, the same logic applies *mutatis mutandis* to different national industries producing the same or similar products in the same global industry (for example, American, European, and Japanese automobiles). If wage increases in the domestic industry made national products more expensive compared with foreign products, oligopolistic firms that care about maintaining their market shares (in either the domestic market or export markets) would cut their profit mark-ups and restrain their price increases in response to wage increases.[14] Although Kalecki's own analysis pertains to domestic wage increases, the same logic evidently applies to a reduction in foreign wages or a currency appreciation, either of which makes domestic wages relatively higher compared with foreign wages when measured in a common currency (see Arestis and Milberg 1993–4).

In this manner, Kalecki's theory of mark-up pricing can be extended to incorporate international competition in two ways: first, it implies that intensified international competition reduces effective industrial concentration and thereby directly lowers mark-ups; and second, it implies that union bargaining for higher wages will reduce profit mark-ups more in an economy that is open to international competition than in a closed economy.

However, these extensions suggest some problems with the conclusions reached by Kalecki in his simplified macro models that ignored these competitive effects.

Consider equation (5.5) above, which shows the inverse relation between national income and the profit share. Note that, if we ignore raw materials and overhead labor, the profit share π is an increasing function of the mark-up rate τ: $\pi = \tau/(1 + \tau)$.[15] Suppose that the workers in national industries win large wage increases, and firms respond by cutting their mark-ups τ but still raise prices to some extent. Now, there will be two offsetting effects on national income. On the one hand, the profit share π will fall, and (by Kalecki's logic) as the income is redistributed to workers who have a higher marginal propensity to consume than capitalists, national income will tend to rise (formally, the income multiplier increases). On the other hand, the higher prices of national products will make them less competitive to some extent (holding foreign prices and the exchange rate constant), thus lowering the trade balance $X - M$ in the numerator of (5.5) with a depressing effect on national income. Thus, in an internationally competitive economy, a redistribution of income toward wages has an *ambiguous* effect on the level of national income, unlike in the simple closed-economy model (ignoring competitive effects) in which such a redistribution is always expansionary. The implications of this point will be explored further below.

International conflict in a two-country model

As noted earlier, Kalecki believed that the positive relationship between trade surpluses and profit realization was the root cause of international conflicts over market shares, as reflected in the economic imperialism of the early twentieth century. Today, conflicts over trade imbalances persist between deficit countries such as the United States and the United Kingdom on the one side and surplus countries such as Germany and Japan on the other. To show more rigorously how such conflict emerges, this section presents a two-country version of a neo-Kaleckian macro model. The model can be seen as a Kaleckian version of the standard Keynesian two-country model with 'repercussion effects.'[16] The standard model is usually applied to analyze the effects of fiscal and monetary policies under alternative assumptions about such factors as the degree of capital mobility and the exchange rate regime. Here, we emphasize instead the effects of changes in the relative competitiveness of national economies (as reflected in their unit labor costs, that is, wages adjusted for productivity).[17] We also take the wage–profit distribution of income into account and emphasize the results for profits rather than national income in each country (although the latter could also be analyzed with our model).

The model developed here uses largely the same notation as the original Kaleckian model presented above, with a few modifications, but adds some complications based on the neo-Kaleckian/structuralist modeling literature referred to earlier as well as features designed to incorporate international repercussion effects. The equations for the 'home' country are as follows:

$$p = (1 + \tau)wa \tag{5.7}$$

$$\pi = (p - wa)/p \tag{5.8}$$

$$C = c_w W + c_r R \tag{5.9}$$

$$I = I_0 + b_1 R + b_2 Y \tag{5.10}$$

$$X = M^* \tag{5.11}$$

$$M = \mu(\rho) + mY, \ \mu'(\rho) < 0 \tag{5.12}$$

$$Y = C + I + G + (X - \rho M) \tag{5.13}$$

$$Y = W + R + T \tag{5.14}$$

$$W = (1 - t_w)(1 - \pi)Y \tag{5.15}$$

$$R = (1 - t_r)\pi Y \tag{5.16}$$

$$T = [t_w(1 - \pi) + t_r\pi]Y \tag{5.17}$$

Equation (5.7) is the mark-up pricing formula, where $\tau > 0$ is the mark-up rate, w is the nominal (pre-tax) wage rate, and a is the labor coefficient (reciprocal of labor productivity). The mark-up rate τ is taken as exogenously given here (it will be made endogenous in the following two sections of this chapter). For simplicity, raw materials and overhead labor costs are ignored. Therefore, the (pre-tax) profit share of value added (which equals the price in this simplified case) is defined by (5.8), and by substituting (5.7) into (5.8) one easily sees that $\pi = \tau/(1 + \tau)$ as asserted earlier. The consumption function (5.9) assumes different marginal propensities to consume (c_w and c_r, with $c_w > c_r$) out of after-tax wage and profit income (W and R, respectively).

The investment function (5.10) includes an intercept term $I_0 > 0$, representing the level of Keynesian 'animal spirits' (the state of business confidence) as well as positive effects of after-tax profits R and national output Y (thus $b_i > 0$, $i = 1,2$).[18] The positive effect of profits is motivated by Kalecki's notion that business investment is constrained by the supply of internal funds or corporate saving, both directly (since a large part of investment is internally financed) and indirectly (since higher internal funds reduce borrowers' and lenders' risks and thereby permit greater external finance). The positive effect of output reflects the need for firms to build ahead of demand in order to maintain a desired level of excess capacity (for example, to deter entry and to allow for future market growth); this may be thought of as the static equivalent of an accelerator effect. The Y term can also be thought of as representing the rate of capacity utilization, on the assumption that full-capacity output has been normalized to unity. The inclusion of a positive output or utilization effect in the investment function (5.10) follows Steindl (1952) more than Kalecki, but has become standard in many neo-Kaleckian macro models.[19]

Exports must be equal to foreign imports (* signifies the foreign country in M^*) according to equation (5.11). Imports are affected by the real exchange rate, $\rho = ep^*/p$, where e is the nominal exchange rate (home-currency price of foreign exchange) and p^* is the foreign price, and by national income, Y. The nominal exchange rate e is assumed to be fixed. For mathematical convenience, the import demand function is assumed to have an additive separable form. The real exchange rate effect is negative ($\mu'(\rho) < 0$) and the income effect is positive, with a constant marginal propensity to import ($0 < m < 1$). Equation (5.13) is the equilibrium condition that national income must equal aggregate demand. All the variables in (5.13) are measured in real terms, with home imports (which are a quantity of *foreign* goods) converted to domestic goods by the real exchange rate (which measures the relative price of foreign goods in terms of domestic goods).[20] Next, (5.14) is an identity linking national income to after-tax wages and profits (W and R, respectively) plus tax revenue (T). Finally, equations (5.15) to (5.17) define after-tax wages, after-tax profits, and tax revenue, respectively, with different tax rates (t_w and t_r) assumed for each type of income. Government spending G is taken as exogenously given.

To make this a two-country model, the foreign country is represented by an analogous set of equations. For equations (5.7) to (5.10) and (5.14) to (5.17), a * is simply added to each variable and parameter and the corresponding equation is obtained for the foreign country. To avoid confusion, the foreign equations involving exports, imports, and the exchange rate are given here explicitly:

$$X^* = M \tag{5.11'}$$

$$M^* = \mu^*(\rho) + m^*Y^*, \quad \mu^{*\prime}(\rho) > 0 \tag{5.12'}$$

$$Y^* = C^* + I^* + G^* + (X^* - M^*/\rho) \tag{5.13'}$$

Given how we have defined the real exchange rate ρ as the relative price of foreign goods, foreign imports (home exports) are a *positive* function of the real exchange rate in (5.12') and foreign imports have to be *divided* by ρ in the foreign national income identity (5.13').

With some rather tedious but straightforward algebraic manipulations, this model can be solved for home and foreign income levels (Y and Y^*) or, alternatively, for home and foreign profit levels (R and R^*), as functions of exogenously given variables and parameters. In the spirit of Kalecki's work, we will focus on the solution for profit levels, but these solutions can readily be transformed into solutions for income levels (and hence employment levels) by using the identity (5.16) for the home countries and the analogous equation (5.16′) for the foreign country. The equilibrium solution can be graphed by showing each country's profit level as a function of the other's, as shown by the lines RR for the home country and $R*R*$ for the foreign country in Figure 5.2. The equations for these lines are:

$$R = \frac{(1 - t_r)\pi\, [I_0 + G + \mu^*(\rho) - \mu(\rho) + m^*\, R^* / (1 - t_r^*)\pi^*\,]}{s(\pi) - b_1(1 - t_r)\pi\, b_2 + \rho m} \tag{18}$$

for home and

$$R^* = \frac{(1 - t_r^*)\pi^*\, [I_0^* + G^* + \mu(\rho) - \mu^*(\rho) + mR / (1 - t_r)\pi]}{s^*(\pi^*) - b_1^*(1 - t_r^*)\pi^* - b_2^* + m^* / \rho} \tag{19}$$

for foreign, where $s(\pi) = 1 - c_w(1 - t_w)(1 - \pi) - c_r(1 - t_r)\pi$ is the marginal propensity to save in the home country, assuming $0 < s(\pi) < 1$ and $s'(\pi) > 0$; $s^*(\pi^*)$ is defined analogously for the foreign country. The denominators of these equations must be assumed positive for stability of the equilibrium.[21]

The upward-sloping dashed line in Figure 5.2 represents balanced trade between the two countries ($M^* - \rho M = 0$), with a slope of $m^*/m\rho$; trade is assumed to be balanced in the initial equilibrium (at point Q_0). Note that points below and to the right of this balanced-trade line represent situations of home surpluses and foreign deficits; points above and to the left of this line represent situations of foreign surpluses and home deficits.

Now, consider the effects of an increase in the home country's competitiveness, in the sense of a rise in the real exchange rate ρ (signifying that home goods are relatively cheaper and foreign goods are relatively more expensive). Note that ρ can be decomposed as:

$$\rho = \frac{ew^*\, a^*\, (1 + \tau^*)}{wa(1 + \tau)} = \frac{ew^*\, a^*(1 - \pi)}{wa(1 - \pi^*)}$$

and thus reflects the following underlying determinants: the nominal exchange rate e, relative foreign unit labor costs (w^*a^*/wa), and the relative foreign mark-up factor $(1 + \tau^*)/(1 + \tau)$ – or, equivalently, the relative home wage share $(1 - \pi)/(1 - \pi^*)$. A rise in any one of these terms would increase ρ.

Starting from an initial equilibrium with balanced trade and assuming that the Marshall–Lerner elasticity condition holds,[22] the RR and $R*R*$ lines both shift up and to the left (to $R'R'$ and $R*'R*'$, respectively) as shown in Figure 5.3. Under plausible assumptions,[23] it can be shown that the new equilibrium point Q_1 lies above and to the left of the initial equilibrium Q_0, implying that

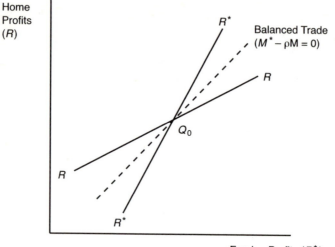

Figure 5.2 Home and foreign profits in a two-country neo-Kaleckian model

profits have been redistributed from the foreign country to the home country. Thus, at least in the short run, for a given set of parameters determining global aggregate demand (for example, fiscal policies in the two countries), there is an inherent conflict between profit realization in the two countries. This is represented by the international profit relationship $\pi\pi^*$ in Figure 5.3, which is the negatively sloped curve through points Q_0 and Q_1. Any improvement in one country's competitive position takes profit income as well as market shares and employment opportunities away from the other (in our example, Y also increases and Y^* decreases). Also, under the same assumptions, it can be shown that the home country will have a trade surplus and the foreign country will have a deficit in the new equilibrium at Q_1, that is, the balanced trade line from Figure 5.2 (which is not drawn in Figure 5.3 to avoid cluttering the diagram) shifts up and to the left *beyond* the new equilibrium point Q_1, assuming that this line originally passed through Q_0 before the increase in ρ.

This Kaleckian analysis of international conflict over profit realizations makes an interesting contrast with the analysis of 'strategic trade policy' in the neoclassical 'new trade theory' literature (see, for example, Krugman 1987; Grossman 1992). The latter analysis is based on models of strategic interaction between national oligopolies in world markets, in which specific forms of 'credible' government interventions can, under certain conditions, shift profits (or oligopolistic 'rents') from foreign firms to domestic firms. Firms are assumed to be strict optimizing (profit-maximizing) agents, and the optimal form of strategic policy intervention (for example, export subsidy or tax) depends on the precise nature of the firms' strategic interaction (for example, Cournot versus Bertrand behavior). Strategic trade policies are generally

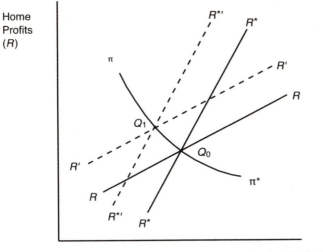

Figure 5.3 Effects of increased home competitiveness (a rise in the real exchange rate ρ) in a two-country neo-Kaleckian model

thought to be of little practical use since – even leaving aside these policies' beggar-thy-neighbor character, which invites retaliation – governments need to have incredible amounts of information about industry structure and behavior in order to choose the 'right' strategic policies, and governments beholden to special interest groups may choose to aid the 'wrong' industries anyway.

The analysis in this section shows that there is another, macroeconomic mechanism with which governments can attempt to capture foreign profits for domestic oligopolists. This mechanism does not rely on any particular form of strategic interaction among rival firms, but merely assumes that oligopolies set prices by relatively rigid profit mark-ups and have excess capacity. Thus, the capacity of governments to engage in profit-shifting policies would seem to be underestimated in the strategic trade policy literature. In a Kaleckian world, any policies that lead to undervalued currencies, reduced wages, or enhanced productivity can potentially capture a greater share of world markets and global profits for domestic oligopolies, without requiring any precise information about industry structure or behavior. Furthermore, in the Kaleckian model, the government does not have to 'pick winners' among national industries; all national oligopolies can share in the benefits of profit-shifting, pro-competitive policies.

Of course, there are ways of ameliorating the international conflict over profits, income, and jobs highlighted by the Kaleckian model. In particular, coordinated fiscal expansions (increases in spending G and G^* or cuts in taxes T and T^*) could shift the conflict frontier $\pi\pi^*$ outward. A fiscal expansion in one country would also shift $\pi\pi^*$ outward, but would leave that country with a trade deficit and give the other country a trade surplus (as in the case of the US fiscal expansion of the mid-1980s).

There are also adjustment mechanisms that could reverse some of a country's gains from increasing its competitiveness. For example, the home currency might appreciate (thus lowering e) as a result of having a trade surplus or, equivalently, home country workers might win higher wages w as a result of tighter labor-market conditions. Foreign wages w^* could also decline as a result of higher unemployment. But these sorts of adjustments (either of which would reverse the increase in ρ) cannot be taken for granted, and even if they occur they are usually far from instantaneous. Especially in a situation in which the home country continues to increase its competitiveness steadily over time (for example, through progressive increases in productivity relative to the foreign country), the home country may give itself persistent trade surpluses with high realized profits and low unemployment rates for a prolonged period of time. As Robinson wrote in her analysis of the 'new mercantilism':

> The chronic condition for industrial enterprise is to be looking round anxiously for prospects of sales. Since the total market does not grow fast enough to make room for all, each government feels it a worthy and commendable aim to increase its own share in world activity for the benefit of its own people . . .
>
> . . . everyone is keen to sell and wary of buying. Every nation wants to have a surplus in its balance of trade. This is a game in which the total scores add up to zero. Some can win only if others lose. The beautiful harmony of the free-trade model is far indeed to seek
>
> (Robinson 1978: 204–5)

International competition, distribution, and growth

In the simple Kaleckian macro model presented above, national income Y is inversely related to the profit share π in the short run, as shown in equation (5.5). This inverse relationship has become known in the neo-Marxian and post-Keynesian literature as 'stagnationism,' in the sense that a redistribution of income toward profits (due to increased monopoly power resulting in higher profit mark-ups) causes a depression of economic activity.[24] Or, put another way, economic expansion in such a system is 'wage-led,' in the sense that a redistribution of income toward wages (that is, a fall in π) causes national income to increase. The intuitive reason for this result is clear: the only macroeconomic consequence of a redistribution of income toward profits in the simple Kaleckian model is to raise the marginal propensity to save, $(1 - c_r)\pi$, and an increase in the marginal propensity to save is contractionary due to the Keynesian 'paradox of thrift' (since more saving requires a fall in consumption demand).

This conclusion does not necessarily hold in more general neo-Kaleckian models, which allow for other macroeconomic effects of income redistribution – on workers' saving, investment demand, tax revenue, or net exports (the trade balance). These more general models open up the possibility of what Marglin and Bhaduri (1990) call 'exhilarationism' or profit-led expansion. Marglin and Bhaduri base the possibility of exhilarationism on a critique of the investment function (5.10).[25] Here, we focus instead on how the exhilarationist possibility is created by openness to international competition.

As discussed earlier, we would not expect profit mark-up rates to be rigid in economies open to international competition. Increases in domestic unit labor costs (wages adjusted for productivity), relative to foreign countries, make home products less competitive and therefore 'squeeze' profit margins (price–cost ratios) if firms attempt to maintain their market shares to some extent. Reductions in domestic unit labor costs have the opposite effect of allowing domestic firms to raise price–cost margins. The assumption of a fixed mark-up rate must therefore be dropped. In this section, we analyze the consequences of making the mark-up rate (and therefore the profit share) an endogenous variable. The first subsection develops a simple model of a flexible mark-up that adjusts to international competitive pressures in an open economy; the following subsection then considers the implications of incorporating the flexible mark-up in a neo-Kaleckian macro model. In both parts, we conduct the analysis for a single national economy, which is assumed to be 'small' in the sense that international repercussion effects are negligible and can be omitted.

A simple model of a flexible mark-up in an open economy

We start with equations (5.7) and (5.8) above, which define the relationships between the price level, the mark-up rate, and the profit share. The nominal wage rate w and the labor coefficient a are taken as exogenously given for simplicity. In a more complex distributive model, there could be equations for wage adjustment and for productivity growth (decreases in a), but such complexities are avoided here as they are not central to the issue at hand.[26] Since we take both a and w as given, then unit labor costs aw are fixed in nominal terms, and the steady-state rate of inflation must be zero. This simplifying assumption is helpful for allowing the real exchange rate to be constant in the steady state, without having to introduce a flexible exchange rate (the domestic currency price of foreign goods, ep^*, is taken as exogenously fixed).[27]

Rather than work directly with the mark-up rate or the profit share $[\pi = \tau/(1 + \tau)]$, it is more convenient mathematically to use the wage share of national income, $[\omega = 1 - \pi = 1/(1 + \tau)]$. Then (5.7) can be expressed as:

$$p = wa/\omega. \qquad (5.20)$$

Also for mathematical convenience, the price adjustment function is specified in terms of differences in natural logarithms. Firms are assumed to have a target mark-up rate τ^f, which is equivalent to a target wage share $\omega^f = 1/(1 + \tau^f)$ (and also to a target profit share $\pi^f = \tau^f/(1 + \tau^f)$]. The price adjustment function for firms is assumed to be:

$$\hat{p} = \phi(\ln \omega - \ln \omega^f) + \theta \ln \rho \tag{5.21}$$

where ϕ is the speed of adjustment of the price when the actual wage share exceeds the firms' target ω^f (which means that the actual profit share π falls short of the firm's target π^f); $\rho = ep*/p$ is the real exchange rate as defined previously (but now $p*$ is taken as fixed); and θ is the sensitivity of price increases to the real exchange rate.[28]

Since $\omega = wa/p$, then the wage share increases at the rate $\hat{\omega} = \hat{w} + \hat{a} - \hat{p}$. Since we have assumed $\hat{w} = \hat{a} = 0$, then $\hat{\omega} = 0$ simply requires $\hat{p} = 0$. Then, the steady-state wage share is easily obtained from (5.21) as follows. First, using (5.20) and the definition of ρ in (5.21), we get:

$$\hat{p} = \phi(\ln \omega - \ln \omega^f) + \theta \ln (z\omega),$$

where $z = ep*/wa = \rho/\omega$ is the ratio of the domestic currency price of imports to unit labor costs (which could also be called the real exchange rate in efficiency-wage units).[29] Then, setting $\hat{p} = 0$, we solve for the steady-state solution[30] (in natural logs):

$$\ln = \bar{\omega} = [\phi \ln \omega^f - \theta \ln z] / (\phi + \theta) \tag{5.22}$$

Taking the partial derivatives of (5.22) with respect to $\ln \omega^f$ and $\ln z$ yields the elasticities of the steady-state wage share with respect to the firms' target wage share and the real exchange rate in efficiency-wage units:[31]

$$\partial \ln \bar{\omega}/\partial \ln \omega^f = \phi/(\phi + \theta) > 0$$

and

$$\partial \ln \bar{\omega} /\partial \ln z = -\theta/(\phi + \theta) < 0.$$

Based on this analysis, we conclude that the steady-state wage share $\bar{\omega}$ can be written as an implicit function $\bar{\omega} = \bar{\omega} (\tau^f, z)$, with $\partial \bar{\omega}/\partial\tau^f < 0$ [recall that $\omega^f = 1/(1 + \tau^f)$] and $\partial \bar{\omega}/\partial z < 0$. Furthermore, since the steady-state profit share is $\bar{\pi} = 1 - \bar{\omega}$, then $\bar{\pi}$ can be written as the implicit function:

$$\bar{\pi} = \bar{\pi}(\tau^f, z), \tag{5.23}$$

with $\partial\bar{\pi}/\partial\tau^f > 0$ and $\partial\bar{\pi}/\partial z > 0$.

What this analysis accomplishes is not only to make income shares sensitive to international competition, but to make them sensitive to domestic wage-setting as well. If workers win a higher nominal wage rate w, for example, $z = ep*/wa$ falls, and this lowers the equilibrium profit share and raises the equilibrium wage share. This occurs because international competition prevents firms from passing through the entire wage increase into a higher price, and thus their profit margin is squeezed. Thus, this model succinctly represents the two ways in which international competition affects mark-ups (and the profit share) in our interpretation of Kalecki's theory: a fall in concentration (which would be expected to decrease the firms' target mark-up τ^f) lowers the equilibrium mark-up rate and profit share, while a rise in the domestic wage (due, for example, to stronger union bargaining) has the opposite effect of creating a 'profit squeeze.'

The open-economy macro model[32]

Now we incorporate the results of the preceding model of distributional shares into a neo-Kaleckian macro model, using a simplified version of the two-country model developed above. For simplicity, we consider only a single, small economy, without any foreign repercussion effects. For algebraic simplicity, we also assume that there is no government spending or taxation. The consumption function and investment function are the same as for the 'home' country above (equations (5.9) and (5.10)). The trade balance, defined as $B = X - \rho M$, is assumed to be determined by the implicit function:

$$B = B(\rho, Y), \quad B_\rho > 0, \quad B_Y < 0 \tag{5.24}$$

The partial derivative $\partial B / \partial \rho = B_\rho > 0$ assumes that the Marshall–Lerner condition holds (starting from a point where $B = 0$); the partial $\partial B / \partial Y = B_Y > 0$ simply assumes that import demand is an increasing function of national income (note that the marginal propensity to import need not be assumed to be a constant m, that is, the income-elasticity of import demand need not be unity). The following identities should be self-explanatory (they are simplified versions of (5.13) through (5.16)):

$$Y = C + I + B \tag{5.25}$$

$$Y = W + R \tag{5.26}$$

$$W = (1 - \pi)Y \tag{5.27}$$

$$R = \pi Y \tag{5.28}$$

By making all the appropriate substitutions into (5.25), we obtain the following equation for equilibrium in the goods market (essentially describing an 'IS curve' in $Y \times \pi$ space):

$$Y = [(c_w(1 - \pi) + c_r\pi + b_1\pi + b_2]Y + I_0 + B[z(1 - \pi), Y] \tag{5.29}$$

which uses the identity $\rho = z\omega = z(1 - \pi)$. However, π is not exogenous in (5.29), and in order to analyze the comparative statics of the relationship between the level and distribution of income in this model, we need to use equation (5.23) to show the determination of (steady-state) π as a function of international labor-cost competitiveness (z) and the firms' target mark-up (τ^f). Thus, substituting $\pi = \bar{\pi}(\tau^f, z)$ into (5.29) and totally differentiating with respect to Y and either z or τ^f, we obtain the following total derivatives:

$$\frac{dY}{dz} = \frac{-(c_w - c_r - b_1)Y\bar{\pi}_2 + (1 - \pi - z\bar{\pi}_2)B_\rho}{1 - c_w + (c_w - c_r - b_1)\bar{\pi} - b_2 - B_Y} \tag{5.30}$$

$$\frac{dY}{d\tau^f} = \frac{-(c_w - c_r - b_1)Y\bar{\pi}_{tf} - z\bar{\pi}_{tf})B_\rho}{1 - c_w + (c_w - c_r - b_1)\bar{\pi} - b_2 - B_Y} \tag{5.31}$$

The denominators, which are the same in both (5.30) and (5.31), must be positive for stability of the goods-market equilibrium. The signs of these derivatives therefore depend on the signs of the numerators, which will determine whether a redistribution toward profits (induced by a rise in either z or τ^f) is expansionary or contractionary, that is, whether the economy is 'exhilarationist' or 'stagnationist.'

Consider first equation (5.30) for dY/dz. This shows the effect of an increase in $z = ep^*/wa$, which could result from a currency depreciation (rise in e), foreign inflation (rise in p^*), productivity improvement (decrease in a), or wage cut (fall in w). Since $\bar{\pi} > 0$, the first term in the numerator of (5.30) is negative if the marginal propensity to consume out of wages is large relative to the sum of the marginal propensity to consume out of profits and the profitability effect in the investment function ($c_w > c_r + b_1$), and positive in the opposite case ($c_w < c_r + b_1$). This term essentially shows the effect of the redistribution toward profits on the *difference* between national saving and domestic investment, an effect which is positive in the former case and negative in the second. In a closed economy, this condition alone would determine whether the economy was stagnationist or exhilarationist.[33]

In an open economy, however, we also encounter the second term in the numerator of (5.30), $(1 - \pi - z\bar{\pi})B_\rho$, which is the effect of increased labor-cost competitiveness on the trade balance and must be positive. We have assumed that $B_\rho > 0$ because the Marshall–Lerner condition holds, and it can also be shown that $(1 - \pi - z\bar{\pi}) > 0$ in our model of distribution,[34] which simply means that the 'squeezing' of profit margins when z rises (that is, domestic unit labor costs rise relative to prices of foreign goods) is not so great as to make home products more competitive rather than less competitive. Thus, even if ($c_w > c_r + b_1$), so that the economy would be stagnationist if it were closed to foreign trade, a sufficiently large competitiveness effect $(1 - \pi - z\bar{\pi})B_\rho$ can make the economy exhilarationist when it is open to foreign trade. The more that import and export demands are price-elastic, the larger is B_ρ and the more likely it is that the open economy is exhilarationist. To see the intuition for this case, consider a *reduction* in the money wage rate w, which raises z. This will redistribute income toward profits according to the mechanism outlined previously, but will also make the country's products more competitive with foreign products. As a result, there are three effects on aggregate demand: a fall in consumption (assuming $c_w > c_r$), a rise in investment (since $b_1 > 0$), and a rise in the trade balance (since $B_\rho > 0$). Only if the first effect ('underconsumptionism') dominates is the economy stagnationist; if the latter two effects dominate, the economy becomes exhilarationist, that is, the redistribution toward profits is expansionary rather than contractionary.

If income shares change because of a change in firms' monopoly power that alters the firms' target mark-up rate τ^f, the results are much more likely to be stagnationist. To see this, note that (5.31) is similar to (5.30) except that the second term in the numerator of (5.31) is negative. This evidently makes it more likely that $dY/d\tau^f < 0$ as compared with $dY/dz < 0$. For example, if the economy is domestically stagnationist ($c_w > c_r + b_1$), then the numerator of (5.31) is definitely negative, that is, satisfying the closed-economy condition for stagnationism is sufficient to ensure that the effects of a higher target mark-up are stagnationist in an open economy. Even if $c_w < c_r + b_1$ so that the economy would be exhilarationist if closed, the negative competitiveness effect of a rise in τ^f makes it possible for the open economy to behave in a stagnationist fashion in this case. Intuitively, the reason for the difference between the effects of increases in τ^f and z is as follows: while increases in either of these parameters redistributes income toward profits, and thus tends to lower consumption and raise investment, increases in τ^f worsen a country's competitiveness and thereby reduce the trade balance while increases in z do the opposite.

Thus, the analysis in this section reveals two important qualifications of the traditional Kaleckian analysis of the relationship between the level and distribution of income. First, there is not necessarily an inverse relationship between the profit share and national income; the relationship can be positive, and is more likely to be so in open economies subject to intense price competition (as reflected in high Marshall–Lerner price elasticities). Second, in an open-economy model with an endogenous profit mark-up rate, the direction of the relationship between the profit share and national income depends on the *source* of variations in the former, that is, the cause of a redistribution of income matters to the macroeconomic effect of that redistribution. Specifically, an improvement in labor-cost competitiveness is more likely to lead to a positive relationship ('exhilarationism') while an increase in firms' target mark-ups (for example, because of increased concentration) is more likely to lead to a negative relationship ('stagnationism').

The preceding analysis has important implications for the political economy of current efforts to further liberalize international trade relations, such as the North American Free Trade Agreement (NAFTA) and Uruguay Round of the General Agreement on Tariffs and Trade (GATT). On the one hand, trade liberalization tends to reduce the effective degree of concentration of markets by subjecting domestic firms to international competition. To this extent, trade liberalization may be thought to lower target mark-ups τ^f globally, with probable wage-led, expansionary effects on the entire world economy. On the other hand, the same exposure to international competition makes it more likely that domestic wage increases squeeze profit mark-ups, with effects that are likely to be contractionary in systems that are 'exhilarationist' for variations in labor cost competitiveness z. To put it another way, this model implies that international competition lessens workers' ability to achieve higher wages without reducing their own employment prospects; rather, international competition tends to foster a competition over job opportunities between workers in different countries which creates a trade-off between domestic wages and employment in any one country. While the net effect of these two changes is unclear, the present analysis suggests that it is important to take these distributional consequences into account in any evaluation of trade liberalization agreements.

At least one policy initiative currently touted as part of so-called 'trade liberalization' – the greater international enforcement of 'intellectual property rights' – may be expected to increase firms' target profit mark-ups, however. The enforcement of these rights strengthens the monopoly power of large multinational corporations in the markets for their technologies and their products. Since increases in τ^f are likely to be contractionary, the promotion of intellectual property rights could potentially have a stagnating effect on global demand – unless the promotion of those rights has a large stimulative effect on the investment activity of the corporations whose intellectual property is thus protected.

Income distribution and the effectiveness of currency devaluation

The model developed in the preceding section also yields insights into a classic issue in open economy macroeconomics: the effectiveness of currency devaluation. The 'effectiveness' of currency devaluation actually refers to two distinct but closely related issues: (a) how effective is a devaluation for improving the trade balance; and (b) how effective is a devaluation for increasing national income and employment. The Kaleckian approach suggests that there is a trade-off between these two objectives due to the distributional consequences of a currency devaluation, which are to redistribute income from wages to profits. As we shall see, these redistributive effects imply that when a devaluation is more effective for either one of these two objectives it is likely to be less effective for the other.

To aid in understanding this implication of the neo-Kaleckian macro model, we shall utilize a diagram commonly found in international economics textbooks for more standard, neo-Keynesian models. Figure 5.4, depicts both the excess of national saving over domestic investment $(S-I)$[35] and the trade balance $(B = X - \rho M)$ as functions of national income Y. In equilibrium, it must be the case that $S - I = B$, that is, the excess of national saving over domestic investment equals the excess of exports over imports, both of which must equal the country's net foreign investment outflow (that is, the increase in the country's net international asset position). Therefore, the intersection of these two functions simultaneously determines the equilibrium levels of national income Y and the trade balance $B = S - I$. We assume that national income does not exceed any constraints of full capacity utilization or full employment of labor.

In the traditional usage of this diagram, a devaluation shifts the trade balance line B up, say to B', assuming that the Marshall–Lerner condition is satisfied. A devaluation has no effect on the $(S - I)$ line, and therefore the new equilibrium lies up and to the right along that line (that is, the equilibrium moves from point E_0 to E_1 in Figure 5.4). A devaluation therefore tends to both raise national income and improve the trade balance, at least in a comparative static sense (that is, ignoring potential long-run adjustments, such as nonsterilized monetary inflows, which could restore balanced trade). The only exception that is commonly allowed for is the Harberger–Laursen–Metzler effect,[36] in which consumers attempt to maintain a target standard of living, and therefore raise their marginal propensity to consume (and lower their marginal propensity to save) in response to the higher cost of imported goods caused by the devaluation. In this case, the $(S - I)$ line rotates down and to the right (becoming flatter), implying that the devaluation is less effective for improving the trade balance (but more effective in regard to income

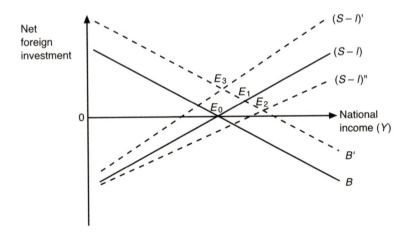

Figure 5.4 Income redistribution effects and the effectiveness of currency devaluation

expansion). This possibility is illustrated by the line $(S - I)''$ and the new equilibrium point E_2 in Figure 5.4.

The neo-Kaleckian macro model developed in the previous section provides another rationale for the $(S - I)$ line to shift in response to a devaluation and shows that this shift may go in either direction (up or down). As we have shown, a currency devaluation is likely to redistribute income toward profits, and this redistributive effect in turn can make $(S - I)$ either rise or fall, depending on the relative marginal propensities to consume out of wages and profits as well as the sensitivity of investment to profits. Formally, note that a devaluation (rise in the nominal exchange rate e) implies a rise in our index of labor cost competitiveness, $z = ep^*/wa$, holding the other factors (p^*, w, and a) constant. Thus, the effects of a rise in e are qualitatively the same as the effects of a rise in z. We have already analyzed the distributional effects of a rise in z in deriving equation (5.23), which shows that π is an increasing function of z. We have also found the comparative static impact of a rise in z on Y in the derivative (5.30), above.

To determine the impact of a rise in z on the trade balance B, we substitute $\rho = z(1 - \pi)$ into (5.24) and use the chain rule of calculus to obtain:

$$\frac{dB}{dz} = B_\rho (1 - \pi - z\,\bar{\pi}_2) + B_Y \left(\frac{dY}{dz} \right) \tag{5.32}$$

in which the first term is the direct effect of a rise in z (the vertical shift in the B line in Figure 5.4) and the second term is the indirect effect (the move along the new B' line to the new equilibrium point). After substituting (5.30) for dY/dz and some manipulation, (5.32) can be solved as follows:

$$\frac{dB}{dz} = \frac{[1 - c_w + (c_w - c_r - b_1)\bar{\pi} - b_2] (1 - \pi - z\bar{\pi}_2) B_\rho - (c_w - c_r - b_1) Y \bar{\pi}_2 B_Y}{1 - c_w + (c_w - c_r - b_1)\bar{\pi} - b_2 - B_Y} \tag{5.33}$$

Relating all these results to Figure 5.4, we note that the redistributive effect of a devaluation on the difference $S - I$ depends on the sign of the first term in the numerator of (5.30), $-(c_w - c_r - b_1)Y\bar{\pi}$. If $c_w > c_r + b_1$, then this term is negative and the $(S - I)$ line in Figure 5.4 shifts up and to the left to $(S - I)'$; if $c_w < c_r + b_1$, then this term is positive and $(S - I)$ shifts down and to the right to $(S - I)''$. Thus, in an economy that would be stagnationist if it were closed to foreign competition (the former case), a devaluation is less effective for stimulating national income when the economy is open to foreign competition. On the other hand, in an economy that would be exhilarationist if closed to foreign trade (the latter case), a devaluation is a more effective expansionary tool.

However, the sign of $-(c_w - c_r - b_1)$ has the opposite implications for the effectiveness of a currency devaluation for improving the trade balance, as can be seen by comparing the new equilibrium points E_3 and E_2 in Figure 5.4. Since $-(c_w - c_r - b_1)$ is multiplied by $B_Y < 0$ in (5.33), the second term in the numerator of dB/dz has the *same* sign as $(c_w - c_r - b_1)$. If the economy would be stagnationist without trade $(c_w > c_r + b_1)$, a devaluation is a more powerful tool for improving the trade balance, precisely because the expansionary impact of the devaluation is diminished by the contractionary effects of the redistribution of income toward profits (which, in this case, tends to reduce consumption and to augment saving to a comparatively large extent). In the opposite case of a country that would be exhilarationist without trade $(c_w < c_r + b_1)$, a devaluation is relatively ineffective for improving the trade balance, precisely because the devaluation is even more expansionary in this case (due to a relatively large stimulus to investment and a comparatively small reduction in consumption or rise in saving).

One last implication of this model concerns the potential for contractionary effects of currency devaluation, a possibility modeled by Krugman and Taylor (1978) based on the earlier suggestion of Díaz-Alejandro (1963). In terms of the graphical analysis in Figure 5.4, for a devaluation actually to reduce equilibrium national income Y, the $S - I$ line must shift up and to the left by a large amount relative to the shift in B (so that point E_3 lies to the left of E_0). This essentially requires that the domestic economy be highly stagnationist while the trade balance is relatively insensitive to changes in relative price competitiveness (that is, import and export demand must be relatively price-inelastic). A sufficient (although not necessary) condition for such a result is the set of assumptions made by Krugman and Taylor, who essentially assume that $B_p = 0$ (that is, rigid import and export demands) and $c_w > c_r + b_1$ (that is, a stagnationist domestic economy).[37] In this case, a devaluation definitely causes output to contract $(dY/dz < 0)$, although (for this very reason) a devaluation is also very potent for improving the trade balance $(dB/dz > 0)$. Krugman and Taylor did not note the opposite possibility of an exhilarationist economy, in which $c_w < c_r + b_1$, and (on their assumption of $B_p = 0$) a devaluation must be expansionary $(dY/dz > 0)$ but actually worsens the trade balance $(dB/dz < 0)$.

Conclusions

This chapter has surveyed the main contributions of Michal Kalecki to international economics and has presented three neo-Kaleckian models which further develop the implications of his theoretical approach for open economies. The first model shows how international trade relations can be conflictive in the presence of oligopolistic industries with excess capacity and mark-up pricing. Changes in competitiveness redistribute profits as well as income and employment between countries, for given aggregate demand conditions (for example, fiscal and monetary policy stances of the governments). The second model shows that allowing for flexible profit mark-ups in countries that are open to international competition can reverse the results of Kalecki's own analysis of the relationship between the equilibrium level of national income and its distribution between wages and profits. When increased relative labor costs put a 'squeeze' on profit margins in the face of international competition, and when commodity trade is relatively price-elastic, a redistribution of income from wages to profits can be contractionary rather than expansionary. The third model shows that the redistributive effects of a currency devaluation (which are to raise the profit share) need to be taken into account in evaluating the effectiveness of a devaluation for the twin goals of improving the balance of trade and increasing national income. If raising the profit share increases domestic expenditures, then a devaluation is likely to be more effective for increasing income but less effective for improving the trade balance, and conversely if raising the profit share decreases domestic expenditures.

All of these results were obtained in fairly simple, highly aggregative, and basically static macro models (except that a dynamic specification of pricing behavior was used to derive the distributional effects of changes in relative cost competitiveness or currency devaluation). The results obtained here therefore need to be incorporated into more complex, dynamic models in order to take full account of feedbacks between all the variables in the models. Just as an example, for simplicity we took the nominal wages and exchange rates as given in this chapter, but one might want to model explicitly how wages and (flexible) exchange rates respond to changes in other parameters of these models (for example, labor coefficients or target mark-ups). Also, some of the other factors in Kalecki's broader work that were omitted here, such as raw materials costs, overhead expenses (fixed costs), and intersectoral relationships, need to be brought back into the analysis.

In a book on post-Keynesian approaches to international economics, it would not be appropriate to conclude without some comment on the relationship between the Kaleckian models presented here and other post-Keynesian perspectives. A post-Keynesian approach emphasizes the idea of a 'monetary production economy' in which 'real' economic activity (production, employment, investment, and so on) is not independent of the financing of asset or debt positions by businesses, households, and governments. Yet, except for the inclusion of a profit term in the investment function (representing financial constraints on investment spending), the neo-Kaleckian models in this chapter have been essentially pure 'real' models without any explicit treatment of money and finance. Among other things, we abstracted here from the monetary policies of the central bank that are required to maintain the assumed fixed exchange rate and given interest rate, and the possible impact of those policies on economic activity. In future work, it will be important to try to integrate the Kaleckian emphasis on the distributional aspects of international trade (both between countries and within countries) with the post-Keynesian emphasis on international monetary relations and payments mechanisms (see, for example, Davidson 1982, 1994). Both approaches will need to be combined in order to develop a complete alternative to orthodox, neoclassical analyses of balance of payments adjustment and exchange rate determination.

Notes

1 See Robinson (1978: 53–60) on Kalecki's relationship with Keynes, and Asimakopulos (1988–9) on Kalecki's influence on Robinson.

2 For example, Kalecki's assumption that industrial firms typically have constant marginal cost and decreasing average total cost (due to the presence of a fixed cost) is now a commonplace assumption in mainstream models of imperfect competition. See, for example, the model of monopolistic competition in Dixit and Stiglitz (1977), which was the basis for Krugman's (1979) model of trade with increasing returns to scale. See also Carlton and Perloff (1994) for a textbook exposition of this type of model. Another example of Kalecki's ideas entering the mainstream is in the new neoclassical literature on financing constraints on investment, in which 'asymmetric information' between borrowers and lenders takes the place of Kalecki's concepts of increasing risks of borrowers and lenders (see Stiglitz and Weiss 1981; Fazzari *et al.* 1988).

3 All page references for Kalecki's work refer to the new set of his collected works (Kalecki 1990, 1991, 1993). The year of first publication of the original article or book cited is given in brackets.

4 See especially Kalecki ([1933] 1990: 165–73).

5 This literature started with the work of Harris (1974) and Asimakopulos (1975) and was then developed further by Rowthorn (1982), Taylor (1983, 1985), Dutt (1984, 1987), and Bhaduri (1986), among others. Dutt (1990) adds the 'Kalecki–Steindl closure' to the list of major theories of economic growth and income distribution, distinguished by its assumption of chronic excess capacity. Later developments in this literature are discussed below.

6 See, for example, the otherwise excellent account of Kalecki's theories in Sawyer (1985) and the discussion of Kalecki's influence on Robinson by Asimakopulos (1988–9).

7 The following exposition draws mainly on the version in Kalecki ([1954] 1991: 239–61). Other, earlier versions are reproduced in Kalecki (1990 and 1991).

8 Robinson ([1971] 1980: 89) attributed this saying to Kalecki, but admitted that she could not find it in his English writings. For similar versions of this saying, see Kaldor (1956: 96) and Harris (1978: 194–5), both of whom quote it without attribution. I am indebted to David P. Levine, Tracy Mott, and Jan Toporowski for assistance in locating these references.

9 We refer here to the standard 'Keynesian' consumption function, $C = C_0 + cY$, where $C_0 > 0$ and $0 < c < 1$, as presented in most macroeconomics textbooks. Such a linear form is not found in Keynes (1936), however, where it is simply postulated that $C = C(Y)$ with $C'(Y) > 0$ and $C''(Y) < 0$. In this respect, Kalecki's specification was more 'Keynesian' than Keynes'! However, Keynes' own formulation can be regarded as a more awkward attempt to build in the idea that the marginal propensity to consume is lower for high income-earners, a cross-sectional concept that he rather misrepresented in a time-series consumption function. Kalecki's formulation (5.3) is a much more straightforward way of representing this idea, assuming that profit recipients can be regarded as the high income earners.

10 In Kalecki's ([1954] 1991: 225–38) original model, π is positively related to total income Y due to the assumption of a given amount of overhead labor, which implies that the labor share falls as income rises. This complexity, which is

incorporated in the models of Harris (1974) and Asimakopulos (1975), is omitted here in order to focus more on the international dimension.

11   However, the same authors sometimes assume a more neo-Marxian specification of developing countries, with full utilization of industrial capacity and capital accumulation constrained by the supply of saving, in their North–South trade models. See, for example, Taylor (1983: 177–89) and Dutt (1988).

12   Such competitive pressures were already building in the late 1960s, but Kalecki took no special note of them in his last article on the topic (Kalecki [1971] 1991: 96–103), published posthumously. This article does give a hint that the results of the analysis differ between closed and open economies, but the point is not pursued.

13   If p is price and u is unit prime cost (average variable costs, that is, production workers' labor plus raw materials costs per unit of output), then p/u is the 'gross margin' (or price–cost margin) and $p/u - 1 = (p - u)/u$ is the mark-up rate. Kalecki's attempts to argue that these ratios were determined by something called the 'degree of monopoly' (or, in some cases, the 'degree of oligopoly') have been criticized as tautological by many economists, including Riach (1971), Asimakopulos (1975), and Kreissler (1988). These authors have also pointed out various technical problems with Kalecki's efforts to construct mathematical models of how these ratios are determined. These technical problems need not concern us here, however, as our focus is on his more substantive, qualitative hypotheses about the factors that influence mark-up rates or price–cost margins.

14   While this is likely to be the response in the short run, firms whose profit margins have been thus squeezed may eventually attempt to weaken their unions, possibly by relocating (or threatening to relocate) production to non-union sites either at home or abroad. Thus, in the long run, it is more likely that competitive pressures will take their toll on wages than on profit mark-ups. An interesting case in point is the United States, where international competitive pressures contributed to the famous 'profit squeeze' in the late 1960s and early 1970s, but more recently have weakened unions and led to declines in real hourly wages.

15   Using the notation of note 13, however, it is easily seen that if $p = (1 + \tau)u$ (or, equivalently, $\tau = p/u - 1$), and if u consists solely of direct labor costs so that p equals value added (that is, there are no raw materials costs to net out), then the profit share is $\pi = \tau u/p = \tau u/(1 + \tau)u = \tau/(1 + \tau)$.

16   This model was originally developed by Meade (1952). For contemporary textbook expositions see Caves *et al.* (1996: 380–3) and Dornbusch (1980: 43–56, 183–6, 199–202).

17   The relationship between relative wages and international competitiveness has been modeled before, for example, by Dornbusch (1980: 70–7, 143–60). However, these treatments have not focused on the issue of the international distribution of profits that was emphasized by Kalecki.

18   An interest rate term could also be added to (5.10), but is suppressed here on the assumption that interest rates are held constant by central bank monetary policy.

19   Marglin and Bhaduri (1990) argue (using the notation of this chapter) that the b_2 coefficient in (5.10) could be negative. Since (ignoring taxes for simplicity) $R = \pi Y$, they argue that the function (5.10) double-counts the effects of output on investment. Holding π constant rather than R, $\partial I/\partial Y = b_1\pi + b_2$, and it is not necessary to assume $b_2 > 0$ in order for $\partial I/\partial Y > 0$. The restriction that $b_2 > 0$ assumes what Marglin and Bhaduri call a 'strong accelerator effect,' that is, that firms would desire to invest more when output rises *even if their profit share falls at the same time* (as would be required to hold R constant). While this is an important issue, the sign of b_2 makes little difference for most of the results in this chapter.

20   Note that domestic and foreign goods are implicitly assumed to be imperfect

substitutes, so that ρ is not constrained to equal 1, that is, purchasing power parity does not hold.

21 In fact, the stronger assumption that sum of the first three terms in each of these denominators is positive is required for some of the comparative static results discussed below (see note 23).

22 This condition is that $\varepsilon + \varepsilon^* > 1$, where ε and ε^* are the elasticities of home and foreign demand for imports, respectively, that is, $\varepsilon = -\rho\mu'(\rho)/M$ and $\varepsilon^* = \rho\mu^{*\prime}(\rho)/M^*$. This is the condition for $\partial(X - \rho M)/\partial\rho > 0$, that is, a rise in the real exchange rate to improve the home trade balance (and worsen the foreign trade balance), starting from an initial equilibrium with $X - \rho M = 0$.

23 A sufficient condition for a rise in ρ to raise R and lower R^* is that (in addition to the Marshall–Lerner condition holding) $s(\pi) - b_1(1 - t_r)\pi - b_2 > 0$ and $s^*(\pi^*) - b_1^*(1 - t_r^*)\pi^* - b_2^* > 0$, that is, the sums of the first three terms in the denominators of (5.18) and (5.19) are each positive.

24 An older term for the same idea is 'underconsumptionism.' This term is often associated with certain nineteenth-century doctrines, which asserted the inevitable collapse of the capitalist economy due to the inability of workers to consume their entire product. Such doctrines obviously ignored the role of investment demand, as well as government deficits and external trade surpluses. Kalecki, of course, did not make such a logical error.

25 See note 19 above.

26 See Rowthorn (1977) and Dutt (1990: 68–86) for more general 'conflicting claims' models of income distribution with positive equilibrium inflation. It should be noted that our approach of modeling price adjustments explicitly but taking nominal wages and productivity as given is consistent with Kalecki's original approach.

27 A version of the model with a flexible exchange rate would be a useful extension of the model.

28 Note that, if the real exchange rate is fixed at unity ($ep^*/p = 1$), then $ln(1) = 0$, and the second term drops out; in this case the equilibrium wage share must equal the firms' target ($\bar{\omega} = \omega^*$) when $\hat{p} = 0$. In this respect, the present model gives firms complete power over workers in the 'class struggle,' *except* for the effects of international competition which allow workers to affect relative shares as will be seen shortly. This parallels the argument in Kalecki ([1971] 1991: 96–103), as summarized in section 2.3 above, in which he argued that increasing money wages has no effect on relative shares *except* for competitive problems, either domestic or foreign.

29 It is easily verified that this model is stable since $\hat{\omega} = -\hat{p}$, and therefore $\partial\hat{\omega}/\partial\omega = -\partial\hat{p}/\partial\omega < 0$.

30 The steady state in this model is not intended to be a long-run equilibrium in which all markets clear with full employment. The steady state of this model is merely a situation of balance in the distributional conflict, with zero inflation and a constant real exchange rate.

31 Recall that, if the firms set a higher target mark-up rate τ^f, this will be equivalent to a *lower* target wage share ω^f.

32 This subsection draws heavily on Blecker (1989a), but recasts the analysis in a simpler framework. See also Bhaduri and Marglin (1990), Sarantis (1990–1), and You (1991) for other open-economy models along these lines.

33 In the simplified case of a closed economy with no workers' savings ($c_w = 1$) and assuming $b_2 > 0$, positivity of the denominator would imply $c_w - c_r - b_1 > 0$, making the model necessarily stagnationist. This is essentially what was assumed by Taylor (1983, 1985) and Dutt (1984, 1987). However, it is clear that this is a special case. Marglin and Bhaduri (1990) argue that $b_2 < 0$ is also possible (see note 19 above), in which case a positive denominator does not rule out $c_w - c_r - b_1$

< 0 even in a closed economy with no workers' saving.

34 Note that $(1 - \bar{\pi} - z\bar{\pi}_Z) = (\bar{\omega} + z\bar{\pi}_Z)$, the sign of which depends on the magnitude of the elasticity $\partial \, ln \, \bar{\omega}/\partial \, ln \, z = (z/\bar{\omega})\bar{\omega}_Z = -\theta/(\phi + \theta)$. Since $-1 < -\theta/(\phi + \theta) < 0$, it follows that $(1 - \bar{\pi} - z\bar{\pi}_Z) > 0$.

35 Note that this is the same as the difference between national income and total domestic expenditures or 'absorption,' that is, $S - I = Y - (C + I + G)$.

36 See Harberger (1950) and Laursen and Metzler (1950) for the original analysis and Dornbusch (1980: 78–81) for a modern exposition.

37 In their article, Krugman and Taylor (1978) actually make investment exogenous, in which case $b_1 = 0$ and the stagnationist result emerges simply from assuming (in our notation) $c_w > c_r$. Krugman and Taylor's specification of production and trade is also different from ours, as they make a distinction between home goods and export goods. But what is important in their specification of trade are the assumptions that (a) the quantity of exports is exogenously fixed by the capacity of the domestic export industries (assuming a small country for which export demand is perfectly elastic); and (b) imports are in a constant proportion to output of home goods – both of which imply that the trade balance is insensitive to relative prices ($B\rho = 0$ in our notation).

References

Arestis, P. and Milberg, W. (1993–4) 'Degree of Monopoly, Pricing, and Flexible Exchange Rates,' *Journal of Post Keynesian Economics* 16, 2: 167–88.

Asimakopulos, A. (1975) 'A Kaleckian Theory of Income Distribution,' *Canadian Journal of Economics* 8, 3: 313–33.

—— (1988–9) 'Kalecki and Robinson: an 'Outsider's' Influence,' *Journal of Post Keynesian Economics* 11, 2: 261–78.

Baran, P. A. and Sweezy, P. M. (1966) *Monopoly Capital*, New York: Monthly Review Press.

Bhaduri, A. (1986) *Macroeconomics: The Dynamics of Commodity Production*, Armonk, NY: M.E. Sharpe.

—— and Marglin, S.A. (1990) 'Unemployment and the Real Wage: the Economic Basis for Contesting Political Ideologies,' *Cambridge Journal of Economics* 14, 4: 375–93.

Blecker, R.A. (1989a) 'International Competition, Income Distribution and Economic Growth,' *Cambridge Journal of Economics* 13, 3: 395–412.

—— (1989b) 'Markup Pricing, Import Competition, and the Decline of the American Steel Industry,' *Journal of Post Keynesian Economics* 12, 1: 70–87.

Boddy, R. and Crotty, J. (1975) 'Class Conflict and Macro Policy: the Political Business Cycle,' *Review of Radical Political Economics* 7, 1: 1–17.

Bowles, S. and Boyer, R. (1995) 'Wages, Aggregate Demand, and Employment in an Open Economy: an Empirical Investigation,' in G. Epstein and H. Gintis (eds), *Macroeconomic Policy After the Conservative Era*, New York: Cambridge University Press.

Brewer, A. (1980) *Marxist Theories of Imperialism: A Critical Survey*, London: Routledge & Kegan Paul.

Carlton, D.W. and Perloff, J.M. (1994) *Modern Industrial Organization*, 2nd edn, New York: HarperCollins.

Caves, R.E., Frankel, J.A. and Jones, R.W. (1996) *World Trade and Payments: An Introduction*, 7th edn, New York: HarperCollins.

Chenery, H. and Bruno, M. (1962) 'Development Alternatives in an Open Economy: the Case of Israel,' *Economic Journal* 72: 79–103.

Cowling, K. (1982) *Monopoly Capitalism*, London: Macmillan.

Davidson, P. (1982) *International Money and the Real World*, London: Macmillan.

—— (1994) *Post Keynesian Macroeconomic Theory*, Aldershot: Edward Elgar.

Díaz-Alejandro, C.F. (1963) 'A Note on the Impact of Devaluation and the Redistributive Effect,' *Journal of Political Economy* 71: 577–80.

Dixit, A. and Stiglitz, J.E. (1977) 'Monopolistic Competition and Optimum Product Diversity,' *American Economic Review* 67, 3: 297–308.

Dornbusch, R. (1980) *Open Economy Macroeconomics*, New York: Basic Books.

Dutt, A.K. (1984) 'Stagnation, Income Distribution, and Monopoly Power,' *Cambridge Journal of Economics* 8, 1: 25–40.

—— (1987) 'Alternative Closures Again: a Comment on "Growth, Distribution and Inflation," ' *Cambridge Journal of Economics* 11, 1: 75–82.

—— (1988) 'Monopoly Power and Uneven Development: Baran Revisited,' *Journal of Development Studies* 24, 2: 161–76.

—— (1990) *Growth, Distribution, and Uneven Development*, New York: Cambridge University Press.

Eichner, A.S. and Kregel, J.A. (1975) 'An Essay on Post-Keynesian Theory: A New Paradigm in Economics,' *Journal of Economic Literature* 13, 4: 1293–1314.

Fazzari, S.M. and Mott, T.L. (1986-87) 'The Investment Theories of Kalecki and Keynes: an Empirical Study of Firm Data, 1970–1982,' *Journal of Post Keynesian Economics* 9, 2: 171–87.

——, Hubbard, R.G. and Petersen, B.C. (1988) 'Financing Constraints and Corporate Investment,' *Brookings Papers on Economic Activity*, 1: 141–95.

FitzGerald, E.V.K. (1993) *The Macroeconomics of Development Finance: A Kaleckian Analysis of the Semi-industrialized Economy*, New York: St. Martin's Press.

Glyn, A. and Sutcliffe, B. (1972) *British Capitalism, Workers and the Profits Squeeze*, London: Penguin.

Gordon, D.M. (1995) 'Growth, Distribution, and the Rules of the Game: Social Structuralist Macro Foundations for a Democratic Economic Policy,' in G. Epstein and H. Gintis (eds), *Macroeconomic Policy After the Conservative Era*, New York: Cambridge University Press.

—— (1997) 'Must We Save Our Way Out of Stagnation? The Investment/Savings Relation Revisited,' in R. Pollin (ed.), *The Macroeconomics of Finance, Saving, and Investment*, Ann Arbor: University of Michigan Press.

Grossman, G.M. (ed.) (1992) *Imperfect Competition and International Trade*, Cambridge, MA: MIT Press.

Harberger, A.M. (1950) 'Currency Depreciation, Income and the Balance of Trade,' *Journal of Political Economy* 58, 1: 47–60.

Harris, D.J. (1974) 'The Price Policy of Firms, the Level of Employment and Distribution of Income in the Short Run,' *Australian Economic Papers* 13, 22: 144–51.

—— (1978) *Capital Accumulation and Income Distribution*, Stanford, CA: Stanford University Press.

Kaldor, N. (1956) 'Alternative Theories of Distribution,' *Review of Economic Studies* 23, 2: 83–100.

Kalecki, M. (1990) *Collected Works of Michal Kalecki*, vol. I, *Capitalism: Business*

Cycles and Full Employment, ed. J. Osiatynski, trans. C.A. Kisiel, Oxford: Oxford University Press.

—— (1991) *Collected Works of Michal Kalecki*, vol. II, *Capitalism: Economic Dynamics*, ed. J. Osiatynski, trans. C.A. Kisiel, Oxford: Oxford University Press.

—— (1993) *Collected Works of Michal Kalecki*, vol. V, *Developing Economies*, ed. J. Osiatynski, trans. C.A. Kisiel, Oxford: Oxford University Press.

Karier, T. (1988) 'New Evidence on the Effects of Unions and Imports on Monopoly Power,' *Journal of Post Keynesian Economics* 10, 3: 414–27.

Keynes, J.M. (1936) *The General Theory of Money, Income and Employment*, London: Macmillan.

Kreissler, P. (1988) 'Kalecki's Pricing Theory Revisited,' *Journal of Post Keynesian Economics* 11, 1: 108–30.

Krugman, P.R. (1979) 'Increasing Returns, Monopolistic Competition, and International Trade,' *Journal of International Economics* 9, 4: 469–79.

—— (ed.) (1987) *Strategic Trade Policy and the New International Economics*, Cambridge, MA: MIT Press.

—— and Taylor, L. (1978) 'Contractionary Effects of Devaluation,' *Journal of International Economics* 8: 445–56.

Laursen, S. and Metzler, L.A. (1950) 'Flexible Exchange Rates and the Theory of Employment,' *Review of Economics and Statistics* 32: 281–99.

Marglin, S.A. and Bhaduri, A. (1990) 'Profit Squeeze and Keynesian Theory,' in S.A. Marglin and J.B. Schor (eds), *The Golden Age of Capitalism*, Oxford: Oxford University Press.

McKinnon, R.I. (1964) 'Foreign Exchange Constraints in Economic Development and Efficient Aid Allocation,' *Economic Journal* 74: 388–409.

Meade, J. (1952) *The Theory of International Economic Policy*, vol. I, *The Balance of Payments*, London: Oxford University Press.

Riach, P. (1971) 'Kalecki's "Degree of Monopoly" Reconsidered,' *Australian Economic Papers* 10, 16: 50–60.

Robinson, J. (1978) *Contributions to Modern Economics*, New York: Academic Press.

—— (1980) *Collected Economic Papers*, vol. IV, Cambridge, MA: MIT Press.

Rowthorn, R.E. (1977) 'Conflict, Inflation and Money,' *Cambridge Journal of Economics* 1, 3: 215–39.

—— (1982) 'Demand, Real Wages and Economic Growth,' *Studi Economici*, 18: 3-53.

Sarantis, N. (1990–1) 'Distribution and Terms of Trade Dynamics, Inflation, and Growth,' *Journal of Post Keynesian Economics* 13, 2: 175–98.

Sawyer, M. (1985) *The Economics of Michal Kalecki*, Armonk, NY: M.E. Sharpe.

Stanford, J. (1996) 'Openness and Equity: Regulating Labor Market Outcomes in a Globalized Economy,' paper presented at Economic Policy Institute Conference, Washington, DC.

Steindl, J. (1952) *Maturity and Stagnation in American Capitalism*, Oxford: Blackwell; reprinted New York: Monthly Review Press, 1976.

Stiglitz, J.E. and Weiss, A. (1981) 'Credit Rationing in Markets with Imperfect Information,' *American Economic Review* 71, 3: 393–410.

Taylor, L. (1979) *Macro Models for Developing Countries*, New York: McGraw-Hill.

—— (1983) *Structuralist Macroeconomics*, New York: Basic Books.

—— (1985) 'A Stagnationist Model of Economic Growth,' *Cambridge Journal of Economics* 9, 4: 383–403.

—— (1991) *Income Distribution, Inflation, and Growth*, Cambridge, MA: MIT Press.

Weintraub, S. (1978) *Keynes, Keynesians, and Monetarists*, Philadelphia: University of Pennsylvania Press.

You, J. (1991) 'Capital–labor Relations and Economic Development,' unpublished PhD dissertation, Harvard University.

Part III

International money and exchange rates

6 International liquidity preference and endogenous credit

Sheila C. Dow

Introduction

The purpose of this chapter is to express Post Keynesian international finance theory in terms of the theories of liquidity preference and endogenous credit creation, theories which have been more fully developed in the context of the domestic economy.

Traditionally, the area of international finance has featured more prominently in Post Keynesian work which addresses particular policy issues than in Post Keynesian theory as such. This has mirrored to some degree Keynes's own treatment of international finance as an area for application of theory than for particular theoretical treatment. Thus, two recent accounts of Post Keynesian theory, Arestis (1992) and Lavoie (1992), deal primarily with the closed economy.

The major exception to this generalisation is the work of Paul Davidson. In *International Money and the Real World* (Davidson 1982), he devoted an entire volume to the development of a Post Keynesian theory of international finance and a drawing out of its policy implications, particularly with respect to reform of the international monetary system. An updated synopsis of this work appears in Davidson (1994), where international economics is given prominence in his statement of Post Keynesian macroeconomic theory. Tarshis (1984) too has focused theoretical attention on the international monetary system, again with a view to its reform.

But more recently, increasing attention has been paid to international finance, reflecting the increasing incidence of issues to be addressed. The tremendous increase in the size and instability of international financial markets since the 1970s, the emergence of the debt crisis, the search for appropriate exchange rate regimes, and the institutional arrangements for the IMF and European Monetary Union have all attracted the attention of Post Keynesian economists.

In the following sections, these various themes which have been developed to address particular policy issues are brought together in a theory of international finance which draws explicitly on the theory of liquidity preference and the theory of endogenous credit creation. This theoretical perspective is laid out in the next section, and applied to questions of analysis and governance of the international financial system in the following section.

International liquidity preference and international credit creation

This section is devoted to setting out a Post Keynesian theory of international finance which uses developments in Post Keynesian monetary theory (see further Cottrell 1994 and Hewitson 1995). These developments have included a bringing together of liquidity preference theory and endogenous credit theory which, for a time, were treated as alternative approaches to Post Keynesian monetary theory. This international version of Post Keynesian monetary theory provides a coherent framework within which to address a range of policy issues.

Liquidity preference is the demand for a perfectly tradable asset with stable value. The theory of liquidity preference underpins Davidson's (1982) analysis of international money. This theory has conventionally been presented as explaining the preferred disposition of a stock of assets among different liquidities. Following Keynes (1936: ch. 17), the motives for demanding liquidity can be classified as:

- *the transactions motive*: this is the demand for money to be used in payment for goods, services and assets. The amount demanded is a stable positive function of transactions, for which income is generally regarded as an adequate proxy;
- *the speculative motive*: this is the demand for money to be held by speculators as an alternative to other assets when it is expected that holding other assets would bring about capital loss. (It is not a demand for money with which to speculate, which would come under transactions demand.) The amount demanded is determined by the strength of expectations as to capital gain or loss on alternative assets;
- *the precautionary motive*: this is the demand for money to be held in case of unexpected requirements. While this has traditionally been treated as a relatively passive element of liquidity preference, represented as a stable positive function of income, attention has increasingly been focused on precautionary demand as the key outlet for instability. Thus, for example, Runde (1994) argues that, while speculative demand reflects decision-making as if there were certainty about expectations of capital gain, precautionary demand reflects uncertainty; the less confidence there is in predictions, the greater the precautionary demand for liquidity.

Within a domestic economy, the national currency is generally the asset which is most liquid and most stable in value. But within the international economy, there is a range of moneys. As long as each has a stable value in relation to the others, then the most liquid of these is generally employed as a means of payment and unit of account; this would normally be the national currency of the economy concerned. But, where the domestic value of the national currency is falling significantly relative to foreign currencies, because of domestic inflation or a depreciating exchange rate, other currencies may better satisfy liquidity preference. This is more likely to be the case the more free is capital mobility, that is, the more liquid is foreign currency. It is a matter of relativities; in cases of hyperinflation, capital controls may not be sufficient to prevent demonetisation and the substitution of foreign currency for domestic currency. It is also a matter of past experience and conventions; where the US dollar has in the past been generally accepted in payment in a non-US economy (whether legally or not), the more easily will the dollar be substituted for domestic currency at signs of that currency weakening.

The relevance of liquidity preference understood in these traditional terms is thus twofold. First, changing domestic and/or foreign conditions may alter what satisfies liquidity preference, and thus alter relative currency demands. Second, changing degrees of liquidity preference at home or abroad may alter relative currency demand depending on which currency satisfies liquidity preference (see Dow 1986-7).

In the first case, suppose that, for a given degree of liquidity preference, there is a loss of confidence in the stability of the value of the domestic currency relative to other currencies, so that foreign currencies better satisfy that liquidity preference. Then capital outflows will put downward pressure on the value of the domestic currency in terms of foreign currencies. If the monetary authorities are committed to maintaining a stable exchange rate, they will have to buy up domestic currency with foreign exchange reserves and put upward pressure on interest rates in order to stem the capital outflows. If the expectation of falling value of the domestic currency is such that the authorities cannot attract sufficient capital inflows, then the limitations on foreign exchange reserves will be such as to cause a crisis, requiring a devaluation. If the exchange rate is floating, the decline in its value may create an unstable situation if it further reduces the capacity of the domestic currency to satisfy liquidity preference; again the authorities may put upward pressure on interest rates to attempt to stem the capital outflow.

In the second case, suppose there is a rise in liquidity preference in a particular economy. Other things being equal, domestic interest rates will rise. If foreign currency is a repository for liquidity preference, there will also be a tendency for capital outflow, requiring that domestic interest rates rise even further than would otherwise be the case in order to make holders of domestic assets satisfied with holding them. At the same time, if the rise on liquidity preference is caused by some deterioration in the domestic economy, foreign investors might be less willing to hold the economy's assets, requiring an even larger rise in interest rates. If the monetary authorities are committed to maintaining a stable value for the exchange rate, then they must hold the exchange value up by selling foreign exchange reserves and by keeping interest rates high in order to stem capital outflows. If the exchange rate is floating, then its value will be free to fall. There is a danger that this fall might change the relative degrees to which domestic and foreign currencies satisfy liquidity preference, so that the two international elements to liquidity preference outlined here may compound each other. In either case, the openness of the monetary system to a range of moneys exacerbates the domestic effects of liquidity preference. But much depends on the cause of the rise in liquidity preference; if it accompanies growth in the domestic economy, capital inflows may be attracted which satisfy the need for greater liquidity.

This discussion has referred to liquidity preference within the domestic economy, regardless of international transactions. But liquidity preference may also be considered specifically with respect to international transactions, that is, a demand for liquidity which would not be present in a closed economy. There is a *transactions demand* for a vehicle for international payments, which bears a stable relationship with the value of world trade. There is also a transactions demand with respect to capital flows, which can be represented as a stable function of the value of these flows. The more unstable are international financial markets, the more the incentive for international capital flows, and therefore the greater the transactions demand for an international means of payment.

The international equivalent of *speculative demand* for money is more complex than domestic speculative demand, since exchange loss from holding one currency is mirrored by exchange gain from holding another. Speculative demand should capture the holding of a stable (as opposed to appreciating) liquid asset in order to avoid exchange or capital loss. This demand may be identified in demand for stable, as opposed to appreciating, currencies, or for gold as an alternative to national currencies. It may also be identified in demand for overnight deposits in foreign currency, to allow for day-to-day exchange speculation, rather than longer-term foreign assets. In the domestic money market, the choice with respect to speculative demand is to hold money or longer-term assets with the prospect of capital gain; a rise in speculative demand puts upward pressure on interest rates. In the international context, the choice is to hold short-term assets in one stable currency (or, often, gold), and in short-term assets rather than longer-term assets. The latter serves to put upward pressure on interest rates in international markets.

The more unstable are exchange rates, the greater the prospect for gains to be made by currency substitution, and thus the greater the demand for liquid balances in one currency or another in order to take advantage of day-to-day changes in the foreign exchange market. Strictly speaking, this demand should be regarded as a subcategory of transactions demand (for speculative transactions). Further, the greater the uncertainty about exchange rates, the greater the demand for liquid international assets in the absence of firmer expectations. This demand is more properly regarded as precautionary demand.

In addition to private sector liquidity preference, there is a need for liquidity for monetary authorities to meet clearing imbalances between themselves; this might be seen as a form of *precautionary demand*, to meet unforeseen imbalances. The level of demand depends on the propensity for imbalance, which depends partly on the degree of economic divergence and the degree to which capital flows allow adequate time for economies to adjust to imbalance. But the incidence of imbalance also reflects the strength of short-term capital flows, that is, on the strength and instability of speculative activity in foreign exchange markets. In addition, the private sector may also have a precautionary demand for international money if there is a general loss of confidence in international assets. This could be a powerful force, the effects being to reduce availability of medium and long-term lending across currencies and rising interest rates. This would also feed back on the precautionary demand by monetary authorities, in that it would be more difficult to fund imbalances with capital flows; official precautionary demand would accordingly increase.

It is of considerable significance whether or not there is an international money other than a national currency, that is, whether or not an increase in demand for international money is also an increase in demand for a national currency. In the Bretton Woods system, the dollar was regarded as providing international liquidity, being easily traded and of stable value. The dollar thus satisfied the need for an international means of payment. Transactions demand for it grew with the growth in world trade and capital flows; the supply of international money in the form of gold or, later, Special Drawing Rights, could not keep pace. But this in itself created a structural imbalance in the US balance of payments, requiring massive capital inflows corresponding to the increasing need for international liquidity; the intrinsic economic conditions in the US itself would rather have warranted capital outflows. The dollar standard broke down in 1971 when the consequence of the dollar's role in the international monetary system allowed the US to run a massive trade deficit which undermined the expected stability of the value of the dollar, that is, its capacity to be acceptable as an international money.

Since then, there has been a tremendous increase also in the demand for international money. The oil crisis, and attempts to deal with its consequences by means of monetarist policies, led to widespread structural imbalances which could not quickly be addressed by conventional adjustment policies. Liquidity was required to finance these imbalances; fortunately, that liquidity was made available by banks recycling deposits by surplus countries. The ensuing instability of international financial markets (including the market in foreign exchange) also increased demand for precautionary balances in order to take quick advantage of expected shifts in exchange rates. Not only did this put upward pressure on interest rates, but it also provided the ready fuel for exchange speculation, adding to the underlying structural imbalance. This increasing demand for international liquidity was still predominantly satisfied by the national currencies perceived to have most stable value and most general international acceptance.

But the 1970s and 1980s were also characterised by the increasing provision of liquidity through the international financial system – the banks – rather than the international monetary system – the IMF and national monetary authorities. Discussion of the international monetary system had focused on the provision of international 'outside money' (balances with the IMF in the drawing and Special Drawing Right accounts), as if international bank money were a stable multiple. This mirrored (and, some argue, influenced) the increasing tendency domestically to focus on bank reserves with the domestic central bank as a means of controlling monetary aggregates. In contrast, the theory of endogenous money was being put forward by Post Keynesians (notably Kaldor 1982 and Moore 1988) to shift attention to bank credit as the causal force, bank reserves being at the end of the causal chain.

The role of the banks in providing credit was the starting-point of Tarshis's (1984) analysis of the international monetary system. What this implies is that the expression of liquidity preference was not restricted to the disposition of a given stock of assets, but in addition influenced the total availability of liquidity. Certainly there was a recycling of payments imbalances within the Eurodollar market. But this coincided with a general expansion in the provision of credit by the banking system driven by competitive forces within the banking system (see Chick 1986). Domestically, banking systems were exercising increasing control over credit expansion, with reserves accommodating this expansion.

The bulk of international banking activity has been channelled through the Eurodollar market, which has expanded at a dramatic pace independent of domestic reserve requirements. It has been argued that, as a wholesale market, the Eurodollar market acted as a pure intermediary rather than a creator of credit (see, for example, Niehans and Hewson 1976). In other words, since its liabilities are not a means of payment, the Eurobanks did not engage in significant maturity transformation; they borrowed and lent medium term. But the Eurodollar market has since shown itself to be capable of changing the degree of maturity transformation as conditions have changed. In particular, when the optimistic expectations of the 1970s proved unjustified and banks faced the possibility of default on sovereign debt, the term of future borrowing shortened. Strange (1986) demonstrates the increasing preference of the banks to keep their assets liquid as the international financial system became increasingly turbulent.

Strange's argument reflects something which was evident in Keynes's own work (see Dow 1997) and which is now increasingly expressed in Post Keynesian monetary theory (see Cottrell 1994 and Hewitson 1995), that the theory of liquidity preference has more general application than households' preferences with respect to a given stock of assets. In particular, it applies also to the banking system itself in its determination of the volume and distribution of credit creation (see Dow and Dow 1989 and Dow 1993: ch. 11). Thus the money supply is best understood as the balance sheet counterpart of the supply of credit, which can be understood in terms of liquidity preference in the credit market. Here the focus is on the precautionary element of liquidity preference.

When firms are confident in their expectations about returns to investment projects, their preference for precautionary balances is low and their willingness to commit themselves to an investment project and a debt contract is high; demand for credit is high. The same applies to investment in financial assets financed by borrowing. When banks share that confidence, their perceived lender's risk is low, and their willingness to extend credit is high. Credit expands when the preference for precautionary liquid balances is low. Correspondingly, when confidence is low and the demand for precautionary balances is high, banks are less willing to expand credit and thus the provision of liquidity is low. Banks differ from other sectors, however, in that their liquidity preference would take the form of holding imperfectly liquid assets (such as interbank loans) rather than perfectly liquid assets.

An equivalent argument can be developed with respect to economies for which the state of expectations is different (see Chick and Dow 1988). Thus, economies for which expectations of economic growth (or at least growth in the value of assets) are held with confidence will express low liquidity preference, resulting in easy credit conditions. Economies for which expectations are not held with confidence will experience tight credit conditions. This phenomenon is illustrated by the balance sheet evidence in the Eurodollar market which shows low-income developing countries maintaining more liquid positions than higher-income developing countries, that is, higher deposits relative to borrowing. This trend became more marked in the 1990s as banks increased their liquidity preference (see Dow 1995). Clearly, this outcome, depending as it does on the confidence with which expectations are held, is to a large extent a product of knowledge, or lack of knowledge. Thus, optimistic expectations about the creditworthiness of developing country borrowers were held with confidence by the banks in the 1970s on the basis of very limited knowledge. But the flimsiness of the knowledge base meant that, once attention was drawn to the risk of default when Mexico announced its intention to default in 1982, the reversal in expectations was very dramatic.

The banks, and firms, have reacted to the confounding of expectations in the 1980s by increasing their liquidity preference, preferring shorter-term commitments. The resulting trend towards securitisation has added to the speculative opportunities offered by exchange instability and the more general instability in international financial markets. Derivatives, developed initially to provide protection from the ensuing risks facing traders, were soon seized on as offering even more opportunity for speculation. By 1991 the notional value of the derivatives market was $8 trillion, or 140 per cent of US GDP (see Kelly 1995: 215).

The current situation can thus be characterised as one of internationally high liquidity preference which is limiting the provision of liquidity to borrowers perceived to pose high risks, but which is fuelling activity in speculative markets where the risks are potentially much higher, but where banks express more confidence in securing a high return. International liquidity is provided by those currencies perceived to have stable value; but that stability is vulnerable to the expectations of international financial markets. In 1992 these markets demonstrated their capacity to pick off currencies at will, breaking up the European Exchange Rate Mechanism and setting back attempts to promote exchange stability in Europe in the run-up to European Monetary Union. Further, the effect of this increase in liquidity preference, and the consequential rise in speculative activity, has been to raise interest rates in international financial markets, with knock-on effects for domestic markets.

Finally, once the focus is put on credit as well as money, the scope for differences in domestic banking systems assumes importance, belying the presumed homogeneity of global monetarism. When considering the impact on domestic economies of higher interest rates and the decisions of international banks with respect to credit availability, attention must be paid to the nature of the domestic banking system. Monetarist theory suggests that any inflow of foreign exchange is homogeneous, adding to the reserves of the domestic banking system, and being multiplied in an expansion of domestic credit. Further, gross substitutability between assets, domestic and foreign, ensures that domestic interest rates will respond to international interest rates. But national banking systems differ in a variety of ways. First, a domestic concern which borrows from an international bank may retain its balances outside the domestic banking system, so the capital inflow is purely notional. Second, the effect of a capital inflow on domestic bank reserves may be sterilised by the domestic monetary authority. Quite apart from the stage of banking development, there are marked differences in formal regulation and in informal convention which influence the relationship between international financial developments and the domestic banking system (see Chick and Dow 1996). Third, if there is an addition to domestic bank reserves there may be no direct effect on domestic credit provision. If confidence in domestic assets is low, the banks may prefer not to be lent to, or to lend outside the domestic economy, cancelling out the capital inflow. Further, banking systems are less constrained by reserves the later the stage of development (see Chick 1986). Highly developed banking systems determine credit creation first and accommodate it with reserves second. While this occurs as soon as there is a lender-of-last-resort, the latitude enjoyed by the banks, and the compulsion to exploit that latitude, increases with banking development. Finally, when banks at different stages of development compete, banks at an earlier stage of development are at a disadvantage; because their redeposit ratio is less assured, their willingness to expand their loan portfolios is accordingly reduced. The effect of international liquidity preference on interest rates may then be exaggerated in domestic banks struggling to compete for deposits with international banks.

In the next section we turn our attention to the various issues addressed in the Post Keynesian literature on international finance, in terms of the design of the international monetary system, given developments in the international financial system. We consider this literature in the light of the theoretical perspective set out in this section.

The international monetary system

The issues facing the international monetary system can be summarised as follows:

- *The need for an international money whose value is independent of the internal policies of any national government, that is, the need for a single asset with assured monetary attributes, whose use does not in itself create adjustment problems for any one economy.* As long as there is a range of moneys, that is, there is a high elasticity of substitution between different moneys, then no one form of money satisfies the necessary requirements of money. Further, if these moneys are national currencies, substitution between them creates both balance of payments problems and opportunities for potentially destabilising speculation, which further reduces the money-like qualities of some of the currencies. Since an asset must inspire confidence in its value, the preferred Post Keynesian option is to design an international money, for which a global agency acts as central bank; that money's attributes must be such as to make it the preferred money, relative to national currencies.
- *The need for greater symmetry in the pressures to adjust to balance of payments deficits and surpluses; the current relative pressure to adjust to deficits lends a deflationary bias to the world economy.* The Post Keynesian focus on distribution issues highlights the distributional consequences of relative power in international financial markets. Deficit countries with a low asset base find it hard to attract international credit to finance the deficit. (This deficit in turn may be the outcome of an unfavourable distribution of power in commodity markets on which many low-income countries depend for export income.) Yet their forced adjustment to the deficit automatically corrects the offsetting surpluses. Further, Post Keynesian macroeconomics does not presume a norm of full employment. Therefore, an undue pressure to adjust by deflating deficit economies has real deflationary consequences for the world economy. The issue of the distribution of the burden of adjustment is thus compounded by the issue of increasing difficulties in maintaining global output and employment.
- *The need to curb the power of international financial markets with respect to the creation and distribution of credit.* The potential instability arising from national currencies acting as international money and the distribution of the burden of adjustment as determined by international credit availability, both rest on the power of international financial markets to switch currencies and to determine the volume and distribution of credit. Because of the uncertainties involved in predicting foreign exchange rates

and in conducting sovereign risk assessment, the markets for foreign exchange and for international credit are speculative and potentially highly unstable, being subject to discrete shifts in expectations; the consequences of these shifts can be real redistributions and real reductions in output and employment. As in the domestic economy, the Post Keynesian approach to financial markets is to consider mechanisms for curbing their power, in order to create a more stable financial backdrop for real activity.

We now consider in turn the various Post Keynesians who have addressed these issues, starting with Davidson. In the absence of an international money for general use, an issue of particular concern is exchange rate arrangements. The exchange instability of the post-Bretton Woods period has cast doubt on the capacity of foreign exchange markets to drive exchange rates to some equilibrium value. Davidson distinguishes between unionised monetary systems (UMS) and non-unionised monetary systems (NUMS), referring to whether or not there is a single currency (or currencies are locked together). In other words, the appropriate distinction is not between national economies and the international economy, but rather between one or more moneys. The significance is that, where there is scope for variation in exchange rates between currencies, there is an additional layer of uncertainty to contend with. Where there is uncertainty, there is a need for liquidity, which raises the issue of the adequacy of the provision of international liquidity. While there is an increased demand for foreign exchange to facilitate speculative transactions, Davidson is referring to the increased demand for precautionary balances to protect traders from a lack of certainty with respect to international values.

Because Davidson identifies international financial problems to a considerable extent with exchange rate variability, his concern is to advocate an increase in exchange rate stability. This argument is reinforced by the argument that floating exchange rates encourage the adoption of an export-led growth strategy. Successful export-led growth causes exchange rate appreciation, which puts pressure on labour to keep labour costs down in order to maintain competitiveness. In aggregate, this strategy cannot succeed; one country's exports success is another's trade balance deterioration. The net result is downward pressure on wages and on domestic demand. A fixed exchange rate system would avoid this outcome.

In terms of the international monetary system as such, Davidson offers a reform plan which owes much to Keynes's plan for an international clearing union. An International Clearing Agency (ICA) would record net payments between countries in terms of an International Money Clearing Unit (IMCU), which would be a money only for central banks (and thus not the object of speculative transactions by the market), the supply of which was in the hands of the ICA. Records of net payments would provide the basis for a trigger mechanism for a symmetrical system of balance of payments adjustment. Like Keynes, Davidson identifies the prevalent asymmetrical pressure on deficit countries to adjust (due to lack of liquidity) as lending a serious deflationary bias to the international economy; a more symmetrical adjustment process would remove that bias. The norm in Davidson's reformed system would be exchange rate stability through agreed exchange rates expressed in terms of the IMCU. But there would be provision for exchange rate adjustment if efficiency wages at current exchange rates were out of line.

While exchange rate stability involving some commitment to announced parities can be regarded as a feature of all Post Keynesian ideas for a reformed system, there is some difference of opinion as to the appropriate exchange rate regime within a non-reformed system. Smithin (1994: ch. 7) argues that any country that chooses to pursue Keynesian demand-management policies (expansionary fiscal policy and low interest rates) in an unreformed international monetary system needs the protection of floating exchange rates. Further, he argues that there is a strong centralising tendency within monetary systems in general. The need for money which commands confidence encourages the centralisation of power in financial centres. Smithin argues that fixed exchange rate regimes encourage such centralisation of power within the international monetary system. In so far as power may be centralised in central banks with monetarist leanings, the scope for achieving low, stable interest rates is thereby limited. Again, floating exchange rates would provide some protection. This argument is reinforced by reference to differences between domestic banking systems. As long as there are differences of regulation, conventions and behaviour between national banking systems, there will be some segmentation in the global banking market. Separate currencies and currencies separated by value (that is, floating) further add to that segmentation, allowing a counter to the tendency for centralisation in banking. Put another way, foreign exchange is less money-like in a floating exchange rate system. In Davidson's ideal reform plan, the more assets that are money-like, the better. But in Smithin's less-than-ideal world, floating exchange rates are offered as a second-best solution.

However, in a more recent account of developments in the international financial system, Smithin (1996) moves further to a more general questioning of the preferability of ending floating. He argues that foreign exchange instability since the 1970s may be the consequence of inappropriate (that is, non-Keynesian) macroeconomic policy than the main cause of macro policy problems. He is therefore much more sanguine than Davidson about the workability of generalised floating as long as governments follow Keynesian policies and coordinate with each other.

But, whatever its cause, the exchange instability which has characterised generalised floating is still widely held to have been a major contributor to a more general instability in international financial markets. Strange (1986, 1994) analyses the growth of this instability, and demonstrates the reaction of the international banks in seeking to increase the liquidity of their portfolios. This has, however, coincided with increased difficulties for individual economies for whom a floating exchange rate has not been adequate to produce external balance. For oil-importing export-dependent developing economies which had borrowed extensively in the 1970s from international banks, the increasing reluctance of banks to continue lending, together with high and variable interest charges on existing debt and weakening export markets, led to the debt crisis.

Tarshis (1984) analyses the debt crisis as a global crisis, not an issue of bank risk assessment at the micro level (see Palma 1995 for a more recent account). He saw the crisis as having arisen in the vacuum left by the IMF as its power in international financial markets diminished with the abandonment of the par value exchange rate system. Like Davidson, Tarshis referred to Keynes's plan for the international monetary system for indications of what had been lacking in the design of the IMF: symmetrical pressure on surplus and deficit countries to adjust to payments imbalance, adequate provision of liquidity, and powers for the IMF independent of the interests of major economies. In other words, the debt crisis had arisen because of undue pressure on developing countries in deficit, inadequate liquidity provision by the IMF to allow adjustment to proceed, and an over-concern with the banks of major Western economies relative to the adjustment burden being imposed on debtor countries. Tarshis's proposals for dealing with the debt overhang include debt forgiveness, and the provision of liquidity to bail out creditor banks in order to maintain confidence in the banking system. But he argued that this support for banks should include acquisition of public equity in bailed-out banks (so that banks would not benefit unduly) and the commitment of the relevant governments to introduce regulation to limit future capacity for credit creation. Indeed, an international regulatory and supervisory agency should be established to ensure the prudential control of the international banking system. Henry Kaufman has made a similar proposal (see Kelly 1995: 227). The endogenous credit theory applied to a domestic economy has shifted attention from monetary policy as a mechanism for controlling monetary aggregates to bank regulation and supervision as a mechanism to promote financial stability (see Minsky 1982). This perspective is carried over to the international context by Tarshis.

Attempts to restore and enhance the role of the IMF with respect to the international financial system seem at face value to run counter to the tremendous increase in financial market power which weakened the IMF in the 1970s. But the debt crisis made clear to the banks the limits to their knowledge of borrowers' economies and their capacity to make borrowers more credit-worthy. As a result they turned to the IMF for assistance. This assistance took the form of requiring borrowers to submit to the conditions attached to IMF credit in order to be eligible for further bank credit. These conditions included structural adjustment programmes, consisting largely of supply-side policies such as financial liberalisation, and monetary controls (supported by tight fiscal policy) to control inflation. The result has been a tremendous cost to debtor countries, whose difficulties in fact had been the result, at least in part, of tight fiscal and monetary policies in creditor countries, as well as of the increasing scale and instability of international financial markets. However, irrespective of the nature of the IMFs policies, the market has demonstrated its need for something akin to a world central bank; indeed, the IMF has in effect been asked to go far beyond the normal activities of a national central bank by intervening in bank-borrower credit relations. A central bank, like the IMF, has superior knowledge in general, superior knowledge of the macro consequences of individual bank decisions in particular, and an established relationship with borrowers and lenders which allows it to take on an intermediation role. If this role were filled along Keynesian policy lines, the IMF could draw in particular on its knowledge of domestic banking systems and their relations with the international financial system.

This is not to say that the IMF currently employs its superior access to knowledge in the best way. The theoretical presupposition of the IMF's structural adjustment programmes is the mainstream one: that saving precedes investment. This contrasts with Keynes, who gave primacy to investment; bank credit can allow investment to precede saving, and other financial instruments can smooth the process of funding investment with saving (see Chick 1983; see also Studart 1995 for a restatement in the context of development finance). The focus then of financial policy with respect to developing economies should be on encouraging financial markets to perform that function effectively. But, as Studart (1995) argues, the IMF emphasis on financial efficiency may impede the funding function. Efficient financial markets, in an increasingly unstable environment, respond by further increasing financial fragility (as evidenced by the behaviour of banks in efficient Western financial markets). Yet the IMF (together with the World Bank) persists in its programme of encouraging financial liberalisation as a means of increasing the provision of saving, despite inadequate evidence that financial liberalisation can play any causal role in the economic development process (see Arestis and Demetriades 1993).

Meanwhile, the increasing fragility of the international financial system itself has been a focus for discussion as to possible control mechanisms. Keynes had advocated some form of control on capital flows even in the 1940s, to allow governments to maintain their exchange rate commitments. If there was adequate reason then for being concerned about the potential danger of capital flows, the rationale must be overwhelming now. The predominant suggestion is Tobin's (1978) tax proposal, whereby a levy would be charged on all foreign exchange transactions, reducing at the margin the return on speculative transactions. As Davidson (forthcoming) argues, however, the tax would have more impact on trade-related transactions, and could not impede the force of speculative flows when foreign exchange gains well in excess of the tax are anticipated. Davidson reiterates the need for a stable international monetary system based on central bank clearing as the appropriate vehicle for eliminating speculation at its root.

An alternative proposal is to route capital flows and trade-related flows through a dual exchange rate system (see Soloman 1989). While it is very difficult to protect such systems from abuse, steps have been taken to classify transactions within foreign exchange markets. Thus, the Bank of England, for example, already distinguishes between foreign exchange risk that arises in the normal course of business and that which is the result of active speculation (see Kelly 1995). Indeed, Kelly argues that this distinction should be applied within derivatives markets. Derivatives trading arose initially in order to provide hedge instruments by which traders could cover their foreign exchange risk. But now markets in a wide range of instruments have developed which redistribute a wider range of risks; the growth of the derivatives market has itself added to the sum total of risk, increasing the fragility of the financial system. Kelly therefore proposes that the right to engage in derivatives speculation be restricted to Special Purpose Vehicles, subject to their achieving high credit ratings. Other market participants would only be allowed to engage on hedging.

Guttmann's (1988) reform proposal, building on Davidson (1982) and Schmitt (1977), returns to the approach of discouraging speculation by means of ensuring a stable international financial environment. But, on the grounds that the international financial system is now dominated by inside money, Guttmann argues that that inside money should be under the direct control of an international authority. Guttmann thus advocates the centralisation of both private and public sector international capital flows, requiring that they all be denominated in Supranational Credit Money (SCM) issued by a New International Monetary Authority (NIMA). National currencies, whose exchange rates with respect to SCM would be fixed, could only be used for domestic transactions. This credit money goes beyond Keynes's (and Davidson's) proposal for an international money as outside money to underpin the structure of private sector international credit. While it removes control of the supply of the international money from government (international and national), it recognises the power which international financial markets have over credit creation regardless of the outside money system, and attempts to separate that power from the international provision of assets in any one national currency.

The replacement of national currencies by an international money is the central aim of the design of European Monetary Union. The intermediate aim is to eliminate structural sources of payments imbalance by means of the economic convergence process, in order to proceed to a locking of exchange rates, and the replacement of national currencies with a European currency, the Euro. Supply of the Euro is to be determined by a centralised European central banking system, along monetarist lines. The design of that system of central banking, as being independent of government, itself entails the monetarist separation of the monetary from the real (see Arestis and Bain 1995). The convergence process is being facilitated by a process of financial liberalisation. The system would then have the same deflationary bias, the same inadequate provision of liquidity to allow time to adjust to payments imbalance, and the same tendency for high interest rates and financial fragility as were evident in the global financial system under the IMF of the 1980s and 1990s. Further, as EU membership expands to include new members of close-to-developing country status, the problems will be exacerbated.

Jespersen (1995) argues that, to be effective, a European central bank should be concerned primarily with promoting financial stability. This reflects a Post Keynesian concern with the stability of the financial environment in terms of the cost and availability of credit and returns on alternative assets, rather than the mainstream focus on stability of monetary aggregates. The significance of the structure and behaviour of the banking system for theory and policy has long been stressed by Chick. She has applied these ideas to European monetary union in Chick (1993a), in which she discusses the centralising consequences of opening up the European financial system to free competition, where the national components of that system have very different histories, structures and behaviour. As Chick and Dow (forthcoming and 1996) argue, the shape of the European financial sector cannot be foreseen without paying attention to the differences in financial behaviour, history and conventions particular to each member. Just as Chick (1993b) argues that monetary theory and domestic monetary policy should be contingent on the particular nature of the banking system at issue, so in considering international finance we must consider the tremendous diversity of banking systems which lurks behind an apparently homogeneous international financial system.

Conclusion

Post Keynesian monetary theory focuses on the intrinsic role of money within the economic process. Money assists the economic process by providing a unit of account for contracts specified in terms of a liquid asset with stable value; that money asset may also be held when confidence in the prediction of the value of alternative assets is low. But money is primarily the liability of the private sector banking system, a by-product of its lending decisions which are also influenced by the state of confidence. If there is a shortage of liquidity relative to demand (regardless of planned saving), then economic activity may be discouraged, and output and employment fall. The Post Keynesian prescription is to attempt to keep interest rates low when economies are operating below full capacity. But above all, policy should be addressed to maintaining stable financial conditions so that liquidity preference does not rise in the first place.

This theory and policy prescription carry over into the international context, but with the significant complication that different currencies offer a range of international moneys. If exchange markets are unstable, then preferences as to which currency to hold as international money may change, creating balance of payments problems for the governments concerned. The greater the degree of payments imbalance, the greater the deflationary bias for the world economy, given the greater pressure on deficit economies to adjust than on surplus economies. Further, the greater the degree of instability in international financial markets, the greater the precautionary demand for liquid balances, and the higher will be interest rates, adding to the deflationary bias.

Of course, all economic units have balance of payments problems, but most do not have the benefit of a separate currency either to segment payments or to change relative values. The deflationary bias in payments adjustment is general; but while separate currencies may potentially reduce the bias, the consequences of exchange speculation enforcing more rapid adjustment than would otherwise be the case (and indeed sometimes unwarranted adjustment) may increase deflationary bias.

The key to adjustment, the potential for steadying its pace and for avoiding it when imbalances are temporary lie with the banking system and its willingness to extend credit. The significant distinction then is not so much between deficit and surplus economies as between deficit economies to which the banks are unwilling to extend credit, on the one hand, and deficit economies which the banks will fund and surplus economies, on the other.

Just as at the domestic level the aim is for financial stability and low interest rates, so at the international level design of the international monetary system should address this aim. (The international financial system operating effectively independently of any global system of governance has shown itself incapable of meeting this aim.) What is required, therefore, is: a mechanism for separating international money from any one national economy, that is, a true international money; strict regulation and supervision of international banking to reduce instability of capital flows and exchange instability and to coordinate financing of payments imbalances; a symmetrical system of payments adjustment involving coordination of adjustment policies. In other words, what is required is an international clearing union and an international credit money, with a forum for policy coordination and a strong bank supervisory system. Given the interdependencies between these functions, they should all be performed within one agency.

References

Arestis, P. (1992) *The Post Keynesian Approach to Economics*, Aldershot: Edward Elgar.
—— and Bain, K. (1995) 'A European Central Bank: a Necessary Evil?,' in P. Arestis and V. Chick (eds), *Finance, Development and Structural Change: Post-Keynesian Perspectives*, Aldershot: Edward Elgar.
—— and Demetriades, P. (1993) 'Financial Liberalisation and Economic Development,' in P. Arestis (ed.), *Money and Banking: Issues for the Twenty-first Century*, London: Macmillan.
Chick, V. (1983) *Macroeconomics after Keynes*, Oxford: Philip Allan.
—— (1986) 'The Evolution of the Banking System and the Theory of Saving, Investment and Interest,' *Economies et sociétés, monnaie et production* 20, 8–9: 111–26; reprinted in P. Arestis and S.C. Dow (eds), *On Money, Method and Keynes: Selected Essays by Victoria Chick*, London: Macmillan, 1992.

—— (1993a) 'Some Scenarios for Money and Banking in the EC, and their Regional Implications,' in I.H. Rima (ed.), *The Political Economy of Global Restructuring,* Vol. II: *Trade and Finance,* Aldershot: Edward Elgar.

—— (1993b) 'The Evolution of the Banking System and the Theory of Monetary Policy,' in S. Frowen (ed.), *Monetary Theory and Monetary Policy: New Tracks for the 1990s,* London: Macmillan.

—— and Dow, S.C. (1988) 'A Post-Keynesian Perspective on the Relation between Banking and Regional Development,' in P. Arestis (ed.), *Post-Keynesian Monetary Economics,* Aldershot: Edward Elgar.

—— and —— (1996) 'Regulation and Differences in Financial Institutions,' *Journal of Economic Issues* 30, 2: 517–23.

—— and —— (forthcoming) 'Competition and the Future of the European Banking and Financial System,' in A .Cohen, H. Hagemann and J. Smithin (eds), *Money, Financial Institutions and Macroeconomics,* Boston, MA: Kluwer.

Cottrell, A. (1994) 'Post Keynesian Monetary Economics,' *Cambridge Journal of Economics* 18, 6: 587–605.

Davidson, P. (1982) *International Money and the Real World,* London: Macmillan.

—— (1994) *Post Keynesian Macroeconomic Theory,* Aldershot: Edward Elgar.

—— (forthcoming) 'Policies for Fighting Speculation in Foreign Exchange Markets: the Tobin Tax versus Keynes's Proposal,' in S.C. Dow and J. Hillard (eds), *Beyond Keynes,* Aldershot: Edward Elgar.

Dow, A.C. and Dow, S.C. (1989) 'Endogenous Money Creation and Idle Balances,' in J. Pheby (ed.), *New Directions in Post Keynesian Economics,* Aldershot: Edward Elgar; reprinted in M. Musella and C. Panico (eds), *The Supply of Money in the Economic Process: A Post Keynesian Perspective,* Aldershot: Edward Elgar, 1995.

Dow, S.C. (1986–7) 'Post Keynesian Monetary Theory for an Open Economy,' *Journal of Post Keynesian Economics* 9, 2: 237–57.

—— (1993) *Money and the Economic Process,* Aldershot: Edward Elgar.

—— (1995) 'Liquidity Preference in International Finance: the Case of Developing Countries,' in P. Wells (ed.), *Post-Keynesian Economic Theory,* Boston, MA: Kluwer.

—— (1997) 'Keynes and Endogenous Money,' in G.C. Harcourt and P. Riach (eds), *The Second Edition of The General Theory,* London: Routledge.

Guttmann, R. (1988) 'Crisis and Reform of the International Monetary System,' in P. Arestis (ed.), *Post Keynesian Monetary Economics,* Aldershot: Edward Elgar.

Hewitson, G.H. (1995) 'Post Keynesian Monetary Theory: Some Issues,' *Journal of Economic Surveys* 9, 3: 285–310.

Jespersen, J. (1995) 'A Post-Keynesian Perspective on Monetary Union and the European Central Bank,' in P. Arestis and V. Chick (eds), *Finance, Development and Structural Change: Post-Keynesian Perspectives,* Aldershot: Edward Elgar.

Kaldor, N. (1982) *The Scourge of Monetarism,* Oxford: Oxford University Press.

Kelly, R. (1995) 'Derivatives: a Growing Threat to the International Financial System,' in J. Michie and J. Grieve Smith (eds), *Managing the Global Economy,* Oxford: Oxford University Press.

Keynes, J.M. (1936) *The General Theory of Employment, Interest and Money,* London: Macmillan.

Lavoie, M. (1992) *Foundations of Post Keynesian Analysis,* Aldershot: Edward Elgar.

Minsky, H.P. (1982) *Inflation, Recession and Economic Policy,* Brighton: Wheatsheaf.

Moore, B.J. (1988) *Horizontalists and Verticalists*, Cambridge: Cambridge University Press.

Niehans, J. and Hewson, J. (1976) 'The Eurodollar Market and Monetary Theory,' *Journal of Money, Credit and Banking* 8, 1: 1–27.

Palma, G. (1995) 'UK Lending to the Third World from the 1973 Oil Shock to the 1980s Debt Crisis: On Financial "Manias, Panics and (Near) Crashes",' in P. Arestis and V. Chick (eds), *Finance, Development and Structural Change: Post-Keynesian Perspectives*, Aldershot: Edward Elgar.

Runde, J. (1994) 'Keynesian Uncertainty and Liquidity Preference,' *Cambridge Journal of Economics* 18, 2: 129–44.

Schmitt, B. (1977) *L'Or, le dollar et la monnaie supranationale*, Paris: Calmann-Lévy.

Smithin, J. (1994) *Controversies in Monetary Economics: Ideas, Issues and Policy*, Aldershot: Edward Elgar.

—— (1996) *Macroeconomic Policy and the Future of Capitalism*, Aldershot: Edward Elgar.

Soloman, R. (1989) 'International Monetary Reform: the Future Is Not What It Used To Be!,' in O. Hamouda, R. Rowley and B. Wolf (eds), *The Future of the International Monetary System*, Aldershot: Edward Elgar.

Strange, S. (1986) *Casino Capitalism*, Oxford: Blackwell.

—— (1994) 'From Bretton Woods to the Casino Economy,' in S. Corbridge, R. Martin and N. Thrift (eds), *Money, Power and Space*, Oxford: Blackwell.

Studart, R. (1995) 'Saving, Financial Markets and Economic Development: Theory and Lessons from Brazil,' in P. Arestis and V. Chick (eds), *Finance, Development and Structural Change: Post Keynesian Perspectives*, Aldershot: Edward Elgar.

Tarshis, L. (1984) *World Economy in Crisis: Unemployment, Inflation and International Debt*, Ottawa: Canadian Institute for Economic Policy.

Tobin, J. (1978) 'A Proposal For International Monetary Reform,' *Eastern Economic Journal* 4, 3–4: 153–9; reprinted in J. Tobin, *Essays in Economics: Theory and Policy*, Cambridge, MA: MIT Press, 1982.

7   The development and reform of the modern international monetary system

*L. Randall Wray**

Introduction

The international financial system could be said to be in crisis. It requires frequent intervention by central banks and other national and international bodies to reduce fluctuations of currencies. It does not tend to eliminate current account deficits or surpluses; exchange rate fluctuations do not lead to movements toward balanced trade, nor do they appear to follow from flows of international reserves: some countries (notably Germany and Japan) run persistent surpluses while others (notably, the US) run persistent (even rising) deficits. Nor does 'free' trade appear to operate according to the Ricardian Law of Comparative Advantage. 'Free' international credit markets do not appear to provide credit in a socially acceptable manner: some countries and activities appear to receive far too much, while others receive too little. The world is experiencing nearly universal stagnation while governments appear to be unwilling, perhaps unable, to do anything about it.

Before moving on to our primary concern, this chapter will briefly present the orthodox view of 'money' – both at the national level and at the international level. In this view, money is primarily a medium of exchange that facilitates the circulation of goods either domestically or internationally. Accordingly, domestic monetary policy should be concerned primarily with control over the money supply in order to minimize inflation. On this view, international monetary policy should be devoted to removing barriers to free capital flows and to the maintenance of freely floating exchange rates. Flexible exchange rates are said to permit independence of domestic policy from international considerations; they also ensure rapid adjustment of international balance sheets to equilibrium.

We next examine the Post Keynesian view of money. This will require a brief excursion into monetary history to make it clear that money was, and is, first and foremost a unit of account. This helps to clarify the nature of various

*   I would like to thank Jan Kregel and John Harvey for comments. An early version of this paper was presented at a seminar at the Economic Policy Institute, and I would like to thank participants for comments.

manifestations of money: credit money, commodity money, and reserve money. We can then move to an understanding of the functioning of the modern international financial system; this will allow us to design a reformed system that will make it easier to deal with some of the previously discussed problems which face the international financial system today.

Finally, this chapter will advocate reformation of the international financial system along the lines of Keynes's famous bancor proposal. However, it will be argued that Keynes's theoretical justification of his proposal was flawed. Using Post Keynesian theory, this chapter will provide a justification for reform that is free from the flaws of Keynes's argument.

The orthodox view of domestic and international money

Let me begin with a quote from Samuelson; this is very similar to the exposition in every money and banking book with which I am familiar. It is also historically incorrect and logically flawed:

> Inconvenient as barter obviously is, it represents a great step forward from a state of self-sufficiency in which every man had to be a jack-of-all-trades and master of none ... If we were to construct history along hypothetical, logical lines, we should naturally follow the age of barter by the age of commodity money. Historically, a great variety of commodities have served at one time or another as a medium of exchange: ... tobacco, furs, slaves or wives ... huge rocks and landmarks, and cigarette butts. The age of commodity money gives way to the age of paper money ... Finally, along with the age of paper money, there is the age of bank money, or bank checking deposits.
>
> (Samuelson 1973: 274-6)

As we all know, the orthodox story begins with a barter economy, which discovers that money can be used to lubricate the market mechanism. While the first moneys are Samuelson's 'furs, slaves or wives' and so on, it is eventually discovered that precious metals serve as better media of exchange (scarcity and physical characteristics ensure their value is high relative to carrying cost; and gold is probably less likely than wives to run off when used as a medium of exchange). Transactions costs are further reduced when the goldsmith accepts deposits of gold, issuing paper money backed by gold reserves. The quantity of gold reserves closely governs the amount of paper money issued so that redeemability is ensured.

Eventually, government fiat money somehow becomes the reserve held by banks against deposits, but this doesn't change anything: the quantity of money is still determined by reserves. Since the central bank determines the quantity of reserves, it controls the money supply. If it supplies too many reserves, the money supply increases too quickly, causing inflation. Thus, according to orthodox economists, money policy should control reserves in order to control inflation: the primary domestic responsibility of the central bank is to serve as an inflation guard dog.

The orthodox view of international money is similarly based on the barter paradigm. As Hahn (1991:1) says: 'The pure theory of International Trade pays no regard to financial matters and deals with non-mediated exchange of regions.' In a simple, moneyless, model, the addition of 'foreign countries' would not complicate the analysis; each country could be treated as an optimizing agent such that an equilibrium vector of relative prices would emerge from barter. If production is added, countries would specialize according to the Ricardian Law of Comparative Advantage, with each taking advantage of its unique national environment (Davidson 1992: 116). If equilibrium were stable, then the process of *tâtonnement* would generate an equilibrium vector of relative prices in accordance with technologies and tastes.[1]

'Free' trade among countries is believed to increase economic efficiency just as 'free' trade within a country would do. In the absence of money and historical time, international trade would always be 'balanced': with all trades executed at an instant of logical time, each purchase of a time-dated commodity by country A would be offset by a time-dated commodity sale by country A. A trade deficit would be impossible, as 'Each region is at all times taken to be in Walrasian equilibrium' (Hahn 1991: 1).

Things become more complicated once we allow for the use of money as a medium of exchange. Of course, as recognized by Hahn (1983), general equilibrium theory (GET) has no room for money but, like the orthodox economists, we will ignore that problem for now. Once money is allowed, we must specify whether our international economy operates with a unified money system (UMS) or a non-unified money system (NUMS) (Davidson 1992). A unified money system is one in which all nations either use the *same* money unit, or one in which different money units are used but in which the *exchange rates* among the different money units are stable and are expected to remain so. (It is not necessary that the exchange rates are *fixed*; it is only necessary that movements are perfectly foreseen.) A non-unified money system is one in which a number of monetary units are used and in which exchange rates are not expected to be stable. It is the NUMS that causes the greatest problems for neoclassical theory (and for real world stability).

Assuming a UMS operating in historical time, a trade deficit now becomes possible: country A can import more commodities than it exports, leading to an outflow of the currency of A. Agents of country B will accept this currency, knowing the rate at which it will exchange against currency B. However, assuming that these currencies are indeed different and that currency A will not be accepted as legal tender in country B, then the agents of B will hold this currency only on the expectation that it will be used later to buy the exports of A. If this is not the case, the currency of A will have to be converted into the currency of B; this might be accomplished by profit-seeking agents specializing in currency exchange (who charge a small fee for the service).

These currency exchanges would have to keep reserves of a variety of currencies in order to accomplish conversions for the currencies of a variety of trading partners; these 'capital' reserves would have to earn a normal return obtained through the fees.

In general equilibrium theory, a gold standard is normally assumed; in this case, each currency is made convertible into gold. Gold can operate as the single reserve, reducing the required reserves of the currency exchanges, resulting in efficiency gains. The currency of any country would be increased whenever a trade surplus led to an inflow of gold reserves; on the other hand, a country facing a trade deficit would lose gold reserves, destroying a portion of the supply of its currency. Seignorage would replace fees as a 'central bank' with the power to issue currency based on gold reserves replaced currency exchanges. As Hahn (1991:1) argues, addition of (UMS) money under a gold standard to GE theory leads to 'no changes in the "real" equilibrium conditions, that is the equilibrium terms of trade'. Just as money is neutral in the domestic economy, in the UMS case, it is neutral in the international economy.

The specie-flow mechanism is supposed to rectify quickly a trade imbalance: the deficit country would lose gold reserves and its money supply would shrink; the prices of its commodities would fall due to the loss of purchasing power of its citizens, attributed to a loss of wealth (as the money supply shrinks); as its prices fell relative to those of competitor nations, its exports would rise; at the same time, its imports would fall due to falling wealth of its citizens. No country could maintain a trade deficit indefinitely for the simple reason that it would eventually run out of gold reserves; before this point was reached, it would have to depreciate the currency, making imports more expensive and exports cheaper. Indeed, a flexible exchange rate, according to the logic of neoclassical theory, would seem to speed the adjustment toward balanced trade. However, a freely flexible exchange rate conflicts with the conditions required to operate a UMS: a flexible exchange rate system could be a UMS only if the exchange rate did not move much, and was not expected to move much.

On the other hand, a freely flexible exchange rate is consistent with a NUMS. Here, while all currencies may be freely convertible into a gold reserve, exchange rates are (or are expected to be) free to adjust to eliminate trade imbalances. According to the efficient market hypothesis, *laissez-faire* will again establish an equilibrium price vector that includes a relative price for each currency; the central bank would merely stand ready to exchange gold reserves for the domestic currency on demand. It is believed that this would promote stability of the NUMS.

Under a NUMS, a trade deficit forces a devaluation to protect gold reserves. This then works 'via the real cash balance effect' to lower domestic spending until the trade deficit is eliminated (Hahn 1991: 1). According to Hahn (ibid.: 6), a 'variable exchange rate is an ideal (although imperfect) substitute' to perfectly flexible domestic prices. For example, assume that wages and prices are rigid in an economy which is subjected to a negative productivity shock. If exchange rates are fixed, this economy can adjust to the shock only by lowering employment and real income; if exchange rates are flexible, however, adjustment is made through depreciation that lowers domestic prices *relative to* foreign prices. Thus, the flexible exchange rate regime is believed to allow adjustment to shocks without adverse employment effects even if domestic prices are not flexible. In this sense, flexible exchange rates are seen as a substitute for flexible domestic prices, and thus *increase* flexibility of a market economy to speed adjustment to equilibrium.

A flexible exchange rate system generates uncertainty about the exchange rate. However, Hahn argues that 'uncertainty' over exchange rates only replaces 'uncertainty' over employment levels – because the fixed exchange rate system would use unemployment as the method for adapting to rigid wages. He thus argues that a flexible exchange rate system is preferred over a fixed exchange rate system in the 'real world' where wages are not perfectly flexible.

In sum, orthodox economists can accept either an international gold standard in which the specie-flow mechanism leads to movement toward trade balance, or a flexible exchange rate system in which fluctuating values of currencies rectify trade imbalances. In either case, the focus is on real variables and money only lubricates the market system. In either case, money is neutral (at least in the long run) but has not been successfully introduced into any rigorous neoclassical model. Freely flexible prices (including the 'price' of the domestic currency in terms of foreign currencies) are supposed to lead to a general equilibrium (although this has never been shown for a model with money). Although it is admitted that a flexible exchange rate system will generate speculation, this is believed to be stabilizing (again, this has never been shown rigorously), and can even offset some degree of rigidity in domestic markets.

Orthodox domestic policy is reduced to guarding against inflation through purported control over the domestic money supply (although the experience of the 1980s has cast considerable doubt among orthodox economists that the central bank can control the money supply – doubters have tended to call for direct control over inflation, but have been unable to get beyond pure mysticism regarding how the central bank is to accomplish this). Orthodox international policy is reduced to hand waves concerning efficient international allocations through free markets with a UMS or NUMS; the latter is believed to impart greater flexibility.

A Post Keynesian view of money

As discussed, the orthodox view of money (whether national or international) begins with barter and with money lubricating trade as a medium of exchange. While it is true that all orthodox economists would also admit a role for money as a store of value, as Keynes remarked, only a lunatic would hold money for such purposes in the neoclassical world. This is because uncertainty of the Keynesian variety is ruled out of existence by neoclassical assumptions. In this section, we will relate the use of money to uncertainty and to private property; in such an environment, money is first and foremost a unit of account – or, as Davidson (1990) argues, as the terms in which private contracts are written. Money is then closely associated with the means of contractual settlement, with the universally recognized measure of wealth, and with the form in which wealth is stored. This is not to deny the importance of the medium of exchange function of money, but an understanding of the origins of money will help to make the nature of money clear. This will aid us in understanding the international money system so that we can reform it.

We will first go through a reconstruction of the history of money and the development of our modern financial system. My view can be summarized as:

1   primitive barter did not lead to the development of market exchange;
2   money did not develop out of barter;
3   credit money predated commodity money and government money – credit money comes first;
4   and the quantity of credit money has never been constrained by the quantity of gold or government money reserves.

Space constraints prohibit a full development of each of these points; a full treatment with citations can be found in Wray (1993a). I will only summarize the major points presented there.

Let's begin with the barter story. Orthodoxy imagines a market economy that predates money; that is, a market based on barter. This is not historically accurate, nor is it logical. The orthodox economist and historian claim to find barter in tribal societies. I will argue that exchange may occur in tribal societies, but it cannot lead to markets or to the use of money: tribal exchange is not markets based on barter, but is very different from market exchange.

For example, Polanyi (1971: 75) argues that the exchanges which occur in tribal societies are 'public acts performed in regard to the status of persons and other self-propelling things'. According to Malinowski (1932: 86), these exchanges have as their main aim to 'exchange articles which are of no practical use'; indeed, Polanyi (1971: 74) says that often 'the identically same object is exchanged back and forth between the partners . . . the sole purpose of the exchange is to draw relationships closer by strengthening the ties of reciprocity'. Furthermore, exchanges were frequently made to *equalize* wealth, rather than to achieve mutually beneficial allocations of resources (Heinsohn and Steiger 1983, 1989). In tribal society, all exchanges were determined by custom. There was generally no fixed exchange rate among exchanged goods – the exchange rates would depend upon the status of the parties to the exchange; and the so-called primitive moneys we observe in tribal society (Samuelson's landmarks, rocks, seashells) are never used as a unit of account to compare the value of different items: there are no free exchanges so there is no need for a unit of account to measure the terms of exchange.

Nor are the primitive moneys ever used as a unit of account to measure debts; there are never any deferred payments, so there is no reason to have a measure of how much one would pay later. In fact, in primitive society, there are no loans in the modern sense of the term. Loans today are always initiated by the borrower and money is used as the measure of how much has to be repaid later. If an individual fails to repay the loan, he or she is subject to sanctions. But in primitive society, loans are always forced by the lender on to the 'debtor.' They will be repaid through a very specific action, with repayment terms fixed by social norms of reciprocity – there is no private negotiation over the terms – and the lender does not expect to receive any economic gain from the loan; the loan is undertaken to destroy his or her wealth, not to increase it, while building ties of reciprocity.

Finally, the 'moneys' are always special purpose – one trades a specific object only in a very specific social setting. For example, a necklace of sea shells is presented to the family of the bride. This does not mean that a wife is worth a necklace; it does not mean that either wives or necklaces are money; obviously, the family certainly doesn't view the woman as money to be used to buy necklaces. It merely means that the primitive valuable, a necklace, is the appropriate gift in marriage. (Dalton 1982). One can't substitute something else; and one never uses the necklace in another social interaction: necklaces are always for marriage and never for 'generalized exchanges.'

Clearly, primitive exchanges do not conform to the orthodox view of profit-seeking market behavior, but represent *conventional* behavior (that is, socially and culturally established norms of behavior) similar to the Western practice of gift-giving at Christmas. Then what are the primitive moneys cited in Samuelson's story? What is the exchange, if it is not an economic exchange designed to maximize individual wealth? The primitive exchange of 'moneys' – primitive valuables is a better term – really was designed to reproduce tribal society, to bring people closer together through social rituals. Tribal exchanges did not lead to the development of the use of money, nor to the development of markets. There is no reason to try to maximize wealth in tribal exchanges; everyone is taken care of to the best of the ability of the tribe.

The institution of private property is a prerequisite of the development of *monetary* production, that is, production *for sale* in markets *for money* to generate profits (Heinsohn and Steiger 1983, 1989). The development of private property destroys the collective security of tribal or command society and generates 'existential uncertainty': each member of society becomes responsible for his or her own security. Each individual household tries to build up a surplus (mainly in the form of grain reserves) to get through bad times. The development of private property leads to the possibility of loans and to the creation of propertyless individuals. If an individual household finds it is not able to produce enough to survive, it must borrow some of the surplus reserves of another household. When private loans are made, the lender gives up private property in exchange for an IOU issued by the debtor, which represents a forward contract.

This private contract must include an interest premium, the size of which is determined by the estimate of the existential uncertainty faced by the lender regarding the possibility that the lender might need the loaned property before payment is due.[2] Thus, all forward contracts involve 'wheat now for more wheat later' propositions, which *are* monetary propositions. The earliest loans were in-kind loans: a bushel of wheat for two bushels later, and so on. In the beginning, interest could be paid out of the natural fecundity of the loaned grain: I borrow a bushel now, and repay two bushels at the end of the growing season.

But eventually, repayment terms became standardized in wheat terms. (As Keynes discovered, the early money of account *was* kept in terms of wheat units.) Temples played a role in standardizing the terms – that is, in development of the money of account. The creditor and debtor needed a neutral witness to (and enforcer of) the contract (there was no writing). Later, writing was invented in the temples to keep track of debt contracts and the tribute that each household had to pay to the temple. The temple would receive payment in kind for the tribute and for witnessing contracts. It also began to act as a depository for the creditors: when a borrower repaid a loan, the temple would hold it for safekeeping for the creditors. Hence, temples accumulated large stocks of grain and animals. To reduce storage costs, the temples encouraged the development of a standard unit of account: at first wheat because its storage costs were lower and because it was fairly uniform in size; but later barley because it was even more uniform. All the early units of account were weight units based on the number of wheat or barley grains. For example, the early money of account used in Babylonia was the mina, equal in weight to 10,800 grains of wheat. The weight units pre-existed money; they were already used to measure tribute paid to temples and they were adopted as the unit of account in which debts were measured. Later, the temple would issue a piece of metal that weighed the same amount as the number of barley grains it represented, stamped to show the value. These stamped metals would merely represent the temple's IOU, measured in the wheat or barley unit of account. When creditors wanted to withdraw a portion of their deposits from the temple, transactions costs were reduced by giving stamped metal rather than counting out the grains of wheat. The metal was then used in private transactions (as a means of payment – or means of contractual settlement) or to pay tribute, but its value was determined by weight in terms of the number of barley grains it represented – again (like the transition from wheat to barley grains), this was a *technical* advance that did not change the nature of money.

Thus, the first money was created as part of a forward contract that involved 'wheat now, for more wheat later.' As the terms became standardized, we have the creation of a money unit of account. The temples did not create money, and money was not first in the form of precious metals. Instead, money was privately created; the temples only played a role in the technical evolution of money. The use of precious metals as money-denominated assets comes later; and the primary reason is not that gold is inherently valuable, but because it is difficult to counterfeit. Even when gold was first used, its value was still determined by its weight equivalent to the barley unit of account. Once there existed a universal unit of account and a method for witnessing and recording private contracts, then privately issued credit money (a privately issued, money-denominated liability – see the next section) could circulate among third parties. It could function as a means of payment, retiring private debt commitments and even perhaps in paying tribute to the temples. So money is first a unit of account and then a means of payment; it does not start as a medium of exchange. In conclusion, money came before markets – it got its start in private loan contracts.

Now of course we don't have written records to prove this. The earliest writing does seem to be records of debt contracts and all early monetary units are weight units, always in terms of a specific number of grains of wheat or barley. This is true for the mina and the shekel; but it is also true for the unit of account used everywhere in Europe: the pound. Whether it is the Roman pound, or the Italian lira, or the French livre, or the Milanese ducatoon, the early money of account was always a weight unit. This is not quite so controversial as it sounds at first. Historians have long written about the ghost money, or imaginary money, of Europe that lasted from the time of Charlemagne through the Middle Ages. There was always an attempt to write debt contracts in an imaginary pound unit of account, even though there often was no equivalent coined unit.

The historians have usually attributed this to confusion or illusion. They think it is strange, for example, to write a debt contract in terms of a pound unit of account, when there are no pound coins. Typically, the only coins were shillings; and over time, the shillings would decline in value so that it took more and more of them to equal a pound unit of account. But this was neither confusion, nor was it anything new. The money of account had always been a weight unit, and it is entirely irrelevant whether there is a coin of the same unit. I'll examine coining later, but money is not the same thing as coins; or, coins are not money. The historian's confusion arises from identifying coin as money, and from emphasizing the medium exchange function of money. If one instead recognizes the fundamental importance of the unit of account in any private property economy operating in historical time, the confusion disappears.[3]

Let's return to the orthodox belief that markets existed before money was invented. However, markets cannot predate money because independence of individuals and private property must exist before markets. In a tribal society, there is no sense in producing things you don't need for the market in order to get things you do need. In tribal society, all needs are already met to the best of the tribe's ability to do so. But, as I argued, once you have private property and independence, you already have the conditions required for the existence of money: the possibility of loans and the existence of uncertainty. The market is not a place for getting things you need; it is a place where you earn the means of retiring debt (or means of contractual settlement) – that is, money. From the beginning, production for markets was production to obtain money – and not to barter for needed commodities. The barter economy is merely a hypothesis obtained by neoclassical economists who take our economy, then drop money and analyze it as if it were a barter economy; then they add money back in as if it came from helicopters. But this leads to a view of money that is completely wrong, and to incorrect conclusions about appropriate monetary policy. Let's look in more detail at a money economy such as ours.

In a monetary economy, production occurs not to satisfy 'needs,' but to satisfy the desire to accumulate wealth in money form. Production is not undertaken by a Robinson Crusoe type agent who is both producer and consumer; instead, there are those who own private property, and those who do not – and so must work for wages. However, the existence of propertyless workers extends market demand, and extends the use of money as a medium of exchange. Unlike production in, say, a tribal society, capitalist production always involves money. The capitalist must hire workers to produce the goods that will be sold on markets. As production takes time, the capitalist must pay wages now, before sales receipts are realized. Furthermore, because the future is uncertain, sales receipts are uncertain. This means that interest must be paid on liabilities and that capitalist production is only undertaken on the expectation of making profits. Thus, capitalist production always involves 'money now, for more money later.'

Since money contracts always include interest, and because contracts always are of the nature of money now for more money later, this means that monetary contracts will always grow over time at a rate determined in part by the rate of interest (Wray 1993b). This generates a logic of accumulation: all monetary economies must grow. If they do not, accumulation falters and nominal contracts cannot be met. The logic of monetary production, then, requires nominal economic growth. It cannot be constrained by a fixed money supply, nor by a commodity money whose quantity expands only upon new discoveries. That is, the money-of-account supply is determined in the private contracts between debtors and creditors; the quantity of wheat-money-of-account can never be constrained by the quantity of wheat in existence. Rather, the quantity of wheat-money created in contracts is constrained by the perceived ability of the borrower to deliver 'more (wheat-denominated) money' later. This leads directly to what is called the endogenous money approach: money has always been endogenous, with its quantity determined in debt contracts denominated in money terms (or the unit of account). The same principles hold regardless of the money unit of account chosen (whether it is the dollar or the yen), and regardless of the medium of exchange used (bank notes, bank deposits, gold coin, or 'fiat' currency), which would be denominated in the money of account.

In order to enhance the ability of privately created money to circulate, IOUs would be 'accepted' by trustworthy individuals or institutions, through an endorsement that guaranteed the IOU. At first, this role was played by the temples; but later, a wide variety of institutions and individuals could perform the role, ranging from governments to merchants, to respected and usually wealthy individuals, and to banks. A good example of such a private IOU was the bill of exchange; indeed, this was by far the most important money-denominated asset used as a medium of exchange and means of payment from the Middle Ages right up to the nineteenth century. It would circulate upon endorsement; in fact, if it was endorsed by a bank, it was called a gilt-edge, meaning that it was supposed to be as good as gold. But it wasn't quite. This brings us to the primary problem of privately created money: its issuer might default. If the issuer defaults, creditors go after the endorsers – but they can default too. So to increase the ability of private IOUs to circulate, they would be made convertible into other media of exchange, such as the precious-metal-wheat-denominated bars issued by temples. Finally, after the development of stamped coins, private liabilities could be made convertible into currency.

Thus, we finally arrive at the 'goldsmith' stage, at which orthodox theory begins, with a commodity money (gold) that is deposited with the goldsmith, who discovers the 'deposit expansion process.' Actually, the process worked in reverse. A commodity money could not have developed before the development of a money of account – which is necessarily the result of private debt contracts. The commodity money is developed for *technical* reasons, but becomes the reserve money *because* privately issued credit money is subject to default risk. It is not that deposits of commodity money make loans and credit money; rather, loans and credit money generate a desire to hold small reserves of commodity money in order to ensure convertibility. Gold, and so on, is not money, nor has it ever been money. Money is the socially determined unit of account; it is wheat money, lira money, or dollar money. But all privately issued money has at least some risk of default, and to make this risk palatable, privately issued credit money is made convertible into other money-denominated liabilities. The commodity money is the risk-free representation of the social measure of value; as such, it is chosen as the 'ultimate' backing for privately issued money. However, the quantity of commodity money available never constrains the money of account supply. This means that wholesale conversion ('liquidation') of private IOUs can never be accomplished in the aggregate. That is, a credit money economy based on a commodity money reserve collapses if there are attempts at conversion.

In all private property economies, money is characteristically a promise to pay. A pyramid of these promises evolves – each backed by (or made convertible into) a promise higher in the pyramid. The rules of the game require that one *discharge* one's IOU using a third-party IOU. (No *private* party is able to issue its own means of payment to be used to discharge its own debt.) Frequently, it is required that the third-party IOU to be delivered is one issued by a party *higher* in the debt pyramid. For example, a bill of exchange liability is discharged through delivery of a bank note; a bank note liability is discharged through delivery of a Bank of England note; the Bank of England note liability is discharged through delivery of gold reserves. Clearly, not all liabilities that serve to fulfill certain functions associated with 'money' fulfill *all* functions; some serve as general media of exchange; others serve as means of payment *only* for those lower in the debt pyramid. Over time, there has been a continual *narrowing* of the types of liabilities that will circulate, to those in the highest reaches of the pyramid. Thus, the financial system has evolved from one in which a wide variety of types of liabilities circulated to one in which government liabilities and the liabilities of banks comprise the vast majority of the circulating 'money supply.' Similarly, there has been a narrowing of the liabilities that are accepted as means of payment that discharge liabilities, although this narrowing has not been as pronounced as that of media of exchange.

The first central banks were created (without exception) to provide government finance. Governments were typically very constrained in their ability to borrow, probably because it was not healthy to be a creditor of a king in financial difficulty. Typically, a government could borrow only if its IOUs were backed by a respected individual. (This, of course, is much different from today, when government guarantees back private liabilities.) The crown was typically seen as the least credit-worthy borrower; it could borrow only with private guarantees; it usually had to pay a much higher interest rate than other borrowers; and crown debts were almost never repaid.[4]

In any case, governments had trouble borrowing, and could not issue fiat money. Government money could circulate only on the basis of the amount of precious metals contained in it. One could say that the whole monetary history of the Middle Ages could be explained as an attempt by the governments either to find gold that they could coin or to debase coin – trying to get more coins out of their gold. Debasement caused the value of coins to fall continually throughout the Middle Ages – sometimes very rapidly. This brings us back to the ghost money. Orthodox analysis attributes the continual loss of the value of government coins to inflation caused by 'too many' coins in circulation – money causes inflation. In reality, it is not that too much money causes inflation; rather, the prices of commodities actually were very stable in terms of the ghost money of account (for example, in terms of the pound). But because government coins were only worth as much as the gold value of the coins, debasement would increase prices in terms of coin, but not in terms of the money of account. Again, this is because one would not accept government debt – a debased coin is really government debt, so it falls in value to the amount of embodied precious metal.

Private institutions did issue money-denominated assets that were stable in value, the so-called giro moneys. As long as people trusted an issuer of a liability, the liability could remain stable in terms of the ghost money; so private institutions could issue fiat money – that is, IOUs denominated in pounds. Because the crown was not trustworthy, however, as it continually tried to get purchasing power by debasing coin or taking gold, its liabilities were worthless, so government money circulated only at the value of embodied precious metals. In fact, the Bank of England was founded because the crown could not borrow from private lenders to finance a war with France as it had recently seized gold that had been deposited for safe-keeping. Thus, central banks were created to buy government debt as they issued their own notes. This development essentially allowed the government to create fiat money: central bank notes could be denominated in pounds – just as any private bank notes were denominated in pounds.[5]

For a number of reasons, central banks gradually took a position at the apex of the pyramid of liabilities. In the case of England, country banks used London banks as their reserve banks, so pyramiding on London was already commonplace. The Bank of England succeeded in passing laws to outlaw note issue by all other London banks, giving it a big advantage. Eventually, London banks made their liabilities convertible into Bank of England notes, leading to the development of a pyramid based on the Bank of England. Thus, non-bank liabilities would be made convertible into bank liabilities, and bank liabilities would be made convertible into central bank liabilities. All capitalist countries developed similar mono-reserve systems, with the liabilities of the central bank acting as the reserve. Under the gold standard, the central bank liabilities would be made convertible into gold, thus gold was the ultimate reserve at the apex.

Later, states discovered that imposition of a tax made payable in terms of the state's own liabilities would generate a demand for government 'fiat' money (that is, government money-denominated short-term liabilities – not essentially different from bank notes). Finally, government debt was accepted as a means of payment and medium of exchange; at this point, neither gold backing nor a central bank was necessary: the government could purchase merely by 'printing money,' gladly accepted by the population as the means with which taxes could be paid.[6] Perhaps because the implications were not fully recognized, states continued to maintain a sort of fiction: 'selling bonds' to the central bank, which then increased central bank liabilities (reserves and notes). While it would have been easier to dispense with the central bank, this might have made matters too transparent; government can always obtain anything for sale in the domestic money of account merely by offering fiat money; taxes ensure a demand for this fiat money.

However, central banks gradually discovered that their position at the apex gave them the ability to function as lenders of last resort – historically, the second major function of central banking (finally understood after the mid-nineteenth century). As they could essentially provide reserves without limit merely by discounting the assets of other banks, they could always stop a run. However, such behavior required that the central bank abandon narrow self-interest, a development that took nearly two centuries after the establishment of the Bank of England to come to pass. This greatly increased the stability of the capitalist system, for it solves the primary problem of a commodity reserve system: the supply of reserves becomes elastic at precisely the moment reserves are needed and maintains orderly markets. But under a gold standard, even the central bank is ultimately limited by its gold reserves, so its ability to stop a crisis is limited. This is why countries invariably went off the gold standard whenever there was a crisis, and this is why a gold standard is not consistent with stabilization of the capitalist economy.

Abandoning the gold standard was a major innovation because it made the supply of reserves completely elastic, and because it eliminated debt deflation and decumulation at the aggregate level. Stabilization requires an elastic supply of reserves, and to the extent that the central bank tries to constrain the growth of reserves, it abandons its responsibility for sustaining accumulation. Thus, the orthodox approach to money and to policy is historically and logically flawed: the monetarist policy prescription (close control over the quantity of reserves) represents a giant step backward, to an unstable system in which accumulation is prone to reversals. Furthermore, monetarist policy would not lead to greater control of the money supply: the supply of reserves (whether of wheat, of gold, or of central bank liabilities) has never determined the quantity of money supplied.

The current system, based on central bank reserves, did not evolve out of a commodity money system. Rather, the commodity money evolved out of an endogenous money system to solve one of the problems with a monetary economy. In any monetary economy, the vast majority of the liabilities denominated in the money of account (indeed, of wealth in general) consists of private IOUs, the value of which depends on the economic condition of their issuers. Thus, commodity money developed as a riskless representation of the social unit of account. Privately issued money was made convertible into commodity money merely to enhance circulation, but it was never constrained by the quantity of commodity money in existence. This helps to make clear that an exogenous money system is not possible in an economy that is based on nominal accumulation. While a commodity reserve system is possible, it is far more unstable than a central bank reserve system. Rather than attempting to constrain the central bank so that its liabilities are supplied *as if* we had a commodity money reserve system, it is far better to maintain the current accommodative reserve system in domestic economies. As we shall see, a similar arrangement is required for the international economy.

The relation between money and credit: a brief digression

Orthodox theory frequently identifies money as a *stock*, used as a medium of exchange to facilitate spending *flows*. On the other hand, *credit* is identified with domestic or foreign saving flows; it is used to finance domestic or foreign investment flows or flows of imports. Some neoclassical economists, such as Tsiang (1980), try to formulate hybrid models in which money stocks that are released through dishoarding can add to the flow of saving to meet the demand for loanable funds. But, as I'll argue, credit is not savings, nor is it dishoarding.

Much of the confusion that arises in discussions of money is generated by an identification of it with certain physical representations of money, such as government paper money and coins, bank notes, checks, or even numbers on computer tapes that record various types of deposits. This focus on physical objects obscures the fact that *credit* really represents a complex social relation. Credit money (as I prefer to call it) is a private, money-denominated liability.

First, credit money is denominated in the social unit of account (the dollar in the US); a unit of account is by its very nature *social*, and it cannot have meaning outside that social context. Second, credit money is 'created' when one agent issues a liability denominated in the social unit of account, and this liability is accepted by another agent. Credit money is never created for inventory or to be thrown on to the market; it is created as part of a social relation between 'borrower' and 'lender.' Enforcement of this credit relation is also *social* – the recording and enforcement of debt contracts has always been undertaken by *society*.[7] Frequently, credit money is created to allow one to 'buy now' on the promise to 'pay later' by delivering a third-party liability denominated in the unit of account at the later date. Even payment (retirement of debt and destruction of credit) is *social* (entailing the delivery of a third-party liability), and ability to do so will depend to a great extent on the economic performance of *society*.

This can be contrasted with the neoclassical view of exchange and 'efficient allocations.' In this view, scarce resources confront unlimited wants; a system of relative prices is generated that allocates the resources in an efficient manner. Credit, however, is not a scarce resource; in some sense there is an infinite supply of credit (the quantity is limited only by the willingness of 'borrowers' to issue liabilities and the willingness of 'lenders' to accept them). In the neoclassical world with no uncertainty, no transactions costs, and no externalities, the 'efficient' price of credit would be zero, as is the efficient price of any good of infinite supply. It is not surprising that the neoclassical world has no use for money contracts.

If there is a price of credit, it cannot be due to relative scarcity facing unlimited wants. Instead, the price of credit has to do with the existence of a preference for liquidity in an uncertain world – liquidity preference.[8] Liquidity preference generates a price system for assets; all financial assets represent liabilities, and each has a price. The price system of financial assets has an impact on the rest of the economy through its effects on investment (and, to a lesser degree, on other types of spending). Capital (that is, means of production) must also have a price; its supply price is determined in the price system for current output, while its demand price is determined in the asset price system; it will be newly produced only if its demand price exceeds its supply price (Minsky 1986). This is where liquidity preference plays a role, as the return to the most liquid asset (usually high-powered money – HPM) is determined by the preference for liquidity. All other assets must have expected returns greater than this return to liquidity in order for them to find homes; thus, asset prices adjust to equalize expected returns. As Keynes (1964) argued, the return to liquidity thus sets the standard return that must be achieved by all assets.

Space constraints do not permit me to go beyond this initial introduction to the role of liquidity preference and its effect on asset prices, except to note that the 'price' of credit is not determined by scarcity.[9] Rather, the 'price' of each liability must adjust so that all expected returns to holders of these liabilities are equal. This means that a liability that promises to pay a 'dollar' one year hence cannot in general obtain a 'dollar' today; it must be discounted, not because of a positive rate of time preference, but due to liquidity preference. Thus, for example, the spot price of this liability today might be 90 cents; the expected return to the holder of this liability is equal to 10 cents over the course of the year. These 'prices' of liabilities do not 'efficiently allocate' credit; rather, they incorporate the discounts required to equate expected returns, which, in turn, are required due to uncertainty which generates liquidity preference. The effect of an 'increase in supply' ('reduction of scarcity') of any particular type of liability has no clear impact on its price (or discount).[10] Similarly, it makes no sense to speak of independence of 'supply' and 'demand' in the case of credit; liabilities are never issued for inventory. Thus, the impact of an 'increase of demand' for credit does not have a simple impact on its 'price.' And it makes no sense to speak of flexible prices of credit ensuring 'efficient allocations' of a 'scarce credit resource.'

In contradistinction to orthodox monetarists who advocate close control by the central bank over the 'money supply,' other orthodox free marketers advocate a 'competitive money system' with complete deregulation. There are many fundamental problems with proposals that would unleash 'free markets' to provide 'mutual funds money' – that is, a privately issued medium of exchange whose value would be market determined – not least of which is a misreading of history and a misunderstanding of 'money.' Money is the social unit of account in which debts are measured; as such, it is the unit of measurement applied to credit. Serious problems arise when liabilities whose values fluctuate relative to the money of account are the basis of the payments system. This is why all capitalist countries now operate with a payments system using liabilities which always trade at par – and why 'free markets' voluntarily abandoned 'mutual funds money' as they attempted to set up giro systems and ghost moneys in which liabilities would exchange at par against the unit of account. This is not due to government intervention into a well-functioning free banking system; it is the result of 2,000 years of evolution and innovation during which experimentation proved that this is the best sort of system. Those institutions which became able to issue liabilities that would trade at par (that is, without discount in spot markets) naturally had an advantage because their liabilities would force others from the payments system. Over time, a pyramidal structure was developed such that liabilities could be converted at par to those higher in the pyramid. This, however, requires that the institution which is higher will substitute its liabilities without limit for its correspondent that is lower. This is why all capitalist countries develop a 'lender of last resort' whose liabilities are provided on demand to ensure that those of institutions lower in the pyramid will maintain parity. Any agent without direct or indirect access to the lender of last resort facility cannot maintain spot parity, thus cannot issue means of payment or media of exchange.

The obvious problem with a 'mutual money' issued by an institution without access to a lender of last resort is that rational behavior leads to a run out of it whenever confidence falls. Self-interest alone will not generate a lender of last resort; the ultimate lender of last resort must act against its own narrow self-interest whenever there is a run in order to save the system as a whole. A system that operates on individual self-interest cannot be stable because the market value of liabilities must be linked to asset values; unforeseen depreciation of assets lowers the 'free market' value of liabilities, inducing a run out of these; par can be maintained only if the run can be stopped so that the issuer can have time for a work-out. This may well involve lender of last resort activity and equity injections; given time, some assets may recover value or the issuer may be able to absorb losses through future profit earnings.

Implications for the international financial system

'Free' market determination of exchange rates in a 'freely' floating regime faces problems similar to those faced by 'mutual funds' money in the domestic economy. A system with mutual funds money is a NUMS, in Davidson's terminology; as mentioned above, 'free float' exchange rates in a NUMS are anchored only by convention. Speculative runs into/out of a currency can easily swamp flows of a currency arising from its medium of exchange function; for this reason, speculation can, at times, dominate over 'fundamentals' having to do with the current account balance.

Free marketers had argued that flexible exchange rates would make adjustment to a balance on current account rapid since a deficit nation would face loss of reserves and depreciation of the currency. In reality, countries in Latin America and the US have run persistent deficits since exchange rates became more flexible. Orthodox economists had also argued that flexible exchange rates would increase the independence of countries to pursue domestic monetary and fiscal policy. This was based on the belief that floating exchange rates could eliminate trade imbalances without necessitating domestic austerity programs. In reality, austerity has been used as the major adjustment mechanism for most deficit nations (excluding the US). Rather than allowing greater independence of nations to pursue policy, flexible exchange rates have increased the need for greater coordination of economic policies among the major developed countries. This results partly from the tendency of flexible exchange rates to lead to speculation; at times, 'capital flows' or speculative demand for currencies dominates purchasing power parity in determining exchange rates so that coordinated intervention is necessary to stem appreciation (or depreciation) of a currency.[11] In short, the 1980s have not been kind to free marketers. The orthodox view that international financial flows merely reflect international flows of goods and services underlies their flawed predictions regarding the benefits of floating exchange rates. An alternative view is required.

Most importantly, it must be recognized that all money-denominated liabilities are assets that carry a price so as to generate expected returns ($q - c + 1 + a$) such that each finds a home.[12] In the case of a foreign liability, the qs come from the explicit interest rate and the as from expected appreciation (depreciation) of the foreign currency; the liquidity of the foreign liability depends on the organization of secondary markets and on the orderliness of these markets – which depends, in turn, on the existence of a market-maker to limit exchange rate movements. Under a freely flexible exchange rate system, the liquidity of foreign liabilities is low; their expected qs and/or as must therefore be high in order to find homes for them. Only foreign liabilities denominated in currencies which are expected to remain stable (or to rise in value) will have orderly markets, thus will be highly liquid. When international liquidity preference rises, there will be a run into these currencies and out of currencies that do not have orderly markets; expected qs of international liabilities must adjust – with those of illiquid assets (especially those denominated in currencies expected to depreciate) rising the most (that is, discounts rise so that prices fall and yields rise).

In the absence of a market-maker, prices of liabilities denominated in those currencies that are *expected* to depreciate must fall quickly – leading to further destabilizing expectations of declining prices. As Davidson (1992) argues, if the elasticity of expectations exceeds unity (more than half the participants in the market expect the currency to depreciate further), then self-interested behavior will cause a cumulative depreciation (through a 'reflexive process') of the currency, generating a run out of it. In this case, a flexible exchange rate system can be made stable only if a market-maker steps in to stop the depreciation by setting a floor to the prices of liabilities denominated in the depreciating unit of account.

Within a UMS, money-denominated liabilities promise to deliver, say, $100 a year hence. These will sell for a spot price of, say, $90 today; the $100 to be delivered will take the form of a means of payment (or means of contractual settlement) – almost certainly a short-term bank liability. As the bank liability within a UMS is guaranteed to exchange at par against the dollar unit of account, there is no uncertainty about the exchange rate of the means of payment that will be used one year hence to fulfill the terms of the forward contract within the UMS. However, in a NUMS, additional uncertainty is generated if the forward contract is written in terms of a foreign currency. Even if the means of payment is guaranteed to exchange at par against the foreign currency, there is, of course, no way to know what exchange rate, between the foreign and domestic units of account, will rule. The uncertainty will be even greater if the foreign means of payment to be delivered is not fixed at par against the foreign unit of account. Modern capitalist countries have eliminated this uncertainty by abandoning 'mutual funds money' within domestic economies through the use of media of exchange and means of payment whose spot price is fixed against the domestic unit of account.

Similarly, attempts have been made to eliminate uncertainty regarding exchange rates among currencies. As discussed above, the gold standard represented a relatively recent attempt to fix exchange rates and to create a UMS. This was not the first attempt, however. The so-called giro moneys and ghost moneys also created a limited UMS. Often, these were privately established UMSs; in other cases, they were set up by governments. The problem with a UMS run by private, profit-seeking institutions, however, is, as discussed above, that the market-making function can conflict with individual self-interest; the problem with a UMS based on gold reserves of a central bank is the inelasticity of reserves.

A lender of last resort is needed to set a floor to asset prices – that is, to establish orderly markets. In the case of assets that are to be used as the dominant media of exchange and means of payment (or means of contractual settlement), the lender of last resort usually ensures that the spot price of the asset equals one, or that it trades at par against high powered money. (This ensures that these are, in Davidson's terminology, fully liquid assets.) Of course, the forward price of these assets need not equal one; the discount will depend on the state of liquidity preference. However, given guaranteed spot prices, forward contracts can then be written within the UMS specifying delivery of the means of payment in the future. Similarly, in the international sphere, a UMS reduces the uncertainty involved in making forward contracts. An international lender of last resort sets a floor to the value of each national unit of account relative to the international unit of account, even if the international unit (say, a ghost pound) doesn't explicitly exist. This is done by keeping relative exchange rates constant. In practice, this can be accomplished by an international lender of last resort for the national central banks; these, in turn, act as lenders of last resort within their domestic economies.

Implementation of fixed exchange rates is not without difficulties. We have long operated within the US with an UMS; this sets fixed exchange rates across all regions of the country. Such a fixed exchange rate system creates various inequities; there is no doubt, for example, that some regions of the country have higher rates of productivity.[13] This has been dealt with in two different ways: the various Federal Reserve Banks were designed to set discount rates independently. This would allow a smaller discount on forward contracts in the disadvantaged regions in the belief that this might stimulate the regional economy. In practice, differential discount rates do not play a major role in the US, perhaps because it is difficult to ensure that the benefits of lower discount rates remain within favored regions. The other way in which we have managed to reduce the inequity of the UMS has been to allow different prices (particularly for inputs to the production process) among regions. (Of course, there is a variety of other policies which have been adopted to deal with unequal development, including various types of fiscal policy – income redistribution, favorable tax treatment, and so on – but these will be ignored here.) As Hahn (1991) recognized, flexible prices within regions represent an alternative (but certainly not 'ideal substitute,' as he had argued) for flexible exchange rates *among* regions.

If an international UMS is adopted, inequities caused by setting the exchange rate 'too high' for some currencies and 'too low' for others will be inevitable. Again, differential discount rates can be used by the international lender of last resort to reduce inequities; a lower discount rate would be offered to those countries whose exchange rate appeared 'too high.' Similarly, countries can also adapt to inappropriate exchange rates through inflation or deflation ('flexible domestic prices') – the method used in the case of the US. However, deflation is especially onerous in any economy which uses forward contracts – that is, in any monetary economy – and significant deflation cannot occur without causing default on nominal forward contracts. For this reason, a country whose exchange rate has been set too high cannot be expected to adjust through deflation; the burden of adjustment can only be carried by those whose exchange rates were set too low, as these can inflate. In a monetary economy, inflation is always preferable to deflation.

However, the preferred course of action would be to readjust the exchange rates. It will never be simple to determine the 'proper' exchange rate for a currency; however, it will be easier to determine this in the absence of speculation against the currency. Once speculation is removed, purchasing power parity is more likely to play a dominant role in the determination of exchange rates.[14] However, speculation cannot be removed without creating the expectation that exchange rates will be fixed. Once this is done, it will be somewhat easier to determine if the exchange rate is 'too high' or 'too low'; in the presence of speculation, this is nearly impossible to determine because the exchange rate is set primarily by convention. To prevent recurrence of speculation, it is necessary for the *expectation* to be that exchange rates will not be changed; thus, changes should be made only rarely.

If we are to move to a world UMS, what is to be used as the international unit of account? One option would be to adopt a universal unit of account for use within each country and among all countries; this, of course, mimics the current domestic UMS used in the US. If this route were followed, the international unit could be based on some existing national unit (say, the dollar) or on a newly created unit (say, a ghost pound). The former would seem to be prohibited due to political considerations. There is apparently a widespread notion that current *de facto* adoption of the dollar for most international trade is unfair because it gives the US an unlimited ability to purchase the output of foreign countries and to run persistent deficits. Actually, of course, when dollar liabilities are issued, these give a claim to holders over US goods, services, or assets. If the holders prefer to hold their dollar-denominated wealth in the form of financial assets, then the US is 'forced' to run trade deficits *because* those with the power to buy US output refuse to exercise this power. Use of the dollar as the international unit of account gives the US no extraordinary advantage – but political resistance to this would be great.

Assuming the ghost pound were adopted, all agents would then be permitted to issue liabilities denominated in the ghost pound; under a single currency system, exchange rates cannot fluctuate. All adjustment would be through one of two price systems: that for current output and that for assets. While all liabilities would be denominated in the ghost pound, the value of any particular liability would be determined by $q - c + 1 + a$. However, each domestic central bank would determine which liabilities maintain spot parity against the ghost pound – through lender of last resort activities that guarantee orderly markets. As each domestic central bank could issue an unlimited supply of reserves denominated in the ghost money of account, it could always set a floor to spot asset prices.

The problem with this arrangement is immediately apparent. Such lender of last resort creates 'orderly' markets, but this removes 'market discipline.' So long as the central bank does not worry about its own narrow self-interest, nationalistic considerations could cause it to widen the lender of last resort activity until all domestic liabilities are covered by guarantees. Essentially, this then violates the rule that one cannot discharge one's debts by issuing an IOU – if the central bank always guarantees one's IOUs, one is never forced to discharge one's debts. The UMS would certainly break down as exchange rates would reappear among the 'ghost pounds' used by different countries.

Perhaps the use of an international ghost pound as the unit of account would work only with world integration – that is, with a truly international financial system and a single central bank – because of the *social* nature of the unit of account. Perhaps the right to determine which liabilities always have spot parity against the unit of the account is the last refuge of national economic autonomy. Keynes seemed to recognize this when he argued that an 'International Clearing Union' (to be discussed momentarily) 'might become the pivot of the future economic government of the world.' (Keynes 1980: 189)

An alternative that is consistent with the 'rules of the game,' but which can provide a way out when necessary, is required. In this spirit, Keynes called for the creation of an International Clearing Union (ICU) based on a bancor unit of account; the bancor, in turn, would be fixed in value relative to gold and then all the currencies of all countries participating in the ICU would be fixed in value relative to the bancor. The bancor would be used only for clearing purposes among countries; countries could buy bancor balances from the ICU using gold, but bancors could not be redeemed for gold. In this way, bancor reserves could never leave the system – eliminating any possibility of a run on bancors.

The initial quantity of bancor reserves would be allocated among countries based on their previous levels of imports and exports. Countries which then ran trade surpluses would accumulate further bancor reserves, while deficit countries would lose reserves. The ICU would provide overdraft facilities to those countries that exhausted their reserves. Since reserves could not leave the system, the ICU could always expand the supply of bancor reserves merely by making advances to deficit countries. In addition, surplus countries could use bancor reserves to make loans to, investments in, or unilateral grants to deficit countries.

The ICU would adopt rules regarding sanctions to be placed on such debtors *and* on countries which ran persistent surpluses (thus, accumulated bancor reserves). Keynes called for a charge on excessive overdrafts *and* on excessive reserve balances of one or two percentage points in order to encourage balanced trade. Other possible actions to be taken in the case of *deficit* countries would include: currency devaluation, capital controls, seizure of gold reserves, and domestic policy 'which may appear to be appropriate to restore the equilibrium of its international balance' (Keynes 1980: 462). Actions to be taken in the case of *surplus* countries include: measures to expand domestic demand, appreciation of the currency, reduction of tariffs and other trade barriers, and encouragement of international development loans (ibid.: 463). Finally, the ICU could use its power to encourage economic development through the use of overdrafts for relief work, for development of buffer stocks of commodities to provide 'ever-normal granaries,' for the establishment of an International Investment Corporation, and to help stabilize prices (ibid.: 190)

Similarly, Davidson (1992) has proposed the use of an international clearing money unit (ICMU) as an international reserve used *only* by central banks in an international UMS. Each country would continue to use its unique money of account for domestic purposes; private agents could choose any of these moneys of account for international purposes. Exchange rates among the international moneys of account would be fixed (with allowance made for adjustments under specified conditions). Clearing among central banks would then take place on the books of an international central bank, kept in ICMUs. The ICMUs would be used only for clearing purposes among central banks. As in Keynes's scheme, sanctions would be placed on countries that continually faced clearing drains, and would also be placed on those countries that continually accumulated reserves of ICMUs. As Davidson explains, this allows creditor nations to share the burden of adjustment with deficit nations; this has three justifications: (a) creditor nations can 'afford' to bear the costs of adjustment; (b) creditor nations may share the 'blame' for deficits of others; (c) placing the full burden of adjustment on deficit countries contributes to worldwide stagnation if it forces them to use austerity. Under the Keynes-Davidson scheme, the creditor nations will lose their ICMU reserves if they don't use them; these would then have an incentive to stimulate their economies so that the ICMU reserves would be used to support greater imports or greater foreign investment; alternatively, excess ICMUs could be given as grants. The international central bank would act as lender of last resort for the deficit countries once they have lost their ICMU reserves. This intervention, however, would come with strings attached, comprised of a combination of rules and discretionary actions taken by the international central bank. Because the creditor nations would be similarly forced to rectify their balance sheet flows, adjustment by the deficit nations would not be so difficult: they would be trying to increase exports precisely when the creditors are trying to increase imports.

Since the ICMU reserves could always be expanded without limit by the international central bank, it could always maintain fixed exchange rates among international units of account by purchasing the liabilities of the central bank of any nation facing pressure to depreciate. Essentially, the international central banker would operate as the ultimate market-maker, with its ICMU at the very top of the debt pyramid. It would guarantee that the liabilities of all central banks were fully liquid *internationally*; each central bank would then choose which liabilities would be fully liquid *nationally*. However, the threat of sanctions to be imposed by the international central banker on those countries that continually experienced a clearing drain would force the national central banker to behave in an appropriate manner domestically. It must be remembered that it is very easy to set a floor to asset prices (whether domestically or internationally); it is much harder to set price *ceilings*. Once fear of failure is removed, 'market discipline' cannot operate to constrain asset prices. The prices of assets are not determined by scarcity, as discussed above, but by $q - c + 1 + a$. If depreciation is eliminated and full liquidity is guaranteed, this is taken into account when asset prices are determined. Thus, lender of last resort guarantees cannot be adopted without a system of sanctions to be applied when intervention does occur.

While the Keynes-Davidson proposal seems to be perfectly consistent with the analysis presented above which focuses on money as a unit of account, the argument used by Keynes to promote his ICU was actually based on a view of money as medium of exchange. Of course, the argument adopted by Keynes was above all *pragmatic*, given the political implications of the proposal. Thus, he may not have been interested in the theoretical basis of his proposal. However, let us briefly examine and critique his argument.

Keynes began with the argument that his goal is to design an international currency system so that the currency exchange will be made to operate as if countries were 'trading goods against goods' (Keynes 1980: 18). 'The principal object can be explained in a single sentence: to provide that money earned by selling goods to one country can be spent on purchasing the products of any other country' (ibid.: 270). The operation of the ICU would be designed to ensure that bancor reserves would not be lost to idle hoards; rather, the reserves of one country would form the basis of overdrafts of another. Keynes argued that his proposal would merely 'generalise the essential principle of banking as it is exhibited within any closed system' (ibid.: 171). This will substitute an *expansionist* tendency in place of a *stagnationist* tendency:

In short, the analogy with a national banking system is complete. No depositor in a local bank suffers because the balances, which he leaves idle, are employed to finance the business of someone else. Just as the development of national banking systems served to offset a deflationary pressure which would have prevented otherwise the development of modern industry, so by extending the same principle into the international field we may hope to offset the contractionist pressure which might otherwise overwhelm in social disorder and disappointment the good hopes of our modern world. The substitution of a credit mechanism in place of hoarding would have repeated in the international field the same miracle, already performed in the domestic field, of turning a stone into bread.

(Keynes 1980: 177)

This is because hoarded reserves lower world aggregate demand and employment; if instead reserves form the basis of loans, world demand and employment would be higher.

According to the perspective adopted above, there are two problems with Keynes' argument. First, an international monetary system cannot be designed as if trade were 'goods against goods.' The fundamental activity of any capitalist economy consists of position-taking in assets that are expected to generate gross income denominated in money terms. So long as foreign ownership of assets is permitted, the international monetary system must be designed with this in mind. While I certainly would not advocate 'free market capital flows,' it does not seem desirable to eliminate 'capital flows' altogether. The goal of Keynes' ICU or Davidson's ICMU is not to limit trade to 'goods against goods,' but to eliminate speculation against currencies that arises from floating exchange rates. In other words, the goal is to remove expected currency appreciation as a component of the expected returns that foreign assets can deliver.[15]

Second, Keynes' banking analogy is confused. While he is correct in his assertion that prohibiting conversion of bancors *into* gold will eliminate the possibility of a run developing on bancors, his argument that the existence of the ICU ensures that bancor reserves will necessarily form the basis of loans is flawed.[16] His plan is not expansionist merely because reserves remain in the system; rather, it is expansionist because it eliminates exchange rate uncertainty, encouraging the use of forward contracts and reducing speculative and precautionary reserve balances. If creditor nations can be encouraged to increase domestic demand for the output of deficit nations, or to employ labor in deficit nations in order to generate foreign investment, then Keynes' plan will indeed be expansionist. On the other hand, if the creditor nation merely prefers to hold its surplus in the form of paper claims on foreigners, then his proposal does nothing to stimulate world demand. The form in which the creditor nation chooses to hold its wealth depends, of course, on the state of liquidity preference; it is primarily the fixed exchange rate system which is expected to lower the return to liquidity that will be required to raise the expected returns ($q - c + 1 + a$) from *capital* investment sufficiently to stimulate world demand.

Conclusion

I hope that the 'Post Keynesian' view of money as a unit of account, and the necessity of maintaining parity of the media of exchange and means of payment against the unit of account, provides a more powerful theoretical argument for Keynes' proposal than that advanced by Keynes himself. If we retreat to the view that money is primarily the medium of exchange and if we focus on 'real exchange' in which money merely lubricates the market mechanism, then the arguments for fixed exchange rates are not strong. A general equilibrium price vector should have room for the inclusion of exchange rates as 'prices' of currencies; if we essentially remain within the barter paradigm of relative prices serving as signals then there can be no justification for fixed exchange rates. As Hahn says, even uncertainty over exchange rates cannot generate a convincing argument for fixed rates since flexible exchange rates reduce uncertainty over employment.

In contrast, the Post Keynesian view leads immediately to a justification for fixed exchange rates; exchange rates are not merely seen as relative prices that emerge from trade, but as ratios of the units of account in which monetary contracts are written. Fixing these ratios as part of a comprehensive reformation of the international financial system will merely apply at the international level the step taken in every developed country at the national level. In the domestic sphere, capitalist countries moved from 'mutual funds money' to 'par money' based on gold reserves, and finally to 'par money' based on central bank reserves. In the international sphere, we moved from 'mutual funds money' to giro and ghost money, to a gold standard and then *backwards* to flexible exchange rates.

In summary, establishing fixed exchange rates, a bancor or an ICMU, and an international central bank has the following benefits:

1   Expected appreciation/depreciation of a currency no longer plays a role in determining asset prices.
2   Use of forward contracts is encouraged because uncertainty over exchange rates is removed.
3   Speculation in currencies is eliminated.
4   The volume of reserves (of gold and foreign currencies) that must be held (for speculative and precautionary purposes) by national central banks and private agents is reduced.
5   A method of dealing with trade imbalances is created that does not rely on austerity. This carries over to the international sphere practices that are frequently adopted domestically. (A nation normally does not force austerity on to a region that runs a trade deficit with the rest of the nation.

Of course, the US could deal with such imbalances more rationally than it has in the past.)

6   It reduces the need for international coordination. In spite of the claim of free marketers, the flexible exchange rate system actually increased intervention into foreign currency markets by governments as they attempted to deal with problems brought on, for the most part, by flexible exchange rates.

7   The bancor or IMCU plan eliminates stagnationist tendencies in world economies, recognizing that capitalist economies *require* accumulation of money-denominated wealth.

Perhaps the primary result of the flexible exchange rate system has been to allow national central banks to pursue control of domestic inflation with single-minded abandon. When combined with the stagnationary influences caused by the asymmetric adjustment problem, whereby trade deficit nations pursue austerity (not matched by expansionary policies of trade surplus countries), this has contributed to worldwide stagnation. Keynes' bancor proposal would encourage surplus nations to undertake expansion and limit the austerity imposed on deficit nations. While it is beyond the scope of this chapter, domestic policy must also be redirected away from concern with inflation; it should be noted, however, that it is ironic that orthodox economists are so concerned with the uncertainty generated in the domestic economy by inflation but are so willing to sweep aside the uncertainty caused by fluctuating exchange rates, even when theory and evidence suggest that the uncertainty caused by moderate inflation is minuscule when compared with that generated by wildly fluctuating exchange rates.

Notes

1   As Ingrao and Israel (1990) demonstrate, the invariant paradigm of general equilibrium theory has been to demonstrate the existence, uniqueness, and global stability of equilibrium. While it has been shown that equilibrium does exist for the hypothesized barter economy under quite general assumptions, uniqueness of this equilibrium can be shown only under unacceptably restrictive assumptions; proof of stability is even more difficult to obtain.

2   Thus, the interest rate is not the rate of time preference. See below.

3   Part of the reason that historians focus on coins is due to the relative abundance of coin and the severe scarcity of surviving evidence of private credit moneys. Not only is evidence of private contracts unlikely to survive due to the physical form it takes (for example, written on paper), but also because once a private contract is fulfilled *there is no reason to preserve it*. When you meet contractual obligations to your neighbor so that your IOU is returned, you destroy the IOU. It would be silly to retain it for posterity.

4   One might wonder why anyone would ever lend. Sometimes, the loans were forced; but some were voluntary in order to get concessions. Sometimes the crown would borrow against future taxes – it would farm out the tax collections to the lenders, reducing the uncertainty.

5   This wasn't actually the first time government fiat money was created – Italian

city states had been able to do it hundreds of years earlier. But this was because all citizens were responsible for city debts. This was not true once you had the development of monarchies: crown debt was not the debt of citizens.

6 See Knapp (1924) and Wray (1993a).
7 Davidson (1990) emphasizes the importance of the existence and enforcement of the 'civil law of contracts' in creating the conditions under which forward contracts in money terms are made possible.
8 Liquidity preference can be defined as a preference for liquid assets, which in turn can be defined as those assets that can be sold quickly with little chance of loss of value. Existential uncertainty is said to be the source of liquidity preference.
9 For a more detailed treatment, see Wray (1992).
10 As Wray (1992) shows, an increase of 'money demand' normally induces an increase of 'money supply'; the effect on asset prices is determined in a very complex way so that this cannot in general be predetermined.
11 According to the 'purchasing power parity' theory, equilibrium exchange rates should ensure that the 'real' price of a commodity will be equalized across currencies (ignoring transactions costs such as transportation); thus, if $1 equals DM2 in foreign exchange markets, then an item that costs $1 in the US should cost DM2 in Germany. If a commodity that sold for $1 in the US were selling for DM1 in Germany, then (again, ignoring transportation costs) it would be profitable to trade $1 for DM2, and then to buy two units of the commodity in Germany for sale in the US (since the dollar could buy only one unit in the US). Exports would flow from Germany, driving up the value of the mark until 'real' prices were equalized. However, this does not appear to hold in the real world, where 'real' prices do not seem to be equalized across currencies. This is because currencies are desired not only for purchases of goods and services, but also for 'capital' transactions (purchases and sales of assets internationally). Indeed, 'capital' transactions currently swamp international trade in goods and services. Capital transactions include 'investment' in real and financial assets, but also include transactions in derivatives and other complex financial instruments. An indeterminate amount of capital transactions is nothing more than speculative behavior.
12 This analysis follows from Keynes (1964). Keynes had defined q as the yield (or coupon) of an asset, c as its carrying cost ('wastage,' depreciation), l as its liquidity return, and a as its expected appreciation/depreciation in nominal terms. The liquidity return is a subjective return, with liquid assets providing greater subjective amounts of liquidity. While illiquid assets obtain very little l, their qs can be large. Carrying cost (c) would be large for physical assets that depreciate (machinery that is used up, wheat that rots), while it would be negligible for highly liquid assets like money. In equilibrium, the total return $q - c + l + a$ is equalized on assets.
13 This implies different equilibrium exchange rates consistent with purchasing power parity if wages are equalized – as Hahn argued, flexible exchange rates can compensate for inflexible wages, so that if government policy or union bargaining equalizes wages across the country, then the 'dollar' in the low-productivity part of the country should exchange at less than par with a 'dollar' from a high-productivity region. This is not permitted within the country, however.
14 This is admittedly nothing more than a guess; no one can know whether deviations from purchasing power parity are largely a function of international speculation. Perhaps capital controls would also be necessary. By the way, Keynes had argued that nothing is more certain than that capital flows must be controlled. (Keynes 1980: 25).
15 Thus, while reduction of currency speculation would move us closer to Keynes' goal (to make the system operate *as if* trade were 'goods against goods' – with 'real' prices equalized as in the purchasing power parity theory – this goal would

never be reached because other capital flows would continue.
16 Indeed, as all who accept the endogenous approach to money are aware, it is *loans* of bancors that create the reserves of bancors held by surplus nations – loans create deposits.

References

Dalton, G. (1982) 'Barter,' *Journal of Economic Issues* 16, 1: 181.

Davidson, P. (1992) *International Money and the Real World*, 2nd edn, New York: St. Martin's Press.

Hahn, F. (1983) *Money and Inflation*, Cambridge, MA: MIT Press.

—— (1991) 'Policy Seminar,' mimeo, Banca d'Italia, December.

Heinsohn, G. and Steiger, O. (1983) 'Private Property, Debts, and Interest, or: The Origin of Money and the Rise and Fall of Monetary Economies,' *Studi Economici*, 21, 3: 3–56.

—— (1989) 'The Veil of Barter: the Solution to the "Task of Obtaining Representations of an Economy in which Money is Essential",' in J. A. Kregel (ed.), *Inflation and Income Distribution in Capitalist Crisis: Essays in Memory of Sidney Weintraub*, Washington Square, N.Y. New York University Press.

Ingrao, B. and Israel, G. (1990) *The Invisible Hand: Economic Equilibrium in the History of Science*, Cambridge, MA: MIT Press.

Keynes, J.M. (1964) *The General Theory of Employment, Interest and Money*, New York and London: Harcourt Brace Jovanovich.

—— (1973) *The Collected Writings of John Maynard Keynes,* Vol. XIV, London: Macmillan.

—— (1980) *The Collected Writings of John Maynard Keynes,* Vol. XXV, London: Macmillan.

Knapp, G.F. (1924) *The State Theory of Money*, London: Macmillan.

Kregel, J.A. (1992) 'Some Considerations on the Causes of Structural Change in Financial Markets,' *Journal of Economic Issues* 26, 3: 733–47.

—— (1993a) 'Alternative Organisation of Financial Markets,' manuscript.

—— (1993b) 'International Financial Markets and the September Collapse of the EMS, or "What George Soros Knew that You Didn't",' mimeo.

Lucas, R.E. (1981) 'Tobin and Monetarism,' *Journal of Economic Literature* 19, 2: 558–67.

Minsky, H.P. (1986) *Stabilizing an Unstable Economy*, New Haven, CT: Yale University Press.

Tobin, J. (1985) 'Theoretical Issues in Macroeconomics,' in G. R. Feiwel (ed.), *Issues in Contemporary Macroeconomics and Distribution*, Albany, NY: State University of New York Press.

Tsiang, S.C. (1980) 'Keynes's "Finance" Demand for Liquidity, Robertson's Loanable Funds Theory, and Friedman's Monetarism,' *Quarterly Journal of Economics* 94, 3: 467–91.

—— (1989) 'Loanable Funds,' in J. Eatwell, M. Milgate, and P. Newman (eds), *The New Palgrave: Money*, New York and London: W.W. Norton.

Wray, L.R. (1992) 'Alternative Theories of the Rate of Interest,' *Cambridge Journal of Economics*, 16, 1: 69–89.

—— (1993a) 'The Origins of Money and the Development of the Modern Financial System,' The Jerome Levy Economics Institute, Working Paper no. 86.

—— (1993b) 'Money, Interest Rates, and Monetarist Policy: Some More Unpleasant Monetarist Arithmetic?,' *Journal of Post Keynesian Economics* 14, 4: 541–69.

Yunker, J.A. (1992) 'Relatively Stable Lifetime Consumption as Evidence of Positive Time Preference,' *Journal of Post Keynesian Economics* 14, 3: 347–66.

8   Exchange rates

Volatility and misalignment in the post-Bretton Woods era

John T. Harvey

Introduction

The market for foreign currency is the largest in the world. A 1989 Bank for International Settlements (BIS) survey concluded that the average daily value of foreign currency transactions (based on April of that year and net of double counting) was around $640 billion (BIS 1990: 208-11). Assuming 250 working days in a year, that translates to $160 trillion annually – enough to finance world trade over 35 times. US GDP that same year was $5,244 billion, or one-thirtieth of the value of currency transactions.

One would think that economists would have an easy time explaining such a large and easily identifiable manifestation of the market system. In fact, just the opposite has been true. Especially since the collapse of the Bretton Woods system, neoclassical economists have had no luck in developing a model of exchange rate determination that has had anything but very limited empirical success (Harvey 1996b, Taylor 1995a and 1995b).

It is my contention that an explanation of exchange rate movements based on Post Keynesian principles would be superior to those offered by the mainstream. To that end, this chapter will employ a Post Keynesian approach to explain the two most salient features of the modern currency market: large and persistent trade imbalances and currency price volatility. Central to the explanation will be the role played by monetary and financial factors in the world economy. In the end, it will be found that foreign exchange rates are determined by international investors' demands for currency as they act to adjust their portfolios, and that the volatility and persistent payments imbalances that mark the modern international monetary system exist because capital flows have grown to dominate the market.

The next section is an elementary explanation of the foreign currency market. Once the basics are outlined, a more detailed examination of the various motivations for demanding currency is offered. Due to the importance of the role of the capital market in this scheme, an extended discussion of its character follows. The volatility of the foreign exchange market is then explained in terms of both the preceding analyses and other psychological and institutional factors. Finally, the reasons for exchange rate misalignment are outlined and concluding comments are made.

Exchange rate determination: basics

In the simplest of terms, exchange rates are determined by the international supplies of and demands for each currency. The greater the demand by US dollar holders for the Japanese yen, for example, the higher the price of yen in terms of dollars. Likewise, as the willingness of yen holders to supply their currency to dollar holders increases, so the price of the yen in terms of the dollar falls.

In the dollar-yen market, all those who are supplying yen are doing so because they demand dollars, and all those demanding yen are offering (that is, supplying) dollars in exchange. In other words, supply of yen equals demand for dollars and demand for yen equals supply of dollars. Unlike product markets, there is essentially no difference between suppliers and demanders. The only difference is the currencies currently held and those desired. Otherwise, their behavior can be examined in the same terms. For that reason, all explanations will be in terms of demand hereafter.

Though an equilibrium exchange rate would be easy to identify in graphical terms, the fact that the demands for currency are rooted in several disparate sources makes operationalizing the model something of a problem. An economic agent may demand foreign exchange for one of several reasons:

1   *importing*: to facilitate purchases of foreign goods and services (for simplicity it is assumed that exporters require customers to bear the burden of currency conversion–it makes little difference in practice);
2   *direct foreign investment*: to purchase foreign assets for ownership purposes (assumed to be held for relatively long periods);
3   *portfolio investment*: to purchase foreign assets for capital gain (assumed to be held for relatively short periods);
4   *official reserve management*: to purchase foreign currency for purposes of exchange-rate intervention.

The overall demand for foreign currency is a summation of the demands associated with each of the above activities. When the price of yen in terms of dollars rises, this must be because there has been a shift among dollar and yen holders toward Japanese goods, services, and/or assets (or toward holding yen as official reserves). Asking what determines exchange rates amounts to asking what determines each of the above four activities. That is done in the next section.

The composition of currency demand

Each of the factors below contributes to the demand for foreign exchange. Of the four, portfolio investment is by far the largest, and therefore most important, factor in setting foreign currency prices. It is also the most unstable, and hence the source of the volatility of exchange rates.

Imports and exports

Importers and exporters require foreign money to purchase goods and services and to translate revenues into their home currency. Roughly speaking, the greater the volume of such trade, the greater the effect on foreign exchange rates. Theoretically, one would expect the demand for goods and services to be tied to both income and price considerations. In practice, the former has been shown to be much more important (see McCombie and Thirlwall, Chapter 3 in this volume). Even large movements in the adjusted price of traded goods and services appear to have little impact on imports and exports, so that only changes in the overall level of economic activity have a consistent effect on trade flows. As Japanese GDP rises, for example, we could expect that Japanese demand for imports would go up, driving the value of the yen down relative to the dollar (*ceteris paribus*). Such is the impact of trade flows on exchange rates. Note that because changes in the level of economic activity will be only slight in the short term, shifting trade flows are not a likely candidate for explaining the volatility of exchange rates. Furthermore, import/export activity appears to comprise only a fraction of daily international transactions.

Direct foreign investment

Direct foreign investment, too, requires foreign currency. Its determination (and therefore its effect on exchange rates) is somewhat more complex, however, as in many respects it is really a microeconomic phenomenon. In general, those enterprises with firm-specific advantages will endeavor to invest abroad (Dunning 1977). One would expect such firms to reside in the developed world, where technology and the extent of the market would be conducive to the creation of barriers to entry and other such advantages. Choice of host country is more difficult to explain. If the investment is vertical, then firms are usually in search of resources and there is no macro-economic rule to where these occur. If it is horizontal, firms are seeking markets and will probably be attracted to growing, stable economies (probably other industrialized countries), but this is a crude approximation. Suffice it to say that however these flows develop, they, like trade, tend to be small and change only slowly (and would therefore not be a contributor to rate volatility).

Portfolio investment

The category of international transaction that dominates world business is portfolio investment (Krause 1991; Schulmeister 1987; Shelton 1994; and

Walter 1991). On a day-to-day basis, the combined volume of trade flows, direct foreign investment, and official intervention is swamped by those seeking short-term capital gain. For all intents and purposes it determines exchange rates.

Purchases of portfolio capital depend on the *expectations* of market participants. As economic agents come to believe that a particular asset may rise in price, so they act to increase the share of that security in their portfolio. The expectations guiding these decisions tend to be volatile and that volatility is superimposed on the foreign exchange market when investors purchase the currency they need to acquire the desired assets. These and related issues are addressed at length below.

Official reserves

Governments purchase foreign currency in order to affect exchange rates. Such intervention is obviously a function of politics. These politics may be supported by well-reasoned economic logic, or they may appear arbitrary and myopic. In any event, it is not possible consistently to link particular economic phenomena to government intervention into the foreign exchange market.[1] Fortunately, this will not prove to be a major obstacle to explaining exchange rates as, since the collapse of Bretton Woods, large-scale intervention has been infrequent.

Capital markets: speculation and enterprise

Above it was argued that, of the four reasons for demanding foreign exchange, portfolio investment is the most important. On the surface of it, this is hardly a controversial statement. But there are crucial differences between the Post Keynesian and the orthodox views of what would determine these flows and how they affect the economy. Before the character of international portfolio investment and its specific impact on foreign exchange prices can be explained, these issues must be addressed.

Neoclassical economists expect the financial or monetary side of the economy to serve as a passive engine of growth for the real side. Financial flows arise only in accommodation of the demands of the real side of the economy, and are not of themselves important. For this reason, neoclassicals perceive little difference between direct and portfolio investment. Both are guided by the subjective preferences of market participants and lead to an optimal allocation of international resources. In either case, it is in the best interest of investors to focus on those factors fundamentally important to the financial success of the entity in question. The only distinction worthy of note is that, because portfolio investment is by nature more liquid, it is likely to react more quickly to changing economic conditions. For this reason, greater liquidity in investment markets is seen as a plus.

Post Keynesians do not share this view. While it may be possible for free markets to encourage 'efficient' allocation of international resources and investment (though this is subject to a number of caveats), the greater the role played by portfolio investment the less likely this becomes. This is so because asset prices play an important role in determining the financial success of the issuing entity. On first issue, higher prices mean greater revenue from the sale. Even as asset prices continue to fluctuate, however, the entity's financial strength (and therefore its ability to control resources) is affected. Not only will higher prices make new issues an attractive option, but the entity in question would find that its credit rating becomes quite high, making other forms of financing very affordable. Managerial stability is also enhanced by high asset prices. The current price of issued assets has an immediate and real impact on the allocation of resources in the economy.

Whether or not the pattern of the prices set in the capital market is conducive to optimal resource allocation depends on whose asset prices are bid the highest. If it is indeed those of the most efficient entities, then optimality is achieved (or at least something approximating to it). This is most likely to occur when the expectations used to guide buy and sell decisions are focused on the long-term performance of the entities in question (assuming no persistent forecasting errors). Keynes calls this activity *enterprise*, or the 'forecasting [of] the prospective yield of assets over their whole life' (Keynes 1964: 158).

Direct investment leads naturally to enterprise. Market participants have a vested interest in the long-term performance of the issuer, which encourages careful and meaningful evaluations of management, products, R&D, market niche, political stability, debt retirement programs, and so on. Asset prices will be derivative of expert opinion of the issuer's credibility, and therefore optimal resource allocation is more likely. Such markets would be fairly stable since the fundamentals determining expectations would hardly change on a daily or even weekly basis, and trading volumes and turnover would be relatively low.

On the other side of the market are those investors seeking to profit from the resale of their assets. If they expect to profit, they must focus on those variables most important to the majority of market participants and then anticipate asset price movements based on those variables. Keynes calls this activity *speculation*, or the 'forecasting [of] the psychology of the market' (Keynes 1964: 158). How this is accomplished is dependent on what sort of activity dominates the market. If it is direct investment, and therefore enterprise, then things are little different than as described in the previous paragraph. There may be somewhat more volatility and turnover, but the ultimate objective of *all* those participating in the market is still the forecasting of the issuers' long-term performance. Portfolio capital investors are forced to pay attention to those issues most important to direct investors because the latter are the primary force setting prices.

But in the event that the market is actually dominated by the speculators, then *the link between asset prices and careful analyses of the issuer's future viability is broken*. Now the game is to guess what everyone else is guessing.

Issuer-specific factors may still be important, but, as speculators are constantly looking for reasons to re-evaluate asset prices and alter their portfolio, the impact of each piece of information is magnified (sometimes well beyond reason). This effect is made greater by the environment of uncertainty in which agents must operate. The end result is higher turnover, greater volatility, and prices that may be driven more by whim than reason. Efficient allocation of resources as defined in the neoclassical model is still *possible*, but cannot be expected.[2]

The current international economy is dominated by portfolio capital flows. It is therefore marked by Keynes' speculation, rather than by enterprise. When the latter dictates market activity, expectations are generally stable and driven by factors that would tend, all other things being equal, to set prices in a way that may encourage the efficiency described by neoclassicals (again, there are important caveats). But, when speculation is the motivating factor, market participants have little reason to care whether or not asset prices reflect the underlying strengths of the issuers. In that case, 'the actual, private object of the most skilled investment . . . is "to beat the gun", as the Americans so well express it, to outwit the crowd, and to pass the bad, or depreciating, half-crown to the other fellow' (Keynes 1964: 155). In such a setting, price volatility tends to be high and there may be extended periods of apparently irrational price movements.

Portfolio capital, expectations, and exchange rate volatility

What this means for the foreign exchange market is that currency prices are driven by the shifting sentiments of international portfolio managers. Because those shifts are speculative in nature it further means that exchange rates do not promote efficient allocation of resources. Though there may be lengthy periods over which they do little harm, there is nothing about the current structure of the international economy that gives reason to believe that currency prices are driven by a benevolent, invisible hand.

To this point, the argument has been developed in a way that implies that international investors' expectations of worldwide asset price movements is what drives the foreign exchange market and currency prices. Though this certainly occurs, it is far from the whole story. Consider the following. First, because of the many thousands of assets available internationally, each requiring considerable investigation if intelligent decisions are to be made, investors are likely to limit their interest to a number of rather generic types. These may include stock indexes, low-risk bonds (especially government), and other standard interest-bearing forms. Second, market participants must take into account the fact that the value of their portfolio is affected not only by own-price changes of assets, but by movements in the value of the currency in which they are denominated. In fact, the latter often swamps the former. This reinforces the tendency to focus on generics, since exchange rate movements affect all assets equally.

Note that these two points lead to an interesting conclusion. If asset value is so closely linked to exchange rate movements, then it must be the case that the latter is a, if not *the*, primary focus of international portfolio investors. This does not mean that other, issuer-specific information will not be of interest; but by and large, forecasting asset value will entail forecasting exchange rates. Hence, *actual exchange rates are driven by exchange rate expectations* (see Harvey and Quinn 1997 for an empirical test of this proposition). When speculators, as a group, predict a yen appreciation, they shift into yen-denominated assets. Since buying yen-denominated assets requires the purchase of yen, speculators cause their prophecy to be fulfilled: the yen appreciates.

This is really no different from any other asset market, except, interestingly, that the currency itself need not be the direct object of speculation.[3] Nevertheless, because the exchange rate is such an important part of the value of any international asset, the potential for fluctuations must be carefully considered. Speculators need never have foreign money as the object of their desire, and yet it will play a central role, both affecting and being affected by portfolio capital flows.

The fact that exchange rates are driven by portfolio capital investors in search of short-term capital gain explains their volatility in the post-Bretton Woods era. Rapidly changing forecasts of future currency price movements have lead to the rapidly changing spot prices. Why would forecasts change so rapidly? The post-Keynesian explanation focuses on six causes: the speculative nature of the currency market; the lack of a true anchor to currency values; the subculture of foreign currency dealers; the particular manner in which people make decisions; the environment of uncertainty in which decisions are made; and bandwagon effects.

When the best heads in the market are focusing on speculation, this alone is sufficient to create greater volatility. The psychological state of mind of market participants will be one that not only expects but welcomes rapid price movements. Their object is to continuously alter their portfolio in a way that leaves them selling assets at a price higher than that at which they purchased them. Price stability is not conducive to achieving this goal. So as investors scour the market for information concerning their investments, they are frankly *looking* for reasons to re-evaluate their portfolio. Thus, inputs into the expectation formation process take on a very different character than they would in a market dominated by enterprise.

It is not only the speculative nature of the market that creates volatility. Because there exists no final end-use for the object of speculation, this means that a solid anchor for currency values does not exist. By contrast, in a market like that for corn futures, the spot price of corn as sold to those who plan to process and sell it to final consumers serves to reign in fluctuations. If the current wholesale price of a bushel of corn is $3, for instance, then speculation of any composition and volume is unlikely ever to drive the futures price far away from that value. Furthermore, the set of factors likely to move futures prices in that market will be well defined *even when speculation dominates the market.*

No such anchor exists in the foreign exchange market. Like corporate securities, foreign currency has no final use. There is the advantage with securities, however, that a clear sense of what should be reflected by the asset price exists: the present value of all future corporate profits (even when that sense of importance is diluted by a speculative market). But of what is a currency value derivative? The most common answer to this question is the underlying strength of an economy; this of course begs the question as to where that strength arises. Is it inflation, unemployment, GDP growth, political stability, or some combination thereof? There is no simple or obvious answer to this question.

Even more fundamental, what is the theoretical justification for the contention that exchange rates reflect the strength of an economy? For that to be true, it must be shown that as an economy becomes 'stronger,' so there is an increase in the demand for its currency. But when the market for an asset with no end use is dominated by speculation, the *only* reason to demand it is in anticipation of an increase in others' demand. We are back to Keynes' musical chairs. Defining the set of variables upon which to focus in making foreign exchange market decisions is problematical.

The only semblance of an anchor that does exist in the market is the prevailing 'sense' among participants that the variables the most popular economic analyses believe to be important are so, at least over the long run (explained in Harvey 1998b). This tendency may create some long-term trends in exchange rate determination, but is far too unreliable for short-run forecasts. Its ability to reduce volatility is limited.

In addition to the lack of a true anchor contributing to the range of currency price fluctuation are the institutional tendencies created by the subculture of currency market participants. Foreign currency trading tends to attract and mold individuals who desire adventure. They crave excitement, and see themselves as 'wrestling with alligators' (Rosenberg 1987: 33) or as having been 'selected for . . . the tribal hunting party' (Feeny and Brooks 1991: 27). This tends to shift their time horizon to the short term, as does their employers' desire not to be seen holding depreciating assets (even when the long-term outlook is otherwise optimistic). Their goal is fast profit on the turn of a price, and they are actively seeking information that they believe predicts such a movement.

Fourth, the particular manner in which people make decisions renders volatility likely. Rather than the deterministic technique of comparing mathematical expected values which mainstream economists claim characterizes choice, real people are far more likely to employ a limited number of heuristic principles (Harvey 1998a). These rules of thumb are not only better suited to the manner in which *Homo sapiens* processes information, but they often give answers not far off those generated by far more complex techniques. Most important to the current discussion are availability and representativeness.

The availability heuristic is used when trying to determine frequency (for the past) or likelihood (in the future). Roughly speaking, the more available something is in memory, the more frequent or likely the decision-maker deems it. This creates a tendency to exaggerate recent and dramatic events and to understate older and mundane ones. It also creates an inclination toward overreaction and rapid re-evaluation of positions as new 'news' becomes available (since it will be overweighted).

Reinforcing this effect is the heuristic of representativeness. Used when the decision-maker is trying to determine the likelihood that object A belongs to class B (where the time horizon may be forward or backward looking), the rule is that the more A resembles (is representative of) B, the more likely A was or will be the result of B. One of the results of this heuristic is that people have a tendency to believe that people expect all events to have a cause. Random fluctuations play no role in most explanations.

Consequently, it is also the case that inputs are almost always expected to have an impact on outputs. As events unfold in the international economic and political arena, so there is a tendency to believe that they must have some impact on prices. The importance of this effect can vary significantly from instance to instance, but it nonetheless adds to the factors causing agents to focus on short-term, rapidly changing events as the causes of future exchange rate movements.[4]

The fifth factor adding to volatility is uncertainty. We cannot know the future, and this has significant implications for market behavior. Realistically speaking, we know neither all the possible future states of the world nor the probabilities to attach to each (as is often assumed in studies of behavior under *risk*). This level of ignorance, combined with the necessity of taking action in the asset market, causes market participants to treat each new piece of information with far more weight than would be appropriate were all the relevant information available. This constitutes yet another reason why events in world politics and economies may cause rapid and unwarranted reactions in the currency market.

Finally, there exist bandwagon effects that cause any movement in the market to have the potential to snowball. These effects are completely independent of the source of the initial change and depend only on the fact that rates are adjusting. The bandwagon effect can be linked to a number of factors, but will be narrowed to two here (see Harvey 1998b for a more complete treatment): faith in the logic of the market and the desire to avoid blame and to take credit. That faith is a result of the representativeness heuristic, the conviction that market outcomes are reasonable and 'correct,' and the sense that individual analyses of market events are never as insightful as those based on the forecasts of thousands of others ('the market is always right'). Consequently, as prices move, there is a strong tendency to believe that the movement is justified by current conditions. If the movement appears to be sustained, there is a very good chance that others will join in on the assumption that the market knows better than they where the rate should go.

The second motivation for jumping on the bandwagon is the fact that doing so may be less damaging to reputation than missing out on a trend. A wrong decision with the trend can be forgiven, but forgoing a profit-making opportunity that the rest of the market 'obviously' saw will be difficult to explain.

Each of the above factors combines to create the volatility that has been the trademark of the floating period. As the market has evolved an increasingly speculative nature, so the factors that determine currency demand have become more variable. The fact that exchange rates are so unstable is not, in and of itself, a bad thing if that instability serves some other purpose. But all indications are that it is simply a byproduct of the casino into which the international financial system has evolved. Resources are not allocated efficiently and the extreme rate volatility adds yet another uncertainty to the ones with which those undertaking international trade and direct investment must contend.

Exchange rates and trade imbalances

The growth of portfolio capital flows has also created the large and persistent trade imbalances that have marked the post-Bretton Woods era. What has made these especially newsworthy and mysterious is that most neoclassical economists did not expect them. In their opinion, the removal of significant government intervention from the foreign exchange market would create a tendency for currency prices to move to offset trade surpluses and deficits.

But this is a logical conclusion only if the sole reason for people to buy currency is to purchase foreign goods and services. In that case, neoclassicals are correct in thinking that an excess of imports over exports would indicate a disequilibrium position in the market for foreign currency, one that would cause exchange rates to move in a way that would eliminate the excess. For example, if we take the US as the home country with a trade deficit with respect to Japan, this would imply that a higher quantity of yen was demanded in the market (for the large US imports of Japanese goods and services) than was supplied (by the Japanese wishing to obtain dollars for purchases of US goods and services). Clearly, this would cause the yen to appreciate. The appreciation makes Japanese imports less attractive to Americans, while at the same time causing US exports to rise. This process would continue until trade was balanced, at which point the quantity of yen supplied and demanded would be equal and equilibrium would be attained. Under these conditions, the actual exchange rate and the one that balances trade would coincide.

But the foreign currency market is not dominated by the activities of importers and exporters, so the scenario portrayed above is based on a false premise. Because it is portfolio capital that runs the market, the equilibrium exchange rate and the balanced-trade exchange are not one and the same. The quantity of yen demanded is not equivalent to US imports from Japan, and the quantity of yen supplied is not equal to Japanese imports from the US. Only if they were would the exchange market serve as a means to balance international trade. Thus, the mere existence of large flows of portfolio capital breaks the self-correcting tendency which many economists hoped floating would bring. Though the specific causes of imbalances may vary, the fact that they exist is a function of portfolio investment.

Conclusions

Nothing has been more important to the post-Bretton Woods international monetary system than the explosive growth of portfolio capital flows. It has changed the very nature of the market and provides an excellent example of the folly of what Keynes (1964: 155) called the 'fetish of liquidity'. In addition to the payments imbalances, resource misallocation, and trade and direct investment diversion this may cause, it reduces government policy autonomy and represents a waste of entrepreneurial talent. This is a problem in all market-based economies, but is even more problematic in the developing world (see Grabel, Chapter 10 in this volume).

Since the 1980s, however, the logic of both mainstream economics and government policy makers has been to equate markets with optimality, raising them to an almost mythical level and offering them as a panacea for all our societies' problems. But markets are only tools. If rational, goal-oriented analysis and experimentation indicate that a market system would best address an issue, then so be it. If not, then let us not be slaves to the ideological residue of eighteenth- and nineteenth-century political thought.

Notes

1   Though a great deal of accuracy may be possible if the particulars of some policy regime are known and stable.
2   Note that it is not necessary that most market participants be in search of short-term capital gain, only that most transactions be of that sort. Given that the number of market transactions undertaken by those focusing on resale will be much greater than those seeking ownership returns, a market can be driven by speculation even if only a minority are so inclined.
3   Of course, many times it is, but this is obscured by the fact that what the speculator actually buys is a foreign asset.
4   Yet another manifestation of representativeness is described below.

References

Bank for International Settlements (1990) *60th Annual Report*, Basle: Bank for International Settlements.

Dunning, J.H. (1977) 'Trade, Location of Economic Activity and the MNE: a Search for an Eclectic Approach,' in B. Ohlin, P.O. Hesselborn and P.M. Wijkman (eds), *The International Allocation of Economic Activity*, London: Macmillan.

Feeney, M. and Brooks, J. (1991) 'The Dealing Room and the Dealer,' in R.

Weisweiller (ed.), *Managing a Foreign Exchange Department: A Manual of Effective Practice*, 2nd edn, New York: Quorum Books.

Harvey, J.T. (1991) 'A Post-Keynesian View of Exchange Rate Determination,' *Journal of Post Keynesian Economics* 14, 1: 61–71.

—— (1993a) 'Daily Exchange Rate Variance,' *Journal of Post Keynesian Economics* 15, 4: 515–40.

—— (1993b) 'The Institution of Foreign Exchange Trading,' *Journal of Economic Issues* 27, 3: 679-98.

—— (1995) 'The International Monetary System and Exchange Rate Determination: 1945 to the Present,' *Journal of Economic Issues* 28, 2: 493–502.

—— (1996a) 'Long-term Exchange Rate Movements: the Role of the Fundamentals in Neoclassical Models of Exchange Rates,' *Journal of Economic Issues* 30, 2: 509–16.

—— (1996b) 'Orthodox Approaches to Exchange Rate Determination,' *Journal of Post Keynesian Economics* 18, 4: 567–83.

—— (1998a) 'Heuristic Judgment Theory', *Journal of Economic Issues* 32, 1: 47–64.

—— (1998b) 'Institutional and Psychological Determinants of Foreign Exchange Rates.'

—— and Quinn, S.F. (1997) 'Expectations and Rational Expectations in the Foreign Exchange Market,' *Journal of Economic Issues* 31, 2: 615–22.

Keynes, J.M. (1964) *The General Theory of Employment, Interest, and Money*, San Diego, CA: Harcourt Brace Jovanovich.

Krause, L.A. (1991) *Speculation and the Dollar: The Political Economy of Exchange Rates*, Boulder, CO: Westview Press.

Rosenberg, M. (1987) 'Traders Make Tradeoffs,' *American Banker* July 30: 33.

Schulmeister, S. (1987) *An Essay on Exchange Rate Dynamics*, Research Unit Labour Market and Employment Discussion Paper 87–8, Berlin: Wissenschaftzentrum Berlin für Sozialforschung.

—— (1988) 'Currency Speculation and Dollar Fluctuations,' *Banca Nazionale del Lavoro Quarterly Review* 167: 343–65.

Shelton, J. (1994) *Money Meltdown: Restoring Order to the Global Currency System*, New York: The Free Press.

Taylor, M.P. (1995a) 'The Economics of Foreign Exchange Rates,' *Journal of Economic Literature* 33, 1: 13–47.

—— (1995b) 'Exchange Rate Modelling and Macro Fundamentals: Failed Partnership or Open Marriage?,' *British Review of Economic Issues*, 17, 42: 1–41.

Walter, A. (1991) *World Power and Money*, New York: St. Martin's Press.

Part IV

Real and portfolio capital flows and the role of technology

9 Globalisation of production and industrialisation in the periphery

The case of the EU and NAFTA

Philip Arestis and Eleni Paliginis

Introduction

The purpose of this chapter is to examine recent economic developments in the periphery of the European Union (EU) and the North Atlantic Free Trade Area (NAFTA) by concentrating on both theoretical and empirical considerations. The theoretical aspects spring from, but go beyond, the model which has come to be known as Fordism and its variant Peripheral Fordism. The empirical aspects evolve around a close study of the experiences of both the EU and NAFTA.

Our own explanation of recent economic developments in these areas may have a great deal in common with Fordist explanations, but it departs from these models at two levels: we emphasise the need of an autonomy of the state to follow appropriate economic policies in promoting economic development; and, also, special attention is paid to indigenous capital accumulation to support the manufacturing sector for sustained economic development.

We begin this chapter with an excursion into the theoretical underpinnings of our thesis. The empirical aspects, where a comparison with the more developed countries is offered, are discussed before we proceed with an examination of the role of state intervention in the process of economic development. Economic policy aimed at enhancing domestic capital accumulation and the role of multinational enterprises (MNEs) in this process are given due attention in the subsequent section, before we summarise and conclude in the final section.

Theoretical considerations

The Fordist model describes a situation whereby capital concentrated in the post-war period into large multiplant enterprises, taking advantage of economies of scale provided by big markets. This concentration was relevant both in terms of industrial production and employment and was thought to be remarkable because of its size and consistency in many countries. A historical compromise manifested itself in the relationship between capital and labour in the core countries of the European Union. Productivity gains produced steady improvements in workers' real incomes, institutionalised as an 'inflation plus' norm for wage deals. The Keynesian welfare state at the same time expanded the social wage along with the private wage. The institutions of collective bargaining, the relation between banks and industry and the role of the state are central issues in Fordism.

However, that Fordist era came to an end by the late 1960s. The problems of inflation, overaccumulation and declining rates of profit, the enhanced bargaining power and political weight of the trade unions, the development of the affluent consumer who rejected standardised, mass-produced, commodities, and so on caused capital to develop new strategies. From about the early 1970s onwards, it is argued, there has been a dramatic change in terms of organisation of production, including the manufacturing sector, and the development of the service sector.

Post-Fordism contends that in response to market and technological changes more flexible units producing *customised* products of different types have become the dominant engine of growth. What has emerged, therefore, is a decentralised form of organising production within both large and small firms. Thus, flexible specialisation whereby tasks and responsibilities are divided into units which are very loosely connected to each other is believed to have produced a most efficient form of production capable of corresponding to the demands of ever-changing markets. The standardised products of Fordism are replaced by the customised products of post-Fordism. The production of the latter is made increasingly cheaper, essentially because of reliance on microprocessor-based technologies. Post-Fordism is very much based on flexible, skilled workers who are prepared to learn new skills and move between jobs according to the wishes of the market.

Another strand of thought sees the crisis in Fordism caused by the collapse of profitability as responsible for an emerging new pattern of capitalist development. MNEs, in particular, in their attempt to recover their profit-ability sought refuge in the new industrialised countries, the peripheral countries, where low-wage and high-productivity possibilities existed. This development is precisely what Lipietz (1987) has labelled 'Peripheral Fordism.' It is Fordism in as much as it involves intensive accumulation and mass consumption by at least some classes in these countries, especially of consumer durables; and it is peripheral in that the centres of 'skilled manufacturing' and engineering are not located in these countries. The local markets of Peripheral Fordism are in consumer durables, where the middle classes are active in these markets, but less so the workers in the Fordist sectors. Exports of cheap manufacturing goods to the centre is the other dimension of the local markets. So an obvious difference between Peripheral Fordism and Fordism itself is that, unlike the latter, the former cannot regulate demand or indeed adjust it to local Fordist branches, given that it is world demand that is involved in this case. So while in traditional Fordism the link of consumption to productivity was met by monopolistic regulation of wage relations, the same is not necessarily true in Peripheral Fordism. Industrialisation is achieved through imports from the centre which are paid for by exporting cheap manufacturing goods to the centre.

Another obvious difficulty with Peripheral Fordism, and one we have touched upon above, is that whilst in Fordism there is a basis of macro-economic control in the form of effective demand regulation, such control is lacking in Peripheral Fordism where industrialisation, such as it exists, is without any national control. Furthermore, since the institutional framework is different in Peripheral Fordism than in Fordism, it becomes impossible to predict from the Fordist model which institutions in the periphery might produce fast growth or the specific countries where growth might take place (Amsden 1990).

The development of both EU periphery and Mexico could be based either on the development of endogenous resources or on the attraction of MNEs. In contrast to Fordism, small to medium enterprises (SMEs) could play an important role in post-Fordism. They offer the ability to respond quickly to the needs of the market. Their role in the development of Emilia-Romagna in Italy raised hopes in the rest on the European periphery for a path to development focusing on the endogenous development potential of the regions. The special conditions in Emilia-Romagna, such as the existence of skilled labour, proximity to very industrialised regions and support from local government, were not present in the rest of the European periphery and therefore the ability to duplicate this path to development became more problematic.

The existence of very weak domestic capital which could not play the innovative role assumed by post-Fordism led to expectations that MNEs could initiate this process by transferring capital and technology to regions which badly needed them. Indeed, MNEs moved to these countries, but the industrialisation of the periphery in the 1960s and 1970s was a *branch-plant* industrialisation with no linkages with domestic capital and with no transfer of skills or technology. Thus MNEs failed to play the role of *growth pole* (Amin and Tomaney 1995).

The structural problems of these economies could be addressed potentially through their incorporation into economic unions/free trade areas. This is based on the classical notion of benefits through free trade. These benefits may arise to partners who are at similar levels of economic development. In both NAFTA and EU we have, none the less, partners at very unequal levels of development. The periphery, in both cases, is dominated by a weak domestic manufacturing sector which could not withstand competition from the manufacturing sector of the core countries. Similarly, the state becomes weaker in directing or assisting the developmental process. Restructuring within the developed economies as a result of global competition, such as the creation of the Single European Market, was intended to strengthen European capital through mergers and the better use of R&D, increasing further the chasm between core and periphery.

It is with these aspects that we deal in this chapter. We thus proceed in the next section to an examination of relevant empirical aspects of the EU and

NAFTA. We then turn our attention to the role of state intervention and economic integration in the process of economic development along with the creation of free trade areas. The impact of industrialisation and of MNEs on economic development is examined before we summarise and conclude in the final section.

Empirical considerations

While Fordism was established in economies which had already reached an advanced level of industrial production and where the agricultural sector was relatively small, Peripheral Fordism encompasses economies with a large and inefficient agricultural sector and a manufacturing sector which is still relatively small and concentrated in areas dominated by MNEs. Further, the banking and financial sectors as well as the overall institutional framework are less developed, expressing, and influencing, the degree of development of these countries. Peripheral Fordism and Fordism are not separated only by a time element. There are fundamental structural differences both between core and peripheral countries today and also between the present structures of the peripheral countries and the structures of core countries in the 1960s, the highest period of Fordism in Europe.

The sectoral distribution of output

The present structure of the peripheral countries of the EU and NAFTA in relation to their most developed partners is highlighted in Table 9.1.[1] In Mexico agriculture comprises 8 per cent of GDP and employs 25 per cent of the population; a similar picture exists in Greece with 13 per cent and 27 per cent respectively, while the equivalent values for OECD average is 4 per cent and 6 per cent (Table 9.1).

The existing structural differences between core and peripheral countries in both NAFTA and EU are reflected in a number of relevant statistics. These reveal the close similarities that exist between the two sets of countries and raise similar questions about unequal economic and political power.

In 1960, the agricultural sector in OECD Europe represented 9.8 per cent of GDP and 25.7 per cent of employment; manufacturing 31.4 per cent and 27.3 per cent respectively (Larre and Torres 1991). At the level of GDP per capita, Mexico and Greece, the two most peripheral countries of NAFTA and the EU, have levels well below that of their richest counterparts, the US and Germany. The US's GDP per capita ($21,449), is 7.3 times larger than Mexico's ($2,930), while Germany's ($18,212) is 2.5 times larger than Greece's ($7,323) (OECD 1992). The relative lower level of GDP per capita points to another difference with Fordism. While the core countries depended on the existence of a relatively well-off working class for mass consumption of these commodities, the same need does not exist within the Peripheral Fordist model. The local market is rather limited to the local middle class. The main

Table 9.1 Selected indicators in the EU and NAFTA, I

	Population (000s)	GDP (US$ PPP)	GDP (per capital, US$)	Employment (%)		
				Agric.	Industry	Services
USA	251,523	5,392	21,449	2.8	26.2	70.9
Germany	63,232	1,152	21,105	3.4	39.8	56.8
Mexico	81,249	n/a	2,930	24.6	25.8	49.6
Spain	38,959	491	12,609	11.8	33.4	54.8
Portugal	9,859	82	6,085	17.8	34.8	47.4
Greece	10,140	74	6,505	24.5	27.4	48.2

Source: OECD, *Economic Survey, 1993*, Paris: OECD

market for the commodities produced in the periphery is the working and middle classes of the core countries.

Employment and unemployment

The level of unemployment is very mixed. It appears low in Portugal, Greece and Mexico while it is very high in Spain. The existence of an over-inflated agricultural sector disguises a serious structural problem of unemployment and the unavailability of jobs in alternative sectors. Further, poor welfare benefits and a supportive family structure lead to unreliable data on un-employment. In countries where there is no developed social benefit system, the registered level of unemployment tends to be low. Thus, the very low levels of unemployment recorded in Greece (8.5 per cent), Portugal (5.2 per cent) and Mexico (2.8 per cent) under-records the existing problem (Table

Table 9.2 Selected economic indicators in the EU and NAFTA, II

	Unemployment (%)	Employed population (%)	GFCF % of GDP (Mach. and equip.)	Wages: average annual change (%)	Prices: average annual change (%)
	1990	1990	1990	1986–90	1986–90
US	5.2	46.8	7.8	2.6	4.0
Japan	2.6	50.6	13.7	3.7	1.3
Germany	5.4	44.1	9.8	4.2	1.4
UK	6.5	46.3	8.5	8.5	5.9
Mexico	2.8	28.8	5.1	5.1	69.7
Spain	16.5	32.2	13.1	13.1	6.5
Portugal	5.2	45.4	13.1	13.1	11.3
Greece	8.5	32.2	8.7	8.7	17.4
EU	8.7	44.0			

Sources: OECD *Economic Surveys*, and Eurostat (1993)

9.2). There is none the less an upward trend in unemployment, even in the official statistics, in those economies.

The high level of unemployment in Spain is a rather new phenomenon. Unemployment there, after a short decline in 1990 to 16.3 per cent, was back in 1992 to 20.1 per cent. Similar trends exist for Ireland, another peripheral EU country, where the level of unemployment in 1991 reached 16.2 per cent. The equivalent levels in the 1970s (average level between 1973 and1979), which was a period of active state involvement in the markets, were 4.8 per cent and 4.1 per cent. It is very difficult to establish the causes for this rise, but the openness of the economy and the EU's neo-liberal attitudes greatly contributed to it.

As unemployment figures are relatively unreliable, employment and population ratios provide a better measurement of the involvement in the work force (see Table 9.2). This ratio is consistently lower for the peripheral countries than for the core ones; the relevant values are: for the US 46.8 per cent, for Germany 44.1 per cent, but for Mexico 28.8 per cent and for Greece 32.2 per cent. The effects of NAFTA and the EU on the levels of employment and unemployment are crucial. Improvements in these areas were expected to come from the liberalisation of the economy and the deregulation of the labour market. In the case of Mexico, despite NAFTA's rhetoric on market forces, these forces apparently operate only in the movement of capital and commodities and explicitly exclude the free movement of labour. Within the EU the apparently free movement of labour is constrained by cultural and linguistic obstacles. In the absence of a substantial movement of labour, capital movements remain the only means for the creation of employment. The unpredictability of the latter, arising out of competition with the rest of the world, is a serious issue, affecting both the overall level of employment and the level of wages. In fact, in the ten years since the liberalisation of the markets, wages in Mexico have fallen. After an increase in wages in the 1970s, they fell by 31.5 per cent between 1979 and 1984, while in Korea in the same period they increased by 14 per cent (Amsden 1990). The minimum wage was eroded in the 1980s and by 1992 was half the 1936 level (Kopinak 1993). Extensive econometric work in this area, for both Mexico and the EU, is speculative and inconclusive.

State intervention, economic integration and development

The analysis so far poses the question of whether economic unions provide a more congenial environment for economic growth in the periphery than alternative forms of operation. We argue that the autonomy of the state and the economic policies pursued are paramount issues in this analysis. An autonomous state following active interventionist policies is essential to the economic development of the periphery. State intervention played a crucial role in determining the form and extent of development in most of the late industrialising countries; indeed, it determined, we would suggest, most of the success stories in these countries. The Asian newly industrialised countries (NICs), and most specifically Korea, offer examples of fast industrialisation achieved through the direct intervention and mapping out by the state of the important areas of expansion.

The autonomy of the state was singled out by Lipietz (1987) as an important aspect of the developmental process in Peripheral Fordism. Although autonomy did not always coincide with parliamentary democracy (Korea), it was crucial in determining policies congenial to growth. In the Asian NICs the state was very dirigiste, determining the areas within the manufacturing sector that were, essential for development and providing the framework which would allow this to happen.

From the turn of the century until now, both within the European periphery and Mexico, economic growth has coincided with periods of economic intervention. In Mexico, as the manufacturing sector was considered the engine of growth, there was extensive use of 'import substitution industrialis- ation' (ISI). Although there were shortcomings attached to these policies arising out of the lack of capital and intermediate goods and lack of a market for the mass consumption of manufactured goods, Mexico, in the period 1955–82, achieved an average rate of growth of 6.5 per cent (OECD 1992). Within the European periphery, there were efforts to enhance the development of the manufacturing sector through import controls and subsidies to domestic capital. In Greece, the average rate of growth between 1961 and 1979 was also 4.5 per cent, dropping to an average of 2.4 per cent in the 1980s (European Economy 1991).

An important factor in the process of catching up is investment as a percentage of GDP. In the 1980s in peripheral Europe the process was unequal. Spain and Portugal experienced a period of euphoria after their membership of the EU began in 1986 and in this period there was an increase in domestic investment financed by domestic savings, as well as an increase in foreign direct investment. Between 1986 and 1990 there was an increase in investment from 22.1 per cent to 26.7 per cent in Portugal and from 19.5 per cent to 24.4 per cent in Spain. This increase in the level of investment created a premature optimism that there was a catch-up which was partly endogenous. Since then, there has been a decline in the level of investment in both countries. Although the levels of investment in the mid-1980s were higher than the immediately preceding period, both Spain and Portugal had experienced higher levels in the past. Spain experienced the highest average level of investment, at 24.6 per cent, in the period 1961–73, while in Portugal, it was 27.8 per cent, in the period 1974–83. Similarly, Greece experienced a high level of investment (22.5 per cent average) in the period between 1961 and 1983. This high level of investment fizzled out in the 1980s when it dropped to an average of 18.5 per cent.

There was an unbalanced growth of international trade from periphery to core in the 1980s within both NAFTA and the EU. Between 1985 and 1991 Greek and Spanish imports from the rest of the EU trebled while exports only doubled. Similarly, in Mexico a surplus in the balance of trade between 1982 and 1988 became a serious and growing deficit from 1989 onwards (OECD reports). Between 1988 and 1991 exports to the US increased from $2,589m to $3,292 while imports increased from $12,607m to $25,032m (excluding the operation of the *maquiladoras*). In this process the peripheral countries became more integrated in the free market areas and provided markets for exports from the core countries. Capital movements, borrowing or financial assistance in the form of contributions to the Common Agricultural Policy (CAP) or Structural Funds were used to finance the deficit.

A further effect of these neo-liberal policies was a process of de-industrialisation of their domestic capital and their increasing dependence on MNEs. The low technology and low productivity associated with domestic production could not survive within an open, unprotected environment. The National Manufacturing Industries Chamber in Mexico reported this process of de-industrialisation and criticised the government for this effect. It estimated that within the first years of NAFTA Mexico would lose 23 per cent of its manufacturing industry and 14 per cent of its jobs (Kopinak 1993). That prediction appears to be vindicated by the experience with Tesobonos, which enabled Mexico to finance a huge current account deficit, equivalent to 8 per cent of GDP, at the cost of stagnant investment. Tesobonos are government bonds denominated in dollars, and are soon to mature. Their size could very well produce another debt crisis compounding the de-industrialisation problem just referred to. The EU periphery has had similar trends and has experienced problems of the same type and magnitude as we have shown elsewhere (Arestis and Paliginis 1993).

These features and statistics stress the extent of the inequalities between core and periphery in NAFTA and the EU and raise the question whether free trade policies could benefit both sets of countries. They also invite the question of whether the open environment of trade associations or economic unions is more congenial to economic growth of the periphery than alternative forms of operation.

Free trade areas and development

The incorporation of these countries into larger free trade areas or economic unions removes the autonomy of the states to follow independent policies appropriate for growth. The regionalization of national states within, eventually, a superstate differentiates and widens the concept of state auto-nomy. The possible effect of it is either the supersession of narrow nationalism and the creation of a new identity or the present situation where new institutions arise, such as the Single European Market and the proposed Independent European Central Bank, which restrict the effectiveness of state autonomy without providing sufficient compensatory alternative mechanisms and institutions. Within Europe today a new identity has not yet been found. Conflicting narrow national interests are still very strong. For the developed economies participation in larger free trade areas or economic unions creates hopes for restructuring their manufacturing sectors, through the guaranteed acquisition of larger markets for their products and the increasing returns of scale associated with this production.

For the peripheral countries, participation represents an effort to minimise their losses. Although their indigenous industries will not be able to withstand competition from the core countries, they hope that their relatively cheaper labour force may entice some MNEs. In the case of the EU, they expect that the Structural Funds will more than compensate them for their losses. The real problem for them is that once the world becomes one where countries are members of larger trade areas, life outside these areas becomes impossible. Within the present structure we do not have yet the institutions and the alternative identity to transcend the national state. The latter may wither away at a later stage, but present experience shows that this may be a long way off.

A recognition of the effects of the Single Market and eventually the European Monetary Union on the poorer states led to a series of measures and funds to compensate them for the effects of 1992 and to assist them towards convergence. Even in the pre-1992 period there were Structural Funds intended to assist countries with lower GDP per capita (less than 75 per cent of the EU average) or to help regions affected by de-industrialisation to redress the imbalance. These funds were neither quantitatively sufficient nor qualitatively appropriate to deal with the problems of peripherality of these countries/regions (Arestis and Paliginis 1993). In 1992, only 24 per cent of the EU budget was directed to the Structural Funds, while 53.3 per cent went to the CAP. Furthermore, the CAP is regressive as it benefits mostly the rich farmers of the developed countries and introduces fundamental distortions in the distribution of funds (Figure 9.1).

The bulk of the Structural Funds together with the Convergence Funds is directed towards building the infrastructure of these countries, on the assumption that its lack leads to slower economic development. The existence of an infrastructure is a necessary but not sufficient condition for the economic development of these countries. Unless further conditions are met, piecemeal construction of infrastructure will not solve their problems. More direct assistance to their productive sector would be more beneficial. Further, since the peripheral countries lack the necessary expertise for undertaking large infrastructure projects, a substantial part of the 24 per cent of the budget for Structural Funds finishes back in the developed countries as payments for capital goods and technical services provided. The periphery thus benefits as consumers of the infrastructure and contributes at the level of unskilled and semiskilled labour in its production. The 53 per cent of the budget directed towards the CAP is for price guarantees. This is a payment to farmers mostly in the core countries. To the extent that farmers in the periphery benefit, a large part of payments from the CAP is spent on consumption goods, most of which are imported from the core countries, as the balance of payments figures show. The funds to the peripheral countries thus represent compensation for the

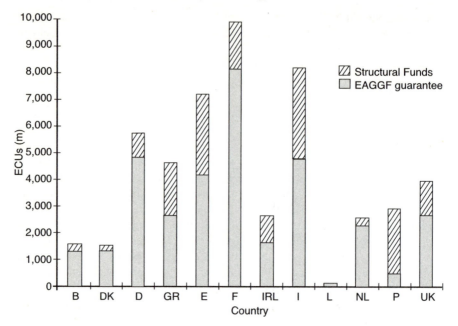

Figure 9.1 EC budget, 1992
Source: *Official Journal of the European Communities*, Court of Auditors,
November 1993

destruction of their domestic industry and a means of acquiring imported goods from the core. Thus the present policies of the EU promoting the creation of the infrastructure in the periphery may not be the most direct way for the latter's development. Although the infrastructure may represent a *sine qua non* for the economic development of these areas, it does not represent a sufficient condition. Companies may or may not be enticed there.

Industrialisation, MNEs and economic development

As historical experience from both the core countries and the NICs has shown, all successful cases of economic development are based on the development of the manufacturing sector. We believe that the development of this sector, when fully integrated into the local structures of these economies, creates the basis for their economic development and is the only solution for their chronic problems of unemployment and underemployment. The manufacturing sector in the peripheral countries was small, fragmented and in some cases controlled partly by MNEs. The main questions are whether the national economies can address this problem and whether the opening-up of the market will impede it.

As we have already discussed, while the Asian NICs developed the basis for the effective control of MNEs, the creation of NAFTA and the EU has effectively removed the ability of states to intervene and protect their indigenous industry. In the core economies, regional problems in the 1960s and 1970 were addressed through the use of Keynesian policies and, despite their limitations, they dealt with regional problems with mixed results. This was achieved under the aegis of the nation state and it was an expression of national identity. The peripheral countries are reduced now to regions without the benefits and protection of the national state. This poses the question of whether, within an open economy and especially in the economic environment of the 1990s, industrialisation could occur through the inflow of foreign direct investment (FDI) in the country instead of remaining dependent on indigenous capital and state intervention.

Although MNEs could play, and in some cases have played, an important role in the developmental process of a country, their role depends ultimately on the national control that is exercised over them. The role of governments is not to deregulate and liberalise the economy, as the neoclassical school assumed, but instead it is to create a regulatory framework, initiate institutional changes, upgrade skills and adopt positive strategies for development. As Dunning (1993: 68) argues, governments, mainly in the East Asian countries, play the role of strategic oligopolists in their relationship with the MNEs. The policies followed by governments in both the EU periphery and Mexico do not follow this model. The NAFTA and the EU neo-liberal framework does not allow these countries to intervene in their economies. In contrast, the East Asian countries did not enter into any free trade agreement with the core countries. Whether a country will benefit from the operation of MNEs depends on the national control exercised over them, the value-added in the periphery and the linkages of MNEs with national capital. All these three conditions were absent from the operation of MNEs in Mexico and the EU periphery. In fact, the value-added in both Mexico and Portugal was low, concentrating in areas such as textiles. The expansion of the automotive industries in Mexico created hopes for a transition to MNEs producing higher-value commodities – but there is no evidence that this has materialised yet.

A general observation about the operation of MNEs is that the operation of these corporations is far from being global. In 1990, 95.7 per cent of the stock of outward FDIs were generated in the developed market economies and similarly, during the same period, 81.2 per cent of the stock of inward FDIs were directed towards the developed market economies (Dunning 1993). Natural endowments and the possession of unskilled labour play a role less central than originally anticipated. 'Increasingly more important are the costs and availability of created assets, including all kinds of information and the capacity to assimilate, interpret and use this information, innovatory capacity, scientific, technical and professional personnel . . . a cooperative and well-motivated labour force, a sophisticated domestic market' (ibid.: 68). This statement none the less does not abstract from the fact that differences in wages for labour of similar skills are important. In 1989 the average hourly compensation for production in manufacturing was in US $14.31, in Germany

$17.53, in Mexico $2.32, in Portugal $2.77 and in Greece $5.48. Ford claims an average hourly compensation in Mexico is $4 while the comparable figure for the US is $30 (Hufbauer and Schott 1992). These wage differentials have created some movement of capital towards countries with lower costs of labour; from Germany and France to Spain and Portugal and from the US to Mexico. The movement to Greece was less than anticipated as there were other political and institutional factors which had a negative overall effect.

In Mexico MNEs were associated since the 1960s with *maquiladoras*, overseas companies which were permitted to import machinery and parts, duty free, and allowed to export the final product abroad, paying tax only on the value added. The characteristics of these enterprises are selective employment policies, the feminisation of production, unskilled labour, relatively low salaries, non-union orientation, the very low value added, and so on. But most importantly, dependence on US economic activity for their operation increased Mexico's dependence on the US. Recessions in the American market have direct effects on exports, employment and GDP. A new wave of *maquiladoras* has moved recently into the automotive industry, creating hopes of higher value added and higher technology transfer. A heterogeneity of technology exists, even sometimes within the same industries, combining sectors which are capital intensive and others which are labour intensive, but there is no evidence that the old *maquiladora* system is disappearing, that the new ones will be more integrated with the domestic industry or that the Mexican government will have more control over their operation.

In the case of the EU, the picture is more confused. MNEs have operated in some peripheral EU countries in the 1970s in an effort to bypass tariff controls and take advantage of lower wages. In Greece, in the early 1980s, as a result of a full membership of the EU and improvements in wages, FDIs declined from $672 million in 1980 to $439 million in 1983 (*IFS Yearbook* 1991) and remained at similar levels for the rest of the 1980s. In Spain and Portugal there was a steep increase in FDIs following their accession to the EU, as a result of the booming state of the European markets at the time. Since 1990 they have declined steadily in both countries, making it difficult to forecast future trends. The influx of MNEs, particularly in Portugal, was associated with production in the low-cost, low-value-added areas, such as textiles, similar to the Mexican experience, while in Spain there were some FDIs in high-value-added areas.

Development through the activities of MNEs is seen as an alternative to active policies initiated by the state. Recent experiences from Europe highlight the problems associated with such policies. Political considerations, geographical proximity as well as wage differentials led to the divergence of EU investments partly from the EU periphery to the central and eastern economies (CEEs). Between 1992 and 1994 FDIs in the CEEs increased from $6,571 million to $11,993 million; the major recipient was Hungary ($6,316 million in 1994), followed by the Czech Republic ($2,820 million) (UN 1994). This move shows that factor and transport cost differentials are important but not the only decisive factor. In 1991, monthly wages were $140 in Hungary and $45 in Poland, but $235 in Portugal and $400 in Spain (Dunning 1993: 433). Low FDIs in Albania and Bulgaria highlight the fact that low labour costs are one of the factors affecting corporate decisions, but it is neither the only nor the most decisive one. FDIs from the EU represented, in 1994, 68 per cent of total FDIs in the CEEs. Although, this increase may not represent a diversification of investment only from the EU periphery to CEEs, specific examples point to a close link between the two. Mitsubishi switched its manufacturing group from Spain and Suzuki from Portugal to Eastern Europe, while Foundation Publishing expanded its typesetting operation to Budapest instead of Greece (Dunning 1993: 435). These moves point to the lack of any commitment by the MNEs towards any country, the unpredictability of their operations and the dangers involved in allowing the process of the industrialisation of a nation rest in their laps.

Further, MNEs tend to have adverse effects on local capital because of their superior access to capital and their ability to offer higher wages. This often leads to the closure of local industries. In fact, linkages with local industries were a requirement for the successful integration of the MNEs into a local economy. The chances of meeting these requirements are low and within an open economy there are no ways to create them. To create these linkages the Mexican authorities insisted that, in the case of the car industry controlled by MNEs, local parts produced by majority Mexican-owned industries should be used (Twomey and Milberg 1994). By 1989, under pressure from the MNEs, the domestic-content rules were relaxed, a further sign of the unequal political power between the core and peripheral countries and the inability of the former to push effectively for their interests.

Summary and conclusions

It has been argued in this chapter that the economic position of the periphery in the EU and NAFTA is different from and inferior to that of the core. Economic unions have not created the necessary institutions which could, and indeed would, promote convergence. If anything, there has been a retrograde move in that state intervention has been weakened substantially. The compensatory funds which were set up by the EU to assist poorer countries with low per capita GDP and to promote convergence do not provide a sound basis for the long-term economic development of the periphery. Multinational capital is not a substitute for domestic capital because of its volatility, the lack of control and the low linkages with domestic sectors.

However, MNEs could play a positive role as part of a controlled and coherent strategy of the type that has existed in some of the more successful NICs. Such strategies do not exist with either the NAFTA or the EU agreements. Control over the flow of MNEs to the periphery is of paramount importance for the creation of the impetus for new investment opportunities and thus sustainable growth.[2] Encouraging indigenous capital accumulation is the preferred way towards industrialisation rather than the strategies which emanate from the theoretical framework of Fordism and its variants discussed above. This is the central message of this chapter.

Notes

1 NAFTA may very well expand soon to embrace other Latin American countries – Chile, Argentina, Brazil, etc. The EU, of course, is already expanding, with the inclusion of other European countries: Sweden, Finland and Austria as from 1 January 1995. The enlargement of both economic blocs will, inevitably, change the nature and problems of the periphery.
2 The type of controls suggested in the text are very consistent with Keynes's (1980) views on capital controls to ensure full employment. In Keynes's view, if fiscal policies are pursued to achieve full employment, regulations on capital are vital, for otherwise capital flight and higher interest rates may very well ensue.

References

Amin, A. and Tomaney, J. (1995) 'The Regional Development Potential of Inward Investment in the Less Favoured Regions of the European Community,' in A. Amin and J. Tomaney (eds), *Behind the Myth of European Union*, London: Routledge.

Amsden, A. (1990) 'Third World Industrialisation: "Global Fordism" or a New Model?,' *New Left Review* July/August.

Arestis, P. and Paliginis, E. (1993) 'Financial Fragility, Peripherality, and Divergence in the European Economy,' *Journal of Economic Issues* 27, 2: 657–65.

Dunning, J. (1993) *The Globalization of Business*, London: Routledge.

European Economy (1991) *Annual Economic Report 1991–92: Strengthening Growth and Improving Convergence*, EC Commission no. 50.

Hufbauer, G. and Schott, J. (1992) *North American Free Trade: Issues and Recommendations*, Washington, DC: Institute for International Economics.

Keynes, J.M. (1980) *The Collected Writings of John Maynard Keynes*, Vol. XXV, ed. A. Robinson and D. Moggridge, London: Macmillan.

Kopinak, K. (1993) 'The Maquiladorization of the Mexican Economy,' in R. Grinspun and M. Cameron (eds), *The Political Economy of North American Free Trade*, New York: St. Martin's Press.

Larre, B. and Torres, R. (1991) 'Is Convergence a Spontaneous Process? The Experience of Spain, Portugal and Greece,' *OECD Economic Studies*, no. 16, Spring.

Lipietz, A. (1987) *Mirages and Miracles*, London: Verso.

OECD (1992) *Economic Surveys: Mexico,* Paris: OECD.

Twomey, M.J. and Milberg, W.S. (1994) 'Transnational Corporations and Mexican Autos: Impacts of Sectoral and Macroeconomic Policies,' mimeo.

UN (1994) *East-West Investment and Joint Ventures*, Geneva: ECE-UN.

10 Emerging stock markets and Third World development

The Post Keynesian case for pessimism

*Ilene Grabel**

Introduction

The 1990s have been a time of dramatic growth in 'emerging' stock market activity in developing and former socialist countries. One index of this rapid growth is changes in market capitalization: emerging market capitalization grew from $146 billion in 1984 to $1.7 trillion in 1993 (IFC 1995).

The turning point for emerging markets came in 1989–90, when portfolio investment inflows to these markets began to increase rapidly. As recently as 1983, there were no net inflows of portfolio investment to emerging markets. By 1989 net inflows had grown to $3.5 billion; in 1993 they reached $13.2 billion. This 277 percent increase between 1989 and 1993 far outpaced the increase in net direct foreign investment (127 percent) and net official development assistance (52 percent) during this period.

Although a brief reduction in emerging market activity occurred following the 1994–6 Mexican financial crisis, investors have continued to flock to emerging markets. And despite Mexico's continuing difficulties, most developing and former socialist country policy makers and (foreign) policy consultants continue to view portfolio investment inflows as an unambiguous benefit to these economies. Inflows of portfolio investment are seen to reflect investor confidence in the ambitious programs of free-market reform implemented in many countries. Inflows are also seen to be an important source of investment finance in capital-scarce economies (WIDER 1990). Perhaps the most appealing facet of portfolio investment is that it seems to be free of the kinds of constraints on national policy sovereignty that have traditionally been associated with direct investment, commercial bank loans, or foreign aid flows.

The constraining effects of direct foreign investment have been well documented (Wolff 1970). In many cases (for example, United Fruit in Latin

* Thanks to Philip Arestis, Paul Burkett, James Crotty, George DeMartino, Gary Dymski, Trevor Evans, David Felix, Harry de Haan, John Harvey, Peter Lange, Anne Mayhew and Roberta Niederjohn, all of whom provided valuable comments on the paper. Jeffrey Judge provided excellent research assistance. The University of Denver Faculty Research Fund and University Internationalization Program provided financial support for this project.

America and International Telephone and Telegraph in Chile), multinationals have intervened directly in site country governance. Bank borrowing and foreign aid have also proven to introduce constraints on policy autonomy as foreign government and multilateral lending institutions have imposed strict conditions on recipient countries. But economists and policy makers have largely failed to consider that the policy autonomy of developing and former socialist countries may also be constrained by undue reliance on portfolio investment inflows.

This chapter develops a post-Keynesian analysis of the consequences for developing and former socialist countries of current efforts to predicate national development strategy on the maintenance of portfolio investment inflows. I argue that a reliance on these inflows introduces two general, mutually reinforcing problems in these economies. These are termed the problems of 'constrained policy autonomy' and 'increased risk potential.'[1]

It should be noted that over the past decade a number of post-Keynesian and other heterodox economists have taken a critical stance towards unrestrained external 'openness' on the part of developing countries (see, for example, essays in Banuri and Schor 1992; Diaz-Alejandro 1985; Felix 1993; Fischer and Reisen 1993; Maxfield 1990; OECD 1993; Taylor 1991). This research has cautioned against unrestrained openness to foreign branch banking, direct foreign investment, aid, external debt and portfolio investment flows. Other post-Keynesian work in this area has also warned that excessive reliance on deregulated market-based financial systems in developing countries introduces destabilizing speculative pressures and can lead to poor real sector performance (for example, Burkett and Dutt 1991; Diaz-Alejandro 1985; Grabel 1995a, 1995b; Singh 1993). With few exceptions (see Stallings 1987), this literature has not addressed the issue of portfolio investment inflows into developing countries.

This chapter is organized in the following fashion. The next section presents general theoretical arguments about the problems associated with reliance on portfolio investment inflows. The subsequent section briefly explores the relevance of the theoretical arguments of the paper to the 1994–6 Mexican financial crisis. Contrary to conventional wisdom, I argue that the Mexican experience is indicative of the types of problems that are apt to occur when any developing or former socialist country relies heavily on uncontrolled portfolio investment inflows. The final section draws out the broad policy implications of the foregoing post-Keynesian analysis, and makes a case for the aggressive management of portfolio investment inflows.

The problems of portfolio investment

Investor interest in emerging markets has its roots in a number of developments of the 1980s and early 1990s. Financial liberalization programs adopted by developing countries from the late 1970s onward (and later by the former socialist countries) have played a key role in stimulating portfolio investment inflows. Financial liberalization introduced dramatic institutional changes in these countries, including the creation of new financial markets and instruments. These changes, coupled with the ensuing investor euphoria, induced speculative appreciation of asset prices, high nominal and real interest rates, and overall shifts in aggregate economic activity toward financial trading and away from industrial activities. In this context price bubbles often emerged as early investor success induced new infusions of capital.[2]

Emerging markets also became more attractive as investment prospects in developed country markets (especially the US) dimmed following the 1987 downturn in US stock prices. The easing of US monetary policy during 1990–3 was particularly important in this regard. In this context, investors were eager to look abroad for more attractive opportunities (Wysocki 1995). At the same time, managers of burgeoning mutual funds in developed countries looked to emerging markets as a means of diversifying their portfolios. These capital inflows to emerging markets comprised not just foreign investors' capital, but also substantial amounts of repatriated (domestic) flight capital as domestic elites gained confidence in newly liberalized economies (Reisen 1993). All of these developments occurred in the context of increasing financial trading.

Constrained policy autonomy

As with other forms of capital inflows, a dependence on portfolio investment inflows introduces constraints (albeit indirect) on site country policy autonomy. The objective of creating an attractive climate for portfolio investment necessitates that governments pursue macroeconomic, exchange rate and social policies that are compatible with portfolio investors' economic interests. Governments may therefore need to adopt and/or maintain tighter monetary policy and higher currency values than might otherwise be warranted (say, for reasons of promoting economic growth). But especially in developing countries, where industrial and agricultural production tend to be highly debt dependent, high interest rates may have a pronounced negative effect on the level of economic activity. Similarly, high currency values may undermine export performance (see Reisen 1993).[3]

It might be argued that foreign portfolio investors – regardless of whether the site economy is developing or developed – may reasonably be expected to be biased toward tight monetary policy in site countries to protect the domestic currency value of their foreign returns (Frieden 1991). In the same vein, all portfolio investors may reasonably expect the government to adopt sufficient measures to keep inflationary pressures under control. While it is generally true that all portfolio investors have a strong anti-inflationary bias, in the particular case of developing countries portfolio investors may be especially concerned that macroeconomic policy be contractionary because of the greater perceived currency, political and inflation risk in these countries. Hence, while the constraint on monetary and fiscal policy autonomy generally obtains today in all countries, it obtains to different degrees in developing and developed countries. Moreover, in the aftermath of a crisis in which investors have been recently harmed by a currency depreciation, their concerns about currency risk might be magnified. This constraint on policy autonomy may exacerbate what are already significant existing constraints on policy autonomy in developing countries which may, for example, stem from foreign creditor or donor influence in economic affairs.

Privatization programs may also be a required component of strategies to create an appropriate climate for portfolio investment. In addition to inducing new capital inflows by creating new investment opportunities, privatization addresses investor concerns that government support of industries or particular firms may fuel budget deficits. In addition, measures to liberalize the economy are likely to be necessary to assure investors that economic efficiency will not be undermined by government intervention. Political repression, involving suppression of labor demands for higher wages or popular opposition to restrictive macroeconomic policy, also may be required in order to demonstrate to investors that the government has the political will to pursue neoliberal economic programs.

In short, a developing country government that seeks to attract and maintain portfolio investment inflows may be severely constrained in an *ex ante* sense: the construction of an appropriate climate for portfolio investment requires the adoption of a fairly restrictive set of policies. Portfolio investors may become the ultimate arbiters of macroeconomic and social policy, to the detriment of economically vulnerable groups and overall economic activity. Investors' 'veto power' is not expressed through conspiracy or brute force, of course – or even through formal conditionality agreements – but through the mechanism of portfolio reallocation (see Frieden 1991). But the indirectness of the threat of capital flight need not reduce its power as a constraint on policy autonomy. Indeed, John Maynard Keynes wrote presciently in 1933 of the constraining effect on domestic politics posed by the threat of capital flight (see Crotty 1983). The dilemma Keynes raised was not confined to Britain in the 1930s; neither is it confined to any region of the world more generally today. In a world in which even the poorest countries have open capital markets offering highly liquid investment opportunities, investors may 'discipline' what they view as errant policy makers through portfolio reallocation.

In addition to what I term the *ex ante* constraint on policy autonomy, there is the possibility of an *ex post* constraint as well. This may obtain if, following an episode of large-scale capital flight or financial crisis, the government is compelled to adopt measures aimed at reversing the outflow of portfolio investment. These measures would probably involve intensification of the policies initially pursued in efforts to market the economy as an attractive site for portfolio investment. For example, Haggard and Maxfield (1996) argue that in the context of a balance of payments crisis, developing country governments are more likely to pursue policies that lead to greater financial openness. This is because domestic political constituencies that favor financial openness may be able to lobby successfully for such measures during crises. Alternatively, governments may use financial openness as a means of signaling to important external actors (such as investors or multilateral institutions) that they are committed to restoring an attractive investment climate.

Governments may also confront an *ex post* constraint on currency depreciations in the context of capital flight or financial crises. In such circumstances, governments may take dramatic steps to protect the value of their currencies in order to prevent an investor stampede. All told, the constraints that obtain in the context of a crisis may exacerbate the pro-portfolio investor policy bias, with detrimental effects on vulnerable groups and overall economic activity.

In the particular case of developing countries, an economic crisis that threatens foreign portfolio investors is likely to induce assistance from foreign governments and/or multilateral institutions. But such assistance introduces a further *ex post* constraint on policy autonomy. Those providing assistance may do so with the proviso that they be given substantial influence over site country policy making via, for example, increasing the role of IMF advisors in domestic policy making. This constraint is particularly problematic for developing countries that may initially welcome portfolio investment inflows as a means of lessening external influence over their economies.

Increased risk potential

The second problem associated with developing country dependence on portfolio investment is termed the problem of increased risk potential. To be clear, this problem does not refer to the multitude of factors that render portfolio investment risky to investors.[4] Rather, the term refers to the manner in which the risk of portfolio investment flight amplifies the potential for macroeconomic instability and financial crisis in site economies.

The increased risk potential of portfolio investment is an outcome of the high degree of liquidity of such investment, of financial openness, and of the volatility of portfolio investors' expectations. As Keynes (1964) noted, liquidity is an important precondition of investment, but it is precisely this liquidity that renders aggregate investment (and hence the macroeconomy) unstable. Given that investor expectations are highly volatile, perceptions regarding the attractiveness of particular markets are subject to rapid change. Investors may be optimistic about portfolio investment in some country for some period, only to reverse that view and turn aggressively pessimistic. Changes in investors' conventional wisdom may be sparked by 'news' (whether accurate or not) or speculation regarding changes in political developments, impending currency depreciations, changes in interest rates abroad, or the emergence of a newer (emerging) market expected to offer even richer rewards. By acting on changes in conventional wisdom, investors force its realization: fears of a market collapse can be self-fulfilling as initial investor flight induces further flight, eventually triggering a crisis (Keynes 1964).

The liquidity of portfolio investment in the context of international financial openness provides investors with an exit option that can give rise to financial crisis and cross-border contagion. While the risk of flight is endemic to portfolio investment in all countries, investors may be more prone to exit suddenly from developing country financial markets given the greater perceived risks in these markets. The greater risk of portfolio investment flight in developing countries strengthens the *ex ante* constraint on policy in these countries.

Not only is the risk potential of portfolio investment greater in developing countries, but its realization is also more costly to the economy. In capital-scarce developing countries, large and sudden withdrawals of portfolio investment may threaten the viability of domestic investment as the resources available for investment finance are reduced. Furthermore, under floating exchange rates, a withdrawal of portfolio investment may trigger or exacerbate a depreciation of the domestic currency in the likely event that the government does not have foreign exchange reserves sufficient to stabilize the currency value.[5] These circumstances are likely to threaten the stability of the macroeconomy, and may trigger a broad-ranging financial crisis.[6]

In the event of portfolio investment flight, the macroeconomy and vulnerable segments of the citizenry ultimately bear the social and economic costs of the austerity measures generally taken in the wake of economic crises (such as reductions in government spending; see Taylor 1991). The loss in purchasing power that stems from sudden currency depreciations may cause dislocation among the significant proportion of wage-earners who are dependent on imported wage goods. Currency depreciation also increases the cost of imported capital goods and external debt-service obligations (which are mostly denominated in 'hard' foreign currencies such as the dollar).

Following financial crises, problems of increased risk potential and constrained autonomy may be mutually reinforcing as measures undertaken to stem crises may further constrain policy autonomy. If governments deplete scarce foreign exchange reserves in efforts to stem losses in currency value, they reduce the resources available to mitigate the consequences of economic downturns. Additionally, the government may be compelled to implement restrictive macroeconomic policies aimed at reducing portfolio investment outflows and inducing new inflows. Hence, not only is the government precluded from taking measures designed to ease the dislocation that accompanies economic crises, but it may also be encouraged to take steps that aggravate the consequences of the crisis. The conditionality that is tied to foreign assistance in the wake of the crisis would exacerbate these pressures.

An examination of the 1994–6 Mexican financial crisis

Twice in the post-World War II period, events emanating from Mexico's financial markets sent shock waves through international markets. The first crisis was Mexico's threatened default on its international loans in 1982. This event marked the beginning of the debt crisis, triggering a drastic reduction in new private bank and bilateral lending to developing countries as a whole.[7]

At the time of the 1982 announcement, contagion scenarios held sway over the US banking and policy communities. These scenarios involved widespread defaults by developing country debtors, resulting in a collapse of bank share prices. The combined effects of these events were, at the time, thought to threaten the stability of the global, and especially the US, financial systems (see Cohen 1991). These fears provided the impetus for the Baker and Brady Plans in 1985 and 1989, respectively. In the event, Mexico's default never came to pass, and the global financial system did not collapse. The real losers from this crisis were the economically vulnerable groups in Mexico and elsewhere in the developing world, who suffered tremendous hardship in the aftermath of the debt crisis and the associated austerity measures.

In less than a decade, portfolio investors returned to Mexican financial markets with a vengeance. The second shock to emanate from Mexican financial markets relates to this development. From 1989 on, Mexico was marketed as a model of successful developing country reform efforts.[8] A recent retrospective on Mexico captures well the spirit of investors' conventional wisdom on Mexico from the late 1980s up until the spring of 1994:

> Mexico was coming to be viewed as a showcase of successful stabilization and economic reform, institutional stability and financial predictability. Mexico was becoming what Chile already had become and what all of Latin America hoped to be . . .
>
> (Dornbusch and Werner 1994: 253)[9]

During this time, Mexico was promoted as the site of one of the world's most dynamic emerging markets. Investment guides and the business press promoted Mexico's newly privatized giants (like Telmex) as extremely attractive investment opportunities.

Several factors abetted the rush to Mexican financial markets. One was the Mexican government's gestures toward political democratization and economic liberalization, which received wide attention in the US. A second, related development was the drive to liberalize trade through the negotiation of the North American Free Trade Agreement (NAFTA). NAFTA was seen to create substantial investment opportunities in Mexico, while further demonstrating Mexico's willingness to pursue neoliberal economic reform. In furthering economic integration between the US and Mexico, NAFTA was also seen to bind together tightly the fates of these two nations, something that foreign investors could count on in the event that Mexico experienced difficulties. NAFTA thus offered a sort of implicit US guarantee on investments in Mexico.

The high returns offered on short-term Mexican government debt were also extremely attractive to individual investors and to pension and mutual fund managers. Both the dollar-indexed short-term bond called the tesobono[10] and the peso-denominated short-term bond called the cete offered returns that far exceeded those available elsewhere, especially in the US where lower interest rates during 1993 encouraged investors to look abroad. Between 1982 and 1989 the cete rate ranged from 44.9 percent to 95.97 percent and between 1990 and 1993 from 14.9 percent to 34.76 percent. The tesobono rate was similarly attractive to investors: it peaked at 29.8 percent in 1988, and was at 10.9 percent in 1991, before falling to 4.08 percent in 1993 (Dornbusch and Werner 1994).

Attracted by these high returns, portfolio investment began to pour into booming Mexican debt and equity markets. Although Mexico experienced a net portfolio investment outflow of $1.7 billion in 1989, within one year the direction of flow was reversed: Mexico enjoyed a net inflow of portfolio investment of $5.9 billion in 1990, followed by net inflows of $19.6 billion in 1991, $21.1 billion in 1992, and $28 billion in 1994.[11] This influx contributed to substantial appreciation in market capitalization, with the stock market index gaining value every year after 1989. Mexican share prices rose 50.09 percent in 1990, 124.67 percent in 1991, 24.45 percent in 1992, and 48.03 percent in 1993 (Dornbusch and Werner 1994; *Economist* 1995a).

As is by now widely recognised inside and outside of Mexico, the peso was fixed at a progressively overvalued rate (in nominal and real terms) by the Mexican government during this period of increased private capital inflows (BBC 1995). While counterfactual estimates of the degree of overvaluation are imprecise,[12] it is clear that the only way that the Mexican government could have maintained the exchange rate during this period was to deplete its foreign exchange reserves.

A tightening of US monetary policy beginning in February 1994 started to diminish the appeal of Mexican portfolio investment (see Fidler 1995; Wysocki 1995). By April 1994 the Mexican bubble began to burst, completely collapsing in December of that year. During 1994 the stock market lost 30 percent of its value and the peso suffered several speculative attacks. In efforts to stabilize the peso, the government depleted $10 billion of foreign exchange reserves (Dornbusch and Werner 1994: 283). The conjunction of this financial instability, the Chiapas revolt, and the assassination of the leading candidate in the presidential election finally led the new President, Ernesto Zedillo, to devalue the peso by 40 percent in December 1994.

Instead of stabilizing Mexican financial markets, the devaluation triggered a mutually reinforcing outflow of portfolio investment and a collapse of the peso, plunging Mexico further into financial crisis (see Lustig 1995). Both foreign and domestic investors exited Mexican portfolio investment. In fact, evidence suggests that Mexican investors were the earliest group of investors to flee (*Economist* 1995i). In January 1995 the Mexican government depleted nearly 50 percent of its remaining foreign exchange reserves (falling from $6 billion at the end of 1994 to $3.5 billion by the end of January 1995) in efforts to calm investors by stabilizing the peso (*Economist* 1995b).

With the peso and Mexican markets entering free fall, the dismal state of Mexican financial markets again triggered fears of global financial contagion. This time, however, the triggering mechanisms of the contagion were different. The first aspect of this scenario involved what was seen as the Mexican government's near certain default on short-term bonds – the cetes and especially the tesebonos.[13] In Ponzi fashion, the Mexican government had been deficit financing its expenditures and obligations with short-term debt, rendering the government vulnerable to a shock from financial markets (Minsky 1986). The depletion of the government's already scarce foreign exchange reserves and the flight of portfolio investment that started in mid-1994 left the government unable to meet its immediate short-term obligations to bondholders (equal to tens of billions of dollars). As of the end of January 1995, the government had spent about $13 billion in order to cover tesobono obligations (Fineman 1995).

The Clinton Administration and financial industry analysts argued aggressively that a default on Mexican government bonds would trigger a general flight from Mexican financial markets and a further collapse of the peso. Not only did this conjure visions of disaster within Mexico, but it was also seen as the harbinger of significant problems within the US, given its deepening integration with Mexico. Specifically, analysts feared that the Mexican crisis (and the austerity measures it would induce) would threaten the anticipated boost to the US economy promised by NAFTA, fuel the uprising in Chiapas, and, in the context of widespread anti-immigrant sentiment in the US, spur a new wave of legal and especially illegal immigration (see *Economist* 1995b). Analysts also began to conjure up US financial crisis scenarios, as institutional and individual holders of Mexican government bonds were left with worthless paper.

The Mexican crisis also led to predictions of systemic financial crisis in the developing world. Analysts feared capital flight from other emerging markets (such as Argentina and Brazil), as formerly bullish investors turned starkly bearish on emerging markets.[14] Indeed, the Argentine government expressed such fears early on (see Sims 1995). In the event, the fears of generalized emerging market flight were well founded: in what became known as the 'tequila effect,' emerging markets in Latin American and elsewhere experienced dramatic portfolio investment outflows. Many also feared a further feedback effect in the form of reversals of the free-market policy reform that had been adopted by developing countries in the 1980s (for example, Lewis 1995). Crisis threatened a return to the past – to nationalist, inward-oriented, state-led development programs.

The Clinton Administration responded to the crisis by pressing for Mexican relief. In exchange for a $20 billion US bailout and $28 billion in additional international loans,[15] the Mexican government committed to further the 1980s reform agenda of privatization, stabilization, and economic liberalization. It also agreed to implement highly restrictive monetary policy, to reduce budget and current account deficits, and to increase the value-added tax and the prices of goods produced by the state (for example, electricity and gasoline). More controversial than the renewed commitment to neoliberalism on the part of the Mexican government were the requirements that: the lion's share of all of the bailout funds be used to cover tesobono and other outstanding bond obligations; the government be able to draw on a $10 billion portion of the bailout earmarked as an emergency fund only at the discretion of the US; the government get permission from the US for most major economic policy decisions; and the receipts of Mexico's state-owned oil company, Pemex, be used as collateral for the US loans and loan guarantees.[16]

On February 22, 1995, the Mexican central bank raised nominal interest rates to 59 percent in efforts to restore foreign confidence in the financial system, to attract capital back to Mexico, and to meet the US bailout conditions. This action precipitated a general increase in the cost of all types of credit. Business analysts have expressed grave concerns that the high level of Mexican interest rates today is contributing to further investment stagnation, recession, and social dislocation (*Economist* 1995c, 1995h; de Palma 1995a, 1995b). Already suffering from large losses, Mexico's banks now confront increasing rates of default on high variable rate loans (Moody's 1995; Smith 1996; see also Grabel 1995a).[17]

Constrained autonomy and increased risk potential

The arguments developed above regarding the general problems associated with developing countries' reliance on portfolio investment inflows speak directly to recent Mexican experience.

An *ex ante* constraint on policy autonomy was apparent in the period following 1989 when the Mexican government implemented the package of economic reforms that was required under the terms of the Brady Plan. These privatization and financial and economic liberalization programs played an important role in signaling to private investors that it was safe to return to Mexico. Coupled with the implicit NAFTA investor guarantees, these neoliberal policies were decisive in attracting high levels of portfolio investment inflows to Mexico after 1989 and 'rehabilitating' the economy. The success in attracting portfolio investment was critically important because new direct foreign investment, private and multilateral lending, and aid flows were all inadequate for Mexico's capital needs.

Once the crisis occurred in 1994, the Mexican government's policy autonomy was further constrained. The government was compelled to try to stem the capital outflow, stabilize the peso, and calm portfolio investors. These steps principally involved the expenditure of vast quantities of foreign exchange reserves. But this strategy did not succeed as investors recognized that the government's resources were well below those needed to make good on its bond obligations. The depletion of foreign exchange reserves also impaired the government's ability to finance ameliorative policies aimed at easing the dislocation associated with the crisis and its aftermath.

The stringent provisions of the bailout provide the most direct indication of *ex post* constraints on policy autonomy. The influence of the US and the IMF on Mexican macroeconomic and social policy has been substantially increased; indeed, the entire direction and import of policy in the post-crisis period are principally aimed at restoring investor confidence. The Mexican government's 'Alliance for Recovery,' signed by government, business and labor leaders in October 1995, reaffirms the commitment to neoliberal economic policies for the foreseeable future. A central feature of the Alliance is an agreement to continue wage restraint.

The arguments advanced above regarding increased risk potential are also germane in the Mexican context. To be sure, the expansion of portfolio investment inflows following 1989 provided the government and private corporations with resources to which they might not have otherwise had access. But the liquidity of this portfolio investment ensured that the December 1994 peso devaluation, coupled with the tightening of US monetary policy in February 1994, would destabilize markets and trigger rapid and substantial portfolio investment outflows. The devaluation was especially destabilizing to tesebono investors who feared that the risk of default on these bonds was especially great (Lustig 1995). When investors again began to exit Mexican financial markets in the spring of 1995, the flight dynamic was self-reinforcing. Thus, the realization of the increased risk potential of portfolio investment had the effect of triggering a withdrawal contagion, and hence inaugurating a downward spiral of flight and financial crisis.

The interaction of increased risk potential and constrained autonomy are also relevant here. In order to try to contain the crisis after December 1994, the bailout provisions necessitated the introduction of greater foreign influence in economic decision making. But by further opening the economy to capital inflows (as the neoliberal tenor of the bailout provisions require), the vulnerability of the Mexican economy to future crises may be exacerbated, necessitating future bailouts and increased foreign intervention in the economy.

Can we generalize from the Mexican experience?

In the aftermath of the Mexican crisis something of a 'Mexican exceptionalism' thesis has begun to emerge among policy analysts. Both the IMF and the World Bank (1995) have contended that the Mexican experience is unique and that it therefore is of little relevance to the former socialist and other developing countries that have become active sites of portfolio investment inflows. Rather than interrogate the Mexican crisis as evidence of the inherent shortcomings of portfolio investment, the crisis has been largely dismissed as an aberration stemming from Mexico's peculiarities. The latter include Mexico's mismanagement of its economic affairs and its political corruption.

Is there merit in this interpretation? The arguments about Mexican economic mismanagement are suspect. This is not to deny the existence of significant current account deficits and low levels of foreign exchange reserves in Mexico. But these economic problems are in no respect unique to Mexico. Other countries facing current account deficits, inadequate foreign exchange reserves, or other important macroeconomic problems are similarly vulnerable to investor flight when conventional wisdom turns bearish.[18] In the context of a speculative bubble, a country's current account deficit may be seen as regrettable, but not so terribly important. However, when conventional wisdom shifts – perhaps because of changes in domestic or international economic and/or political conditions – these economic problems themselves become reasons for a self-exacerbating investor withdrawal made possible by financial openness.

It is noteworthy that the exceptionalism thesis overlooks the most important aspect in which Mexico is unique. Mexico enjoys a special relationship with the US. Over the past two decades the economies of these two countries have become increasingly integrated; the NAFTA agreement codifies the general trend while symbolizing the unusual relationship that has emerged between a developing country and an economic superpower. The question that should be broached, then, is whether this peculiar relationship does make the Mexican crisis anomalous.

It may be true that NAFTA euphoria increased the rate of portfolio investment inflows into Mexico, leading to price bubbles that would otherwise not have occurred. But, if true, this validates the post-Keynesian arguments developed here regarding the riskiness of predicating economic development on highly volatile portfolio investment flows. Moreover, investor euphoria about Mexico in the early 1990s also stemmed from numerous other circumstances that are not in any way unique to Mexico. Specifically, financial liberalization and privatization programs created investment opportunities for those individual and institutional investors in developed countries who were looking abroad for investment sites, especially after US monetary policy eased. These circumstances created investor interest not just in Mexico, but in numerous developing and former socialist countries that have been active sites of portfolio investment.

But on balance it might be concluded that the special relationship between Mexico and the US should have decreased the likelihood of the kind of crisis that Mexico experienced. Given the strategic importance of Mexico in the US campaign to liberalize trade and investment flows in the Americas and the degree to which successive US Administrations have invested political capital in ensuring Mexico's success, investors should have been reasonably certain that the US government would intervene forcefully to prevent financial instability in its southern neighbor. What is remarkable about the Mexican experience, then, is that the implicit *ex ante* guarantee of the US counted for so little when investor sentiments about Mexico changed in the face of disturbing political and economic news. The special relationship with the US may have counted more in managing the crisis after the fact – but if so, then we may rightly conclude that what was anomalous about the Mexican crisis is that it was not more severe. In this case, other site countries can take little solace from the notion that Mexico is somehow 'different.'

Is financial autarky the answer?

I have argued that developing country dependence on portfolio investment could have unanticipated and undesirable consequences for these countries. The shift away from direct foreign investment, lending and aid, while thought to resolve concerns about foreign control and capital scarcity, could exacerbate problems of constrained autonomy for developing countries and introduce increased risk into the economy. These problems are self-reinforcing. While the arguments presented here are highly general, they are certainly germane to the dynamics of the recent Mexican financial crisis. Moreover, the Mexican crisis itself cannot be written off as a strictly anomalous event. Dynamics similar to those evidenced in Mexico could easily obtain in the very large number of developing and former socialist countries that are today active sites of largely unregulated portfolio investment. Indeed, the freewheeling nature of the Russian stock exchange has received much attention of late (for example, see Reisen 1995; Middleton 1996).

What do these arguments imply about the means by which developing countries should meet their capital needs? At the broadest level, it implies that financial openness and policies aimed specifically at attracting portfolio investment introduce and exacerbate significant problems. In particular, the high degree of liquidity of portfolio investment makes it a problematic solution to the capital scarcity faced by developing countries. If portfolio investment is to be encouraged at all, developing country policy makers would be advised to manage it aggressively, even at the risk that such management will reduce the overall volume of inflows.

Management of portfolio investment itself may take a variety of forms.[19] The most extreme measure would involve outright restrictions in the form of stringent capital controls, especially aimed at outflows. These measures might be in the spirit of Keynes' (1933) prescriptions. Given that any individual developing country today undertaking such measures would be placed at a competitive disadvantage in attracting funds, such measures would have to be pursued on a regional or South–South basis (see, for example, Taylor 1991).

But are South–South capital controls impractical in today's global economy? It may be argued that capital controls are at odds with the *Zeitgeist* and IMF mandates, both of which celebrate openness, that they are not feasible politically, that they are not effective because they are too easily evaded, and that they might trigger a crisis in emerging markets as investors flee these markets in anticipation of controls. However, the inevitability and immutability of openness should not be taken for granted. Multilateral organizations such as the UN and the OECD are beginning to investigate the complicated effects of openness. They have begun to examine the viability and desirability of damping openness and reducing the hyperliquidity of capital markets (see UNDP 1994; Fischer and Reisen 1993). For example, a recent OECD study of financial openness in developing countries argues for the 'late' removal of their capital controls (Fischer and Reisen 1993). That is, the study identifies the achievement of sound government finances and an appropriate institutional and regulatory structure for financial sector supervision as important preconditions for the removal of capital controls. Against these criteria, many developing countries today appear to be good candidates for capital controls.[20]

The successful use of stringent capital controls by South Korea and Japan during their periods of rapid economic development is instructive in this regard. Despite the World Bank's (1993) recent 'revisionist' analysis of the lessons of East Asian successes, the consensus of the literature on East Asian development confirms that capital controls were an integral part of the achievements of these developmental states (for example, Amsden 1989; Hart-Landsberg 1993). During Japanese industrialization, for example, there was an outright prohibition on foreign ownership of securities and equities. In South Korea, violations of prohibitions on overseas capital transfers were punishable by a minimum sentence of ten years in prison and a maximum sentence of death (Amsden 1989: 17).

It is unfortunate (though not terribly surprising) that in the wake of the Mexican crisis and in view of the success of East Asian capital control policies, the IMF and the World Bank have failed to call for developing country control over portfolio investment inflows (see Dadush and Brahmbhatt 1995). In fact, a recent World Bank (1995) study acknowledges that short-term, liquid capital inflows are potentially volatile. The Bank argues that the tequila effect is avoidable, provided domestic policy makers maintain sound macroeconomic policies (for example, minimize current account deficits), channel inflows to 'productive' uses, and avoid excessive reliance on short-term capital inflows. Indeed, this is seen by the Bank as a key distinguishing feature separating those countries that have successfully harnessed private capital inflows (that is, East Asian countries) from those that have not (that is, Latin America and Mexico, in particular). Hence, the Bank dismisses outright the efficacy of capital controls in accounting for the financial stability and macroeconomic performance of East Asian countries.[21]

An alternative to capital controls is the use of volume- or price-based restrictions on asset purchases and sales as means to manage portfolio investment and to slow the pace of flight during crises. Similarly, the implementation of 'circuit breakers' which essentially stop sales during periods of crisis could accomplish the same aim. A variety of measures aimed at damping financial market volatility and encouraging investors to lengthen their time horizons are currently in place in some developing countries (see *Economist* 1995f). For example, in Colombia foreign investors are free to engage in (less-liquid) direct investment, but are precluded from purchasing debt instruments and are discouraged from purchasing corporate equity. In Chile, foreign portfolio investors are required to keep their cash in the country for at least one year.

The tax system can also be used to damp portfolio investment volatility and to provide some compensation for the costs of liquidity, as Tobin (1978) has proposed (see also UNDP 1994: 70). This uniform, global transaction tax has been taken up recently by the United Nations and several prominent development economists (Felix 1993; Singh 1993; see also Diaz-Alejandro 1985: 22). These taxes are designed to throw sand in the gears of portfolio churning so as to reduce volatility and lengthen investor time horizons. Moreover, as Felix (1993) points out, there are already a variety of measures in place globally and within the G7 countries that establish a framework for supranational financial policy and cooperation. These comprise agreements to share tax information, coordinate macroeconomic policy, and impose uniform capital standards and bank regulation. It may also be the case that developing countries could pursue a uniform South–South tax in the event that a global tax proves at present to be too difficult to negotiate.

It is certainly the case that any of the measures outlined here would diminish the attractiveness of portfolio investment in developing and former socialist countries by reducing the market's liquidity. But if the arguments presented here are correct – as the Mexican experience suggests – then a reduced level of portfolio inflow may be a worthwhile price to pay for enhanced macroeconomic stability and policy autonomy.

Notes

1 Grabel (1996b) compares the effects of portfolio investment inflows to those of direct foreign investment, external loans and foreign aid. The following discussion draws heavily on this work.
2 Grabel (1995a) discusses the implementation and consequences of financial liberalization programs in developing and former socialist countries.
3 It is obvious that under floating exchange rates a currency appreciation may also result from high levels of portfolio investment inflows. When trade performance is undermined under these circumstances, the Dutch disease effect is said to occur. What is important about the Dutch disease is that it shows that portfolio investment inflows (and not just outflows) can be also be problematic.
4 Investors bear numerous risks. For example, bonds carry default risk, equity investments are associated with commercial risk, foreign investment carries exchange rate risk, and in countries with histories of high inflation, the returns on portfolio investment may be undermined by inflation risk.
5 Under floating exchange rates, portfolio investor flight may not only result in real currency depreciations but it can also be triggered by real currency depreciations (or expectations thereof) (see, for example, Taylor 1995).
6 See Eichengreen and Portes (1987), Krugman (1991) and Wolfson (1986) for a

general discussion of the contagion or transmission mechanisms for domestic and international financial crises. See also Taylor's (1995) generalization of Minsky (1986).

7   Felix (1994) and Reisen (1993) argue that there are important parallels between the dynamic and (likely) outcome of the over-lending/over-borrowing of the 1970s and the 'over-investing' taking place today.

8   See Dornbusch and Werner (1994) and *Economist* (1995e) on the 'rehabilitation' of Mexico after 1982 until the current crisis.

9   Similar views were echoed by US Treasury Secretary Robert Rubin (see Sanger 1995).

10   The initial dollar-indexed vehicle, the pagafe, was replaced by the tesobono in 1990–1.

11   Other Latin American countries experienced similar inflows. From 1989 to 1990 Brazil received $40 billion and Argentina $10 billion in portfolio investment (*Economist* 1995b).

12   See Dornbusch and Werner (1994) for one such estimate.

13   For example, see accounts in *Economist* (1995b), Sanger (1995) and Fineman (1995).

14   For discussions regarding the fear of systemic flight from emerging markets, see, for example, *Business Week* (1995); de Palma (1995a); *Economist* (1995b, 1995d, 1995e, 1995g); Lewis (1995a, 1995b); Sanger (1995).

15   See *Financial Times* (1995) for details on the bailout package.

16   Note that in January 1997 the Mexican government repaid its US government obligations.

17   In 1993, 7.1 percent of total loans were classified as non-performing (Dornbusch and Werner 1994: 284). The 'bad loan problem' seems to be worsening following the rise in interest rates. In fact, by as early as February 1995 the finance ministry had already lent $1 billion to assist troubled banks (*Economist* 1995c). By January 1996, past-due loans exceeded $17 billion – 18 percent of outstanding loans made by Mexican banks (Smith 1996).

18   Indeed, the likelihood of persistent current account deficits is increased by the attainment of conditions necessary to the creation of an attractive climate for portfolio investment.

19   Note that the discussion here does not address what can be done on the 'supply-side' to curb the volatility of portfolio investment. See Grabel (1996a).

20   Crotty and Epstein (1996) develop a case for capital controls, and explore a range of policy instruments that might achieve that goal.

21   Reisen (1993) argues that the key to East Asian success in preventing capital inflows from undermining trade (and hence macroeconomic performance) is not the use of capital controls, but the sterilization of 'hot money' inflows.

References

Amsden, A. (1989) *Asia's Next Giant*, New York: Oxford University Press.

Banuri, T. and Schor, J. (eds) (1992) *Financial Openness and National Autonomy*, Oxford: Clarendon Press.

British Broadcasting Corporation (BBC) (1995) Speech by the Mexican finance secretary to deputies on the economic situation, January 23; original source: Television Azteca, Mexico City.

Burkett, P. and Dutt, A. (1991) 'Interest Rate Policy, Effective Demand, and Growth in LDCs,' *International Review of Applied Economics* 5, 2: 127–53.

Business Week (1995) 'Mexico's Quake Rocks Argentina,' January 23: 32.

Cohen, B. (1991) 'Whatever Happened to the LDC Debt Crisis?,' *Challenge* 34, 3: 47–51.

Crotty, J. (1983) 'On Keynes and Capital Flight,' *Journal of Economic Literature* 21, 1: 59–65.

—— and Epstein, G. (1996) 'In Defence of Capital Controls,' in L. Panitch (ed.), *Socialist Register: Are There Alternatives?*, London: Merlin Press.

Dadush, U. and Brahmbhatt, M. (1995) 'Anticipating Capital Flow Reversals,' *Finance and Development* 32, 4: 3–5.

de Palma, A. (1995a) 'Economy Reeling, Mexicans Prepare Tough New Steps,' *New York Times* February 26: p. A1.

—— (1995b) 'The Mexicans Rise up Against "Fiscal Terrorism",' *New York Times* May 13: 4.

Diaz-Alejandro, C. (1985) 'Good-bye Financial Repression, Hello Financial Crash,' *Journal of Development Economics* 19, 1–2: 1–24.

Dornbusch, R. and Werner, A. (1994) 'Mexico: Stabilization, Reform and No Growth,' *Brookings Papers on Economic Activity* 1: 253–315.

Economist (1995a) 'Hong Kong: The World's Emerging Markets All at Sea,' January 28: 68–71.

—— (1995b) 'To the Rescue,' February 4: 13–4.

—— (1995c) 'Mexican Finance: Band-Aid,' February 25: 79.

—— (1995d) 'A Rough Ride,' March 11: 71–2.

—— (1995e) 'The Mexico Syndrome and How to Avoid It,' March 18: 73–5.

—— (1995f) 'The Tequila Hangover,' April 8: 65–6.

—— (1995g) 'Rising Markets, Sinking Feeling,' May 13: 71–2.

—— (1995h) 'Mexico's Economy: A Real Turkey?,' August 5: 68–9.

—— (1995i) 'Sorry, Gringos,' August 26: 65.

Eichengreen, B. and Portes, R. (1987) 'The Anatomy of Financial Crises,' in R. Portes and A. Swoboda (eds), *Threats to International Financial Stability*, Cambridge: Cambridge University Press.

Felix, D. (1993) 'Developing Countries and Joint Action to Curb International Financial Volatility,' *UNCTAD Bulletin* 21: 7–9.

—— (1994) 'International Capital Mobility and Third World Development: Compatible Marriage or Troubled Relationship?,' *Policy Sciences Review* 27, 4: 365–94.

Fidler, S. (1995) 'More Liberal Flow of Funds Creates Instability,' *The Financial Times*, January 27: 4.

Financial Times (1995) 'Bitter Legacy of Battle to Bail out Mexico,' February 16: 4.

Fineman, M. (1995) 'Mexico Uses $4 Billion from US Bailout to Pay Investors,' *Los Angeles Times* April 5: A1.

Fischer, B. and Reisen, H. (1993) *Liberalising Capital Flows in Developing Countries: Pitfalls and Prerequisites*, Paris: OECD.

Frieden, J. (1991) 'Invested Interests: the Politics of National Economic Policies in a World of Global Finance,' *International Organization* 45, 4: 425–52.

Grabel, I. (1995a) 'Speculation-led Economic Development: a Post-Keynesian Interpretation of Financial Liberalization Programmes in the Third World,' *International Review of Applied Economics* 9, 2: 127–49.

—— (1995b) 'Assessing the Impact of Financial Liberalisation on Stock Market Volatility in Selected Developing Countries,' *Journal of Development Studies* 31, 6: 903–17.

—— (1996a) 'Financial Markets, the State and Economic Development: Controversies within Theory and Policy,' *International Papers in Political Economy* 3, 1: 1–42.

—— (1996b) 'Marketing the Third World: the Contradictions of Portfolio Investment in the Global Economy,' *World Development* 24, 11: 1761–76.

Haggard, S. and Maxfield, S. (1996) 'The Political Economy of Financial Internationalization in the Developing World,' *International Organization* 50, 1: 35–68.

Hart-Landsberg, M. (1993) *The Rush to Development*, New York: Monthly Review.

International Finance Corporation (IFC) (various years) *Emerging Stock Markets Factbook*, Washington, DC: IFC.

Keynes, J.M. (1933) 'National Self-Sufficiency,' *Yale Review* 233–46.

—— (1964) *The General Theory of Employment, Interest and Money*, New York: Harcourt Brace Jovanovich.

Krugman, P. (1991) 'International Aspects of Financial Crises,' in M. Feldstein (ed.), *The Risk of Economic Crisis*, Chicago: University of Chicago Press.

Lewis, P. (1995a) 'Socializing Risk to Foster Free Markets,' *New York Times* February 11: C8.

—— (1995b) 'Preventing the Next Peso-style Crisis,' *New York Times* February 12: C3.

Lustig, N. (1995) 'The Mexican Peso Crisis: the Foreseeable and the Surprisable,' *Brookings Discussion Papers* 114.

Maxfield, S. (1990) *Governing Capital: International Finance and Mexican Politics*, Ithaca, NY: Cornell University Press.

Middleton, T. (1996) 'For the Brave, an Open-end Russia Fund,' *New York Times* April 28: F6.

Minsky, H. (1986) *Stabilizing an Unstable Economy*, New Haven, CT: Yale University Press.

Moody's (1995) 'Mexican Banks Face Severe Challenges,' January 23.

OECD (1993) *Financial Opening: Policy Issues and Experiences in Developing Countries*, Paris: OECD.

Reisen, H. (1993) 'Capital Flows and Their Effect on the Monetary Base,' *CEPAL Review* 51: 113–22.

—— (1995) 'For US Investors, Russia Rates Caution,' *Wall Street Journal* October 23: A16.

Sanger, D. (1995) 'The Education of Robert Rubin,' *New York Times* February 5: C1.

Sims, C. (1995) 'Argentina, a Victim of Mexico Peso's Fall, Tries to Recover,' *New York Times* March 12: C14.

Singh, A. (1993) 'The Stock Market and Economic Development: Should Developing Countries Encourage Stock Markets?,' *UNCTAD Review* 4: 1–28.

Smith, G. (1996) 'Tossing a Lifeline to Mexico's Banks,' *Business Week* January 22: 80.

Stallings, B. (1987) *Banker to the Third World*, Berkeley, CA: University of California.

Taylor, L. (1991) 'Economic Openness: Problems to the Century's End,' in T. Banuri and J. Schor (eds.), *Economic Liberalization: No Panacea*, Oxford: Clarendon Press.

—— (1995) 'Financial Fragility: Is an Etiology at Hand?,' in G. Dymski and R. Pollin (eds), *New Perspectives in Monetary Macroeconomics*, Ann Arbor: University of Michigan Press.

Tobin, J. (1978) 'A Proposal for International Monetary Reform,' *Eastern Economic Journal* 4, 3–4: 153–9.

United Nations Development Programme (UNDP) (1994) *Human Development Report*, Oxford: Oxford University Press.

Wolff, R. (1970) 'Modern Imperialism: a View from the Metropolis,' *American Economic Review* 60, 2: 225–30.

Wolfson, M. (1986) *Financial Crises*, Armonk, NY: M.E. Sharpe.

World Bank (1993) *The East Asian Miracle*, Oxford: Oxford University Press.

—— (1995) *Global Economic Prospects and the Developing Countries*, Washington, DC: World Bank.

World Institute for Development Economics Research (WIDER) (1990) *Foreign Portfolio Investment in Emerging Markets*, WIDER study group series, no. 5.

Wysocki, B. (1995) 'Some Painful Lessons on Emerging Markets,' *Wall Street Journal* June 22: A1.

11 A primer on technology gap theory and empirics

*Bruce Elmslie and Flavio Vieira**

Introduction

The notion that international and interregional trade flows are related to systematic, country-specific differences in technological knowledge has a long history in economic thought. This line of thought can be traced from David Hume to David Ricardo, and from Ricardo to modern technology gap theory. If unifying themes can be found in this disparate body of thought, it is in the non-public-good aspect of technology, and in the link between trade patterns and macroeconomic outcomes. The mainstream view of technology and trade suggests that technology's importance in determining trade flows diminishes over time because of the easy of technology transfer.[1] The transfer of new technological innovations allows theorists to assume that each country maximizes welfare according to identical production functions. Technology gap theory, while it allows for the important public-good aspect of technology, views technological asymmetries as important long-run determinants of trade flows. Moreover, it also captures interactions between trade flows and changes in long-run growth patterns and levels of employment.

This chapter attempts to review the current state of the theoretical and empirical literature in technology gap theory. We utilize an aspect of the existing theoretical literature to more fully link the interaction between comparative and absolute advantage in technology gap models. Our discussion of the empirical literature generates ideas and suggestions for future research into the overall importance of technological asymmetries in determining both industry net trade flows and each country's overall trade balance.

The rest of the chapter is organized as follows: the next section reviews the theoretical literature and develops a model of technology gap that links comparative and absolute advantage into a single explanation of trade flows. Subsequent sections critically review the empirical literature, and provide

* A draft of this paper was presented at the Southern Economic Association Meetings, Washington, D.C., November 23–25, 1996. The authors thank Robert Blecker, William Milberg and other participants of that session for helpful comments.

suggestions for future research into the role played by sector-specific technological gaps in determining trade flows.

Theory

In the beginning: a suggestive history

A review of the literature of any field in economics can begin virtually anywhere. The analysis of the origins of concepts and theories are often limited not by accurate historical accounts but by limited space, time and interest of the authors. This brief history will attempt to outline two of the important beginnings of modern technology gap theory by first reviewing the origin of an important conceptual link between the dynamic and once-and-for-all static gains from trade, and second, by developing a model of technology gap that was first written by Josiah Tucker in the mid-1700s. As will become clear, Tucker was the first writer to posit a 'formal' model which made use of dynamic gains from trade in accounting for the evolution of trade patterns. In other words, Tucker developed a cumulative causation model of trade in which the gains provided by specialization from trade create new opportunities for further growth and trade.

Mercantilist writers have been lauded and criticized in the literature on foreign trade at least since Hume's *Political Discourses* in 1752. While both have been present in the literature, the latter is by far the more prevalent. Mercantilists have been criticized for everything, from their views regarding the gains from trade to their self-promotion of the merchant's role in society as being important. Yet, throughout almost all criticisms of mercantilist thought lies one 'lesson' which is claimed to have been missed by mercantilist writers: the economy naturally tends to full employment. In other words, mercantilist writers of the Thomas Mun stripe assumed that the economy will generally operate at a pace that leaves resources – land and labor – idle. This 'flaw' in the logical foundation of mercantilist thought was not corrected, many stories go, until Hume and Smith set the record straight.

From the perspective of many modern writers working on technology gap theories, this 'flaw' of mercantilist logic proves to be interesting because of a natural link that such logic necessitates. This is the link between international trade and changes in macroeconomic activity. In such models of economic activity, trade flows can influence the aggregate level of employment. As Thomas Mun, the great spokesman of late mercantilism stated:

> the true form and worth of forraign Trade [is], *The great Revenue of the King, The honour of the Kingdom, The Noble profession of the Merchant, The School of our Arts, The supply of our wants, The employment of our poor, The improvement of our Lands,* ...
>
> (Mun [1664] 1986: 88, original emphasis)

With this link between an economic policy and economic activity in mind, Mun made an interesting distinction between 'Natural' and 'Artificial' wealth.[2] Natural wealth 'proceedeth of the Territorie itselfe,' while artificial wealth 'dependeth on the industry of the Inhabitants' (Mun [1621] 1986: 48–9) In Mun's view, natural wealth consisted of what we now call natural resources but also included items such as 'Corn, Victuals [grains in general], Hides, Wax, and other natural Endowments' (Mun [1664] 1986: 71). Artificial wealth, on the other hand, consisted of the 'Art' or skill and labor which manufactures add to the natural wealth.

The question that most interested Mun in making this distinction was how countries limited in natural wealth (Holland) could compete in international markets with countries such as England which were abundant in natural wealth. Mun's answer was that abundance of natural wealth makes the people of the country lazy, uninventive, and cowardass. While the lack of natural wealth 'enforceth Vigilancy, Literature, Arts and Policy' (Mun [1664] 1986: 82). Thus, the issue for Mun was to break this vicious link between a state of 'general leprosie' and abundance of natural wealth. For, 'our wealth might be a rare discourse for all *Christendome* to admire and fear, if we would add *Art* to *Nature*, our *labour* to our *natural means*' (ibid.: 73).

From a modern perspective, it is tempting to conclude that Mun was grasping for a distinction between resources that exhibit diminishing returns and those that exhibit increasing returns. While no evidence of this exists, it is true that such a distinction would be made in the 1750s by Josiah Tucker in his development of a logical model of trade based on technology gaps.

Tucker was profoundly interested in the relationship between the growth of poor countries and that of rich ones such as his homeland, England. Specifically, several writers had expressed concern that England's export markets would be taken over by poorer countries that could produce goods cheaper because of their lower wages and other costs. Tucker responded with an increasing-returns argument that demonstrated the cost advantages of richer countries in the production of the most complex commodities:

> [The rich country possesses] established Trade and Credit, large Correspondences, experienced Agents and Factors . . . also a great Variety of the *best tools and Implements in the various kinds of Manufactures, and Engines for abridging Labour*; – add to these good Road, Canals, and other artificial Communications . . . And in respect to Husbandry and Agriculture, it is likewise in Possession of good Enclosures . . . great Stocks . . . a great Variety of Plows, Harrows, &c. suited to the different Soils; and . . . every other superior Method of Husbandry arising from long Experience . . .
>
> (Tucker [1776] 1974: 30, emphasis added)

Each of these stocks that allow the rich country to undersell the poor one at any point in time also sets the conditions for further gains. Thus, the rich country not only has the best tools and technologies, but also the 'superior Skill and Knowledge (acquired by long Habit and Experience) for inventing and making of more' (ibid.: 31). Moreover, the rich country need not rely only on the 'genius' of its own manufacturers and farmers to maintain this pace of innovation. The high wages, easier access to capital, and greater 'Exertion of Genius, Industry, and Ambition' will cause the best and brightest inhabitants of the poor countries to emigrate to the rich ones, draining the 'Flower of its [the poor countries] inhabitants' (ibid.: 32) This brain drain opens 'larger Correspondencies; – it presents us . . . with the Inventions and Sagacity of other Nations, creates more Imployment for the Natives, helps and improves our old Manufactures, and sets up new ones; – thus impoverishing our Rival, and the same Time that it enriches ourselves' (Schuyler 1931: 81).

From this analysis of markets, one may conclude that the rich country will come to dominate all trades, leaving no export markets for poorer countries. However, this is a mistaken presumption. Tucker seems to have had some rudimentary notion of the principle of comparative advantage, in the sense that he understood that one country could never dominate all markets. Based upon his knowledge of scarcity and his increasing-returns philosophy, Tucker developed a technology gap theory of trade in which a country is competitive in goods based upon some relation between the complexity of the good's production process and the country's level of development. Poor countries produce simple commodities cheaply, while the more complex commodities are cheaper in the rich countries:

> [I]t may be laid down as a general Proposition, which very seldom fails, That *operose* or *complicated Manufactures* are cheapest in rich Countries; and *raw Materials* in poor ones: And therefore in Proportion as any Commodity approaches to one, or other of these *Extremes*, in that Proportion it will be found to be cheaper, or dearer in a rich, or a poor Country.
>
> (Tucker: 36, original emphasis)

This may be termed Tucker's general rule of trade.

The logic of Tucker's model leads us directly to a modern model of the technology gap within a comparative advantage framework, developed in Krugman (1990).

Models of comparative advantage

Two models of technology gap within a strictly comparative advantage framework will be discussed. First, a model developed by Krugman (1990) is analyzed which hypothesizes a 'niche' of export goods for each country based on the country's level of technology. A second model by Pasinetti (1981) is then reviewed which posits a relation between changes in trade flows and the relative pace of technological progress by sector.

Krugman develops a model of trade based on technology gaps between countries at various levels of development in which trade flows are driven by comparative advantage. He utilizes a Ricardian model with a continuum of goods first developed by Dornbusch *et al.* (1977), and subsequently utilized by many technology gap models of trade (see, for example, Dosi *et al.* 1990; Cimoli and Soete 1992; Cimoli 1988, 1994; Maggi 1993; and Elmslie and Milberg 1996). The model posits that countries which are more advanced technologically have a comparative advantage in technology-intensive goods, the intensity of technology embodied in goods being measured along the continuum. Krugman then utilizes this framework to analyze the effects of expanding and narrowing the technology gap between countries.

The model assumes that a 'best-practice set of techniques of production' (Krugman 1990: 154) exists which is constantly being improved. This set of techniques is measured by a unit labor requirement a^* which follows a rate of technological progress g. Thus, for any good (z) at time (t) we may write:

$$a^*(z) = e^{-g_z t} \tag{11.1}$$

All other countries lag behind the best-practice country by λ, country i's lag is given by λ_i:

$$a_i(z) = e^{-g_z(t-\lambda_i)} \tag{11.2}$$

Comparative advantage is determined by each country's relative lag λ such that more-advanced countries have absolute advantages over less-advanced countries in all goods, but productivity advantages for each good are determined by g_z. For any two countries (i and j), the advantage of i is given by:

$$a_j(z) / a_i(z) = e^{g_z(\lambda_j - \lambda_i)} \tag{11.3}$$

where $\lambda_j > \lambda_i$.

The general result of the model is that countries specialize in goods along the continuum which match the technology intensity of goods with the relative technological development of the country. In other words, '[e]ach country has a 'niche' in the scale of goods; the higher the country is on the technology ladder, the further upscale is the range of goods in which it has a comparative advantage' (Krugman 1990: 157).

As will become clear, while Krugman (1990) does present a model of trade based on technology gaps, it is not recognized among the well-established models. Most models maintain a role for absolute advantages in the determination of trade flows in technologically intensive goods. Krugman avoids this by making the restrictive assumption that countries are capable of producing similar varieties of all goods. Once this assumption is eliminated, absolute advantages combine with comparative advantages to determine trade flows.

Several authors (for example, Dosi *et al.* 1990; Dosi and Soete 1983) have suggested that the analysis of structural change developed by Pasinetti (1981) may provide important theoretical foundations for technology gap models. A detailed analysis of these foundations is undertaken in Milberg (1991) and repeated with further evidence in Elmslie and Milberg (1992). Specifically, Pasinetti (1981) develops a model of the determination of relative changes in trade patterns based on structural change occurring in each country relative to trading partners. In an *n* country, *n* good model with many countries exporting the same good, Milberg states this relation as follows: *ceteris paribus*, industry *i* from country *H* will improve, worsen or maintain its world market share as:

$$\left(\frac{Z_{iH}}{R_H} \right) \begin{array}{c} > \\ < \end{array} \left(\frac{Z_{iW}}{R_w} \right) \tag{11.4}$$

where *W* represents the rest of the world, Z_{ij} represents the rate of technological change in sector *i* for country *j*, and R_j represents the average rate of technological change over the *n* sectors in country *j*. Milberg refers to expression (11.4) as the Pasinetti Trade Hypothesis (PTH).

Milberg tests the PTH by utilizing input–output data from the US and Canada over the period 1961–72. He develops direct and indirect labor coefficients or vertically integrated labor coefficients for 33 sectors in each country to measure the rate of technological progress as changes in these coefficients over time for each sector and for the average rate of technological change for each country. Milberg finds a significant positive correlation between relative rates of technological progress and import penetration, supporting the PTH.

Comparative and absolute advantage

Technology gap theory has been searching for stronger theoretical foundations since its beginnings in the 1960s. The first model developed in Posner (1961) attempted to build on the dominant Heckscher–Ohlin (H–O) approach by explaining an aspect of trade that H–O could not: changes in trade patterns in manufactured goods based on changing technology gaps.[3] However, since Posner much of the work on technology gap theory has attempted to more completely dissociate itself from mainstream analysis because of many of the unrealistic assumptions made by H–O vintage models. Specifically, technology gap theorists have attempted to examine three areas which are often assumed away by mainstream theory. First, in technology gap theory a major role is given to absolute advantages in the explanation of trade flows between advanced countries. Second, a link is maintained between changing patterns of international trade and the level of macroeconomic activity, much as we showed in Mun's approach. Finally, cumulative mechanisms are built into the models so that the present pace of technological advance is a function of past advances; in other words, the growth of knowledge is dependent on the existing stock of knowledge. As we have noted already, this conception of the growth of knowledge can be traced back to Tucker.[4]

While many technology gap models exist, the specific model that follows will attempt to pull together the three major themes described above. Various aspects of the model can be found in Dosi *et al.* (1990), Cimoli and Soete (1992), and Cimoli (1994).

Following Krugman (1990) and many others, the model assumes a Ricardian single-factor economy with a continuum of goods which can be ordered by technology intensity along an interval z. Two types of goods, Ricardian and innovative, are specified along the interval. Ricardian commodities are standardized and capable of being produced in both countries in a two-country world. Innovation in Ricardian goods is defined as process innovation if that technological progress lowers unit labor requirements. Thus, a change in the pattern of process innovation changes comparative advantages between the countries. Innovative goods are differentiated so that each specific good is only produced in one of the countries. Technological change in these goods takes the form of product innovation which changes absolute advantages. By assumption, Ricardian commodities $[0, z_0]$ are lower on the scale of technology intensity than innovative goods $[z_0, z_1]$. Wages are assumed to be determined exogenously by institutions specific to each country. This assumption allows the model to pursue issues not considered by labor market clearing models relating to the relationship between changes in trade flows and changes in the macroeconomy. Finally, import demand functions are allowed to differ between countries so that price and income elasticities may differ.

Assume two countries, 1 and 2. For Ricardian commodities, the technology gap is measured by the absolute difference in unit labor requirements per commodity between the two countries. Thus, a function $A(z) = a_1(z)/a_2(z)$ may be defined as an increasing function in z such that country 1 has an advantage in the least technologically advanced commodities. On a continuum $[z_0, z_1)$, country 1 specializes in $[0, \bar{z}]$, while country 2 specializes in $[\bar{z}, z_1]$. Innovation goods are placed on the continuum from $\bar{Z}_1$ to Z_1 with $\bar{Z}_1 \geq \bar{Z}$. Thus, country 2 is the sole producer of the innovative goods $[\bar{z}_1, z_1]$. Holding product innovation constant, net trade in Ricardian commodities is determined by unit labor costs in the two countries. Country 1 exports those which follow the following:[5]

$$a_1(z)w_1 < a_2(z)w_2 \qquad (11.5)$$

The non-traded or border commodity(ies) is given by the equality of equation (11.5) and may be defined by:

$$\omega = w_2/w_1 = A(\bar{z}) \qquad (11.6)$$

The borderline commodity is thus a function of the relative wage (w) and the technology gap (A):

$$\bar{z} = \bar{z}[\omega(t), A(z, t)] \tag{11.7}$$

The sensitivity of changes in the border commodity to changes in the relative wage is written as an elasticity of $\bar{z}$ with respect to w:

$$e = (\omega / \bar{z})d\bar{z} / d\omega = -1 / T \tag{11.8}$$

where T is the elasticity of the technology gap (A), $(z/A)dA/dz$, with respect to z.[6] Thus, the larger the initial technology gap, the smaller the effect on the border commodity from changes in relative wages.

A detailed model of technology gap is developed in Appendix A. However, issues that arise from the model can be addressed without such detailed treatment. What should technology gap theory focus on as its major theoretical concern? This theory must be interested in developing both a theoretical and general empirical understanding of the institutional framework which generates new technologies as well as determines the extent of technology transfer between countries. The number of studies that pave the way toward improving understanding of how these institutions differ between countries is slowly increasing (see Nelson 1993). Next, we must develop models in which to build an understanding of the effects of changing patterns of technological progress and transfer on trade flows between countries. A complete under-standing must include an analysis of the relationship between comparative and absolute advantage.

Most analysis concentrates on trade based on comparative advantage, in which each country has the technological ability to produce each good. However, the model described above and developed in Appendix A is general enough to capture trade based on absolute advantage in one particular form. Trade can be based on technological asymmetries that are based on product innovations as well as the process innovations already explored. In such cases, trade is based on country-specific absolute advantages. The technology, or product, is particular to the innovative country.

In the model, product innovations are assumed to be confined to the more advanced country. This assumption is made to simplify the analysis of trade along the continuum of goods so that country 2 is the only producer of the innovative goods $[z_0, z_1]$. The inclusion of innovative goods in the model does act to modify the pattern of trade in the Ricardian goods. Absolute advantage trade increases the number of Ricardian goods that country 1 specializes in along the segment $[0, z]$.

Innovative goods may also be introduced so that both countries produce these goods. Assume that balanced trade exists in Ricardian goods. Then, in order for the balanced trade condition to hold over all traded goods as in equation A11.8, trade must also balance in innovative goods.

The theoretical model allows for technology gaps to initiate trade on the basis of comparative and absolute advantage. The next section critically analyzes the empirical literature regarding trade based on technological asymmetries. One of the questions to be addressed regards the relative importance of comparative versus absolute advantage in the analysis of trade flows. Since plausible models can be developed that emphasize both types of country-specific advantages, the question of importance becomes an empirical one.

Empirical evidence

The main goal of this section is to analyze the recent literature in terms of developing empirical models which are able to provide an explanation of the relation between technology, trade flows, and growth.

This part of the chapter is divided in the following way: first, we discuss how technology is usually measured (patents or R&D expenditure), specifying the advantages and disadvantages of adopting one or the other proxy for technology; then we analyze the difference between adopting a static (cross-section) or a dynamic (time-series) model specification; finally, we present models that have been used in the literature and the empirical results derived from them, and briefly address the issue of comparative versus absolute advantages as the main source in explaining the relation between technology and trade.

Different measures of technology

Technology gap theory attempts to capture the impact of technology on trade flows between countries. In doing so, it must deal with the question of which proxy best measures technology. Essentially the literature uses either the number of patents or R&D expenditures as a proxy for technology; each has advantages and disadvantages, which are analyzed below.[7]

The use of patents as a proxy for technology has been eschewed by most of the traditional international trade analyses largely because patent data between countries are very sensitive to specific legislation within each country, making it difficult to derive robust conclusions and to establish a reasonable base of comparison.

Studies using patents as a proxy for technology also must deal with the problem of using either the number of patent applications or the number of patents granted for each country as the relevant proxy. Dosi *et al.* (1990) argue that the results derived from these models suggest that the number of patents granted is a better measure of technology output than the number of patent applications. They also argue that foreign patents are a superior and more reliable indicator of technology output than are domestic patents.[8] The main distinction between using patents or R&D expenditure as a proxy for technology is that the former is a technology output indicator and the latter indicates technology input. Even though Soete (1981) argues that foreign patents are a better proxy for technology, it is still an imperfect one because it is only able to capture the endogenous technological performance of each country: it does not take into account technology which is imported through trade, licensing, or other modes of transfer.[9]

Other problems associated with using patents are that not all innovations are patented, and some patents may also be registered in other foreign countries as a policy adopted by firms in order to diminish the possibility of having competitors. Last, but not least, it should be mentioned that technology when measured by patents seems to be less relevant to trade for those manufacturing segments which are considered 'very high tech' either because, in general, they involve a large amount of government (military) funds for research or because of security reasons, because patenting implies publication of the innovation.

In spite of these criticisms, Hulst *et al.* (1991) and others defend the use of patents in preference to R&D expenditure because the latter is a measure of technology input rather than of technology output. They also argue that any proxy used should be able to be a comparative measure in terms of comparing industries across countries, which was done by transforming the patent data into what they called RTA (Revealed Technological Advantage) indices.[10]

The main purpose of the RTA index is to have a comparative measure of the technology performance (competitiveness) among industries. The revealed technological advantage index is calculated by dividing country j's share of patents granted in sector i by the total patent share of country j. The expression that represents the RTA index is given by:

$$RTAi,j = (P_{ij} / \Sigma_j P_{ij}) / (\Sigma_i P_{ij} / \Sigma_i \Sigma_j P_{ij}) \tag{11.9}$$

The use of R&D expenditures as a proxy for technology has been criticized on several levels. First, as mentioned above, it is an input variable and thus is an inadequate measure of the output of innovation activity, which is the main objective of econometric models used by technology gap theory. As an input variable, R&D expenditure does not provide a straightforward link to understanding how the innovation process is affected, especially in models using disaggregated data at the industry level. Second, studies which use R&D expenditure also find problems in terms of establishing international comparisons because exchange rates do not usually equalize R&D input costs across countries. Third, using an input variable like R&D expenditure to measure technology allows for little or no control over the efficiency of resource use, rendering it impossible to make consistent inferences from any data set of R&D expenditure concerning technology and innovation.

Considering the brief discussion above on the limitations of using both patents and R&D expenditure as measures of technology, it is clear that the first-best option would be to have some internationally comparable innovation data; but this is not available. This argument should not be viewed as an element discouraging future empirical research on the impact of technology on trade and growth, but rather that it is necessary to search for and develop new data which contain information on technology that can be compared on a country-to-country basis.

One final point that should be mentioned is that patents and R&D expenditure are complementary, implying that any empirical study using both of them should expect a positive correlation between the two activities. After all, both patents and R&D are imperfect measures of technology, but they are certainly important variables to be considered in any empirical research which intends to capture the relation between technology, trade, and growth.

Empirical implications of using cross-sectional or time-series data

The literature on the relations between technology and international trade has shown since the 1960s that on both methodological or empirical grounds there are relevant problems in attempting to capture the dynamic process of technological development and its relation to growth and trade. The main issue to be addressed is whether a static or dynamic model should be used. Incorporating a static model implies working with cross-sectional data among countries and industries while a dynamic one involves time-series data.

The primary objective of models using time-series data is to understand the dynamic impact of technology gaps on trade between countries. Time-series models are a better empirical tool for capturing long-run effects because they do not merely compare industries from different countries at a given point in time, as is usually done by models based on cross-sectional data. Another advantage of the dynamic setup is that it allows consideration of the stock of patented inventions from previous time periods, and not merely of the patents granted in a certain year. The stock specification proxy is the cumulative nature of technological knowledge.[11]

The first models of the impact of technology gaps on trade among countries were originally based on cross-sectional data which compared industries in different countries at a given point in time. They were able to derive some comparative statics and conclusions but not in terms of determining patterns of trade because they do not incorporate the time dimension into the theory, having problems in capturing the dynamics of the international trade flow, which is an essential element for technology gap theory. This basic deficiency was probably the main reason why, since the beginning of the last decade, studies have started using time-series data.

Most studies using cross-sectional data, such as Soete (1981), try to minimize the static problems by using the capital–labor ratio and geographical variables to incorporate the level differences between international trade share. This procedure was done in order to provide a more complex and accurate basis on which to compare each country's international trade share which depends on how these variables change. The argument against this is that these variables do not have a significant variation during the relevant period of time when compared to the nominal variation (price, technology, and investment indicator) of the other variables. The static models using cross-sectional data usually show a significant correlation between technological capabilities and export performance but they cannot capture the dynamics of the impact of variables such as exchange rates, technical change, and changes in input prices on the flow of exports, which is the dependent variable.[12]

The evolutionary approach to technological change and trade is a more flexible model in terms of not imposing many restrictions on the dynamic results that could be generated by time-series data. On the other hand, it implies some additional difficulties in terms of linking theoretical and empirical results, which is a serious methodological constraint for this kind of analysis.[13] This limitation arises from the necessity for any theory that intends to be treated as scientific not only to provide strong predictions which must be empirically testable but also to be corroborated by evidence. This depends in a large extent on the ability to establish a connection between empirical results and the theory.

It is quite reasonable to expect dynamic models of technology and trade to dominate the theoretical and empirical scenario in the development of the theory in the future especially, because of their relevance in explaining patterns of trade.

Model specifications and empirical results

We briefly address questions which arise from the use of comparative or absolute advantage in evolutionary models of international trade. We then present three representative models which are a synthesis of what has been developed in empirical research on the impact of technology on trade.

Posner's (1961) original model was developed to capture the impact of technology and innovation on trade, using absolute advantage as a theoretical explanation of the differences in industry competitiveness among advanced countries. Many technology gap theorists still argue that the relation between innovation and its effects on trade is mainly a matter of absolute advantage between countries:

> 'competitiveness' is an 'absolute' concept, in the sense that it is independent of intra national comparison of the activities in which a country is 'better' or 'worse', although it obviously compares one country with the rest of the world.
>
> (Dosi *et al.* 1990: 190)

Dosi and Soete (1983) argue that technology gap models measure the impact on international competitiveness of factors such as differences in the degree of innovativeness, and changes in labor productivity, or the mechanization of production, which are all sources of absolute advantage (disadvantage). The composition of trade among countries is primarily determined by technological gaps, while comparative advantage plays only a secondary role.[14]

The final argument used by the technology gap theorists concerning the adequacy of using absolute advantage to explain differences in international competitiveness is that comparative advantage is determined by the relationship between absolute productivity advantages and relative wages. Therefore, they are not able to provide a complete explanation of differences in international competitiveness, which can only be done by emphasizing the primary role of technology gaps in explaining the composition of international trade and not so much by comparative advantage considerations.

Most of the theoretical and empirical work using comparative advantage as the main explanation of the relationship between trade and innovation considers the relation between wage rates and average technology levels of each country as the parameter which defines each country's relative position in terms of comparative advantage or disadvantage. The models of the determinants of international competitiveness within a comparative advantages framework use the concept of Revealed Comparative Advantage (RCA) as a proxy for comparative advantage or disadvantage. The RCA measures the actual distribution of exports between countries and is formally expressed as the ratio of the competitiveness of each sector to the competitiveness of the entire economy. The formal expression for RCA is given by:[15]

$$RCA_{ij} = (X_{ij} / \Sigma_j X_{ij}) / (\Sigma_i X_{ij} / \Sigma_i \Sigma_j X_{ij}) \tag{11.10}$$

where:

X = some indicator of international competitiveness
i = sector or industry
j = country

To determine X, the most typical kind of model used to capture the impact of technology on trade simply regresses some variable which represents export performance for a particular country on a set of input requirements by commodity, which is mainly represented by the industry R&D expenditure variable for each country (R&Dj). This is represented by the following expression:

$$X_{ij} = a_i + b_i E_j \tag{11.11}$$

where:

X_{ij} is the variable of export performance;
E_j is the set of input requirements by commodity;

i = country
j = commodity
b_i = desired resource availability for country 1.

In contrast to the above model, there is another setup which is concerned with explaining trade flows among countries for some particular commodity or industry. Here the attention is on inter-country variations in innovation and international trade performance. This kind of model is considered by Soete (1981) as the basis for the technology trade gap theory. The equation which represents this model is:

$$X_{ij} = a_j + b_j E_i \qquad (11.12)$$

where:

X_{ij} = export performance variable;
E_i = resource availability by country;
b_j = input requirements for each industry;
i = country;
j = industry.

The above equations representing each model are quite similar but their implications are not. In the second model specification, the logic is that the observation of resource availability in each country (E_i) will enable one to estimate the input requirements for each industry (b_j) and compare them to the actual value of input requirements (E_j).[16]

The model represented by equation (11.12) is concerned with the issue of how innovation changes across countries, which is one of the main theoretical elements of the technology gap theory.

On the other hand, the first model observes input requirements by commodity (E_j) to estimate the resource availability for the desired country (b_i), and then it proceeds to validate each (b_i) by looking at their correlation with all countries' resource availability (E_i).

The best regression result found by Soete (1981) was one which estimates for each of the industries considered using XSHA (the share of each country's i exports of industry j in the total OECD exports of industry j) as the dependent variable and four independent variables:[17]

$$\ln XSHA_{ij} = \beta_{0j} + \beta_{1j} \ln PSHA_{ij} + \beta_{2j} \ln KL_i + \beta_{3j} \ln Pop_i + \beta_{4j} Dist_i \qquad (11.13)$$

where:

$PSHA$ = share of each country i's US patents in industry j in total OECD US foreign patents in industry j for some period of time;

KL   = relation between gross fixed capital formation and total employ-
           ment for each country *i*;
Pop   = population of each country *i*;
Dist   = Linnemann's distance proxy.[18]

Soete's (1981) model and the test developed is considered as one of the
most important in the literature. It uses a static cross-sectional analysis and it
is commodity-specific. The empirical results of static models such as this are
that innovation is a crucial determinant of international trade flows for most
industries. This kind of model is among those that attempt to capture the
impact of comparative advantages on trade performance by adopting the
concept of RCA, even though the best results do not include RCA as an
independent variable.[19]

The general conclusion of models using cross-sectional data and foreign
patents as an output-technology measure is that international trade performance depends on each country's technological performance in what are
called 'innovative industries.' These industries are characterized by a high and
significant elasticity of technology and they are generally technology-
intensive.[20]

By the early 1990s there were some new empirical studies which, in the
present chapter, constitute the second representative model. One such model
was developed by Cotsomitis *et al.* (1991) and attempts to capture elements
such as price competition and an indicator of domestic demand by including
the exchange rate and country size variables, respectively, in the determination
of trade flows. The main difference between this model and earlier ones is that
it uses bilateral trade balances (BTB) as the dependent variable instead of
export performance.[21]

The BTB index is calculated using the following expression:

$$BTB_{i'ij} = (X_{i'ij} - X_{i'ij}) / (X_{i'ij} + X_{i'ij}) \tag{11.14}$$

where:

$X_{i'ij}$ = exports from country (i) to (i') in industry j;
$X_{i'ij}$ = exports from country (i') to (i) in industry j;
i and i' = countries;
j = industry.

The interpretation of the BTB is that it is an index formulated to measure
the relative size of the difference in exports between two countries in a specific
industry in relation to the trade flow between them with respect to this
industry. In one word, the BTB is a measure of net export pattern.[22]

The use of bilateral trade balances as the dependent variable has a huge
implication in terms of reflecting a conceptual option for absolute advantages
as the main source in explaining the relation between technology and trade,

rather than comparative advantages as was assumed by the models working with export performance as the dependent variable. The implications of adopting BTB as the dependent variable is usually to be able to explain differences in international competitiveness and the composition of trade based on the existence of technology gaps (absolute advantage).

The econometric procedure used by this new model is to regress BTB in a two-by-two country setup against the following independent variables:[23]

TG = stock measure of technology gap (lagged three periods);
REX = real exchange rate (lagged two periods) and using the purchasing power parity (PPP) concept and manufacturing wholesale prices;
POP = country size (population).

The model is represented by the following expression:[24]

$$BTB_{i'ij} = a + b_1\, TG_{i'ij-3} + b_2\, REX_{i'i-2} + b_3\, POP_{i'i} + e \qquad (11.15)$$

where:

X = exports
i and i' = countries
j = industry
e = stochastic error

The empirical findings of this model were somewhat different from those found by Soete, especially concerning the low percentage of cases where the technology gap coefficient (b_1) was significant. The model also found many cases where the sign of the technology gap effect was the opposite (negative) of what is expected. In general the empirical results point out that the technology gap variable (TG) has little explanatory power regarding bilateral trade balance. The results for the country size impact on BTB were significant in most cases. The exchange rate results show that it is somewhat significant but has problems of unexpected signs.

Finally, we have the third and last representative model used to measure the impact of innovation on trade. These models are called 'empirical models of export market shares (performance) with explicit supply-side effects'.[25] Magnier and Toujas-Bernate (1994) find empirical evidence that price effects have a weak and sometimes perverse impact on competitiveness, implying that an increase in labor costs and export prices do not seem to result in lower growth rates of exports or GDP. The authors adopt a time-series specification because it allows for different values for the parameters estimated, either between countries or between industries. They also assume that the differences between the elasticities of technology across industries are the same for all countries, which is a restrictive assumption but justified based on some data problems for R&D expenditures.[26]

The model regressed an export market share ratio (MSX_{ij}) variable for country i, industry j on a set of independent variables (F_{ij}) which includes relative prices, R&D expenditures and fixed investments in the following way:

$$MSX_{ij} = \alpha_{ij} + (\beta + \beta_i + \beta_j)F_{ij} \tag{11.16}$$

where $\Sigma_i \beta_i = \Sigma_j \beta_j = 0$.

The above specification incorporates the idea that each elasticity is the outcome of a sum of an average effect (b), a country-specific effect (b_i) and an industry-specific one (b_j), respectively expressed by the beta parameters above. The model uses a partial adjustment mechanism of export market shares to its long-run level (MSX^*) and it captures the effects in terms of industries and countries. The expression for this is:

$$\Delta MSX_{ij}(t) = \mu[MSX^*_{ij} - MSX_{ij}(t-1)] \tag{11.17}$$

where t = time.

Magnier and Toujas-Bernate (1994) run four different models, all of which have the long-run level of export market shares (MSX^*) as the dependent variable. The difference among them is that in the first one the only independent variable is the indicator of price competitiveness (PC), the second includes the relative fixed investment (IN), the third incorporates price competitiveness (PC) and R&D expenditure (RD), and the last has all the above three independent variables.[27] The estimation of the models used variables in terms of log deviations from their temporal mean value in order to assure dynamic specification and conclusions. The estimation was done by adopting the two-step feasible generalized least squares (2SFGLS) procedure in trying to detect any problems of grouped heteroskedasticity.

The empirical result of the models of export market shares is that including non-price effects increases the explanatory power of the model. This element supports the technology gap theory since export market shares depend not only on price but also in terms of investment and R&D expenditure which is emphasized by the theory. In formal terms this was done by including variables (RD and IN) along with the relative price indicator (PC).

Another important empirical finding is that export prices have a large impact on export market shares regardless of the inclusion of non-price effects. Considering R&D expenditures and fixed investments separately (not treating both at the same time as independent variables), it has also been found that they have a significant impact on export market shares. The final empirical result is that the best model is the one which includes all three variables (RD, IN, and PC) to explain the long-run dynamics of export market shares among countries engaged in international trade. This is in accordance with the theoretical framework of the technology gap theory which put emphasis upon the relevance of variables like R&D expenditure to explain differences in international competitiveness.

Table 11.1 is designed to provide a general list of the most important empirical results from the technology gap literature, dividing them in two classes of models: cross-section (static) and time-series (dynamic).

The empirical results listed on the table are able to provide some general conclusions regarding the technology gap theory. First, it is reasonable to argue on the relevance of innovation to the determination of international trade performance both at the country or at the industry level. Second, one can say that either foreign patents or R&D expenditure have advantages and disadvantages in measuring technology but both are still the best options in

Table 11.1 Technology gap model: comparison of empirical results

Static models using cross-sectional data
- Foreign patents are a superior measure of technology than domestic patents.
- For most industries innovation is a crucial determinant of international trade flows.
- International trade performance of each country depends primarily on the performance of the innovative industries.
- Distance from the major foreign market reflects crucial advantage for many industries.
- Crucial role of the technology variable in explaining the intercountry changes in export performance for most of the industries.
- Company R&D is more relevant than total R&D in explaining innovative activity.
- Skilled labor has a positive impact on innovation.
- Large-firm employment share has a positive impact in innovation.
- Number of patents is negatively related to concentration and it is not significantly dependent on advertising.
- Capital/output ratio is positively related to the number of patents but it does not have a significant impact on innovation.
- R&D expenditure by company is strongly correlated to patent activity.
- Technological specialization does not unambiguously imply trade specialization.

Dynamic models using time-series data
- The coefficient for the stock measure of technology gap is not significant in explaining bilateral trade balance.
- More likely to find cases where the technology gap has opposite (negative) sign.
- Country size has a significant impact on bilateral trade.
- The exchange rate variable has a significant impact on trade but it shows unepected signs in some cases.
- Weak and sometimes perverse impact of price on competitiveness.
- Increase in the explanatory power of the model by including non-price effects.
- A model including R&D expenditure, fixed investment and a price competitiveness variable provides a better explanation for the long-run dynamics of export market shares.
- Most empirical results do not support the Posner–Hufbauer technology gap theory (increase in the technology gap between two countries was supposed to result in an increase in the volume of trade between them).
- Changes in wages and in the exchange rate have only short-run impact on changing the degree of competitiveness.
- The technology effects on trade have a long lag structure.

terms of data availability for technology gap models. Finally, it is important to include non-price effects to explain changes in export market shares (international competitiveness).

Conclusions: where should the theory go?

In the near future, technology gap theory should direct an effort to develop stronger theoretical foundations to include a better specified model that is able to incorporate the dynamic impacts of technology gaps on trade without losing empirical fitness, as has happened during recent tests. On the empirical side it is necessary to have a more appropriate data set for international technology comparison; the empirical analysis generated from it could then be tested to see how well it corroborates the theoretical propositions. Future empirical work on technology gaps should also include variables such as the number of researchers, labor skills (human capital), and the level and means of technology transference between countries.

The evolutionary approach to trade and technology must continue to use the concept that technology gaps are not merely an outcome of comparative advantages based on endowments, as assumed by traditional trade theories, but rather a result of a dynamic process with some specific characteristics both in a country or in a sector, involving elements like innovation, imitation and organization changes. These elements are more likely to give each country or sector absolute advantages/disadvantages.

One further comment on the theoretical model should be made. A great failing of the theory developed in this chapter is that it makes no effort to link developing or narrowing technology gaps to a theory of firm or industry evolution. The theory is extremely mechanical. The search for stronger theoretical foundations must include the development of a formal link between the analysis of trade flows, and the creation and destruction of specific technology gaps. These gaps are opened and closed at the level of the firm. Thus, technology gap theory must have its foundations firmly planted in an evolutionary theory of the firm, perhaps as has already been developed in evolutionary economics (see Nelson 1995).

Appendix A

To analyze the model in detail, we may differentiate (11.7) to obtain:

$$\overline{z}' = e[(\hat{w}_1 - \hat{w}_2) + (\hat{a}_1 - \hat{a}_2)] \tag{A11.1}$$

where $\wedge$ represents relative growth rates. Thus, the exact relationship between a relative change in either wages or unit labor requirements is dependent on the existing technology gap as related through e. Where the technology gap is smallest (related by a more elastic relation) changes in relative wages and unit requirements have the largest impact on trade flows.

Several issues remain to be resolved in a technology gap model. First, how is $\hat{a}$ determined, and second, how does the relationship between changes in wages and changes in unit labor requirements affect trade flows? For purposes of the model under consideration, we will assume that, at any point in time, a_1 and a_2 are constant and determined by cumulative output and learning capabilities, as in Vaglio (1988) and Cimoli(1994).[28] Following a generalized form of Verdoorn–Kaldor's law, we may specify the following:

$$a_1 = \kappa_1^{\alpha}, 0 < \alpha < 1,$$
$$a_2 = \kappa_2^{\gamma}, 0 < \gamma < 1, \tag{A11.2}$$

where a and g represent learning capabilities which may differ between the two countries. International learning may take place and is modeled through cumulative output (or knowledge) variable k as:

$$\kappa_1(t) = \int_0^t \left(X(t)_1 + \delta X(t)_2 \right) dt$$
$$\kappa_2(t) = \int_0^t \left(X(t)_2 + \delta X(t)_1 \right) dt \tag{A11.3}$$

where X_i is the output of country $i = 1,2$, and d represents the technology spillover, where $d = 0$ implies no spillovers and $d = 1$ implies no lag in the international transmission of new knowledge. In order to maintain institutional flexibility in the determination of changes in relative wages over time, we assume that relative wages move with changes in relative productivity, but the exact relation may differ from country to country:

$$\hat{w}_i = \lambda_i \hat{a}_i, \text{ for } i = 1,2, \text{ and } \lambda_i \leq 1 \tag{A11.4}$$

The exact relation between changes in trade patterns and technological change is found by substituting (A11.4) into (A11.1):

$$\overline{z}' = e[(\lambda_1 \hat{a}_1 - \lambda_2 \hat{a}_2) + (\hat{a}_2 - \hat{a}_1)] \tag{A11.5}$$

From (A11.5), it becomes clear that relative changes in productivities (as determined by differing rates of technological progress as determined by (A11.2) and (A11.3)) influence trade patterns through two vehicles; first, as shown in (A11.1), through the existing technology gap, and second, through the institutional mechanisms determining relative wages. Thus, for any given change in relative productivities, the influence on trade patterns will be larger (smaller) the less (more) relative wage changes reflect the changes in relative productivities.

The pattern of specialization is stable only in two special cases:

$$\bar{z}' = 0 \left\{ \begin{array}{c} e = 0 \\ \hat{a}_1 / \hat{a}_2 = (\lambda_2 - 1) / (\lambda_1 - 1) \end{array} \right\} \tag{A11.6}$$

Thus, trade patterns will be unstable in the face of technological change unless very specific circumstances occur (for example, the institutional forces relating wage increases to average productivity increases are the same in both countries, $\lambda_1 = \lambda_2$).[29]

To close the model, we need some assumption regarding the determination of the trade balance. Several authors (for example, Milberg 1994) have argued that a model of trade which attempts to describe trade and markets in any realistic sense must utilize a monetary model which allows for long-run imbalances in trade flows. In other words, it is necessary to incorporate a monetary theory of production into realistic trade models. To put matters succinctly, we have no such model here. Instead, we choose to make the simplifying assumption of balanced trade (we have no money in the model) but allow import demand functions to differ by country and by commodity. Thus, we allow for the realistic possibility of income and price elasticities differing for each z_i.

Given that income is only derived from labor and that labor is normally less than for fully employed, we write the income for each country, Y_i for $i = 1, 2$, as:

$$Y_i = w_i N_i \text{ for } i = 1 \text{ and } 2 \tag{A11.7}$$

with $N_i \leq L_i$ where N and L are employment levels and labor supplies respectively.

The demand functions are written as import demand functions for each country since reciprocal demand for each country's exports determines the trade balance. Assuming balanced trade, the constraint is written as:

$$Y_1 \int_{\underline{z}}^{z_1} \beta_1(z) dz = Y_2 \int_0^{\bar{z}} \beta_2(z) dz \tag{A11.8}$$

where b_i for $i = 1$ and 2 is the per capita import expenditure of each country.

From this formulation, we develop a link between trade and overall macroeconomic activity. The quantity of each commodity produced is determined by the pattern of specialization and the per capita demand for each good. It is '[t]echnology gaps [that] determine the set of possible patterns of specialization and the asymmetry in demand [that] determines the different effects on the quantities produced and exported of each commodity' (Cimoli and Soete 1992: 43-4) The form that b_i takes is given by:

$$\beta_i = p(z) \, m_i \, [z, w_i, p(z)] \, / \, w_i \qquad\qquad (A11.9)$$

where $p(z)$ is the price of each good (z_i), and $m_i(z)$ is the per capita demand for imports for $i = 1$ and 2. Differentiation of (A11.9) allows for an analysis of the relation between the trade balance and relative price and income elasticities (see Cimoli and Soete 1992 and Cimoli 1994).

Notes

1 There is, of course, some interesting work on trade with technological asymmetrics being conducted by theorists not aligned with technology gap theory (see Trefler 1995).

2 Mun was by no means the originator of this distinction: it also appears in the writings of Gerard de Malynes, Samuel Fortrey, and Nicholas Barbon among others. See Johnson (1937).

3 Other important early models of trade based on patterns of technological change are Vernon (1966) and Hufbauer (1966).

4 See Elmslie (1995) for a complete analysis of Tucker's views.

5 With the current formulation of the model, we assume that only country 2 produces innovative goods and that quantities of each commodity traded will adjust to allow for their one-way trade. This will be discussed in more detail when the balanced trade condition is addressed.

6 Several papers (for example, Cimoli and Soete 1992, and Cimoli 1992) refer to e as a technology gap multiplier, but it is better interpreted as an elasticity.

7 The literature on technology measures is quite extensive. See, for example, Soete (1981); Acs and Audretsch (1989); Dosi *et al.* (1990: ch. 3).

8 Further discussion of the models and regressions used to get these results will be given below.

9 See Elmslie (1994) for a discussion of the importance of foreign sources of technology and empirical results from Portugal.

10 For more details on the RTA indices and how they were constructed, see Hulst *et al.* (1991: 252–3, esp. fn 1).

11 Using the stock of patents as a measure of technology gap was done by Cotsomitis *et al.* (1991); this contrasts with the well-known test developed by Soete (1981) which uses patents as a flow variable.

12 The static cross-sectional model using a commodity-specific analysis like the one in Soete (1981) is presented on page 261, equation (11.13).

13 It should be mentioned that models using time series are better able to incorporate dynamic increasing returns, which has become an important theoretical issue in international trade since the late 1970s with the development of the New International Trade Theory and the discussion about intra-industry trade characterized by increasing returns and economies of scale.

14 This kind of model of technology gap is trying to develop a theoretical framework which is compatible with the classical hypothesis of cost-based adjustment.

15 See Dosi *et al.* (1990: 161). The idea of RCA is to measure each country's market share in a particular industry divided by its overall market share among all countries.

16 This is known as Leamer's external validation.

17 All variables were considered in natural log (ln) terms except for the Linnemann's distance proxy (Dist).

18 The Linnemann's distance proxy is intended to capture the physical distance of various countries with respect to what is called the 'world centre'.

19 The complete set of four regressions with a different specification is given by Soete (1981: 646–7).

20 In studies such as Soete (1981: 649–51), the technology elasticity is captured by the parameter b_1 on Tables 2 and 3, which is the (b_j) variable as specified by equation (11.12) in the present work.

21 One of the most recent empirical studies using *BTB* as the dependent variable is Verspagen and Wakelin (1995) which formulates a model where *BTB* is influenced by real factors like R&D expenditure, investment, and wage costs for a set of developed economies.

22 Recent studies in the literature, such as that by Verspagen and Wakelin (1995: 5–6), uses change in bilateral trade $(BT_t - BT_{t-1})$ as the dependent variable, where the initial trade balance is measured at time $(t-1)$.

23 Measuring *TG* in a stock specification is done in the following ways:

$$TS_{ijt} = \Sigma P_{ijt} \cdot F_{t-k}$$

where:

i = country
j = industry
t = year
P_{ijt} = total number of patents issued by the US to country i in industry j for a given year t
F_{t-k} = weight accorded to the foreign patents in terms of their age $(t-k)$.

Therefore,

$$TG_{i'ij} = TS_{ij} - TS_{i'j}.$$

In the case of the country-size variable, *POP* we have:

$$POP_{i'i} = DP_i - DP_{i'}$$

where *DP* is domestic population.

24 The parameter estimation was done by a OLS regression, and the Cochran–Orcutt test for detection of autocorrelation problems was adopted.

25 See Greenhalgh (1990) and Magnier and Toujas–Bernate (1994). Both models adopt a time-series (dynamic) specification and discuss the issue of price and non-price competitiveness.

26 The technology elasticity captures the sensitivity of export market shares to technological innovation.

27 For further details, see Magnier and Toujas-Bernate (1994: 504).

28 For a more complicated formulation which allows relative productivity growth to vary across sectors, see Elmslie and Milberg (1996).

29 Cimoli (1994) provides more details on the possibilities for dynamic relations between patterns of specialization and technological change.

References

Acs, Z.J. and Audretsch, D.B. (1989) 'Patents as a Measure of Innovative Activity,' *Kyklos* 42, 2: 171–80.

Amendola, G., Dosi, G. and Papagni, E. (1993) 'The Dynamics of International Competitiveness,' *Weltwirtschaftliches Archiv* 129, 30: 451–71.

Cimoli, M. (1988) 'Technology Gaps and Institutional Asymmetries in a North–South Model with a Continuum of Goods,' *Metroeconomica* 39, 3: 245–74.

—— (1994) 'Lock-in and Specialization (Dis)advantages in a Structuralist Growth Model,' in J. Fagerberg, B. Verspagen and N. von Tunzelmann (eds), *The Dynamics of Technology, Trade and Growth*, Aldershot: Edward Elgar.

—— and Soete, L. (1992) 'A Generalized Technology Gap Trade Model,' *Economie appliquée* XLV, 3: 33–54.

Cotsomitis, J., DeBresson, C. and Kwan, A. (1991) 'A Re-examination of the Technology Gap Theory of Trade: Some Evidence from Time Series Data for OECD Countries,' *Weltwirtschaftliches Archiv* 127, 4: 792–9.

Dornbusch, R., Fischer S. and Samuelson, P.A. (1977) 'Comparative Advantage, Trade and Payments in a Ricardian Model with a Continuum of Goods,' *American Economic Review* 67, 5: 823–39.

Dosi, G. and Soete, L. (1983) 'Technology Gaps and Cost-based Adjustment: Some Explorations on the Determinants of International Competitiveness,' *Metroeconomica* XXXV, 3: 197–222.

——, Pavitt, K. and Soete, L. (1990) *The Economics of Technical Change and International Trade*, New York: New York University Press.

Elmslie, B. (1994) 'International Trade and Technical Progress: the Role of Capital Good Imports in Portugal,' *International Review of Applied Economics*, 8, 3: 227–50.

—— (1995) 'The Convergence Debate between David Hume and Josiah Tucker,' *Journal of Economic Perspectives* 9, 4: 207–16.

—— and Milberg, W. (1992) 'International Trade and Factor Intensity Uniformity: an Empirical Assessment.' *Weltwirtschaftliches Archiv* 128, 3: 464–86.

—— and —— (1996) 'The Productivity Convergence Debate: a Theoretical and Methodological Reconsideration,' *Cambridge Journal of Economics* 20, 2:153–82.

Greenhalgh, C. (1990) 'Innovation and Trade Performance in the United Kingdom,' *Economic Journal* 100, 400: 105–18.

Hufbauer, G.C. (1966) *Synthetic Materials and the Theory of International Trade*, London: Duckworth.

Hulst, N. van., Mulder R. and Soete, L. (1991) 'Exports and Technology in Manufacturing Industry,' *Weltwirtschaftliches Archiv* 127, 2: 246–64.

Johnson, E.A.J. (1937) *Predecessors of Adam Smith: The Growth of British Economic Thought*, New York: Prentice-Hall.

Krugman, P.R. (1990) *Rethinking International Trade*, Cambridge, MA: MIT Press.

Maggi, G. (1993) 'Technology Gap and International Trade: an Evolutionary Model,' *Journal of Evolutionary Economics* 3, 2: 109–26.

Magnier, A. and Toujas-Bernate, J. (1994) 'Technology and Trade: Empirical Evidences for the Major Five Industrialized Countries,' *Weltwirtschaftliches Archiv* 130, 3: 494–520.

Milberg, W. (1991) 'Is Absolute Advantage *Passé*? Towards a Post-Keynesian/ Marxist Theory of International Trade.' in M. Glick (ed.), *Competition, Technology and Money: Classical and Post Keynesian Perspectives*, Aldershot: Edward Elgar.

—— (1994) 'Structural Change and International Competitiveness in Canada: an Alternative Approach,' *International Review of Applied Economics* 5, 1: 77–99.

Mun, T. ([1664] 1986) *England's Treasure by Forraign Trade*, New York: Augustus M. Kelley.

—— ([1621] 1986) *A Discourse of Trade, from, England unto the East-Indies*, New

York: Augustus M. Kelley.

Nelson, R. (1993) *National Innovative Systems: A Comparative Analysis*, Oxford: Oxford University Press.

—— (1995) 'Recent Evolutionary Theorizing About Economic Change,' *Journal of Economic Literature* XXXIII, 1: 48–90.

Pasinetti, L.L. (1981) *Structural Change and Economic Growth: A Theoretical Essay on the Dynamics of the Wealth of Nations*, Cambridge: Cambridge University Press.

Posner, M. (1961) 'International Trade and Technical Change,' *Oxford Economic Papers* 13: 323–41.

Schuyler, R.L. (1931) *The Elements of Commerce and Theory of Taxes*, New York: Columbia University Press.

Soete, L. (1981) 'A General Test of Technological Gap Trade Theory,' *Weltwirtschaftliches Archiv* 117, 4: 638–60.

Trefler, D. (1995) 'The Case of the Missing Trade and Other Mysteries,' *American Economic Review* 85, 5: 1029–46.

Tucker, J. ([1755] 1931) *The Elements of Commerce and Theory of Taxes*; reprinted in R.L. Schuyler, *Josiah Tucker: A Selection from His Economic and Political Writing,* New York: Columbia University Press.

—— ([1776] 1974) *Four Tracts on Political and Commercial Subjects*, 3rd edn, New York: Augustus M. Kelley.

Vaglio, A. (1988) 'Static and Dynamic Economies of Scale in Export-led Growth,' *Economic Notes* 2: 61–81.

Vernon, R. (1966) 'International Investment and International Trade in the Product Cycle,' *Quarterly Journal of Economics* 80: 190–207.

Verspagen, B. and Wakelin, K. (1995) 'Trade and Technology from a Schumpeterian Perspective,' unpublished.

Author Index

Subject Index